The Working Class in American History

Women in American History

*Lists of books in the series appear
at the end of this volume.*

DISHING IT OUT

DOROTHY SUE COBBLE

Dishing It Out

Waitresses and Their Unions in the Twentieth Century

UNIVERSITY OF ILLINOIS PRESS
Urbana and Chicago

Publication of this work was supported in part by a grant from
the Andrew W. Mellon Foundation.

This book is printed on acid-free paper.

Portions of this manuscript originally appeared as "Organizing the Postindustrial Work Force: Lessons from the History of Waitress Unionism," *Industrial and Labor Relations Review* 44 (April 1991): 419–36; "Rethinking Troubled Relations Between Women and Unions: Craft Unionism and Female Activism," *Feminist Studies* 16 (Fall 1990): 519–48; and " 'Practical Women': Waitress Unionists and the Controversies over Gender Roles in the Food Service Industry, 1900–1980," *Labor History* 29 (Winter 1988): 5–31. Figure 1 appears by permission of Michigan State University Press.

Library of Congress Cataloging-in-Publication Data
Cobble, Dorothy Sue.
    Dishing it out : waitresses and their unions in the twentieth
century / Dorothy Sue Cobble.
        p.   cm. — (The Working class in American history) (Women in
American history)
    Includes bibliographical references and index.
    ISBN 0-252-01812-5 (cl : acid-free paper)
        1. Waitresses—United States—History—20th century.   2. Trade-
unions—Restaurants, lunch rooms, etc.—United States—
History—20th century.   3. Women in trade-unions—United States—
History—20th century.   I. Title.   II. Series.   III. Series: Women
in American history.
HD6073.H82U53   1991
331.4'78116479573'0904—dc20   90-22629
                                                              CIP

*To Lucy Kendall
and to John and Ava Marron*

Contents

Preface

There have been few points in my life when I have felt that my Southern working-class heritage and my intellectual, feminist aspirations were not in tension. This book represents one such moment. Like the novelist who must somehow write first her autobiography, no matter how disguised, I knew that my first major academic project would be a response to my life experiences as well as to those of the classroom.

My interest in unionism—and more specifically unionism in a traditionally female occupation—undoubtedly had its roots in my own particular family history and my desires to recast that history. From my father I learned male union traditions, both noble and shortsighted. The railroad brotherhood gave him a route to dignity and an alternative to upward mobility, but the battles against technological change, an inept railroad management, and the dissolving fraternity of craftsmen inspired more bitterness than hope. His union culture also offered few resources for a revaluing of the contributions and power of those outside the white male craft brotherhood. In contrast, my mother operated in inclusive ways and seemed infinitely flexible in the face of political, social, and economic upheaval. Yet she found it difficult, if not impossible, to see her own work in a nonunion department store as worthy of romance and a living wage.

Was there a working-class institution that captured the best of these traditions? One that could lay claim to rights, provide a sense of identity and power to its members while granting the same to those outside its ranks? An institution to which I as a woman could belong? Perhaps only a union built by women could forge such a vision. What I found, however, was that history resists mythology, and that my desire to revise the work and union histories of my parents was not to be fulfilled in the ways I anticipated.

The jobs I held also left their mark on this book, as did the years I spent working with and teaching trade unionists. My union job (longshore work) offered more money than I had ever seen, a reasonable, self-regulated work pace, autonomy, and pride, and—had I been a man—would have provided a remarkably tight-knit workplace community. My nonunion jobs (magazine editor, waitress, art model, file clerk, receptionist) all paid close to minimum wage, and only the editing job compensated with status and expensive annual company luncheons. How were these extremes to be explained? Because all my nonunion jobs were also "women's jobs," I could hardly look simply to the gendered nature of the work. What would it mean to "women's work" for it to be unionized?

Because my string of working-class jobs and my frustrated urge for time to read, think, and write were fast propelling me back into school and into an academic career, I decided that my approach to answering such questions would be through historical texts rather than through the accumulated bruises of personal experience. The trade unionists I was teaching and my deepening involvement in labor politics gave me yet another set of questions. What would be the future of trade unionism and hence of worker power in the new postindustrial society? Could labor appeal to the growing female-dominated service work force, or was it historically and irredeemably linked to the anchor of the blue-collar male worker?

The history of waitresses and of waitress unionism only gradually revealed itself as the door behind which I might find answers. My one stint as a waitress had been short-lived—I was fired for not smiling enough—and I, like most of my generation, hardly associated waitressing with union solidarity. Yet, as I began to explore the histories of various female-dominated occupations, waitressing emerged as one of the few in which women had organized viable unions and had sustained those unions.

My book began formally as I worked on my dissertation in history at Stanford University. As a graduate student I was the lucky beneficiary of wise counsel from faculty and fellow students. My advisor, Carl Degler, was a model for me as a scholar and mentor: forthright in his criticisms, yet genuinely supportive of my work. Throughout my graduate years, Carl Degler treated me with respect personally and intellectually, took my work and my ideas seriously, and expected from me the highest standards of scholarship. Estelle Freedman offered keen theoretical insights and painful but sound editorial advice. Friends and colleagues in my Stanford dissertation group and in the Bay Area Labor History Workshop read various drafts and saved me from numerous grammatical and theoretical lapses. David Brody, Tony Fels, Michael Kazin, and Ruth Milkman read my unwieldy first drafts and have continued to give me substantive comments that have been instrumental in shaping my overall arguments.

My greatest debt then as now is to Lucy Kendall, a veteran waitress, political activist, and self-taught intellectual, who devoted countless hours to making this book a reality. Lucy worked with me at every step, from typing the initial correspondence to libraries and unions, to spending hours tracing obscure references, to offering critical comments on my successive written attempts to bring her world—the world of waitressing and of waitress unionism—alive. I will never quite understand how I became the lucky recipient of Lucy's research and clerical skills and her boundless energy, but I do know that if Lucy had not been there with flashlights, gloves, and steel nerves, the records lying untouched for fifty years in the cellar under the basement of the San Francisco restaurant workers' union might still be there collecting yet another layer of dirt and mold.

When I somewhat reluctantly left the Bay Area after fifteen years, my book project traveled with me to Rutgers University. In New Jersey I entered another community of scholars who took me into their fold and shared their diverse and stimulating perspectives. I owe a great deal to the thoughtful promptings of Ava Baron, David Bensman, Patricia Cooper, Adrienne Eaton, Mary Hartman, Alice Kessler-Harris, Suzanne Lebsock, Patricia Roos, Deborah White, and the members of the Industrial Relations Seminar at the Institute of Management and Labor Relations. In particular, Dee Garrison and Michael Merrill have been generous friends and intellectual companions.

The labor education department at Rutgers University provided me with financial and research assistance. Thanks go to Steve Meicke, Karen Behmke, Su-Fen Chiu, Seth Grodofsky, Rochelle Suster, Larry Evans, Carmen Martino, Mary Paige Lang, Mary Alice Fuster, Maria Nogueira, and Aline LaBorwit for tracking down elusive references and patching botched footnotes. Irene Bouton and Angie Jackson offered clerical help; Mamata Datta, Eugene McElroy, and Majorie Watson, librarians at the Institute of Management and Labor Relations, added their research skills. I also received critical funding for research and travel from the National Endowment for the Humanities; the American Council of Learned Societies; the Henry J. Kaiser Family Foundation, Archives of Labor and Urban Affairs, Walter Reuther Library; the Albert J. Beveridge Foundation of the American Historical Association; the Rutgers University Research Council; and the Faculty Academic Study Program of Rutgers University.

This book would never have been written had not certain individuals from the labor movement offered their resources and support. Charles Lamb and Sherri Chiesa, officers of the Hotel Employees and Restaurant Employees Union, Local 2, gave me access to their materials and guided me to sympathetic international officers. Jack Kenneally, former general vice president of the Hotel Employees and Restaurant Employees International Union, and Anne Esper, administrative assistant to the general president, opened the voluminous files of the international union to me, patiently answered my inquiries about various extant locals, and made my stay in Cincinnati a pleasant one by taking me to numerous union restaurants and bars. (Firsthand observation was an indispensable aspect of my research, I then decided.) I am also grateful to Cindy Young, Jackie Walsh, Jeri Powell, Flo Douglas of HERE Local 2 in San Francisco, the late Charles Paulsen, international organizer of

HERE, Florence Farr of HERE Local 24, and the other men and women in the culinary industry who discussed their work and life with me. Bob Dixon, editor of Local 24's *Michigan Hotel Bar Restaurant Review*, I'm sure, spent more time than he would like to remember sorting through long-forgotten boxes of photographs and newsclippings.

No researcher can do justice to a topic without the help of archivists and librarians. Debra Bernhardt guided me through the considerable collection at the Tamiment Institute Library, Robert Wagner Labor Archives in New York City, helped me contact the officers of HERE Local 6, and spent a week with me in yet another damp unlit basement culling unaccessioned records. Jerry Hess from the National Archives and Records Service, Bette Eriskin in the Social Science Library, University of California, Berkeley, and Jim Knox and Hallie Perry of the Stanford University Green Library were extremely helpful. Special thanks also go to Richard Wentworth, Karen Hewitt, and Mary Giles of the University of Illinois Press for their sympathetic and meticulous attention to the project through the various stages of the production process.

Finally, I want to thank John Marron for his love and support; I only hope he realizes how much that has meant.

Introduction

For twenty-seven years, the restaurant had been a "haven for many West Hollywood singles, old and young." The menu was nothing fancy—"the usual eggs and burgers available all over town"—and the decor was "all-American coffee shop," but customers were fiercely loyal, "drawn by what one called the waitresses' good will." Yet when a new owner took over in 1984, he replaced "the doting middle-aged women—many of whom had been at the job 10 years or more" with younger help. The fired employees, ranging in age from sixty to seventy, organized as "the granny waitresses" and refused to go quietly. They hoisted picket signs proclaiming "Good Loyal Service Demands Honest Recognition" and began walking back and forth in front of the restaurant, sometimes for eight hours a day. The close-knit workplace community the waitresses enjoyed spilled over into the picket line. Waitresses brought each other "baked noodles and sandwiches, and pass[ed] the time discussing diets, illnesses and customers—just like it used to be on the job." One sixty-year-old waitress volunteered matter-of-factly that she picketed in part because she missed her co-workers of fourteen years.

The collective response of the granny waitresses was nurtured by their occupational community, pride in their service, and sense of connectedness with their work and customers. "You know when you get up in the morning, put a cup of coffee on the table for your husband? That's the kind of relationship it was with the customers," explained one veteran of the coffee shop. Once on strike, the waitresses relied on tactics traditional to their craft: they convinced the public to honor their lines; they reached out to the middle-class women's community—gaining the pledge of the National Organization of Women "to take the plight of senior waitresses around the country"; and they turned to their male allies in the labor movement. Because the new owner legally could ignore the previous union contract, hire permanent nonunion replacements, and enjoyed statutory protection from secondary boycotts and sympathy strikes, however, the waitresses settled in for a long battle. As one picketer said, "I worked here for 14 years. I guess I can walk that long."[1]

When I first began thinking about waitresses as a subject for a book, I had no idea I would find the story of the granny waitresses reenacted in various guises as I leafed through the archives.[2] Neither did I anticipate how fully those waitresses—with their intense ties to each other, to their customers, and to their work and union—were products of a different era, one that by the 1980s had disappeared almost completely. I knew little about the historical evolution of waitress work, the values engendered by its performance, or the workplace practices and organizations waitresses created. No book-length historical study of waitresses had been written; in fact, only a few studies from any disciplinary perspective existed.[3]

Yet the more I read about their history and the more I thought about their variegated reality, the clearer it became that here was a subject that had appeal at many levels. In some ways, waitressing is the quintessential female job. Probably more women at some point in their lives have held waitress jobs than any other. And, as the New York artist Jerri Allyn has said in one of her many performance pieces about food, money, and work, "waitressing is not just a job but a metaphor." All women are waitresses because all women feed and nurture those around them. Waitresses are simply the "professional nurturers."[4]

Waitressing reveals the deeply gendered expectations surrounding the world of work. In the theater of eating out, the waitress plays multiple parts, each reflecting a female role. To fulfill the emotional and fantasy needs of the male customer, she quickly learns the all-too-common scripts: scolding wife, doting mother, sexy mistress, or sweet, admiring daughter. Other customers, typically female, demand obsequious and excessive service—to compensate, perhaps, for the status denied them in other encounters. For once, they are not the servers but the ones being served.

The food service encounter is structured by a gendered and class-bound culture. Yet the specific content of that interaction arises from the symbolic, unconscious emotional lives of the participants themselves. More than food is being consumed at the restaurant site. And those who serve it are responding to hungers of many kinds. Eating stirs sexual and emotional associations of the most primitive order. "For there are expectations and intimacies and memories tied up with food," one journalist has written, that no one escapes.[5]

Waitress work is also prototypic of the new service work force. If present labor force trends persist, the personal service worker will be more representative of the postindustrial economy than the computer programmer or the data-entry clerk.[6] Projections target building cleaners, nurses, cooks, and waiters—all personal service jobs—as among the fastest-growing occupations. Waiting work, already one of the most frequent occupational "choices" for women, is second only to retail sales in the number of new openings projected for the 1990s.[7]

Waiting work, however, was not always a prominent occupation for women. In 1900, barely a hundred thousand people worked as waiters, and only a third of these were female; as late as the 1920s, men still retained close to a half of all wait jobs. But by 1970, more than a million people served food, and 92 percent were women.[8]

Yet despite the feminization and expansion of food service, sexual and racial stratification persisted. Invariably, men monopolized the better-paying, more prestigious jobs where formal service was the rule, with white waiters occupying the choicest positions. Women worked where remuneration was the lowest: in coffee shops, in tea rooms, and on the breakfast and lunch shifts of neighborhood cafes and full-service restaurants. Waitresses were also primarily white. The few black women who found employment in the trade— black women averaged only 7 percent of all waitresses over the course of the twentieth century—toiled in the worst waiting jobs or accepted employment as "busgirls" or waitress assistants.

Yet research on service work, particularly personal service occupations, continues to lag despite the centrality of such work to the burgeoning post-industrial economy and the daily lives of countless individuals. Without such research, a critical sector of the work world will remain understudied, and the research biases of the past will go unchallenged. Basic sociological and historical assumptions—from theories of "alienation" to concepts of "militancy," "working-class culture," and "skill"—have rested on studies of male, blue-collar labor and are increasingly ill-suited as generalizable theoretical frameworks.[9] The empirical base must be broadened to encompass the service sector as well as the female worker.[10]

To my delight, as I delved into the archives I realized that the history of waitress unionism, unfolding daily before my eyes, also offered intriguing scholarly possibilities. Although many groups of women workers developed strong work cultures, waitresses were one of the few to institutionalize their informal workplace practices and build permanent labor organizations.[11] Beginning in 1900 with the founding of the Seattle waitresses' local, waitresses formed all-female unions in Chicago, San Francisco, and other communities across the country; they also joined mixed culinary locals of waiters, cooks, and bartenders. In contrast to the sporadic organizing among women telephone operators, clericals, and other female service workers, waitresses sustained their organizational impulse for more than seventy years.[12] At their peak in the 1940s and 1950s, union waitresses represented nearly one-fourth of the trade nationally. In such union strongholds as San Francisco, Detroit, and New York, a majority of female food servers worked under union contract.[13] Indeed, only the institutions built by women in the garment trades appeared to rival waitress unions in terms of influence and longevity.[14]

Union waitresses also enjoyed a degree of institutional independence and autonomy experienced by few other groups of organized women. Throughout the twentieth century, union waitresses were affiliated almost exclusively with the Hotel Employees and Restaurant Employees International Union (HERE), a male-dominated international representing primarily bartenders, cooks, and waiters. Yet from the earliest days of unionization, waitresses resided in their own separate craft- and sex-based locals. With the rise of industrial unionism in the 1930s and 1940s, waitresses increasingly joined mixed-sex and mixed-craft organizations, but the all-female waitress locals, almost all of which had been initiated before 1930, remained among the largest and most powerful organizations within HERE until the 1970s.[15] Because of this decentralized, craft structure, waitresses elected their own female officers, developed their own bylaws and constitutions, devised their own bargaining agenda, and determined their own stance on legislative matters. In addition, the local market economy in which bargaining took place in the hotel and restaurant industry reinforced the autonomy of culinary locals.[16]

The extensive and previously untapped records of these female-led and female-dominated organizations offered an unusually direct and unmediated view of the attitudes and perspectives of wage-earning women.[17] Looking at union institutions, particularly those constructed by women, seemed to open new vistas on working-class culture, the social construction of gender, workplace activism, and a myriad of other issues.[18] Indeed, writing a national history of waitresses and their unions would allow for a synthesis of the new labor history with the old. The study would not focus on a neighborhood or a workplace per se as has been the dominant approach of the new labor history. But by reconceiving of the union as a community and as a site of cultural inquiry, the methods and the concerns of the more locally focused studies would not be lost. They would simply be used in a new arena.[19]

I began to formulate the group of questions which would constitute the core of my project. I wanted to know why this particular group of women chose unionism, how they sustained their collective impulses, and what difference gender made to their unionism. What issues would they define as central? What distinctive strategies for collective advancement, if any, would be forged by these women unionists? And how would their story reshape the conventional concepts and narrative of labor history, if at all?

Many waitress locals, in fact, defined their goals in explicitly sex-conscious ways, announcing their intent "to further the rights of working women" and to bring about economic and political equality with men.[20] What did "equality" and "advancement" mean to working-class women? How did the meaning(s) of these concepts change over time? And, of equal importance, what would a consideration of waitress unionism disclose about the class dimensions of female consciousness and activism?[21]

The answers any historian finds to questions like these are partial. The sources fall silent at critical junctures; generalizations based on a single occupational group are risky at best. Only as more case studies of female unionism and of working-class female institutions are written will definitive propositions be forthcoming.[22] Yet as the documents accumulated and the contours of the history of waitresses began to take shape, I found myself reaching a number of conclusions—conclusions that suggest fresh perspectives on several emerging scholarly debates.

A study of waitresses and the unions they created throws into relief the gendered nature of our understandings of work and unionism. Despite the pathbreaking work of Mary Blewett, Joan Scott, Patricia Cooper, and others, many labor historians have continued to write the history of male unionism in a fairly unself-conscious fashion.[23] Few disclaimers are offered about the possible gender biases of conclusions; few attempts are made to speculate about which elements of that history are distinctive to male or female trade unionism and which elements are universal. Waitress unionism diverged sharply from the male-dominated labor movement; it also resembled it in surprising ways. Both the differences and the similarities are instructive.

The goals waitresses pursued, for example, were often at odds with those espoused by their union brothers. Waitresses vehemently opposed the men in their International who argued for legislative and contract provisions preserving liquor service for men. They also initially took umbrage at equal pay proposals advanced by male co-workers because they believed that with the protective laws restricting women's hours, equal pay would mean the loss of their jobs to men.

Even when waitresses shared similar goals with male workers and voiced these objectives in language common among trade unionists, the words themselves held different meanings for women than for men. The very definition of terms was gendered. For the majority of male workers, the "family wage"— or the "sum necessary to sustain family members" was reserved for men only. In contrast, waitresses argued that any wage earner, male or female, whose contribution to family support was crucial deserved a "family wage." For them, the term legitimized higher wages for women rather than deference to male financial needs.[24]

The definition of skill was reformulated as well. Waitresses claimed to be skilled craftswomen despite the larger societal view of their work as unskilled and despite the fact that they acquired most of their training and experience on the job. For them, "skill" encompassed social abilities. "Nurturing" and "caring"—what sociologist Arlie Hochschild has called the "emotional labor" in women's service jobs—deserved respect and compensation just as did physical strength and "technical" know-how.[25] Although they never achieved the power and prestige accorded the "elite" trades, unionized waitresses did gain many of the protections and benefits that organized men enjoyed. Their history demonstrates that, for workers, *craft* and *skill* were flexible terms encompassing a wide range of ability and job know-how. The achievement of skilled status was based on workplace struggle, not simply on some "objective" measure of expertise.

Likewise, the achievement of such union objectives as "respectability" occurred on gendered terrain. Respectability for women was intimately intertwined with sexual respectability. For waitresses, respectability proved elusive because waiting work involved close personal interaction with male strangers in an environment laden with sexual overtones. Sexuality was always a double-edged sword for waitresses because its expression enhanced their earnings while lowering their status. What image could be projected by the waitress which would achieve both the respectability of being "well-paid" and morally upright? And how could the more explicitly sexualized service encounters be controlled so that the server maintained her dignity as well as her earning potential?[26]

Waitresses, along with other women workers, devised different routes to achieve their ends than did their male counterparts. First, as personal service workers with strong bonds to their clients, they relied on their customers for both individual and collective advancement. Historically, "sexual service" work has been one of the few ways for women to earn a living wage.[27] Companionship, sexual flirtation, and more explicit sexual services were offered in exchange for money. Only through this primitive exchange relationship with individual men could working-class women earn more than a poverty wage. Waitresses also relied on patron support in helping pressure employers into union recognition and bargaining breakthroughs. To the degree that good service and strong personal bonds built patronage, waitresses had a leverage with their employers that workers in many other occupations lacked.

Second, waitresses looked to cross-class alliances with their sex more frequently than did male workers, and in part because of these ties, they also used the legislative arena to a greater degree. Waitresses in New York, Chicago, and other cities, for example, depended on the Women's Trade Union League (WTUL) for assistance in leadership training and legislative activity. Their legislative activism spanned the course of the twentieth century, from Progressive Era campaigns for wage and hour legislation to the drives after World War II for equal pay, maternity leave, and sex-based wage and hour laws.

Despite these considerable differences from the unionism espoused by men, waitresses thought of themselves as craftswomen, and in certain crucial ways, their unionism was similar to that devised by male craft unionists. They spoke of their work as a skilled craft, and they engaged in practices that have long been associated with craft unionism: organization along craft lines, emphasis on craft identity and specialization, restrictive membership rules, and union monitoring of performance standards.[28]

Recognizing the essential craft nature of waitress unionism extends the reassessment of male craft unionism that has emerged in the writings of Michael Kazin, David Montgomery, and Christopher Tomlins. The earlier monolithic view of craft unionists as a conservative, apolitical elite who were hopelessly out of touch with the rank and file by the 1930s has crumbled in the face of the new revisionist scholarship. The poor reputation of the AFL—a reputation fostered in part by the industrial unionists of the CIO and taken up uncritically by labor historians sympathetic to the "new unionism"—has also come under reconsideration.[29]

Michael Kazin's work on the building trades in San Francisco during the Progressive Era attacked the conventional wisdom at its core. A group long thought to be the archetypal, apolitical business unionists were revealed as prominent urban progressives who combined a practical wage-worker consciousness with a social reform mentality whose roots lay in the nineteenth-century soil of antimonopoly and producer republicanism. David Montgomery's *Fall of the House of Labor* undercut yet another aspect of the traditional portrait. All kinds of unionists found a home in Montgomery's AFL: unskilled and semiskilled, immigrant and native born, socialist and republican. Christopher Tomlins moved the reassessment into the 1930s. In a 1979 essay, one of the first to challenge the standard interpretation of the 1930s as the triumph of the CIO, Tomlins contended that labor's resurgence was based in large part on the success of AFL organizational drives. His later book, *The State and the Unions*, also evidenced sympathy for the AFL's belief in the inherent right to collective activity and its goal of creating a more neutral state.[30]

My work moves further along this revisionist road. If the history of waitress unionism is any indication, craft unionism encompassed semiskilled and unskilled workers in the early decades of the twentieth century, and these workers voluntarily adopted the craft perspectives pioneered by skilled workers. Moreover, rather than dismiss craft unionism as conservative and dysfunctional in advancing the interests of workers by the 1930s, I contend that the craft style of organization was crucial to the survival of unionism among many groups of workers. In short, craft union approaches had a vitality and a durability that have gone unrecognized.

Many trades, especially those connected with manufacturing, faced "de-skilling" in the late nineteenth and early twentieth century, or, in the words of other scholars, were being moved from "batch production" to "mass production" technologies.[31] And for these workers, a new unionism was necessary. The transformation of their work, however, and their subsequent need for a new form of unionism should not blind researchers to the much different history of the nonmanufacturing trades. De-skilling may not have occurred until much later, if at all, for service workers, and they continued to work primarily in small shops with informal systems of work organization.[32] It is not surprising that their different relation to work resulted in the creation and maintenance of a different form of unionism.

In an industry of small employers and a highly mobile labor force, such as the restaurant sector, for example, workers needed to be bound together by more than antiemployer animus or the promise of protection from unjust discharge and discipline. The emphasis on building solidarity through craft identity, on upgrading the status of the trade by monitoring entrance standards and workplace job performance, and on providing benefits and services that would travel with workers from jobsite to jobsite all created sources of loyalty among workers that allowed unions to sustain themselves and exert power over multiple small worksites.

True, certain aspects of the craft union model could result in negative consequences. Rigid jurisdictional rules bred intercraft bickering and a "protect-your-own" mentality. The extensive web of craft rules that provided protection from employer abuse could also inhibit workplace flexibility and reinforce a hierarchical system of highly specialized job classifications. And, most disturbingly, the exclusionist tendencies of craft unionism often meant that union membership was reserved for white workers only. Waitress unionism fell prey to these problems just as did male craft unionists. Nevertheless, an awareness of the deficiencies of craft unionism should be combined with a recognition of its innovations and strengths.

The organization of workers along craft and sex-based lines held advantages for women workers as well. The few writers who have explored the relation between union organizational structure and women's subordinate status have emphasized the superiority of industrial unionism. As sociologist Ruth Milkman has observed, the "logic of industrial unionism" has often meant the admittance of women into unions whereas "craft logic" dictated their exclusion.[33] Yet, the success of waitress unionism demonstrates how an organizational structure based on the logic of craft, rather than being incompatible with female mobilization, proved instrumental in its creation and maintenance. The separation of workers by trade provided women with a space apart from male hostility and allowed the development of female perspectives and leadership skills. The tradition of local control and decentralization—so characteristic of craft unionism—also allowed for female autonomy. In contrast to the experience of women organized primarily into mixed-sex, industrially based locals, waitresses enjoyed an unusual degree of participation within their International union and an institutional base from which they could and did raise issues of concern to women. Thus, although industrial union structures were more conducive to the entrance of women into unions, craft structures may have been superior in sustaining female participation and leadership.

Further, twentieth-century craft unionism was in fact quite radical in its demands for workplace control and self-management. The collapse of the "progressive bloc" within the AFL in the 1920s, as David Montgomery has suggested, certainly dampened the struggle for workers' control, but the demise of the radical traditions of nineteenth-century craft unionism has perhaps been overdrawn. Twentieth-century AFL craft workers sought not simply "bread and butter" advances in their negotiations with employers, but what Selig Perlman called "liberty in the shop" or what I have termed "peer management."[34] The work rules and contracts devised by these mainstream craft unionists remained intact into the 1960s, and although they did not involve a challenge to state power or to the ownership of their enterprises, in the context of American management's exceptional penchant for unilateral control, their demand for power on the shopfloor was a radical assault on a central tenet of capitalism as practiced in the United States.[35] In short, any analysis of the AFL or of craft unionism that purports to assess its achievements in representing workers, both male and female, must look to its accomplishments in the collective bargaining arena as well as its activities and pronouncements in the political realm.

Finally, the history of waitress unionism suggests that a different kind of unionism did develop in the 1930s and 1940s, but that its distinguishing characteristics have been only partially understood. The industrial form of unionism meant a more inclusive approach in which a multitude of trades coexisted in one organization unit, but it also meant a new system of organization and shopfloor representation. A critical paradigmatic shift was occurring: from what I call "occupational unionism"—an approach which emphasized the occupational identity of the worker and tied union power to control over those within the occupation—to what can be seen as "worksite unionism"— a form of unionism where rights and protections were linked to a particular worksite.[36]

In other words, I am suggesting a new typology of unionism—one that parallels the conventional craft/industrial typology but recognizes the distinctive workplace representation systems adopted by unions as well as their decision to organize horizontally (by trade) or vertically (by industry). Hopefully, the use of a new typology of unionism and the adoption of new terms to describe the dominant union forms in the twentieth century will call attention to the problematic nature of the terms *craft* and *industrial* unionism and open up for debate the question of what in fact has distinguished different forms of unionism historically.

The history of waitresses also intersects with many important streams of research in women's history. Scholars of women increasingly have been concerned with differences among women, primarily of class, race, and ethnicity, and the ways in which the history of these marginalized groups forces a rethinking of the standard conceptual frameworks in the field. Assertions of a homogeneous cross-class culture for women and a single explanatory schema have been reevaluated.[37] One important aspect of this new scholarship has involved the reconstruction of the distinctive values and experiences of wage-earning women.

Sarah Eisenstein, for example, argued that working-class women rejected specific elements of Victorian morality, in particular the notion that female wage work in the public sphere was incompatible with moral womanhood. Other scholars such as Jacquelyn Hall, Joanne Meyerowitz, Christine Stansell, and Kathy Peiss have posited a separate female working-class morality which held distinct views on the boundaries of acceptable female behavior, condoning the expression of female sexuality, sexual mixing with men, and even premarital intercourse.[38] My research on waitresses confirms many of these observations. Waitresses held views toward female participation in the paid work world, female sexuality, respectability, and other issues that diverged from the dominant middle-class ethos.

Waitresses also articulated and acted upon a feminist vision that was shared historically by many working-class women and their allies, but that has been almost completely eclipsed by the more middle-class feminist perspectives that became dominant in the 1960s.[39] Middle-class feminist activists of the 1960s emphasized "equal treatment," "equal opportunity in the workplace," and "integration of the spheres." Often these approaches were conflated with "feminist" thinking; other strategies were viewed as antifeminist or "false consciousness." In the last decade, however, a renewed awareness of the multiplicity of feminisms and of the rich, diverse traditions of female consciousness has emerged.[40] The working-class feminism advocated by waitress unionists represents one of these lost traditions.[41]

Waitresses advocated a feminism that stressed "difference" and "separateness" rather than "sameness" and "integration." Rather than abandon the advantages of special protections, of sex-based legislation, of separate-sphere alternatives in their workplace and their union, they tried to reconcile such differences in treatment with concepts of equality and "equal opportunity."[42] They wanted equality and special treatment and did not see the two as incompatible.

They also sought a feminism that balanced the needs of the individual woman with the needs of the working-class community and the family of which she was a part. They argued that economic justice and fair treatment for the majority of women can only be provided through employee representation and collective power not individual upward mobility. Rather than focus primarily on moving individual women into the higher-paying jobs held by men, they opted for improvements in the jobs traditionally held by women. Upward mobility for a few did not seem as important as the economic security of the larger group. Class loyalties and communitarian "class" values shaped their concepts of justice and equality.[43] Advancement meant being better able to fulfill the responsibilities (and enjoy the pleasures) of motherhood and family life as well as improving life at the workplace.[44] Although their perspective differed in fundamental ways from other forms of feminism, waitresses were no less committed to the advancement of their sex.

Neither did their perspectives always set them apart from other feminist activists. In the Progressive Era, waitresses advocated separate, all-female locals and "woman-centered" organizing and bargaining. They defended such sex-based protective legislation as wage and hour statutes, night work, and laws restricting women from occupations seen as "morally and physically dangerous." These approaches resonated with the dominant ideology emanating from the feminist movements of middle-class and elite women.

But after World War I, waitresses found themselves at odds with emerging feminist groups such as the National Woman's party or the National Federation of Business and Professional Women's Clubs who advocated "equal treatment," stressed the similarity of the sexes, and pushed for individual opportunity rather than collective advancement through unionization. Waitress unionists maintained ties with other similarly inclined working-class and middle-class feminists through the Women's Bureau and the Women's Trade Union League, however, and carried on their feminist vision, advocating sex-based legislative and contract provisions as well as pay equity and other forms of equal treatment.[45]

In the 1960s, a new consensus arose within the women's movement that united warring middle-class factions and eventually drew in certain union and working-class women.[46] In part because waitresses worked in jobs where sex-typing partially insulated them from direct competition with men, in part because of their own continuing distinct ideological perspectives on sexual equality, and in part because their roots lay in craft- and sex-based organizations, waitresses were one of the few organized women's groups who continued to advocate sex-based legislation, sex-based organizational structures, and a separate "female sphere" within the work world.[47] Throughout the 1970s, they opposed the Equal Rights Amendment, arguing that it would decimate sex-based protective statutes, in particular those mandating limits on overtime and those requiring maternity benefits, rest breaks, seats, and other amenities. Waitresses insisted that the advantages of these "protections" outweighed whatever economic opportunities might become available in the absence of such laws. They also defended their sex-based locals against legal assault and pushed for the upgrading and revaluing of women's jobs. Rather than end the sex-labeling of jobs and move women into work traditionally done by men, they sought to preserve and extend the female sphere.

Because of these stances, waitress leaders were often marginalized and misunderstood. To many younger activists, the older, working-class generation's concern with sexual differences appeared rigid, inhibiting, and acquiescent to male privilege. Class tensions aggravated the breach. The most prominent waitress spokeswoman in this period, Detroit's Myra Wolfgang, railed against Betty Friedan as "a middle-class college 'intellectual'" who knew nothing about working women's real problems; she also saw ERA supporters as privileged women who wanted others to sacrifice on "behalf of a mythical equality" that would benefit only elite women. Yet Wolfgang considered herself devoted to women's equality, and she agitated for extensive public child-care support, equal pay, equal opportunity legislation, and campaigns to "expose male chauvinism."[48]

In the 1980s, critics began reevaluating the strategies of the 1960s, pointing out the drawbacks of moving women into men's jobs and of rewriting divorce statutes and protective laws to ensure equal treatment.[49] New feminist voices assumed gender differences and revalued those differences.[50] An alternative tradition, carried on by waitresses and others, was resurfacing.

The adherents of the new gender politics of the 1980s differed in important ways from those who recognized difference in the past: they saw sex differences as more mutable and were more optimistic about men taking on greater responsibility in the domestic realm. Yet the recognition of the "dual role of women," the importance of "accommodating difference," and the inadequacies of "equal treatment" and "affirmative action" have all been prominent themes. The comparable worth movement, for example, rested squarely on the assumption that women's sphere must be upgraded and revalued and that women should not have to become men in order to be respected and well-compensated for their work.[51]

In seeking to compare the sensibility of waitresses with their male working-class counterparts as well as with their more elite sisters, I have thus far stressed the unanimity among this group of working-class women. Sisterhood and class solidarity had very real limits, however. The majority of waitress locals, for example, excluded black and Asian women from membership until the 1930s and 1940s. Although a few locals pursued issues of racial discrimination in hiring and promotion once the racial barriers fell, minority women continued to be relegated to the lowest-paid, least-desirable positions in the industry and remained underrepresented in the occupation as a whole.[52] In addition, although waitress consciousness contained elements of class and gender identification, the strongest, most consistent aspect of their ideology appears to have been trade identification. When the interests of their trade conflicted with the larger interests of their class or sex, the needs of the craft often came first.

Throughout much of the twentieth century, the identity of white waitresses with the principles of a "craft sisterhood" overrode such divisive issues as just exactly what constituted "sexual respectability" and "women's work," and held at bay the competitiveness of waitresses over customers, tips, and individual gain. It was the commitment to the collective advancement of the sisters in the craft that allowed waitresses to organize and maintain a collective presence. By the 1950s and 1960s, however, even that long-standing consensus had begun to unravel. Increasingly, the differences among waitresses came to undermine their unity of purpose and spirit. The story of waitress unionism is one of disintegration and conflict as well as growth and solidarity.

Dishing It Out is an attempt to address scholarly controversies. It is also an attempt to recreate the lives of a group of very nontraditional women. Waitresses worked in an occupation that historically was judged as immoral and degrading; they organized and sustained female unions with a vehemence unmatched by few other groups of women.

The story begins with the work itself. Chapter 1 details the expansion of commercial food service and its transformation into a female occupation. Particular attention is paid to what the case of food service reveals about the larger social processes of occupational segregation and feminization. Chapter 1 also recreates the work world, ethnicity, and family characteristics of waitresses.[53] In contrast to descriptions of wage-earning women that stress their primary identity with their family role and their perception of themselves as temporary, secondary wage workers,[54] I argue that waitresses exhibited a strong attachment to their work and their occupational community; they also developed a work culture rooted in a realistic appraisal of their needs and status as primary wage earners.

Chapters 3 and 4 present the story of the building of unions among waitresses and analyze the forces that promoted and inhibited their success. The case of waitress unionism refines the emerging theory concerning the conditions under which collective action among women could occur and endure.[55]

Chapters 5 and 6 detail the impact of waitress unionism in the workplace and establish the essentially craft-like character of the organizations waitresses built. Here the achievements as well as the limitations of waitress unionism as a vehicle for class and feminist impulses become clear.

Chapter 7 traces the changing perspectives of both black and white waitresses on such questions as liquor service, equal pay, night work, and bartending for women and contrasts their views with those of their male co-workers. Chapter 8 focuses on the strategies devised by waitresses to enhance their power within their union and returns to the question of the sources of female activism and leadership among waitresses.

Dishing It Out concludes with an analysis of the decline of unionism among waitresses. In the decades after World War II, economic, political, and social forces radically reshaped the nature of work and labor-management relations

within the hotel and restaurant industry, leaving only a few fundamentals intact—waitresses continued to serve up daily their coffee, good humor, and
sassy repartee. What were the implications of these changes for unionism in
the industry? And what, if anything, can the history of waitress unionism
reveal about the prospects for organizing waitresses today?

PART I

The Occupational Community of Waitressing

Waitressing as an occupational category is bound by the thinnest of common threads: all waitresses serve food. Beyond this commonality one encounters diversity in the nature and duties of the occupation; the environs in which the work is performed; the wages, hours, and working conditions; and the attitudes toward the occupation by the public and the waitress herself. Yet despite these differences, many women who entered waitressing in the twentieth century perceived their work as a discrete craft and identified themselves as members of an occupational community of waitresses. These female service workers never defined their work as a "career"—the term used by middle-class working women—but neither did they dismiss their work outside the home as merely a "job." Waitresses derived social and personal identity from their work, and many evidenced a primary commitment to their trade and their community of co-workers. The strong occupational identity of waitresses and the group ties they forged partially explain why waitresses, unlike women in many other female-dominated occupations, engaged in widespread political and economic activity directed toward transforming the workplace and why ultimately they were able to sustain their union organizations.

CHAPTER ONE

The Rise of Waitressing: Feminization, Expansion, and Respectability

Children love to sleep in houses other than their own, and to eat at a neighbor's table; on such occasions they behave themselves decently and are proud. The people in the town were likewise proud when sitting at the tables in the cafe. There, for a few hours at least the deep bitter knowing that you are not worth much in this world could be laid low.

—Carson McCullers, "The Ballad of the Sad Cafe"

George Smith, a veteran waiter, was "not worried" about competition from waitresses, a Detroit union journal headlined in 1942. According to Smitty, a few women could "carry a tray with the best of men and dish out first class service," but "to work in the best jobs" you had "to learn to whisper in the dining room and holler in the kitchen." Most waitresses, he insisted, simply got confused. They were "either delicate flowers who whisper[ed] both places, with the result that the chef [did not] . . . get the orders straight, or Amazons who holler[ed] in the dining rooms as well as the kitchens, thereby grating the nerves of the guests."[1] Few observers have shared Smitty's particular prejudices regarding female "waiteresses," but historically most have agreed that men were more suitable for waiting work, especially in "first-class" establishments.

Although women served food in the earliest colonial hostelries, and nineteenth- and twentieth-century women worked in boardinghouses, tea rooms, coffee shops, and cafes, the majority of commercial food and lodging establishments employed men until the 1920s.[2] Before the twentieth century, most women food servers worked in private homes as domestics. The formation of a group identity among female food servers in the twentieth century, then, rested on two historical transformations: the commercialization of food service (or its removal from the isolated home realm into the commercial sphere) and the growing acceptability of women in this new public waiting work.

Early Dining and the "Professional Waiter"

In colonial American cities, public food service work took place in taverns and inns that were also centers of political, literary, and social exchange.
Meals, when available, typically were prepared and served by the male vic-
tualer with the aid of his wife and family. Outside helpers, if required, assisted
in a variety of tasks: food preparation (including harvesting from an adjoining
garden), food service, and household cleaning.[3]

As water, rail, and stagecoach transportation developed in the nineteenth
century, the business of feeding and lodging changed character. Numerous
small hostelries expressly for travelers sprang up in out-of-the-way villages and
at road and rail crossings. In urban areas, especially on the East Coast, larger,
more elaborate structures were erected beginning in the 1830s. These first
"hotels" provided accommodations for transients and facilities for community functions on a scale far exceeding the early inns. The Tremont House
in Boston, for example, opened in 1829 with 170 guest rooms, ten public
rooms, and a main dining room that served two hundred diners at a single
setting. Many catered to male travelers and were reluctant to provide shelter
to unaccompanied women, let alone hire them.[4]

Later in the century, luxurious, multistoried hotels catered to a growing
urban wealth and taste for extravagance. Monuments to conspicuous consumption, these hotels indulged every culinary whim of their guests. Despite
widespread reliance on the American plan, in which meals were included in
the price of lodging, hotels vied for patronage by offering the finest in cuisine
along with impeccable service. As befitted European traditions of formal dining, "impeccable service" invariably meant male personnel, including male
waiters in the dining rooms. Men were also stronger, employers explained,
and could more easily climb stairs with trays loaded down with heavy silver,
glassware, and food.[5]

American hotels differed from those in Europe, however, in that diners
often were served by black men. In the decades after the Civil War, employers
frequently relied on waiting crews composed entirely of black men. The shortage of white male immigrant and native-born labor, the availability of black
job seekers, and the southern tradition of black servants in the home all contributed to this American departure. Black men—especially those outside the
South—lost the more desirable service jobs to white men by the end of the
nineteenth century, and they fell further behind once feminization gathered
speed in the early decades of the twentieth century. But as Table 2B in the
Appendix shows, black men maintained a disproportionate share of the work
until the 1940s. As late as 1930, one-fourth of male waiters were black.[6]

In the decades before and after World War I, as a stratum of hotels opened that was a notch below the highly touted palaces preceding them, the real boom in hotel employment began. Exemplified by the Buffalo Statler Hotel built in 1908, these new hotels met with instant success. Appealing to businessmen and travelers, they provided the modern conveniences and privacy of the finest hotels at a moderate price. They also adopted the European plan, in which travelers paid separately for room and meals. Informal dining typified the commercial hotel, with a cafeteria or coffee shop as the common eating arrangement.[7]

Initially, male waiters, black and white, predominated in these scaled-down dining rooms as well as in the older, exclusive hotel restaurants, but a few employers experimented with female help. Employers hired women of all races and ethnic groups in these early decades, but nine out of every ten jobs went to white women.[8] Ellsworth Statler hired white waitresses for the 2,257-room "inn" he had built as an exhibit for the 1904 St. Louis World's Fair. Women waiters "proved to be a curiosity," attracted clientele, and helped Statler turn a profit. Resort and summer hotels, especially those catering to couples and families, also replaced their male help with female. Non-southern black waiters in particular lost ground. Those working in the most elegant establishments faced competition from newly arrived white male immigrants; others were replaced by white women. The owners of the Hotel Chalfonte, a prominent resort in Atlantic City, brought 250 white waitresses from Boston in a special guarded train to replace the hotel's black male crew in 1909.[9]

As the supply of male labor contracted during World War I, even more hotel owners looked to women. At the war's end, some rehired "the old-style professional waiter—a hallowed institution in the hotel world," but others retained women on a permanent basis.[10] In addition, when waiters, cooks, and other male culinary workers joined the labor walkouts of the postwar era, employers in some of the "biggest and best" hotels engaged women as strikebreakers. In 1919, New York City "bosses hired girls to take the places of the men" for the first time, New York City's fledgling culinary worker tabloid headlined after four thousand food workers quit their posts.[11]

Although "nothing could have induced" some hotel proprietors "to give women a chance if the strike of the [New York City] waiters had not forced them into it," a different verdict emerged in the strike's aftermath. Women were superior employees, proprietors now determined: they were more obedient and compliant than waiters and cost much less. Employers defended the "radical step" of using women by pointing out the "greater cleanliness, tact, efficiency, and adaptability" of waitresses. Proclaiming his newfound fondness for women, the dining-room manager of New York's Waldorf Hotel announced that "no matter what the conditions of the labor market will be in the future, women will serve the banquets and be part of the dining service at the Waldorf." Other employers agreed, arguing that if busboys did the hauling of heavy food trays and wine stewards served the liquor, all obstacles to female employment would be removed.[12]

By the early 1920s, male waiters still held the majority of jobs in the most exclusive hotel restaurants, but their dominance in the industry as a whole had ended. As the golden era of luxury hotel dining faded in the 1920s and 1930s, the larger hotels replaced their posh dining rooms with smaller, informal restaurants and coffee shops, the change in ambience facilitating the shift from a male to female staff.[13] And, as in the preceding decades, the number of black men declined disproportionately because they were being displaced by white men as well as white women.[14] The growth of restaurants outside of hotels, particularly those catering to the working and middle classes and to the increasing number of female diners, also transformed the nature of food service work and spurred feminization.

Harvey Girls, Hashers, and Tea Room Maids

The feminization of food service in the independent restaurant sector resembled that of hotel dining: the kinds of jobs held by women multiplied much faster than those held by men, and women displaced men in jobs that had traditionally been reserved for male personnel. Before the twentieth century, waitresses could be found serving food in boardinghouses, music halls, private clubs, and such commercial establishments as Fred Harvey's famous chain that fed railroad passengers along the Santa Fe system, but the vast majority of independent restaurants relied on male waiters.[15] Waiters predominated in the more elegant restaurants where "fashion demanded the superior presence of the male" and in numerous other environments thought improper for the nineteenth-century working girl: aboard ocean vessels, in railroad dining cars, and in the saloons and bars set up for the urban working man.[16] Having replaced the old-style tavern and corner grocer as the favorite urban drinking dispensary by the mid-nineteenth century, saloons competed for patrons by offering free food with the purchase of a 5 cent schooner of beer. Typical establishments provided a buffet from 11 to 3, a hot meal at 5 o'clock, and a final repast about midnight. One Chicago saloon employed five full-time countermen just to carve the meats and fill the platters for hungry patrons.[17]

In the 1910s and 1920s, waiting jobs opened up to women as new types of restaurants prospered and "eating out" became a pastime no longer reserved for the rich or the single male businessman or traveler. Between 1900 and 1930, the number of restaurants nationwide more than tripled, and by 1938 more than one million people were employed in eating establishments.[18] The new consumer demand for restaurant dining arose for a variety of reasons. The wealthy, accustomed to fine continental dining when away from home, began patronizing fashionable restaurants in their own local communities. Smaller, apartment-style homes and the loss of domestic help—between 1900 and 1940 the ratio of servants to private families fell 36 percent—also sent many of the wealthy into the public sphere in search of lavish service and culinary elegance. But the largest group of additional restaurant patrons came from the middle and lower classes.[19]

Changes in the living patterns of the urban working classes fostered more dining out among the general public. In the late nineteenth and early twentieth century, boardinghouses had provided the comforts of home (in a limited fashion) to unattached men and women. Then, rooming and lodging houses dominated the trade, offering living quarters for newly arrived immigrant workers as well as for the army of clerks, stenographers, and shopgirls streaming into the inner cities from the surrounding countryside. But, unlike boardinghouse keepers, few proprietors in the furnished room districts prepared culinary fare, and fewer still provided kitchen facilities.[20] Consequently, a small but thriving industry of cafes, tea rooms, "hash houses," lunchrooms, and cafeterias sprang up to serve this new clientele—a large portion of which was female—and to compete with the older working-class taverns.[21] The "roomers" were joined by the growing throngs of urban commuters, middle-class female shoppers, and tourists, all clamoring to be fed. Drugstores added soda fountains; department stores offered lunch counters and even full-menu restaurants. During World War I, servicemen and the newest female labor force entrants frequented commercial eating establishments as well.[22]

Restaurant entrepreneurs competed for this new mass market with simplified food delivery systems that lowered costs while increasing convenience. Customers in the Childs Dairy Lunch or the Thompson's or Waldorf chain sat at one-armed desk seats and bused their own trays. Drive-ins and prepackaged mobile lunch cars opened their awnings. The Automat, introduced by two Philadelphia lunchroom operators, Joseph Horn and Frank Hardart, took self-service one step beyond the cafeteria—"the restaurant industry's first attempt at emulating the assembly line." The Automat relied on a mechanized service approach in which patrons retrieved precooked dishes from under glass cubicles by simply dropping in the right combination of coins. Some lamented this new style of food consumption: "Eating is no longer a 'fine art,'" protested an observer in 1932, "but is becoming a sort of 'hit and run matter.'" Despite protests, the trend continued.[23]

The move toward inexpensive, simple dining added to the demand for women. The cheaper labor of women was necessary where employer profits were lower. The quick yet personable service needed in informal eateries also clashed with the leisurely, aloof style of the male waiter, traditional in full-service, formal restaurants and upper-class homes. The presence of a friendly, attractive female server suited owners perfectly. As one Cleveland manager confided: waiters simply "did not respond to his suggestions for courteous and smiling service."

With employers emphasizing beauty, sex appeal, and a pleasing personality, waiters found it difficult to compete. According to one: "It is hard to overcome the prejudice of the bosses regarding the small items wherein we constantly fall down, to-wit, lacking neatness in our appearance, forgetting how to smile, demonstrating our animosities toward one another for all to observe." The only exceptions were restaurant owners of "certain nationalities who accept our [male] service because of old customs which were established in the land of their birth . . . where waiters typify high-class standards." Other waiters were more sanguine, believing that waitresses would be limited to "drug and other stores with lunch counters." They argued that there was "still a place in the sun for the real service waiter" or the "first class waiter" who worked "in the best jobs."[24]

In the 1920s, restaurateurs also began experimenting with restaurant decor, hoping to appeal to the growing consumer taste for style and novelty. Restaurants lagged behind department stores and other retail businesses in responding to the "new ethos of consumption which emphasized color, spectacle, and sensual pleasure," but by the 1920s many recognized that restaurant dining could fill psychological and social needs as well as dietary ones. Concerned with creating "an atmosphere divorced from everyday reality," one Los Angeles businessman designed an interior that "captured the feeling of a redwood forest." A neighboring cafeteria resembled a tropical paradise—complete with simulated rainfall. Others strove for more modest effects: a relaxed, "homey" atmosphere familiar to the new, non-elite diner or a subdued upper-class drawing-room environment suitable for female teas and luncheons.[25]

By and large, employers preferred women in these new-style eateries. Few of the exotic "theme" restaurants called for men: women were more suited for the role of decorative object. One of New York's most popular restaurants hired young, attractive waitresses to match its elaborate color scheme: "service in the Fountainette room is by waitresses with red hair; in the main dining room, blondes; in the lunch room, brunettes." Indeed, one industry analyst in *Restaurant Management* recommended matching waitresses to each other, observing that "a corps of waitresses of uniform size and color" could add as much to a restaurant interior as expensive or unusual furnishings. Even employers who worked the more traditional theme of "family-style dining" preferred female servers to complete the effect; in this case, however, they looked for the nurturing, motherly type. Tea rooms, department store restaurants, and other light luncheon spots that catered to a predominantly female clientele hired women as well, admonishing them to act and dress like maids in upper-class homes.[26]

The advent of Prohibition in 1920 opened up further opportunities for women. Overnight, bars were transformed into soda fountains, luncheonettes, or coffee shops. "Practically all the eating houses established . . . where bars were formerly located are employing girls," a Los Angeles culinary union organizer observed. Victorian society demanded higher standards of morality from women than from men; women were expected to abstain from drinking, serving, or mixing liquor, or even being in the presence of liquor consumption. Without liquor, many drinking and eating spots became more acceptable places for both female patrons and servers. Owners also sought the cheaper labor of waitresses because restaurants without liquor made less profit. "We old-time hams have become obsolete since the service houses have dispensed with the handling of alcoholic beverages," a veteran waiter wrote.[27] By the end of the 1920s, women claimed 59 percent of all table service jobs nationwide (Table 1).

Although black women had never comprised a large percent of the occupation, their proportion dropped precipitously after 1920 and never recovered. In 1920, 12.1 percent of waitresses were black, by 1930 only 7.6 percent (Table 2A). Because of their sex, black women had been excluded from the waiting jobs in which black men had found acceptance—those in elegant hotels, trains, and other situations that catered to travelers and businessmen, did not require a homelike, informal, or intimate atmosphere and hence were more amenable to black and male personnel. Yet because of their race, they were at a disadvantage in competing for the new jobs opening up to women.

By the 1920s, employers were becoming more self-conscious about their public image. They sought out waitresses who conformed to the white American standard of beauty—a standard now largely rooted in a "fashion culture" that emphasized appearance over spiritual beauty. Most employers preferred white applicants almost exclusively. Some even followed the advice of management consultants who urged the hiring of a mix of "blondes, brunettes, and redheads." Few agreed with the New York City tea room proprietor who "installed colored women as waitresses" in 1921 because of their "gentle sweetness, innate love of beauty," and exalted spiritual qualities. Tea rooms, in fact, were somewhat unusual in that a "crew of colored women" could as easily "complete the atmosphere" as could a corps of white women, since in the tea room setting the ideal waitress resembled the domestic in an upper-class home.[28]

Black women continued to find work in the small number of black-owned restaurants or in those catering to an all-black clientele. Others were hired because they were cheaper. The cost advantage, however, had to be fairly substantial. A "domestic service" specialist in the U.S. Employment Service found that when the minimum wage law for women and minors went into effect in the early 1920s in Washington, D.C., "practically all of the hotels and restaurants immediately discharged Negro workers and took on white ones." Some explained that whites were more efficient, but most simply said that $16.50 a week was "too much to pay Negroes."[29]

Black waitresses also may have lost food service jobs as black migration

into the northern cities increased after World War I. Although an estimated
half-million blacks headed north between 1916 and 1921, few moved into
waitressing.[30] In the South, black women were more acceptable in visible
public service jobs than in the North because southerners were accustomed
to intimate social interactions with black servants in both the private and
public realms. In the North, blacks found themselves competing with immigrant women who, unlike white southerners, were less inhibited about taking
on personal service work—work that in the South was associated firmly with
black labor.[31]

Finally, employers turned to women in the 1920s, particularly white
women, because, unlike white men, they were plentiful. In the 1920s, many
white, native-born men had better-paying and more gender-appropriate job
options than those opening up in the expanding restaurant sector. The passage of the 1924 Immigration Act also ended the traditional source of white
male restaurant labor: the European-trained, immigrant cook or waiter. In
contrast, native-born white female applicants, many escaping the shrinking
opportunities in rural America, eagerly sought out waitressing jobs. These
farm recruits were joined by their urban sisters who were spending more years
of their lives in the paid work force. Many "chose" waitressing because it required little training and promised the possibility of a living wage. Of equal
importance for some, however, was the change in public attitude toward the
occupation.[32]

"One Step Ahead of a Hussy"

The 1920s marked a watershed in public perception of waitressing as the
work lost many of its disreputable overtones. During the Progressive Era and
earlier, waitress work was judged an "improper trade" for women because it
was performed in surroundings deemed incompatible with Victorian respectability.[33] Waitresses interacted daily with male strangers, conversing freely
with them in public settings. They might work where liquor was sold or worse
still, dispense it themselves. Moreover, because of the server's economic dependence on the tip, she often flirted or "jollied along" her male customers.
Middle-class moralizers who assessed waitresses using their own refined criteria of 'polite conversation' and strict segregation of the sexes found much to
condemn. For them, a waitress crossed the line of impropriety the moment
she crossed the threshold of the restaurant.

Indeed, the intimacy of food service, the tip exchange, the decided departure of waitresses from middle-class standards of gentility, and perhaps the
association—often unconscious—between eating and sex led to the denun-
ciation of waitresses as "loose women" and even as prostitutes. Shocked by the
willingness of waitresses to date numerous men, to engage in frank and unin-
hibited sexual banter, and to frequent the "cabaret life," sociologist Frances

Donovan decried their "lives of semi-prostitution" and "the low, common, vulgar" state to which "economic independence" had brought them. Proclaiming them to be "genuine Bohemians," Donovan added tellingly: "They appeared to be happy, too, not cast down and ashamed of their degradation." [34]

Although in all likelihood waitresses were "more free and easy in manners and speech than other wage-earning women," as the 1912 U.S. Senate report on the conditions of women and children observed;[35] nevertheless, little evidence was ever offered that waitresses as a group engaged in sexual liaisons or offered sex in exchange for money more frequently than women in other working-class occupations. Prostitutes, however, often claimed to be waitresses when arrested in taverns and bars—thus reinforcing the negative image of the trade—even though former prostitutes (when speaking frankly) rarely listed waitressing as a former or current occupation.[36] Moreover, middle-class observers often did not recognize that the sexual jokes and innuendos between waitresses and customers were a commonly accepted aspect of working-class culture and did not necessarily lead to sex for pay or multiple sexual partnerships by waitresses.[37]

During the 1920s, the loosening of restrictions on female interaction with male strangers and the advent of Prohibition combined to elevate the moral status of the occupation. Waitressing as a legitimate occupation became disentangled from waitressing as a front for prostitution or as an occupation linked to liquor. With the expansion of opportunities for waitresses in luncheonettes, in tea rooms, and in family dining settings, the typical environment in which waitresses worked became more sanitized and respectable in the eyes of the public.[38]

As expanding employment demands brought in more native-born, white, lower-middle-class women, social attitudes adjusted accordingly. In the decade of the 1920s alone, the number of native white waitresses more than doubled, jumping from seventy-seven thousand to more than one hundred and eighty thousand. "It is the class of people in the occupation which makes the job unattractive," one vocational study declared. Luckily, "the hasher of a generation ago [whom] everybody agreed was an untidy, uneven-tempered, unpredictable creature" was being replaced by a more genteel, "high class" type who had been thoroughly drilled in table etiquette, neatness, diction, and proper personal hygiene. The introduction of training courses also helped "professionalize" the trade. Restaurants, unions, and public schools started their own training programs for table servers, some subsidized by funds from the Vocational Education Act of 1917. Reformers hoped that training programs would upgrade waitressing, raising it to the level of "the so-called refined occupations." [39]

But critical assessments of waitressing lingered among some segments of the population. One 1920s waitress remembered the indignation of her father, a factory worker in Elizabethton, North Carolina, when she brought home her first tips. Another waitress who attempted to join the women's auxiliary of her husband's fraternal group in a small town in the Northwest in the 1920s recalled the hostile reactions she encountered. "At the first meeting I attended, a lady asked me what I did, was I a housewife, what did I do, and I told her I was a waitress, and she soon left her seat and started whispering with some other ladies, and I began to feel like an outcast because I was a waitress. I resented that and didn't ever return to a meeting of the organization." Decades later, waitresses still complained of male customers who automatically assumed waitresses were sexually available and of haughty, moralistic female customers who "looked down their noses" at food servers and prejudged them as "unprincipled and unstable." To them "a waitress is one step ahead of a hussy and losing ground fast," one Illinois veteran of the craft explained. "Some day I'm going to ask one of these butterflies to try on my apron, just for size."[40]

The New Order: Feminized and Segregated

The feminization of food service proceeded throughout the 1930s. A dwindling number of employers heeded the president of the New York City Society of Restaurateurs, who argued in 1935 that waitresses would never "as a class come up to the requirements of the adept knights of the napkin"—those expert waiters who were "thoroughly familiar with wines and fine liquors" and knowledgeable about complicated recipes and food preparation techniques. Under pressure from both the depression crisis and the persisting consumer preference for inexpensive, simplified dining, employers broke with tradition and replaced men with lower-paid women. The demand for female servers was so great in the 1930s that state agencies like the Pennsylvania State Employment Service set up training programs "to fit inexperienced girls for waitress work."[41]

Not surprisingly, in the midst of depression, black male and female servers suffered heightened job discrimination. More whites were available for service work, and their labor could now be secured more cheaply. Black men dropped from 25 percent of the male wait force to 12 percent, losing jobs to white men as well as to women. Similarly, the percentage of black female servers reached a nadir of 4 percent in 1940. Despite the expansion *and* feminization of food service employment in the 1930s, even the *absolute* number of black waitresses declined (Tables 1, 2A, and 2B). Those blacks who managed to retain their food service jobs suffered downward mobility. Black waitresses were either relegated to the worst-paying jobs or reduced to the status of "busgirl."[42] To a degree, southern blacks were insulated from direct job competition with whites because, as Julia Blackwelder and others have noted, white southerners were more reluctant to "trespass" into jobs formerly held by blacks, but even in the South, a disproportionate number of the new jobs went to whites.[43]

With the expansion of the economy during World War II and the shortage of men, women of all races and ethnic groups entered wait work. They "invaded" traditional male bastions such as hotel room service, railroad dining, and ocean cruise work. And with the suspension of state protective laws prohibiting night work for women, female servers moved into the late-night and dinner trade. The domestic upheaval of wartime also altered the eating habits of the public, expanding the number of job openings. As families separated and women worked long hours in defense plants, people who before the war rarely ate a meal outside their home now did so daily.[44]

The hunger for inexpensive, commercially prepared food showed no sign of abating in the postwar era. With Americans eating one in four meals outside the home by 1951, hamburger chains, drive-ins, and twenty-four-hour coffee shops mushroomed along highways, in suburban developments, and in small towns across the country. These changes paralleled the development of cost-saving technologies in commercial food preparation and service, the growth of two-income families, and the boom in auto tourism. The abandonment of home cooking became a permanent habit for the average American, opening thousands of jobs for waitresses.[45]

By the 1950s, food service had become not only a thoroughly female-dominated occupation, but also one of the principal means by which women earned a living. Four out of five servers were female, and waitressing emerged as the sixth-largest occupation for women, outranked only by clerks and typists, secretaries, saleswomen, private household workers, and teachers.[46] The ensuing decades simply extended these trends (Table 1). By 1970, women comprised 92 percent of the trade and waitressing maintained its status as one of the fastest-growing occupations for women.[47]

Yet despite the upheavals of feminization and expansion, the second-class status of female servers remained intact, ensured by a persistent sexual division of labor within the occupation. Although the type of waiting jobs classified as "women's work" differed depending on the era and the region, the practice of sex-typing jobs as either male or female was ever-present. Throughout the twentieth century, waiting work remained sexually segregated by firm type, that is, whether formal dinner house or neighborhood cafe, and by shift and station assignment within an individual establishment. The racial stratification persisted in the face of changing racial ratios as well. Generally, waiters monopolized employment at higher-priced, fancier restaurants requiring formal service, with white waiters holding the best of these positions. Women worked in tea rooms, drugstore counters, cafeterias, and coffee shops and other establishments where checks and gratuities were low. Nonwhite women either took the worst of these jobs or dropped out of the occupation.[48] In establishments that employed both men and women such as neighborhood cafes or lower-grade steak houses, women were found on the breakfast and lunch shifts; waiters historically picked up the lucrative dinner trade and liquor service. Invariably, the better-paying, more prestigious jobs were held by men, primarily white men. The sex segregation of food service in part reflected the domestic division of labor which necessitated women at home to care for their children and family in the late afternoon and evening, but it also rested on discrimination. Women could always be found dishing out midnight specials at lonely truckstops and twenty-four-hour cafes, while tuxedoed male waiters served elegant lunches to corporate executives.[49]

The sex-based division of labor partially explains why the feminization of food service work occurred at different rates in different locales. Women dominated the occupation first in small towns and in the less urbanized West because of the shortage of available male labor and the greater number of lower-paying food service jobs. In large metropolitan areas, even on the West Coast, male service personnel retained their majority into the 1960s, claiming the exclusive dining rooms of the best hotels as their preserve.[50]

But what does the history of women's entry into waiting work reveal about feminization as a sociological phenomenon? Overall, the forces that spurred the changing sex composition of waiting work appear similar to those delineated for other feminized occupations such as clerical work and bank tellers.[51] Yet the complex and variegated ways in which those factors interacted in the case of food service calls into question the search for a single explanatory schema for all occupations. For example, such external forces as Prohibition, economic crisis, immigration restrictions, and the two world wars underlay shifts in both the supply and demand for female labor and are all critical for understanding the move toward female labor in waiting work. Technological innovations, however, were less important in spurring feminization than in other occupations such as clerical work and printing.[52] The evolution of personal service work also differs from nonservice occupations in the key role reserved for consumer preference—whether it be for inexpensive eateries or for young, attractive, white women.[53]

Moreover, the case of waiting work reveals the inadequacies of current theory in explaining the processes of feminization among a nonprofessional, multiracial work force. Sociological research has stressed the importance of "male flight" out of declining occupations in facilitating female entry, yet the resistance of male waiters, both black and white, to changes in sex composition indicates that the movement of men out of blue-collar and low-paid service occupations may not always be voluntary. Especially when feminization involves the direct substitution of white women for minority men, as in waiting work, the resistance of men will be heightened because minority males traditionally have had fewer alternative occupational choices.[54] Of equal importance, the interplay between race and sex has been underexplored. Although the evidence is only fragmentary because many of the sources fail to discuss race explicitly, in food service white women displaced both white men and black, while nonwhite women competed primarily with white women (and to a much lesser degree with black men) for the other, less desirable jobs.

Finally, the rate of feminization and the resilience of sex and race-segregated work patterns were in large part a result of employer actions, as other histori-cal accounts have argued.[55] Nevertheless, as later chapters will explore more fully, the changing gender and racial ideologies of workers themselves, both men and women, also shaped the contours of the industry.[56]

The Women Who Wait: Ethnicity, Age, and Marital Status

Waitresses work in a bewildering variety of environments and come from diverse backgrounds. They might be "serving chicken dogs at the Vet or foie gras at [the Four Seasons], or taking drink orders in a club in stiletto heels and a satin corset."[57] Sitting down to a meal, the patron is as likely to be greeted by a thin, tired, young mother of three as a robust, wise-talking, middle-aged divorcee. Yet despite the seeming diversity, over the course of the twentieth century the majority of waitresses shared certain distinguishable characteristics. Indeed, waitresses as a group exhibited a notable degree of homogeneity, especially in regard to ethnicity, family status, and economic situation. These shared characteristics differentiated them from women in other female-dominated trades and facilitated the formation of a work-based community.

By and large, waitressing in the twentieth century was an occupation re-served for white women drawn from the "old" Northern European immigrant groups (English, Irish, German, Scandinavian, and Welsh). In the fifty-year period from 1910 to 1960, black women averaged only 7 percent of all wait-resses (Table 2A). Over the course of the century, waitresses became eth-nically homogeneous as well. Numerous pre-World War I studies noted the scarcity of Southern and Eastern European immigrants in hotel and restaurant work and commented on the Irish, German, or Scandinavian backgrounds of individual servers.[58] Early data gathered on the ethnicity of "servants and waitresses" provides another supporting piece of evidence. In 1900, more than 40 percent of foreign-born Irish, Swedish, Danish, and Norwegian immi-grants were "servants and waitresses," but fewer than 15 percent of Italian and Russian immigrants.[59]

As native farm women of Irish, English, German, Welsh, and other North-ern European backgrounds flocked to waitressing in the 1920s, the "old" immi-grant cast became even more pronounced. As early as 1917, Frances Donovan, relying on the participant-observer method, described Chicago waitresses as native women from small towns in the Midwest, of foreign or native parent-age, typically Methodist, Lutheran, or Catholic. Even in New York City, with its unusually high concentration of Southern European immigrants, a 1931 study found that "the English, Irish, Scotch, German, and Swedish predominate" as waitresses and that many came from small towns in New England or were "immigrants of Northern Europe."[60]

Of course, most employers sought English-speaking servers and thus drew heavily on the larger pool of native-born applicants among the older immigrant population, but language proficiency does not explain the continuing bias against second-generation Jews or Italians. Indeed, a 1931 New York City report commissioned by the Emanuel Federated Employment Service in part because of its concern with the lack of Jewish waitresses concluded that restaurant employers had a "decided preference" for the " 'Nordic' race—those that are tall, blonde and fair-skinned," and that the "dark swarthy appearance" of many Greek, "Latin," and Jewish women kept them from being hired, even by owners from their own immigrant background.[61]

In contrast to their ethnic and racial homogeneity, waitresses varied greatly by age and marital background. This diversity set them apart from such female-dominated occupations as clerical work or teaching in which young, single women congregated or domestic service where the bulk of the work force was older and married. They more closely resembled saleswomen in department stores, in part because the retail sector hiring strategy (like that in food service) included both young and old, married and single.[62]

The majority of waitresses were under thirty-five throughout the twentieth century, but a significant number were older, even in the pre-World War I era. In 1916, the New York branch of the National Consumers' League concluded that two-thirds of the women who worked in restaurants were under thirty. Yet Frances Donovan reported that waitresses "may be of any age. There are grandmothers in the waitress group." A 1929 New York Department of Labor study found 17 percent of the waitresses surveyed to be over forty-five. Cafeteria managers, for instance, traditionally hired women thirty-five and over. Other employers viewed older waitresses as appropriate for an older female clientele or in family-style restaurants catering to children.[63]

In the 1940s and 1950s, the rapid expansion of food service made securing an adequate supply of younger workers difficult. As a result, older women were hired into a greater variety of food service jobs. A Women's Bureau study in the 1950s argued that restaurant owners now regarded mature women as desirable employees, finding them to be "stable, courteous, dependable and cooperative." In particular, married women between thirty and forty and "women without young children" were seen as good hiring risks. Despite the more flexible stance of employers in the postwar era, most continued to seek waitresses "between eighteen and thirty." Their quest was unsuccessful, however. In 1950, the average age of waitresses was 30.8, just slightly below the average age of all women workers (31.1); in 1960 it was virtually unchanged.[64]

In contrast to the popular image of the young, single waitress, a large proportion of waitresses also were married (Table 3). An anonymous reporter, recounting her brief stint as a waitress in 1908, confided that "the majority are really married women . . . and many bring their children to the meetings of the union." The Consumers' League was also "rather surprised" in 1916 "to find so large a proportion of married women in the work"—some 33 percent. This figure surpassed the percentage of married women found in the overall female wage-earning population: in 1910, 24 percent of working women were married; in 1920, 23 percent. Waitresses maintained their greater tendency to marry as late as the 1960s, according to Census Bureau figures tabulated in Table 3. Thus, even the postwar waitress of the 1950s and 1960s was more likely to be married than her sister workers in other occupations.[65]

The Waitress as Primary Earner

The most distinctive characteristic of waitresses, when compared to other occupational categories, was the large number who were divorced, separated, or living apart from their family of origin. In one pre-World War I study, only 3 percent of waitresses reported being divorced and 11 percent widowed—comparable to the 15 percent of all working women who reported being widowed or divorced. But Frances Donovan estimated that of the waitress work force she observed in 1917, 50 percent were married, 10 percent unmarried, and a full 40 percent divorced. Representing herself as a waitress rather than an outside authority, Donovan probably obtained more candor from her subjects and hence constructed a truer portrait of the personal backgrounds of waitresses. In addition, later regional studies consistently presented waitressing as an occupation employing large numbers of married women with husbands absent, as well as many divorced and widowed workers. A 1929 New York Department of Labor survey tabulated the marital status of women workers by industry: 35 percent of waitresses were either widowed, separated, or divorced, more than twice that of any other occupational group. The statistics compiled by the Census Bureau for the 1950s and 1960s reveal the same phenomenon. In 1950, for example, 28 percent of waitresses but only 22 percent of all working women were divorced, widowed, or separated.[66]

Likewise, a disproportionate number of single waitresses lived apart from their families. A 1912 study of Chicago waitresses stated that "the majority of girls do not live at home," while a Consumers' League survey in 1915 found that 34 percent of the female hotel and restaurant workers lived with friends, with the proprietor, or in furnished rooms separate from their place of work, rather than with families or relatives. According to the Bureau of the Census, in 1920 only 31 percent of waitresses lived with their husbands or their parents in contrast to 73 percent of the overall female labor force. Fully 38 percent of waitresses were boarders (the highest of any occupational category),

10 percent lived with the employer, and the remainder with their children and other relatives. Thirty years later, when Women's Bureau researchers asked hotel and restaurant women about their living arrangements, 30 percent still reported living apart from their families. No other union-affiliated group surveyed reported more than 20 percent living apart from their families.[67]

In part because of their diminished ties to the traditional family, waitresses as a group were more likely to be the primary contributors to their own upkeep and that of their families than women in other occupations. Not only were the large numbers of divorced and separated waitresses responsible for their own support, but the single and married women in the trade also carried heavier financial burdens than their counterparts in other occupations. Donovan noted that "the waitress is dependent entirely upon her own resources, and does not, like the shopgirl and the office girl 'live at home'. . . . She needs all she makes." But neither an independent residence nor a marriage license guaranteed relief from family obligations. Many "women adrift" sent money to their families, and a majority of the married waitresses surveyed in Connecticut in 1916 claimed to be the primary support of their family. Later comparative studies, conducted in the 1940s and 1950s, confirmed that the number of waitresses who were the sole contributors to their families was considerably higher than for any other female group studied.[68]

Many waitresses, of course, worked part-time to "supplement" their family income, as did women in other trades. Significantly, however, waitressing was an occupation dominated by full-time workers until the 1960s. The part-time, "one-meal" girl accounted for only a small proportion of the trade. In addition, in the early decades of the twentieth century, part-time, seasonal, and student workers were concentrated in the resort trade as opposed to the year-round restaurant and hotel trade. Only in the post-World War II era did waitressing become a haven for married women seeking part-time work and for college-age youth not yet ready to move into a "real" career. As late as 1950, 71 percent of all waitresses worked full-time, and industry consultants could still advise restaurant managers to seek "a source of recruits largely untouched"—college students looking for part-time work.[69]

The relative long-term occupational tenure of many waitresses may have also reinforced a sense of themselves as permanent workers. Although commentators frequently remarked on the high turnover rate among this "fickle class" of workers, rapid turnover reflected a short length of stay in any one position rather than a short workplace tenure. Waitresses were notorious migrants, picking up and leaving jobs after a few months. But they were leaving a particular job or employer, not the occupation itself. Because many were the sole support of themselves and their families, even those who did marry or had children often returned to the occupation rather quickly. "I've been here for twenty-five years," one waitress commented. "I even worked the first eighteen years without taking a vacation because I couldn't afford it, raising kids . . . the whole bit." Since waitress work, unlike factory work or even domestic service, had flexible hours and shifts that could be adjusted according to the needs and hours of young children, waitresses also were able to combine work and raising children more frequently than women in other occupations and hence dropped out of the work force for a shorter period.[70]

Union records, newspaper accounts, and interviews all attest to the long careers of waitresses. Many started working in their teens and could still be found waiting tables in their old age. As one mused in the 1970s, looking back over her succession of waiting jobs, "I waited tables all my life. Just a born waitress, I guess." Numerous locals awarded life membership to retired waitresses with extensive years in the trade. In 1952, the national journal of the Hotel and Restaurant Employees Union reprinted an article from the *Chicago Daily News* about one of the more popular waitresses in the Chicago local. Born on a farm outside of Chicago, she had migrated to the city at the urging of an older girl friend working in a Chicago restaurant. Upon arriving in Chicago, the young farm girl took a job in the Sherman Hotel Coffee Shop and kept it for close to thirty years. Referred to as the "Mother of the Sherman Hotel," she illustrates the older waitress as a folk type—one who had worked in a place so long that she, more than any other person or feature of the restaurant, came to represent the establishment. She had outlasted a changing management, clientele, and neighborhood.[71]

Thus, as waitressing emerged in the twentieth century as one of the principal jobs for women, it was distinguished by certain characteristics that enabled female servers to formulate and sustain a culture of solidarity at the workplace. Most female food servers shared a similar racial and ethnic background. The relative ethnic and racial homogeneity of waitresses fostered group cohesion as it has for other groups of workers, men and women.[72] In addition, more than women in other occupations, waitresses lived outside a traditional family setting and hence turned quite readily to their workplace community for friendship and support.[73] If young and single, they often chose to live apart from their families, frequently residing with other waitresses in small apartments or rented rooms. The high proportion who were divorced, separated, or widowed lived alone, with friends, or with dependent relatives or children. Unable to rely financially on their family of origin or on a husband, waitresses were often primarily self-supporting and attached to the work force in a permanent fashion.

These characteristics in particular set waitresses apart from other female wage earners and fostered group identity and union consciousness. And, as the next chapter will detail, the problems and pleasures accompanying waitressing work also reinforced the allegiance waitresses felt for their work and for each other.

CHAPTER TWO

Work Conditions and
Work Culture

A waitress, when asked the effect of the work upon her, answered,
"Sore feet and a devilish mean disposition."

—An anonymous waitress, 1915[1]

"We [the waitresses] used to pull more jokes on those men [the
customers] than anything. And there was one man, Bubby, he
was the greatest . . . weighed close to 300 lbs. So this friend of
mine, Kathleen, she said, 'Bubby, come here. I want to ask you
something. Do you like bear meat?' 'Oh, God,' he said, 'I'd love
some. I haven't had any since I left home.' 'Well,' she said, 'take
a bite of my behind. That's wild meat for you.' Well, I thought he
would die."

—Valentine Webster, waitress and
union official, speaking about her
waitress days in Butte, Montana,
in the 1920s and 1930s[2]

Thrown onto her own resources by a marital separation, Joan Crawford in
Warner Brothers' 1945 film *Mildred Pierce* wanders the streets in search of
work. Exhausted and demoralized, Crawford stops for a cup of tea at a downtown restaurant. In desperate need of waitresses, the crusty head hostess, Eve
Arden, agrees to "give her a trial." Crawford proves her mettle, meeting the
physical and emotional demands of the job; she even finds herself enjoying the
tips and the bustling atmosphere of the restaurant. Crawford soon opens her
own restaurant and then another and another, eventually becoming wealthy.
In the end, the film is ambivalent about Crawford's stint among the working
classes, at times portraying her manual work as ennobling and purifying, at
other moments siding with Crawford's husband and daughter, who see her as
forever tainted with the "smell of grease." Clearly, however, Crawford's decision to become a "hasher" had put her claim to middle-class respectability to
the test.

Few waitresses achieved Crawford's financial heights and few suffered such
emotional abuse from their children and spouse, but many found waitressing

surprisingly fulfilling. Food service work appealed to many women because of the possibility of earning a living wage, the camaraderie among workers on the job, and the rewards of the service encounter. Nevertheless, the grueling workpace, long hours, and a condescending public could make life difficult.

Whether or not the pleasures outweighed the problems depended on many factors: the type of restaurant where one worked, the personality of the manager, and the strength of the protection afforded through the collective efforts of one's co-workers. A few waitresses were lucky enough to secure positions in restaurants where tips were adequate, the pace decent, and the employer fair, but most worked in hectic, low-priced establishments and endured an arbitrary, "personalized" management or the "militaristic" regiment of chain outfits dedicated to standardization in both food and service. In response, waitresses devised various strategies for combating their job-related woes. Some pursued individual solutions such as upward mobility through entrepreneurship or marriage. Others helped create a supportive work culture that countered the abuse of employers, maximized the positive aspects of customer interaction, and in general made food service work more tolerable. And, as later chapters will detail, a sizable number of waitresses also attempted to formalize their work-based group culture through the establishment of waitress unions.

Long Hours and Low Wages

Food servers before the 1940s worked extremely long hours. For those working in boardinghouses, hotels, or other situations where waitresses lived-in, a "day" resembled the twenty-four-hour, on-call situation endured by domestic servants, beginning with breakfast duty at 6 and continuing until 8 or 9 at night with only a brief period off for meals. The server might also be expected to return at 10 or 11 for a "party" that could last into the next morning. Live-out situations guaranteed some hours off the job, but employers cut into leisure time by scheduling split shifts. When the work was spread out over one or two "splits," the employee ended up on call for upwards of fourteen hours or more, although she technically "worked" nine or ten. According to one investigator, the problem was "not always one of long actual hours of work, but of a long overall day with intervals between hours of duty arranged so as not to be of much use to the worker." Some waitresses worked part-time, coming in for a breakfast or a lunch shift, but few could afford this "one-meal" option. Before World War II, at least four-fifths of the women in the trade were full-time, steady workers who either worked the hours demanded by the employer or moved on in search of another waitress job.[3]

Although the hours required of waitresses declined over the course of the twentieth century, waitresses continued to work longer than workers in other trades. In the pre–World War I era, the seven-day week was common in the hotel and restaurant industry. One-third of the employees surveyed in 1915 had no day of rest. Moreover, 35 percent were engaged more than sixty hours a week, while only 4 percent of factory workers were so engaged.[4]

During and after World War I, the six-day week, ten-hour day became more common, especially in independent restaurants. A typical, full-time restaurant waitress worked six days a week from seven in the morning until eight at night with a three-hour break between shifts in the afternoon, usually from two to five. Hotels, however, worked their employees longer hours, dismissing this abuse as inherent in the nature of a "domestic industry." Only a few adopted the "revolutionary practice" which appeared in other industries of granting a full day off.[5]

During the depression, hours returned to pre-1920 levels. According to government surveys, work days for waitresses in Delaware extended over thirteen hours; in Florida, 90 percent worked seven days, and "70 percent of the white women, principally waitresses, had an overall spread of 12 hours and over." One sufferer complained to Secretary of Labor Frances Perkins that at a local bakery and luncheonette the waitresses were "compelled to work 12 hours a day without even [being] allowed to sit down and eat their midday meal in peace." Every third week, they received one day off.[6]

The Hotel and Restaurant Codes enacted under the National Industrial Recovery Act did little to remedy the situation, setting an abysmally low minimum wage—"too low for even an adequate standard of living"—and a fifty-four-hour maximum work week. To make matters worse, employers defied even these minimal standards with little fear of government reprisals. A report appearing in the Women's Bureau newsletter, *The Woman Worker*, revealed that 23 percent of workers in independent restaurants and 63 percent of hotel workers still had a seven-day week in 1939. Another survey found that fully 40 percent of the stores violated both the six-day clause and the twelve-hour daily maximum for work "on premises" or "on call."[7]

Employers rationalized continued ill-treatment of workers by pointing out the similarity of hotel work and domestic labor. The Hotel Code itself reflected these employer sentiments: "Hotel workers perform a purely domestic service . . . and should not rightfully be likened to industrial workers. They are primarily and essentially the type of workers employed in private homes." And like housework, it was argued, personal service work was unskilled, performed only intermittently, and required less physical strength than industrial work. Hotel employees spend "much of their time . . . simply in evidence, awaiting a call for service."[8]

In the 1940s, as a result of unionization, state minimum wage and maximum hour legislative coverage, and the increased competition for workers, working hours finally lessened. The average weekly hours dropped to forty-eight—still considerably higher than the forty-hour week achieved in other industries. This pattern prevailed until 1966, when hours dropped again after the inclusion of the industry under federal wage and hour coverage.[9]

In return for long hours, many waitresses received minimal cash compensation from their employers, barely enough to sustain themselves, let alone their families. Throughout the century, hotel and restaurant employees received a lower average *cash wage*—the wage paid after room, meal, and other deductions and exclusive of tips—than any other occupational group except domestic servants. Weekly cash wages for waitresses before World War I averaged $4 to $5 a week, while salesgirls "had a nearly even chance of earning the living wage of $8 a week," and stenographers took home even more. In the 1920s, cash wages climbed to $8–$12 a week but still fell short of the $14–$15 minimum weekly income for a single woman determined by various state minimum wage commissions.[10]

Wages plummeted in the early thirties. In 1934, the New York WTUL concluded that "the hotel and restaurant industry is paying in net cash wages a lower rate than any factory industry or occupation in the State of New York . . . [a rate] only equaled by domestic service and industrial homework." Despite the protests of such reformers as Mary Anderson, chief of the Women's Bureau, and the passage of a revised NRA code, the situation remained unchanged. The New York State Department of Labor contended in 1939 that "the earnings of many women and male minors in the [culinary] industry are not sufficient to provide adequate maintenance and to protect health and are not commensurate with the value of the services rendered." Two years later, an Illinois study of fifteen thousand female restaurant workers reached a similar evaluation: 97 percent of waitresses and 90 percent of countergirls received less than a living wage. Some employees, in fact, received no cash wages at all; they simply bartered their labor for meals and a roof over their head.[11]

The situation improved in the 1940s, but as late as 1953 the New York State Department of Labor could state the "average taxable wages in the restaurant industry are below those in all covered industries in the State." In California in 1952, $104–$111 per week was required for a "commonly accepted standard of living," but weekly cash earnings in restaurants and taverns were $62.21.[12]

The almost universal practice of employer fines reduced cash wages below these reported amounts. Fines for breakage were the most frequent ones imposed on employees but not the only ones. Waitresses recounted stories of fines for "giving a girl cashier a portion of wheatcakes which had been left over and paid for by a customer, . . . for forgetting to serve a guest with a finger bowl, . . . for dropping a knife, . . . [or] for drinking in the pantry some of the coffee left by a guest." Waitresses who filled water jars or butter dishes after guests were seated might also have such a failure "credited against" them. Employees were held responsible for lost silverware, with or without evidence as to how it disappeared. New York City waitresses, interviewed by the WTUL in the 1930s, objected strenuously to repeated deductions for lost items, tardiness, and mistakes on customer checks. On top of these "legitimate" fines, a few bosses had servers "kick-back" a portion of their wage to keep their job.[13]

Until the late 1950s, most restaurants either required waitresses to pay for their uniforms or to rent them from the employer. Employees might also be responsible for laundry bills and the costs of other items such as their pads and pencils. Costs mounted if one worked for a whimsical employer who adopted every new uniform fashion or frequently changed dining-room supervisors. "A few weeks ago we got a brand new manager," one waitress wrote in 1931. "New orders and new regulations are floating all over the place . . . to show that he knows more than his predecessor, is the order of the day." New regulations meant added expenses, including "two new uniforms for which we have to pay about ten dollars [and] new stockings and new shoes to match."[14]

Some employers had stringent dress codes that resulted in additional costs for employees. Many large restaurant chains and hotels required hairwaves and manicures. "The standards of the daily inspection are such that home-done manicures and waves will not pass," the WTUL reported. One waitress interviewed in 1935 complained of having to buy a new pair of expensive sheer stockings every week to wear with her short uniform. These were necessary, the employer told her, because her legs would be more attractive to the traveling salesmen who made up her clientele.[15]

Employees lost money through sickness, injury, and early retirements; few restaurants before the 1950s provided paid sick leave or retirement benefits. Food service work was heavy physical labor and could result in poor health and exhaustion. "The occupation is one of the hardest a woman can enter," Lillian Matthews wrote in 1901. "A waitress must carry heavily loaded trays, weighing from fifteen to twenty-five pounds over a slippery floor, every muscle being strained by the lifting, balancing, and walking required by her task." One waitress wondered why the government neglected the regulation of their work when it would "not allow an army mule to walk more than 13 miles in the same day." Indeed, because of the physical demands of the work, the long hours, and the frantic pace, a waitress (especially in the early decades of the twentieth century) could expect her work life to be shortened by ill health. In addition, injuries from falls on slippery floors and stairs, burns and lacerations from kitchen equipment, and heavy lifting meant days without pay.[16]

Even for those in good health, waitressing was not always steady work. Lay-offs for lack of work could last for months or occur daily when no customers appeared. Employees lost pay between jobs and often ended up paying a fee to an employment agency or a local saloonkeeper for a referral to their next job. Older waitresses suffered the most, as some employers fired older women the minute a younger, more attractive applicant walked in. Employees controlled few of these occurrences; as a result they experienced insecurity and anxiety.[17]

Peculiarities of Service Work:
A Room, Meals, and Tips

Culinary workers depended on supplementing their meager cash earnings with a free room and meals from employers, and tips from customers. In the eyes of employers and much of the public, low cash wages were justified because of these touted fringe benefits, but in reality generous room and board allowances coupled with substantial tipping were rare. All too often, waitresses were stuck with minimal cash wages, a stingy clientele, and substantial employer deductions for a room and meals.

The practice of boarding was widespread among waitresses and was often a requirement of employment in the first two decades of the twentieth century. Living-in arrangements meant increased availability of employees for the seven-day, around-the-clock schedule. The costs of providing lodging for employees was small where hotels and boardinghouses had extra rooms and beds available. Some establishments set aside certain areas for "help lodging"; others actually built separate living accommodations for their employees. The Fred Harvey chain of independent restaurants invested in elaborate dormitories and hired strict matrons to ensure that their female servers conformed to Victorian standards of propriety. Living-in declined in the interwar years as more waitresses worked in restaurants apart from hotels, public attitudes toward wage-earning women altered, and hours shortened. By the 1950s, the majority of employers, with the exception of resort owners, no longer required boarding.[18]

Boarding also diminished because employees preferred live-out situations. In keeping with the traditions of domestic service where servants were denied a private life, live-in workers were forbidden to receive visitors in their rooms and were expected to remain on the employer's premises around the clock. Live-out arrangements allowed more personal autonomy, the possibility of a family life, and increased social contacts.[19]

In addition, accommodations provided by employers rarely were worth the cash value deducted from wages. One waitress revealed that in the fashionable hotel where she worked, "the girls are put in the garret on the fifth floor . . . without windows and without heat. . . . A tiny washroom with one bathtub and one washstand . . . accommodate[s] 30 girls, but on Wednesdays and Saturdays this room is used by the guests of the hotel who use the dance hall on the same floor. Then we are forbidden to use the room." At swank summer resorts in the 1950s, waitresses told of "two hundred employees . . . housed in a dormitory containing three bathrooms." All two hundred were "served next to the garbage room with filthy china and silver." Their diet consisted of "fish, fish, and more fish."[20]

Although boarding declined, employers continued serving food to their employees. They found it profitable, convenient, and believed it discouraged food pilfering. In the 1930s, 90 percent of restaurants in New York City and 82 percent of those in upstate New York furnished free meals to their employees. Decades later, the majority of food service workers nationwide still received at least one free meal a day. Ironically, the lowest-paid workers were often the ones denied meals. Woolworth paid its lunch-counter workers rock-bottom wages and forbid them "to eat or drink on the firm." According to a 1939 national Women's Bureau study, food servers who received one to three meals a day earned a larger cash wage than those receiving no meals at all.[21]

Having meals provided could operate as much to the employee's detriment as to her advantage. Employers offered meals in lieu of wages and deducted amounts beyond the actual value of the food. Meal charges were levied despite the desires of workers to eat with friends and family. Workers were denied expensive food such as steak or lobster and often served the cheapest staple day after day, or given leftover and rotten dishes. Waitresses complained of receiving "stew everyday" or "spaghetti without sauce" on a regular basis. One compiled her typical 1935 menu: "Lunch—leftover vegetables (all rotten), coffee; supper—soup, rice pudding, coffee." Another explained that although she worked in one of the highest-priced hotels in Atlantic City, she and her co-workers received such atrocious food that they strolled the boardwalk every night after work hoping someone would buy them dinner.[22]

Complaints abounded over eating conditions. Interviewed in 1936, a waitress described the help's kitchen: "there are no chairs, only benches; and on them are heaped dirty dishes, clothes, everything, so we usually eat standing up. We have to wait until the last customer is out and at night this means 10 o'clock." After serving customers in the grandest of halls, waiters and waitresses might be relegated to the kitchen or a damp pantry to eat their own meals.[23]

Poor eating and lodging accommodations particularly irritated restaurant employees because they were aware of the better facilities provided for clientele. The most luxurious, spotless interiors could open onto employee quarters with badly ventilated kitchens, crowded and unclean locker areas, dirty washrooms and toilets, and cramped, dismal dining halls. Such glaring status divisions could wear on employees as much as the physical demands and emotional stress of their work.[24]

Lacking adequate cash wages or fringe benefits, waitresses relied on the generosity of their customers to lift them out of poverty. And indeed, in certain situations and during certain points in their careers, waitresses made substantial earnings through tips. Frances Donovan proclaimed waitressing the "most lucrative occupation open to untrained and uneducated women" in 1917 and declared that overall income "compared very favorably with that of the average teacher, stenographer or well-paid saleswoman." Her enthusiasm sprang from her tips, which were "as great or greater" than her wages. Other

studies confirmed that with good tips waitresses in 1922 made more than most
women industrial workers and in 1931 "as much, if not more, than the average
stenographer." Waitresses themselves declared the occupation "the one where
you could make the money."[25] The financial *possibilities* of waitressing, then,
did exceed those in many other female-dominated trades. Nevertheless, few
attained these financial heights, and fewer still sustained them.

Tip income for many waitresses was small, unreliable, and at times non-
existent, especially before the 1940s. Because of the sexual segregation in the
industry, female servers worked in lower-priced establishments where tips were
meager or absent. Most table service waitresses could count on tip income,
but not those serving at department store lunch counters, dairy lunches,
cafeterias, and chain restaurants. In the late 1930s, only 65 percent of independent restaurants listed tipping as a customer practice, and 42 percent of
counter waitresses and 89 percent of variety store waitresses received no gratuities at all.[26] A young, attractive waitress might secure employment in one of
the better-tipping restaurants, but generally her tenure was short-lived. Even
when she held onto her lucky find, as she aged, tips from many of the male clientele could decline. For waitresses, as for other women in the sexual service
sector, appearance could count more than experience and skill in determining
income.[27]

Even in the best of circumstances tips were never certain. They fluctuated
from week to week and from house to house. Financial security was impossible.
In periods of business downturns, the public cut back on tipping as an easy step
in managing shrinking incomes. Waitresses lost tips due to co-worker mistakes
(a cook's bungling or a hostess's rudeness), poor station assignments, or slow
business. Assignment to "side work" such as cleaning washrooms, scrubbing
tables, and washing silver, reduced tips to a trickle. Waitresses resented such
tasks, especially when all the extra work fell to the women. Beulah Compton, a Seattle waitress during the 1930s and 1940s, remembered with chagrin
that "men got the best stations . . . and the women would work the counters
and do all the cleanup work. That really used to annoy me because a waiter
could stand in his tux, with his arms folded, and the waitresses had to clean
the side stands and do all the dirty work right around him; never did you see
a waiter cleaning a fountain or doing anything like that." Another waitress
remembered: "They'd get the tip and the girl wouldn't get nothing."[28]

Furthermore, the custom of tipping was not entrenched on a national basis
until the 1940s, and even then the "acceptable" amount remained quite modest. In the early part of the century, a vocal and organized reform movement
arose that viewed tipping as "un-American" in its encouragement of social
distinctions and class superiority. "Tipping is what we left Europe to escape,"
declared one early reformer. "It is a cancer in the breast of democracy." Numerous pamphlets, articles, and books condemned the practice; major restaurant

and hotel employers courted public favor by forbidding tipping on their premises; and a handful of states actually passed anti-tipping legislation. Between
1909 and 1918 seven states—Washington, Mississippi, Arkansas, Iowa, South
Carolina, Tennessee, and Georgia—enacted anti-tipping laws. Some of the
laws aimed at the takers of tips exclusively; others punished the givers as well.
Laws proved futile in stopping the practice, but their passage indicates that a
large portion of the population frowned on tipping.[29]

Early female social reformers and union activists opposed the practice as
well. They worried less about the so-called "un-American" character of the
tipping system and more about its perceived potential to reinforce low wages
and encourage immorality in women dependent on male customers for their
livelihood. One Progressive Era reformer recommended the abolition of tipping because "in the hands of a vicious man the tip establishes between him
and the girl a relation of subservience and patronage which may easily be
made the beginning of improper attentions." Elizabeth Maloney, a respected
Chicago waitress union official, condemned tipping because it created friction
between workers and "made it pretty hard for a [waitress] to draw the line—
where the line of propriety should be. She knows that the man is going to
leave her a dime or a quarter, and, . . . while she resents things that are said
to her . . . she hesitates about it because she wants the money."[30] Industrial
Workers of the World (IWW) activists opposed tipping because it encouraged
the receiver to "become servile, slavish, mealy-mouthed and beggarly: and to
succumb to 'the easier way' of loose morals."[31]

The anti-tipping movement culminated in the 1920s, but opposition to
the practice resurfaced sporadically in the ensuing decades. Food servers continued to complain of being regarded as "menials" because of the tip and of
employers who defended low wage rates for employees by pointing to their
tip-earning potential.[32] In 1938, state minimum wage administrators—many
of whom were middle-class female social workers and reformers—agreed at
a Women's Bureau conference that "tips shouldn't be considered in setting
minimum wages" and that a 10 percent service charge should replace tipping. A few employers posted signs discouraging the custom, and customers
withheld tips on principle. An *Atlantic Monthly* columnist in 1946 proclaimed
tipping to be "undemocratic, dishonest, and destructive" and urged American citizens to refrain from the habit. As late as 1951, the Illinois legislature
considered a bill subjecting anyone who tipped to fines that ranged from
$5 to $25.[33]

As public antipathy toward tipping cooled, the practice became more widespread and the amount of the tip increased. In 1916, the custom was "to give
10 percent of the sum paid for the lunch or dinner." Early arbiters of social etiquette also advised that 10 cents was the minimum tip "except at a restaurant
of humble pretensions, where five will be gladly accepted by the waitress." A

veteran waitress from Montana recalled the tipping habits of her affluent customers in the 1910s and 1920s. "Today they tip but they didn't do it in those days. I'd be tickled to death to get a dime." By the 1940s, the recommended rate had inched up to 12 percent and soon shifted to 15 and 20 percent. In the post-World War II era, earnings from tips could be substantial, even for women servers who were concentrated in lower-priced restaurants where the percentage system of calculating gratuities worked to their disadvantage. Indeed, after the 1940s, food servers received as much if not more in tips than in wages. By the 1970s, estimates ranged from half to some two-thirds of waitresses' total income derived from gratuities.[34]

With the help of high-tipping clientele, then, an individual waitress could bring home more money than a woman in sales, factory, or clerical work. But few sustained such high incomes. The overall earnings profile for waitressing resembled the "relative high but flat" earnings chart Claudia Goldin has graphed for domestic service. In the beginning, especially, waitress income might compare favorably to income levels in higher-status jobs, but unlike her sisters in saleswork for example, the long-term financial possibilities for waitresses were poor.[35]

Ironically, although the tipping system kept many individual waitresses out of poverty, it militated against the achievement of a stable, living wage for the occupation as a whole. One industry analyst concluded that "earnings are undoubtedly lower than would be the case if all income were derived from contractual wages; with consumers paying directly for the services they receive." Moreover, the tipping system aggravated income stratification within the industry. Employer-paid cash wages bore an inverse relation to the value of tips earned: those with the lowest cash wages received the least tip income. In restaurants catering to a working-class clientele, for instance, both wages and tips commonly were lower than those in higher-priced places. Consequently, the distribution of food service compensation was bifurcated, with most male incomes falling near the top and most female at the bottom.[36]

Although tipping permitted a certain amount of autonomy in service work, it also fostered individual entrepreneurship, competitive behavior, and dampened the ardor for collective effort. With its "remnants of use value," tipping lay outside the commercial exchange system; this intimate transaction created a more ambiguous kind of worker consciousness than the classic adversarial "us versus them" attitude. Some servers chose to rely on the ephemeral, sporadic tipping system rather than join with their co-workers to push for higher cash wages. Tipping also weakened the potential alliance between customer and worker. At times, workers perceived the customer rather than the employer as responsible for their feeble income. And to a large degree, employers convinced the public that low wage rates were justified because servers received tips and special fringe benefits such as room and board.[37]

Arbitrary Management and a Demanding Public

Added to their other problems, waitresses endured individual employers
who were discriminatory, arbitrary, or downright abusive. Less-favored employees could be assigned to the poorest shifts, the least-frequented stations,
the bulk of the "side-work," or harassed by fines and verbal abuse. Promotions
rarely were based on seniority or awarded in an even-handed fashion. Older,
less attractive, or minority women were the last hired and the first laid off.[38]

Management treatment of black employees differed from that of white.
They expected an extra dose of servility from black workers and often punished
certain "high-handed" behavior by blacks while tolerating it in whites. A ceiling existed on the advancement of blacks in the restaurant industry, human
relations theorist William Whyte found. Ironically, the same employers who
refused to promote blacks expected top-notch service from them and were
perplexed by their "lack of motivation."[39]

Sexual harassment plagued young and old, black and white. Male bosses
were not above pressuring their female staff for sexual favors and encouraging
waitresses to use their sexuality to attract customers. "The boss, accustomed
to looking upon his employees with the same attitude that he regards a coffee
urn, does not see why he cannot use the waitress's body for other purposes
than waiting on the table," one server explained. "After many suggestive approaches, such as walking into the dressing room when she is donning her
uniform, attempting caresses and so on, he states the issue bluntly, 'be nice
or else.'" Refusal of such "offers" was a "common reason that girls are unjustly
discharged" and "is well known to any female food worker who has been in
the business any length of time," she insisted.[40]

Looking back over some thirty years in the trade, a worker categorized the
types of waitress jobs available. Tellingly, her categories were not based on the
type of customers or the style of service, but on whether the jobs were "with
or without pleasure." If you had to sleep with the boss in order to secure and
keep the job, it was a "with pleasure" position. Even on those jobs technically
"without pleasure," the boss might pressure the waitress to indulge the patrons
sexually. When Loretta Szeliga worked as a "bargirl" in a speakeasy during
the 1920s, the tavern would get a percentage of any drinks men bought her.
"Then they thought because they bought you a drink, they could feel you
up," Szeliga recalled, still with a touch of indignation. "The owner—a friend
of mine—begged me to quit because I wouldn't allow it. He told me I was
ruining his business. I thought, 'Why let the bums pinch my fanny so I could
hold this job?'"[41]

Customer abuse of waitresses could operate independently of the employer,
of course. Regardless of employer practices, some male customers expected
intimacies or sexual favors in exchange for the tip. One waitress "unloaded on

the subject of cafe Romeos" in an interview with an Illinois labor reporter in the 1950s. She began by explaining that "the wisecrack often heard in union halls . . . that you can tell a guy is middle-aged when he pays more attention to his food than he does to the waitress . . . may draw smiles all around—but never from a waitress." Illustrating the seriousness of the situation, she spoke "bitterly" of the "few boneheads . . . who can't keep their hands to themselves" and suggested that "waitresses who serve the evening trade should be issued a 38-caliber automatic as part of their uniforms."[42]

Haughty and disrespectful customers proved vexing as well. "Ninety percent of the waitresses when asked about their work complained about one thing or another [first], . . . then came complaints of bad treatment by the public." In hearings before the Minimum Wage Board of New York City in 1947, one waitress strayed from the topic at hand and spoke resentfully "of the smile the waitress must always have for the insolent guest on whose tip she is depending to buy something for her child or some stockings she needs herself." The Irish waitresses at Schrafft's complained of the older women customers who would treat them like personal servants. " 'Where's my maid?' the women [customers] had been known to call out, and the maidlike uniforms and aprons that the waitresses had to wear reinforced that image."[43]

Customer maltreatment of waitresses, in part rooted in the tipping system, in part inherent in the unequal financial relation between customer and service worker, was fueled by the condescension of the public toward food service work. Although waitressing had lost its immoral cast in the eyes of the public by the 1920s and 1930s, the status of the work remained low. Waitressing was seen as menial, unskilled work, and waitresses were to be treated accordingly. "The notion that serving food could be as complicated a task to learn and to do as, say, making furniture, never impressed itself on public opinion." Personal service workers also suffered from the stigma of dependence: instead of having a formal contractual arrangement that provided a living wage, they relied on customer largess.[44]

In addition to demanding sexual favors or servility, customers looked to waitresses for the fulfillment of other psychological needs. The act of eating and of being fed is overlaid with powerful associations. Diners transferred unconscious memories connected with food onto the waitress. Some had insatiable appetites for recognition, mothering, and emotional nurturance; others wanted witty conversation, entertainment, or a friendly nod as they recounted their daily triumphs and defeats. "Where else can I find a friend and get my lamb chops at the same time?" one customer queried. The waitress herself was part of the consumption exchange.[45]

A few needed to let off steam, and the waitress was an available and nonthreatening target. Waitresses saw the public at its worst: the day could start with crabby, before-coffee breakfast-eaters for whom "if there is one wrong

wobble in that poached egg, you've got trouble," move to the hectic noon-
time crowd—"a wave of anxious eaters who hit like a tornado"—and end with
maudlin or quarrelsome drunks.[46]

By and large, waitresses fulfilled the public's expectations admirably. As
one frequent restaurant-goer rhapsodized in the *Los Angeles Times Magazine*,
waitresses "are the cement of society. In diners as bleak and lonely as an
Edward Hopper painting, they feed the hungry, cheer the weary, solace the
defeated and rally the disunited." And at times, playing the part of temptress,
nurse, mother, or entertainer could be gratifying to a particular waitress. Few
approached O. Henry's fantasy waitress in his short story "The Brief Debut of
Tildy" who could sing out witty retorts while juggling heavy trays of roast beef
and potatoes. But many performed ably in the theater of dining out, shaping
the service encounter to meet their own emotional and financial needs as well
as those of the customer. Nevertheless, patron demands could be overwhelm-
ing, especially in situations where the employer interfered with the exchange
between customer and waitress.[47]

The New Service Ideal:
"Personality and Pulchritude"

Many employers held up artificial and unnatural standards of employee behavior that reduced the control of waitresses over their work and undermined
their power in the service interaction. Some attempted to copy the scientific management reforms of their industrial counterparts. They insisted on
uniformity in food and service and developed extensive rule books governing dress, grooming, customer interaction, and the elements of proper table
service. Chain stores pioneered in this work regimentation, but more family-
style restaurants, especially the larger ones, also moved from an informal to
a more bureaucratic management style. "Every gesture . . . every word she
utter[ed] to any guest and . . . every detail of her appearance" was scrutinized
by management, one chain store waitress reported in 1940. White Castle, a
chain popular in the interwar period, bragged to customers that those who
serve "are guided by standards of precision which have been thought out
from beginning to end. They dress alike; they are motivated by the same
principles of courtesy." Being "a Stouffer's girl" in the 1950s meant wearing
"five-eyelet oxford shoes, full slips, no hairpins or jewelry and passing the daily
girdle check."[48]

Employer definitions of good service varied according to the clientele and
were modified over time in response to the shifting tastes of the public. Few
required as did the Glacier National Park employee manual of 1918 that waitresses "daily provide their tables with fresh wild flowers which grow in pro-
fusion not far from any hotel," but many specified in endless detail just what
devotion to service meant. In restaurants catering to the wealthy, the ideal

resembled the standards set for domestic servants in upper-class homes: unobtrusive, meek, and respectful. Faultless table service consisted in "absolutely
noiseless movements," and the most perfect waitress was "one whose presence
was not felt in the dining room." Social interaction between customer and
server should be avoided, and in no instance were customer wishes or opinions
to be contradicted.[49]

In contrast, in restaurants serving the working-class, the waitress had much
more leeway in her exchange with customers. The equality in social status
allowed a greater degree of familiarity. Rather than formality and deference,
banter and barbed exchange were common. Working-class customers felt at
home with waitresses who reminded them of their wife or mother—the figures who were most likely to serve them in the home—and politeness was not
expected. A devoted regular observed: "I've been coming in here for 10 years
and I doubt if they've ever said ten civil words to me . . . they don't put up
with nothin.' I get treated here same as I do at home." Another explained
the appeal of Sam's Breakfast Cafe, a waterfront hangout for sailors and lob-
stermen: "Good food, good value, pleasant company, and a lot of guff from
the waitresses—what more could you ask for?" In one working-class restaurant
studied by William Whyte, the waitress informed him that, "in this place the
customer is always wrong, and he knows it—God bless him."[50]

In the 1920s, a different service ideal came to dominate. Restaurants
serving an exclusively working-class clientele continued to tolerate a free-
wheeling, sassy independence in their waitresses, but the majority of restaurants now attracted a more heterogeneous clientele. They adopted the
"bourgeois style" of the middle-class—one that encouraged friendly encounters tempered by deference and emotional restraint. Good waitresses possessed
an "indestructible good humor," practiced "sweet-tempered, patient service,"
and cultivated "a pleasant voice and a friendly smile." Stouffer's eight-week
course for waitresses on "the finer points of serving a critical public" flatly
advised: "a good waitress does not argue with the customer."

Childs restaurant offered a "charm course" for its employees in 1937 in
which waitresses were "thoroughly drilled in the psychology of making the
customer happy with life in general, as well as with hot cakes and maple
syrup." The Childs chain even formulated rules for wives based on "the charm
formula" followed by servers. Their "tips for wives" with grouchy husbands included: "don't answer back, no matter what he says. Get his breakfast quickly
and as efficiently as possible. And the way *he* likes it. Don't do any little
thing which irritates him, such as tapping your foot, rustling the newspaper,
or slamming things. No matter what he does, don't be ruffled."[51]

The changing expectations of food service employers paralleled shifts
occurring in the workplace at large. As Peter and Carol Stearns have shown, by
the 1920s employers emphasized "managed friendliness" as well as more tra-

ditional values such as employee obedience and docility. In short, employers now laid down rules that aimed to control feelings as well as behavior.[52]

In some ways, this new style was more "natural" in that waitresses no longer had to strive for invisibility. Yet it was also more demanding. Waitresses found they had to work hard at emanating certain traits—cheerfulness and eagerness to please—while suppressing anger, grouchiness, and irritability. As Arlie Hochschild argued in her study of flight attendants, service workers who must always be polite even when customers are rude, belligerent, and demanding find this "emotional labor" as exhausting as mental or physical work. It was hard for Clela Sullivan, a Butte waitress, when she left "hashslinging" in the 1940s and began serving "the hoi paloi. I would snarl at them. If they gave me a bad time I gave them one right back. Then I was warned . . . you learned to smile." Denying one's own natural responses to unpleasant external stimuli can also lead to increased stress and anxiety levels or to a state of denial—what C. Wright Mills has called "self-alienation."[53]

The new service ideal asked waitresses to enter into a closer emotional relation with their clients but left them with few weapons to use in this heightened emotional interaction. They lacked the "status shield" of masculinity that inhibited customer abuse.[54] And, both invisibility and "snappy repartee" were now discouraged. Maintaining one's dignity became increasingly difficult.

The new uniforms employers adopted after the 1920s only aggravated the problem. Abandoning the maidlike black dress embellished with lace-trimmed apron, cuffs, and cap, employers dressed female servers in eye-catching fantasy outfits or sexually provocative styles. The possibilities were limitless: majorette uniforms with short skirts, heavy boots, and a military top hat or a peasant maid ready for a roll in the hay. One "award-winning" uniform design featured waitresses in Chicago-style gangster outfits, wearing pin-striped suit coats but no pants. Restaurants like Schrafft's and Stouffer's with their emphasis on sensibly dressed, unobtrusive female servers were now more the exception than the rule. Mixing "gustatory pleasures with the visual delights of comely lassies in abbreviated uniforms," made good business sense in 1940 to the owners of Houston's biggest drive-in. Applicants needed "good figures, health cards, and come-hither personalities." They also had to be willing to "endeavor to sell large orders of food, work in seven and a half hour shifts, six days a week," and live on their tips.

The sexual tease aspects of the service encounter peaked in the 1960s. Playboy Clubs reached their zenith; airline stewardesses shed their wholesome, all-American-girl image and served meals wearing thigh-high skirts, fishnet hose, and buttons reading "Fly Me." Always "on parade," the days when one could focus solely on efficiency and promptness were over. "Personality and pulchritude" were at the heart of the new service ideal.[55]

"Working the Circuit"

Waitresses responded to their working conditions in a variety of ways. Before the 1920s, when conditions were at their nadir, most workers deemed it a victory to survive and maintain their health and sanity. Few had the energy or time for outside reform activities. One journalist who worked in the trade to research an article on waitresses wrote in 1907 that she was "too tired to bathe; . . . too tired to organize." She either slept during her afternoon off or lay around scheming about how she could get back at the mistress. Much to her surprise, she observed herself turning into a "typical shiftless servant" who no longer cared about her work, her appearance, or improving her situation.[56]

Like their journalist sojourner, waitresses surveyed in 1915 had little inclination for group activities. They evidenced a singular lack of "group interests and social life" outside of work, the Consumers' League remarked. Of the girls attending the local settlement house educational activities, fewer than 1 percent were restaurant workers. The Consumers' League concluded that they did not have the time or the physical strength for such interests. Exhaustion did at least numb the working girl to insults and criticism. Status concerns must have appeared marginal when ability to survive the day's toil was at stake.[57]

Fearing unemployment and loss of pay, waitresses avoided individual confrontations with employers or customers. Some got even with the employer through petty theft and through ridiculing managers and customers when they were out of earshot; others, unburdened by family or spouse, moved on. Employment opportunities equally as good or better might be available across the street, the next town over, or out West. Waitresses moved in a never-ending treasure hunt for the big-tip positions. There was always the hope—and the possibility—that one would luck into that rare situation with all the right ingredients: a fair employer, a thriving business, and a generous clientele.

Waitresses were a roving lot: few stayed more than a year in any one job and many changed jobs every few months. Some were fired or laid off; others would simply try out a job for a few days and then quit if it were not to their liking. But typically, rather than move in and out of the industry, waitresses, like construction workers, kept within their line of work and sought other jobs waitressing.

Some waitresses "tramped" from job to job as a way of "picking up the trade" or "broadening their experience." Blanche Copenhaver, a self-described "born traveler," left her farm in Lowell, Wyoming, as a seventeen-year-old during World War I and spent the next twenty years as a migrant waitress, touching down in towns throughout Texas, Arizona, and Wyoming before settling in Butte, Montana. "I loved seeing the country" was her only explanation. Others moved in response to the seasonal fluctuations in their industry. Like her society clientele, a waitress might winter in the South and summer in the mountains. At times, waitresses traveled as part of a crew. One resort waitress explained the system: "The chef would move his whole crew from one resort to another. We'd work all three meals seven days a week for twelve weeks straight, then we'd have two months off. We really got along—like a family it was." One vocational counselor remarked that the "gypsy impulse" of waitresses engendered a "feeling of superiority which help[ed] compensate for the undesirable features of the trade. A waitress in Podunk is merely a . . . waitress, but she who ha[s] . . . carried trays in Seattle and Frisco and New Orleans and Chicago becomes thereby more of a person in her own estimation." In recognition of their wandering habits, waitresses were referred to as "boomers"—working-class slang for migratory workers or those who followed "boom" times—by workers in other trades; no other female-dominated occupation earned this epithet.[58]

Despite the high turnover among waitresses, few moved into better-paying, higher-status positions. The waitress expression "working the circuit," vividly conveys the circular, horizontal movement of their work lives: most moved in and out of "nearly-identical positions." Men occupied most of the server positions in finer restaurants, and even though small service establishments promoted hourly employees to low-level supervisory positions more often than large industrial or financial establishments, first-line supervisory positions for women remained scarce. Dining rooms that employed women usually lacked head waitresses; the hostess (who often made less money than a regular waitress) performed the duties instead. Vocational guides enthused over the opportunities for women in food service, but rather than promote from within, employers hired a better-educated college woman or (as characterized by the *New York Times*) "a cultured girl tired of too much leisure." Tied down by dependents, most waitresses lacked the time for the training or education necessary to qualify for dining room supervisor or restaurant manager. "Restaurant work is a 'blind alley' trade," one sociological investigation bluntly stated. "There is little opportunity for development or advancement." The situation had changed little by the 1970s when researchers confessed, "there is little prospect for increased earnings because most high-priced restaurants use waiters rather than waitresses and because females are usually not recruited or promoted to the kitchen or to management positions that provide higher salaries."[59]

Opportunities for female entrepreneurs did exist in food service—an industry where the work, "feeding mankind, ha(d) always been peculiarly woman's business." Between 1910 and 1930, the proportion of women proprietors of eating and drinking places moved from 9 to 24 percent and remained steady over the next few decades. But few of these female entrepreneurs were former waitresses. Only the rare waitress could accumulate the capital necessary to open a restaurant. Saving or borrowing money was difficult for any working-class woman in a low-paying occupation but particularly so for waitresses, who so often were the primary support of themselves and their families. Not all waitresses desired business ownership either. Idoniea Duntley opened her own restaurant in the early 1920s after working a long stint as a server. She "couldn't stand the responsibilities. . . . It just got me down." She returned to waitressing even though her restaurant prospered. Indeed, rather than scaling the heights of their profession, most waitresses experienced downward mobility over the course of their working careers. As they aged, their range of employment possibilities narrowed and their ability to attract tips declined. They were relegated to cafeterias, hash houses, and counter service where wages and tips were the lowest.[60]

Some waitresses escaped wage work through marriage, but most returned to the workplace after a minimal break or no break at all. They had little choice: the economic survival of their families depended on both incomes; their husbands died or abandoned them or they divorced or separated. Hilda, the "democratically-minded" Harvey girl in Edna Ferber's story "Our Very Best People," married an Irish brakeman and rose with him in his ascent to general manager of the Santa Fe; she was living the fantasy of many but the reality of few.[61]

In sum, few waitresses escaped difficult working conditions through upward mobility or marriage, and as isolated individuals, their power to alter their situation was also limited. In frustration, an ever-growing number turned to formal group action, agitating for legislative reform and collective bargaining. Simultaneously, waitresses organized informally, creating a supportive workplace culture that carried over from job to job and countered condescension and abuse from customers and bosses.

Waitress Work Culture

The values, ideas, and practices developed and transmitted by and within a particular occupational group constitute a work culture.[62] Work cultures are shaped by the experience of the workplace as well as by the gendered values of family and community that workers bring with them into their place of employment. Many occupational groups have created their own culture at the workplace, and waitresses were no exception.[63] Indeed, because of the nature of restaurant work and the strong personal ties that formed among female servers, waitresses developed a particularly rich occupational culture, replete with its own distinctive jargon, humor, and group norms.

The group customs developed by workers on the job typically eased the stress of employment and provided some measure of autonomy. These cultures were not "automatically oppositional" to the employer, however, nor did they always facilitate union organization. Clerical work culture, for example, has

been found to "both reinforce and challenge management control." Other
female work cultures, such as those developed by department store employees,
were perhaps less accommodating to employer demands than clerical work culture yet still did not lead to unionization.[64] Waitresses, however, devised a
system of ideas and practices that served as a primary form of resistance to
the intrusion of employer power and as a basis for successful workplace unionization. Waitress work culture drew on aspects of women's culture or the
experiences common to all women: reproduction and domesticity. Yet it also
was shaped by the realities of their lives at the workplace. Indeed, waitress
work culture resembled the militant craft work cultures of male printers and
cigar makers as much, if not more, than the domestically rooted work cultures
attributed to other female-dominated trades.

Waitress work culture was based first and foremost on the positive assessment of the occupation held by individual waitresses. To a surprising degree,
waitresses valued their work and derived both pride and pleasure from service.
Although burdened with adverse employment conditions and stigmatized for
engaging in personal service, many working-class women preferred waitressing to the other jobs available to women with little education and training,
such as factory, domestic service, or sales work. The attraction was based in
part on objective criteria: flexible shifts that could be adjusted to the sleeping
and school schedules of young children or a working husband; the possibility
of earnings above other working-class jobs; and the security of regular meals
and board.

But waitresses also volunteered more qualitative, intrinsic factors in explaining their choice of waitress work: the opportunity to interact with co-
workers and customers and to meet new people, the pleasure of leaving a customer satisfied, the gamble and immediate gratification of the tip, the general
excitement and challenge of work where face-to-face contact was required.
One waitress explained why she preferred food service to secretarial: "I just
can't feature sitting at a typewriter all day trying to make out what some long-
winded big shot made me Gregg down. Now getting him in a good humor
with a sandwich and a cup of coffee, I adore that. I just plain get a kick out
of feeding people." Another emphasized the appeal of ever-changing social
encounters: "I have to be a waitress. How else can I learn about people? How
else does the world come to me?"[65]

The actual work experiences of individual waitresses led many to assessments of their skill and status that differed from the critical judgments of their
employers or the public. Employers maintained that waitress work, being one
of the domestic trades, required neither skill nor ingenuity; some bragged that
they would not hire an experienced man or woman. "All I want is a clean,
healthy body," one said. "I get better results if they are not too brainy." The
Hotel Statler in Buffalo conveyed its condescension toward employees by in-

cluding in its employee code a description of service workers as "the persons who are to fetch and carry . . . whose portion it is to render intimate, personal service to others. Since time immemorial, this class of servitors has been of the rank and file."[66]

Waitresses, however, recognized the skills of judgment and memory involved in waitressing and the dignity that attends a basic human service provided in an expert manner. Drawing on the positive aspects of female socialization and women's culture, they defined service as important and skilled work. As one explained: "it's a good experience to serve; I think everybody should have to serve sometime in their life. Serving is giving, as corny as it sounds." Another waitress of twenty-three years considered her work to be "an art." "When I put the plate down, you don't hear a sound. When I pick up a glass, I want it to be just right. When someone says, 'How come you're just a waitress?' I say 'Don't you think you deserve being served by me?'" A former farm girl who became a waitress in Memphis told Works Progress Administration interviewers of her thrill in learning the trade. "I was just tickled to death with myself when I got expert. Ten different orders in my head without getting coffee crossed with Coca-Cola was going some for a country girl."[67]

Waitresses also knew that although employers considered servers unskilled workers who contributed minimally to the enterprise, employers acted in ways that belied their pronouncements. Employers established training programs for waitresses and at times even agreed to unionization without strike or boycott pressure because the union offered competent, skilled employees. Routinely, employers apprenticed younger waitresses to older experienced workers. "The head waitress trained me," Clela Sullivan remembered. "How to set the tables, how to take the orders, how to turn them into the kitchen, how to put them down properly. . . . If you served a piece of pie, you'd better have the point just so. . . ." Training could last six months or more before a waitress had her own station. A certain number of apprentices never graduated; they simply were not cut out for the demands of the trade.[68]

Waitresses recognized that their performance could be critical to the success of a business. Many patrons responded more to the personality of the food server than to the quality of the decor or food. Minnie Popa, for instance, was "more than a waitress; she was an attraction." She pulled in the customers no matter where she worked. "With all the feasting and flirting and merry exchange of wit," some restaurants came "near being a salon," with the waitress for their "Madame Récamier." Even the most determined employer was unable to exert complete control over this service exchange. Waitresses could hurt business by suggesting the least expensive menu item, ignore the poor tippers, offer food and drink on the house, or simply provide lackluster, uninspired service, even though it jeopardized their own tip income. Waitresses could also go out of their way to add that special attentive, anticipatory touch that would cement the customer's patronage.[69] Anticipating customers' needs or "getting the jump" on the customer along with "suggestive selling" could impact on customer spending and hence increase the size of the tip as well as the profit margin.[70]

Like most service workers, the relationship with the customer gave waitresses a measure of control over their work environment, no matter how intrusive a boss they had.[71] Employers defined certain boundaries for acceptable behavior with customers beyond which the food server could not cross, but within those parameters, waitresses exercised a considerable amount of latitude. The sphere of autonomy provided by face-to-face interaction with the customer both strengthened waitress group ties as well as undermined them. On the one hand, the independent relation to the customer promoted a recognition of skill and provided a basis for assertion in the face of employer hostility. On the other hand, waitresses sometimes saw themselves as successful entrepreneurs who did not need group solidarity because they could rely on their own individual "bargaining" with their clients and employers.[72]

Although the social science establishment generally relegated waitresses to the lowest rung on the status and skill ladder,[73] a handful of scholars confirmed what waitresses already knew: their work was demanding emotionally, physically, and mentally. In addition to needing physical strength and endurance, waitresses "must be quick and alert, must remember vaguely-given orders accurately, must often meet unreasonableness and insult with amiable indifference," a turn-of-the-century researcher observed. Twenty years later, Frances Donovan cited the older waitress, who, having refined her social skills over a long period, knew how to control interactions with customers and co-workers.[74]

Sociologist William Whyte elaborated on Donovan's insights in his postwar studies of human relations in the restaurant industry. By observing a number of waitresses and the points at which they "cried" or broke down, Whyte zeroed in on the emotional maturity and interpersonal skills essential to the makeup of a successful waitress. He concluded that women with strong verbal ability and quick reflex intuition regarding human nature were drawn to waitressing. Such women performed admirably in the trade because they succeeded in "taking charge" in their interactions with customers and co-workers. By being assertive without being offensive, these women minimized the psychological burdens and maximized the economic benefits of the trade.[75]

The work culture waitresses created helped them learn these tricks of the trade. It also sustained waitresses' positive but beleaguered sense of their dignity as personal service workers. As one team of researchers concluded, the cocktail waitress finds a positive self-image "in a group of associations which affords her the understanding, sympathy, and self-enhancement not found on the job or in society at large. In reference groups she may take pride in her efficiency, knowledge of the work, her strategies and general resourcefulness in a manner that may not be recognized as legitimate by the larger community."[76]

Waitress work culture was rooted in and nurtured by the strong personal ties that developed among waitresses on the job. Waitresses spent a considerable amount of time socializing and eating meals together. They might arrive early "to smoke cigarettes and drink coffee," eat their meals as a group on work time, spend their off-hours between shifts together, or go out dancing or drinking after hours. Restaurant work attracted those in need of companionship. As one young waitress writing for *Collier's Magazine* in 1929 testified: "It's very unpleasant thinking about being a girl in a big city who . . . must sit down alone and eat. The waitress, however, doesn't do this. When her work is done, she sits down with the other girls at a table and eats a good meal." Workers who lived-in during the early decades of the twentieth century perhaps formed the closest relationships, but many waitresses who resided off the employer's premises lived with other waitresses in small apartments and furnished rooms. Writing in the 1940s, Whyte found that many waitresses "developed passionate loyalty" to one or two co-workers. "The group life in the waitress world [is what] makes it appealing," he concluded. Decades later, first-hand accounts of waitressing frequently stressed "the closeness" and "sisterhood" among waitresses. "I think it comes from suffering the same indignations and receiving the same pleasures," one explained.[77]

Although waitresses worked and socialized with other culinary crafts, their community of interest lay directly with other waitresses. The demands on each craft within the larger structure of the restaurant often created friction between crafts while solidifying the ranks of each individual craft. Waitresses needed food and liquor immediately if their customers were to be satisfied; cooks and bartenders, removed from the watchful and hungry eye of the customer, responded more to their own inclinations for steady, unpressured control of their work pace.[78] Often settled best through group pressure, the arguments between waitresses and other food service crafts promoted waitress solidarity and group strategizing.

The richness of waitress work culture is most evident in their use of a language peculiar to their occupation and their reliance on group-devised work rules and trade secrets. Older waitresses trained new workers in the basic etiquette of table service and helped apprentices learn the first prerequisite of the work culture: the "restaurant vernacular." Being accepted "into the fraternal order of restaurant workers"—as one new waitress described it—meant learning the language of that particular workplace, where a non-tipping customer was a "stiff" and a reprimand from the boss was another appropriately phallic term, "cigar." Instructions to cooks from waitresses were unintelligible to the uninitiated. Adam and Eve on a raft, draw one, and lazy two in a kimono might be a typical early morning communication from a waitress whose customer wanted two fried eggs on toast, a cup of coffee, and two donuts to go. Although use of pejorative names for customers might "be reason for instant dismissal," food service workers had a well-developed vocabulary of terms for customers. Besides the stiff or dead-beat, waitresses contended with the "squawker," the "lonely heart," the "train catcher," and the "cafe casanova." Categorizing customer types helped the greenhorn waitress determine the appropriate serving behavior and, when used behind the customer's back, could be a source of considerable humor and catharsis. "Soda fountain lingo," according to one analyst, lightened the work load through the use of abbreviation, relieved monotony, mystified the public, and encouraged esprit de corps among the initiates.[79]

Inexperienced waitresses had to master other aspects of workplace culture in addition to the language. Group norms defined acceptable service styles, governed which tasks waitresses would perform, and which of the employer's rules could be broken. Idoniea Duntley recalled how as a young waitress she was expected to carry food on her arms, even when trays were available. It was part of the pride of waitressing. "Spot four coffee cups on one arm and you're looking at . . . [the waitress] in top form," as one commentator volunteered. Waitresses agreed to "neglect" tasks such as sweeping and vacuuming floors, scrubbing walls, and washing bathrooms that they considered porter work. Stealing customer's possessions was viewed as theft and frowned upon, but "fiddling schemes," in which the waitress got extra meals from the kitchen and pocketed the payment, were regarded "as a legitimate entitlement—a part of wages." The "acceptable" amount of food one could steal or "fiddle" was regulated by the group, however. These collectively set rules countered the arbitrary, informal reward system practiced by bosses in which favored employees would be offered less side work, "access to pilferage privileges," or other perks.[80]

The elaborate group work rules devised by workers rivaled the most sophisticated personnel systems. Workers created job rotation schemes and regulated station assignments. In one restaurant, the waitresses took turns calling in sick when they felt the supervisors had overstaffed. Waitresses assisted each other, but each had her regular customers and other waitresses were expected to honor those previously developed relationships. Valentine Webster explained "the way *we* worked it" when a new worker arrived. "I'd show . . . [her] what to do and I'd take the heavy load until . . . [she] learned the ropes." Whyte unearthed layers of informal work practices regulating work flow and crises; he concluded that without these work groups the business of feeding would grind to a halt.[81]

Older waitresses passed on to younger women their stock of knowledge about pleasing and controlling customers as well as their techniques for gaining cooperation from cooks and bartenders. Their understanding of diners—

which, as one journalist observed, was as valuable to a waitress as "wood lore to a trapper"—involved knowing the exact degree of intimacy or formality desired, anticipating and shaping the needs of customers, and recognizing customers to avoid. In a situation "potentially fraught with subservience and sexual subtexts," waitresses handled offensive diners by ignoring them, by humorous putdowns, by adopting "dramaturgical devices," or by pure humiliation. They were "at once, warm and welcoming, brusque and wisecrack-y." The trick was to influence customer behavior so that the work of serving them was bearable, without losing the customer's sympathy and hence forfeiting the tip. During the social reformer Maud Younger's first day on the job in 1907, an experienced co-worker exhorted her "to jolly your customers along. You've got to build up a little trade for yourself. Now, if a man says to me, 'Is that order coming?' I say something funny. Sometimes I say, 'Yes, so's Christmas.'" Another waitress, writing in the *New York Times*, unconsciously revealed the group-devised nature of these tricks by her use of the pronoun *we*. "When a slightly inebriated customer asks you to knock off work and do the night clubs with him, we have a good answer. We just tell him we'd love to, but we're married and is it all right if we ask our families to come along too." A third waitress revealed how "we dealt with stiffs. If a stiff came in with a large party, we'd give him the check." Although we "might lose 50 cents," she added, it was a "worthy sacrifice."[82]

Waitress work culture also helped women realistically interpret the flirtations and sexual games of male customers. Unrestrained by masculine ears and oblivious to the dominant culture's strictures, waitresses talked candidly with each other about sexual matters and the power relations that existed between men and women. These group appraisals of male behavior must have saved many a waitress from being swept off her feet by flattery or from being rushed into a mismatched courtship and marriage.[83]

The occupational culture developed by waitresses departed in significant ways from the conservative peer culture of women workers depicted by some historians.[84] The waitress subculture, worldly and pragmatic, hardly reinforced romantic visions of escape into marital bliss. The kinds of stories repeated in the workplace by the older divorced and separated waitresses more often than not put the younger women on guard against members of the male sex who, by all appearances, rarely functioned satisfactorily in their roles as providers and companions. As one divorced truck stop waitress retorted when told by a male patron that she'd have a good man to take care of her if she wasn't so mean: "You listen here, I'm good enough woman for any man but all you guys want are chippies." Many waitresses, Donovan noted, took on male lovers rather than marry because they believed that the men around them could not provide them with domesticity. The answer to one waitress's question—"What did I get by gettin' married?"—was frequently "nothing at all."[85]

Furthermore, the nature of service work itself discouraged idealization of the male. Unlike many working women who were either segregated from or subordinate to men at work, waitresses interacted constantly with male customers, supervisors, and co-workers, often "initiating action" with bartenders, cooks, and customers rather than responding to their demands. They were confronted daily with the foibles of men and could observe first-hand the battleground of the sexes by watching the stratagems of other waitresses in dealing with male customers, co-workers, and bosses. Waitress Mame Dugan's reaction in O. Henry's short story "Cupid à la Carte" was rather extreme: she refused to marry because "after watching men eat, eat, eat . . . they're absolutely nothing but something that goes in front of a knife and fork and plate at the table." But many waitresses had "met man face to face" and discovered "that the reports in the Seaside Library about his being a fairy prince lacked confirmation." The work of serving food and the peer culture developed at the workplace undermined rather than reinforced romantic fantasies.[86]

In conclusion, the very nature of the work, the social organization of the workplace, and the pragmatic close-knit work culture among food service workers fostered a positive occupational identity among waitresses and an activist orientation. Waitressing was difficult, demanding work, but work that encouraged assertive behavior and provided those doing it with a positive assessment of their skills. The division of labor at the workplace reinforced occupational and gender ties, while the frequent social interaction between men and women and the candid waitress subculture inhibited a female peer culture based on romantic fantasy and marital escape. These workplace experiences interacted with the particular ethnic, family, and economic characteristics shared by waitresses to create a consciousness that valued work-based collective activism. Unlike workers in most other female-dominated occupations, waitresses created an occupational community that not only fueled the formation of waitress unions but also sustained those unions for more than half a century.[87]

San Francisco waitresses escort Waiter's Local 30 Labor Day float. (*Mixer and Server*, December 1905)

What appears to be an atypical scene from Butte, Montana: white waitresses on duty at an Asian restaurant, probably the Mai Wah Noodle Parlour, n.d. [1890–1910]. (Paul Eno Collection, Montana Historical Society, Helena)

Labor Day float, Chicago Waitresses' Local 484, 1913. (Local 1, Chicago)

Trustees of the Waitresses' Recreation Home, Seattle Waitresses' Local 240, around 1913. (Nell Ranta)

A MOVIE
OF THE RESTAURANT WORKER

I 7 A.M. The Waitress arrives —15 minutes for breakfast	**V** 3 to 5 P.M. "Free" and nowhere to go
II 7.15 to 10 A.M. Customers must be served	**VI** 5 to 8 P.M. Carrying trays and walking many miles
III 10 to 12 A.M. She sorts folds and polishes	**VII** 9 P.M. Exhausted Home and to bed
IV 12 to 3 P.M. With heavy trays she walks about five miles	**VIII** 6 A.M. The daily grind be- gins again

HER PROGRAM FOR ⟨ **ELEVEN HOURS A DAY!**
SEVEN DAYS A WEEK!

"A Movie of a Restaurant Worker."
(*Survey*, 18 November 1916)

Detroit Woolworth waitresses
and retail clerks occupy their
store in February 1937. (Library
of Congress)

PART II

Waitresses Turn to Economic and Political Organization

Before the 1930s, few American workers were organized: in 1920, at the peak of pre-New Deal organizational strength only a fifth of the nonagricultural work force belonged to unions. The situation changed dramatically during the 1930s and 1940s as workers flocked to the labor movement and for the first time in American history gained collectively bargaining agreements in such major industries as steel, auto, and communications. Nevertheless, by the early 1950s, union growth sputtered to a halt, reaching a high-water mark in 1954 with 35 percent of the nonagricultural labor force organized.[1]

Although the patterns of union growth among wage-earning women paralleled the membership fluctuations of the larger labor movement, the proportion of organized female workers consistently remained below that of male workers. Before the 1930s, fewer than 7 percent of women belonged to unions. The organizing successes of the Congress of Industrial Organization (CIO) and the American Federation of Labor (AFL) in the 1930s and 1940s swept women as well as men into unions for the first time, but when the dust had settled, fully 85 percent of the female work force remained unorganized.[2]

The success of waitresses in organizing labor unions stands as a significant achievement, particularly for women outside of manufacturing. Organization occurred among women telephone operators, and even clerical workers and salesclerks in the Progressive Era and the 1920s, but these unions were short-lived. In the New Deal era, organization spread once again to women outside of manufacturing, but the campaigns met with limited success. By the late 1940s, organized office workers were rare, and women store clerks lacked the protection of union contracts outside of a few urban centers.[3] In contrast, waitresses founded permanent unions in the Progressive Era that survived into the 1970s; during the peak unionization period in the 1940s and 1950s, close to a quarter of the trade claimed union representation. In certain cities, waitress locals achieved considerable power, wresting major concessions from employers and reshaping the nature of labor-management relations in the food service industry.[4]

The following two chapters trace the rise of union activity among waitresses from 1900 to the 1950s and analyze the forces that propelled and inhibited organization in this female-dominated occupation.

CHAPTER THREE

The Emergence and Survival of Waitress Unionism, 1900–1930

[Where] waitresses' unions are strong, the business is on a high plane, the hard work fairly paid and the working women who are engaged in it are self-respecting and respected by all who know them. They are distinctly high class, and so it can be here, if the girls will get together and work.

—Anonymous journalist writing for
the *Independent* in 1908[1]

The historic barriers to female unionism before the 1930s were formidable: women's lack of permanent wage status, the ambivalence emanating from a trade union movement overwhelmingly male, the class tensions between female wage earners and their elite sisterly allies, and the objective difficulties in organizing "unskilled" workers with little strike leverage.[2] Moreover, as recent scholars have argued, many women workers may have preferred to exert collective power in ways other than unionization.[3] Yet waitresses not only chose unionization as their vehicle for expressing militancy, but they also managed to build all-female union institutions in these early years that provided them with an impressive degree of power and dignity.

Waitresses turned to unionization as early as the 1880s, forming separate all-female unions as well as locals that included male waiters and other food service crafts. With the help of the Federated Trades Council of San Francisco and the International Workingmen's Association, San Francisco waitresses organized a separate local on May 25, 1886, while Los Angeles waitresses united with male culinary workers in requesting that the White Cooks, Waiters and Employees Protective Union of the Pacific Coast charter a mixed-gender and craft local. Many of these earliest locals affiliated briefly with the Knights of Labor, but by the mid-1890s most had either disbanded or cast their lot with the newly emerging AFL.[4]

In April of 1891, the AFL chartered the Waiters and Bartenders National Union with an initial membership of 450. The Waiters and Bartenders National Union, later to change its name to the Hotel Employees and Restaurant Employees International Union (HERE), made little progress until the first years of the twentieth century: in 1899 the total membership of the union had not passed a thousand. By World War I, however, membership climbed to sixty-five thousand: HERE had established itself as a permanent fixture in the industry.[5] The Industrial Workers of the World also experimented with organizing the "foodstuff" industry in this era but with notably meagre results. IWW culinary locals sprang up in a few Western IWW-dominated mining and lumbering towns, and the IWW inspired strikes in New York and other immigrant centers, but their organizations were short-lived and geared primarily to male waiters and cooks.[6]

Choosing Separatism

Substantial gains in organizing female culinary workers did not occur until after the founding of separate HERE-affiliated waitress organizations. The first permanent waitress union, Local 240 in Seattle, received its charter on March 31, 1900. Over the next decade, HERE waitress organizations took root in at least a half dozen other communities. By the World War I era, at the height of the movement for separate female organizations, more than seventeen permanent waitress locals existed and approximately 70 percent of organized HERE waitresses belonged to separate locals. These female working-class organizations survived the open-shop campaigns of the 1920s, the initial shocks of the depression, and forged ahead in membership and influence during the favorable climate of the New Deal and the 1940s. The majority maintained their separate female identity and organizational structure until the early 1970s (Tables 6–8).[7]

The impetus for separate gender organization among women workers has been poorly understood by scholars. Although many unions barred women from membership or relegated them to second-class citizenship, separate-gender organization was not merely a product of nor a reaction to the discrimination of male workers. In many industries, the sex segregation of work decreed that membership in locals organized by trade or department would be either predominantly one sex or the other. Moreover, although a consensus on separatism as a strategy never existed among working women, in certain periods and in certain trades, women themselves pushed for separate-sex organizations.[8]

Waitresses had strong affinity for separatism. They initiated numerous separate locals before the 1930s, and their commitment to separatism sustained many of these locals into the 1970s. In part, their preference for separatism derived from their ethnic and cultural orientations. As Susan Glenn has suggested, Americanized, native-born women tended to be greater supporters of separatism because of their unencumbrance with the strong community and class ties of recent immigrant women and their closer connection with the native-born variety of feminism rooted in the separate spheres traditions of

American middle-class womanhood.[9] The particular workplace experiences and family status of waitresses also nourished their inclinations to organize autonomous, all-female locals—locals that could address "female" concerns and provide women with an "initiating," leadership role.

The desire of waitresses for separate organization prevailed over the mixed-gender model suggested by the organization of food service work. In contrast to many workplaces where divisions along sex and craft lines were synonymous, female and male servers belonged to the same craft. Simply following the craft logic of the food service workplace would have resulted in a mixed-sex craft division in which waiters and waitresses belonged to the same craft local. The formation of separate waitress locals necessitated a rationale beyond craft identity: the legitimacy of gender concerns had to be put forward.

Moreover, female culinary workers faced opposition from male unionists who supported integrating women into mixed-sex locals or organizing them into separate but subordinate branches of the male local. A separate, autonomous female local would create problems. Some men feared conflict over wage scales, work rules, and distribution of jobs; others were reluctant to lose dues-paying members.[10] The International union pursued neutrality: they officially encouraged organization by craft "regardless of race, color, sex, or nationality" but allowed for the formation of separate organizations based on race and sex. Section 49 of the 1905 HERE Constitution read: "there shall not be more than one white or colored local of the same craft in any city or town, except waitresses who may obtain a charter." In short, women workers had to take the initiative in establishing their own locals, and they did so.[11]

Fifty Seattle waitresses applied for a separate charter in 1900, braving "the strong prejudice against working women mixing in unions, and the even stronger prejudice against women forming their own unions," as their union newspaper recorded. The union's historian bragged that although "a good many people thought an organization run by girls would not last long," the local thrived. Its first president, Alice Lord, an aggressive native-born organizer and Irish, remained the principal officer for close to forty years, holding off marriage until her fifties. Over the years, Lord relied on the assistance of Agnes Quinn, who left to head up the Portland waitresses in 1921, Dorretta "Dyna" Landon, a former activist in the telephone operators union and the office employees, and Pauline Newman Fuhr, who had joined the local in 1907 at age fifteen. Lord, however, credited the loyal rank and file for the accomplishments of the local. Laying claim to an American tradition that abhorred inequalities, she bragged: "the girls belong to a race whose forefathers fought for the liberty of humanity in 1861–65, and they are fighters too—this time for the liberty of the wage earner." The Seattle waitress local soon had sister organizations in St. Louis, Cleveland, and Chicago.[12]

The problems of operating within mixed locals led San Francisco waitresses to conclude that their interests as women trade unionists would be better served through separate-sex organizations where they could define their own organizational goals and practices. Much to the surprise of the waiter officials of San Francisco's Local 30, not only the bartenders but "the waiteresses too" began "asking for an organization" in 1901. By April, sixty-three waitresses had formed a branch of the waiters' union; five years later, having "decided that a separate organization was desirable," they petitioned their male co-workers for "a local of their own." Once the waiters voted approval, the new two hundred and fifty member local installed its first officers on February 21, 1906.[13]

Like its sister organization in Seattle, the San Francisco local enjoyed continuity and vigor in its principal leaders. The waitresses elected Minnie Andrews as president and first business agent. Andrews guided the local through its first decade, later becoming one of the first women organizers on the International staff. Louise Downing LaRue—a firebrand agitator for women's suffrage and a veteran officer of the mixed culinary locals in St. Louis and San Francisco—took a leading role as did Maud Younger, a native-born San Francisco heiress (known locally as the "millionaire waitress") who devoted her life to suffrage and social reform. By the 1920s and 1930s, the reins of leadership passed to Montana-born Frankie Behan, a 1922 transfer from Seattle who served as an officer into the 1950s, and Lettie Howard, who devoted thirty-nine years to the union, broken only by her absence in 1919 when she helped organize waitresses in Los Angeles. There were others such as Julia Marguerite Finkenbinder, Elizabeth Kelley, and Laura Molleda, almost all of whom were native born and of Northern European background.[14]

Portland, Oregon waitresses persevered for a separate local despite opposition from their male colleagues because, as they explained it, they wanted to elect their own female officers and conduct union affairs by their own standards. Gertrude Sweet, a carpenter's daughter from Napa, California, who served as recording secretary for the mixed local during her first year as a member, recalled that "many of the waitresses were not happy with the way the waiters were conducting the business of the union. Two or three times we had to call in police officers because they were not sober and they were fighting on the floor." By 1921, "there were no waitresses serving as officers," Sweet continued. "We were in the majority, and we decided it was time that we ran our own union."[15]

Male unionists in Portland resisted the exodus of women from their local. "In regards to . . . the separate charter for the Waitresses, organizer [Harley] Johnson and I have held it off and discouraged it for more than a year," a local waiters' union official wrote. But "the girls won't be satisfied until they get a separate charter." In the end, the male officers relented and sent the waitresses' application to the International, promising in an accompanying note a detailed account of the "disagreeable scenes enacted recently and in the past few years" and "the causes leading up to this move on the part of the girl members." [16]

When the International president finally granted the waitresses' request in late 1921 and "the divorce" was final, the new union, Local 305, blossomed. Agnes Quinn, recently arrived from Seattle where she had been president of Local 240 for seven years, was elected business agent and reelected every year until her retirement in the 1940s. Gertrude Sweet became Waitress Local 305's first president at the age of thirty-one and remained a HERE official into her eighties. As salutatorian of her high school class, Sweet had dreamed of being a medical missionary, but a college education proved financially impossible. Sweet worked as a waitress, raised four children, and learned of unionism from her husband's involvement with an AFL loggers' local. By her thirties, she had found her life's work as a waitress official. [17]

The history of Local 457 in Butte, Montana, provides further confirmation of the preference of waitresses for separate, all-female organization. In 1890, Butte women service workers—waitresses, cooks, and laundresses working in boardinghouses where the local hard-rock miners and other laborers lived—formed the Women's Protective Union (WPU). Although the early relation between the WPU, the local Knights' Assembly, and the Butte Miners Union (which took in trades other than miners) is unclear, by the turn of the century the WPU was acting as an autonomous union affiliated directly with the local Silver Bow Trades and Labor Assembly. They also briefly joined the Industrial Workers of the World in 1905. In 1907, the WPU applied for a HERE charter and became Local 457 of the Hotel Employees and Restaurant Employees. On the front lines of the new HERE local were single-minded, no-nonsense women like Lena Mattausch, an officer from 1913 until the late 1950s, and Bridget Shea, a formidable Irish woman who "never wore anything but black" and raised five children while managing the local. [18]

Local 457 faced mounting pressure for amalgamation in the 1920s. In 1921, Butte Cooks and Waiters' Local 22 asked for jurisdiction over all women in the trade; Local 457 refused, countering with a proposal that the sexual division be reinforced: they wanted the removal of the word *persons* in Local 22's contracts. Local 22 backed off after receiving bargaining assistance from the larger, more powerful WPU and the jurisdictional division by gender appeared resolved. In 1926, however, after having lost members to the WPU despite concessions to employers, Local 22 sought the aid of the International in consolidating the two locals. HERE President Edward Flore and other International officers visited Butte to quell "the dissension" and to put the question to a referendum vote. On October 1, 1926, Butte women voted 177 "in favor of remaining a separate local" and 26 in favor of amalgamation. A year later, Local 457 delegates to the HERE 1927 convention must have felt vindicated when they delivered their report on mixed locals "showing where they were a failure in many places."[19]

Employer Opposition and Waitress Tenacity

These first waitress locals encountered considerable obstacles in sustaining their fledgling organizations. In addition to the ambivalence of their own culinary brothers, they faced bitter feuds with employers, condescension from middle-class "uplift" or moral reform groups, and divisions in their own ranks. Nevertheless, many locals weathered these trials and established themselves permanently in the industry.

Typically, female locals faced their greatest battles with employers after they demonstrated significant bargaining power. Employers often underestimated the organizational potential of their female employees and, taken by surprise, were forced to grant concessions. These initial union victories, however, sparked employer counterorganization and open-shop campaigns. Employers in Seattle took the offensive after waitresses won wage and hour concessions in 1908. The restaurant keepers refused to abide by the union's work rules and proposed a return to the seven-day week. Local 240 "did not think the same, so . . . everyone voted to go out." With only one "black sheep" scabbing, the restaurant owners capitulated after twelve hours.[20]

Chicago waitresses also maintained the upper hand with employers in their early years. With the assistance of the milk wagon drivers' union and the Chicago Federation of Labor, forty-one waitresses formed their own organization in March of 1902. Within a few months, a majority of their trade—some 1,500—had enrolled. On an appointed day, all union members appeared in their restaurants wearing union badges and demanding a reduction of hours and an increase in wages. Taken by surprise, the employers, almost without exception, yielded. Guided by the fiery oratory and "fervent heart" of Irish-born Elizabeth Maloney who officered the local from 1902 until her death in 1921, Local 484 secured signed agreements with numerous Chicago restaurants, expanded its membership, and moved into its own headquarters in the Chicago Labor Temple. Their success was evident in the Chicago Labor Day parade of 1905. The International organizer assigned to Chicago reported that of all the Chicago culinary locals, only Local 484 participated in the parade. "Over 60 members rode in automobiles with flags flying and a magnificent banner. The girls got the greatest reception along the line of march I ever saw; they certainly did credit to themselves and our organization," he added.[21]

Except for a few isolated strikes and picketing at individual restaurants, the local experienced relative peace until confronted with a major employer backlash against unionism in 1913. Angered by their concession of "one day's rest in seven" or the six-day week, some one hundred employers formed the Chicago Restaurant Keepers Association and demanded a return to the seven-day week. The waitresses responded by striking all association restaurants. For the next year and a half, Local 484 and restaurant owners locked horns. The waitress local received little help from its weaker brother culinary locals, but it did receive aid from "the society women who have appointed committees and are assisting us in their own way"; the Hull-House settlement workers who held protest meetings, picketed alongside the striking waitresses, and appointed a committee to call on the mayor and the police chief; and the bakers and the bakery wagon drivers who honored the waitresses' picket line.

In defense, the Restaurant Keepers Association marshaled its own formidable arsenal of weapons. They brought in black female strike-breakers and hired picketers to harass the union marchers and advertise the employers' point of view. They employed labor spies and gunmen to intimidate the strikers, and they obtained sweeping court injunctions against the union which prohibited "striking, picketing, organizing, boycotting, conspiring, resigning [from work], or in any way interfering with their [the employer's] business." The employers also set up a rival employer-dominated waitress association modeled on the waitress union, with club rooms and job referral services. After more than two hundred arrests, the employers prevailed. They broke the waitresses' control over the labor supply and reinstituted the seven-day week in some restaurants. The Chicago local continued to represent some 30 percent of the trade, but they did not regain their former dominance until the 1930s.[22]

The San Francisco waitresses in their first two decades experienced similar cycles of advance followed by employer backlash and defeat. After the union began pressing for the ten-hour day in 1901, the local Restaurant Keepers Association gained the backing of the San Francisco Employer Association and precipitated a strike. After enjoining union picketing, the owners held out for six months, operating their restaurants with scab labor. The union lost considerable membership—union waitresses had trouble getting jobs and some were forced to leave town or assume false names—but the local followed the strike defeat with a remarkable period of rebuilding. In part, the unprecedented surge in membership resulted from the waitresses' decision to pursue "more subtle means than direct action," according to one early authority on the union. The waitress union dedicated itself to an educational campaign that brought results both in working conditions and increased membership. Although many restaurants refused to bargain or sign agreements, by May of 1902, a handful of establishments instituted working conditions in conformity with the standard 1902 Waitress Wage Scales and Working Agreement: employment of union members only; six-day week; and $8 a week for day work, $9 for night work. In December 1903, the waitresses survived a second open-shop campaign and lockout by the employers. With the assistance of Mayor Eugene Schmitz, recently elected by San Francisco's Union Labor party, they emerged victorious with a new one-year agreement that reduced hours to nine a day.[23]

By the time the separate waitress charter became official in 1906, union waitresses had signed up a majority of their co-workers. Relying on "silent picketing" to foil court injunctions and the new union strategy of "monthly working buttons" worn conspicuously by all union waitresses—an idea that can "accomplish . . . what the Union label has secured for the printers and other craftsmen"—the local steadily increased its numbers and influence, even adding cafeteria waitresses to its ranks after 1910.[24] In 1916, however, when San Francisco culinary workers struck for the eight-hour day, the employers regained the upper hand. The strike, dubbed a "complete failure" by more than one analyst, was called off after three months, but not before membership defections left the waitress union reeling. In particular, the cafeteria women disregarded the strike order and remained on the job. As a result, the Waitress Union lost the cafeteria workers and did not regain them until the 1930s.[25]

Some waitress locals disappeared completely during these years. In New York City, Waitresses' Local 769 had the support of the Women's Trade Union League (WTUL) and such well-known reformers as San Francisco's Maud Younger, but it went under in 1908 after only a few years of activity.[26] In 1912 and 1913, the International Hotel Workers Union, a syndicalist-inspired, independent organization, agitated among New York's hotel and restaurant workers, drawing in a few waitresses. IWW organizers Elizabeth Gurley Flynn and Joseph Ettor, who lent their talents to the organization, urged novel tactics such as exposing adulterated food and "scientific sabotage"—defined variously as dropping trays of food on the floor, spilling "gravy on the shirt-fronts of well-dressed patrons," and confusing orders—but few if any concessions were wrested from employers. The WTUL picked up the refrain for a separate waitress union in 1914, but a credible organization was not in place until 1919.[27]

Waitress unionism revived during World War I. Long-established HERE locals gathered steam, and new HERE units such as Local 729, representing the employees of the Harvey eating houses, sprang to life. In Minneapolis, department store waitresses held out for $9 a day and a guaranteed return to their posts in the tea room, preferring "to be silent picket[s] and pace the sidewalk with [their] message than be turned into inexperienced and inefficient glove or ribbon sales[women]."[28]

Most locals incurred losses in the labor turmoil following the war, but by the mid-twenties membership resumed its upward spiral. By 1927, female membership in HERE had more than quadrupled from pre-World War I figures. Women now represented more than a fifth of the total membership of the International union, a sizable leap from 5.4 percent in 1910 and 9.3 percent in 1920,[29] and for the first time, women outnumbered men in some of the mixed culinary unions, prompting workers in the industry to label these communities "girls' towns."[30] These changes resulted partially from the resiliency of the female unions during this period and the feminization of food service work; the declining vitality of the male-dominated locals also contributed to the changing sex ratio.

The advent of Prohibition and the employer campaigns of the 1920s cut deeply into the male membership of HERE. Having peaked in 1918, the number of male culinary unionists dropped precipitously after the passage of the 18th Amendment and plunged downward throughout the 1920s, hitting bottom in 1933. The 18th Amendment, in effect nationwide by January 1920, wrecked the all-male bartending constituency within the union. Numerous waiter and cook locals also folded up for lack of membership and finances. After the passage of Prohibition, employers who previously had been sympathetic to unionism because of the higher profit margins accompanying liquor service adopted tough bargaining stances. Speakeasies, operating in a subterranean fashion, did not yield to traditional organizing methods. The public attention generated by unionization usually resulted in the bar or restaurant closing.[31] In addition to these industry-specific problems, the union faced a climate inhospitable to any brand of unionism. The American Plan destroyed locals across the country, and employers' liberal use of court injunctions, yellow-dog contracts, and employer-dominated culinary associations stymied union advance at point after point.[32]

At first, even some of the stronger female organizations were overwhelmed. Chicago waitresses struck in 1920 to enforce their new agreement, but "the bosses came out on top." Unable to appeal to the young women flocking to the new soda fountain lunches and small sandwich shops, the Chicago local declined in membership and influence.[33] By the mid-1920s, however, female locals in Kansas City, Buffalo, and other towns told of the return of "old members who had wandered from the fold," and of local membership figures inching back to their World War I level. In particular, locals in the West gained ground.[34] Butte's WPU rebounded after a 1920 strike and brought "every cafe in the city in line." By 1926, in a strange twist of circumstances, the Butte Miners' Union appealed to the stronger WPU to have union-minded wives pressure their unorganized miner husbands. The Miners' Union even proposed that the Silver Bow Trades and Labor Council "declare the women from the WPU . . . who were married to non-union miners . . . unfair to organized labor."[35] A few western locals, having organized a majority of the waitresses in their community, petitioned the International for jurisdiction over other female service workers such as soft drink dispensers, cooks and laundry workers, maids in boardinghouses and small hotels, and even "telephone girls."[36]

Female membership also grew as waitress unionists adopted more flexible tactics in dealing with employers, reevaluating their early reliance on strikes and picketing. Although waitress locals did not abandon adversarial tactics, increasingly they replaced strong-arm methods with rational persuasion and an appeal to the employer's business savvy. Female organizers now approached employers directly in the hope that union recognition would be granted voluntarily. And, for various reasons, some proprietors—always a minority before the 1930s—complied. A few shop owners, having been union members themselves, believed in the value of the services the union provided its members. Others realized the possible benefits of unionization to their own business survival: union houses received free advertising in union publications, patronage from union workers increased, well-organized locals provided a reliable supply of competent, trained help, and standardization of labor costs enhanced industry stability and eliminated cut-throat competitors. Female organizers frequently employed these arguments in meetings and discussions with employers. Even when organizers found picketing and boycotts necessary to gain recognition, they later emphasized their willingness to act cooperatively. Delia Hurley, one of the first female organizers on the International staff, announced after gaining union recognition through picketing that "we in turn, are and will continue to make what amends we can for the injury done, by announcing at every meeting we attend of the house being fair."[37]

"Then they are not brothers"

Organized male culinary workers seldom erected formal constitutional barriers to the entry of women, but their reluctance to organize women retarded the growth of waitress organizations and at times was as much of an obstacle as the hostility of employers. Women HERE members from their first days of union participation appealed to their male counterparts for organizing support, but the majority of men resisted these calls to action until the 1930s.

As early as 1906, Alice Lord, the secretary of the Seattle waitresses, called attention to the needs of unorganized women workers in the pages of the HERE national journal, *Mixer and Server*. Lamenting that the subject of organization among waitresses had never been addressed in the opinion section of the journal, Lord explained the rationale for independent waitress locals and the importance of organizing female workers. In the next issue of the journal, waitress activist Myria Koomey endorsed Lord's position, adding indignantly that "the male contingent of our organization have shown by their indifference of the past, that they either don't want to see the waitresses organized or are afraid to tackle the job." Koomey followed this indictment by pointing out the inconsistency in male behavior whereby they "put forth every subtle art known to show how swell they think of us, but we don't seem to be worthwhile when it comes to . . . [helping us] establish a union that will assist us to make a living and put a few clothes on our back." In her final volley, Koomey questioned men's right to call themselves trade unionists while they ignored their sister co-workers. "If organization is good for the men and will help them to obtain conditions then they are not brothers if they don't aid the women to organize and get conditions."[38]

Lord and others continued agitating in these early years, and in the end won a few concessions from the International union.[39] HERE initiated an organizing campaign among waitresses in 1908 and introduced a resolution at the AFL convention that same year asking for "moral assistance" in their "endeavor to establish . . . unions of these female workers . . . employed in the hotels, restaurants and similar public service establishments." A year later, however, the organizing staff consisted of six bartenders and three culinary workers—all male. The first female organizers were not appointed until female unionists secured passage of a resolution at the 1909 HERE convention requiring the appointment of women.[40]

As World War I approached and female workers moved into jobs vacated by men, the top HERE officials recognized the seriousness of the threat to male standards and began pressing for increased attention to unorganized women. General Secretary Jere Sullivan's alarmed editorials appeared in virtually every issue of the national journal during 1918 and early 1919. Sullivan paused briefly in the early 1920s to write of other concerns, but a steady barrage of calls to action greeted readers in the mid-1920s, prompted by another wave of female workers flooding the industry.[41]

At first, Sullivan appealed to the higher nature of his audience. He gently chided Local 20 waiters in St. Louis, urging them to "assist the girls in building up their local" and "not be so blinded by their own success as to forget the promises they have made." By 1918, his editorials stressed male self-interest. Waiters who in the past were unconcerned about "what became of the girls" must wake up to the fact that their wages are being "forced to a lower level." Like the cigar-makers and printers, they must recognize "the menace of allowing the women of the trade to remain unorganized."[42]

Local culinary unionists heeded Sullivan's advice for the brief period of the war. For the first time, women organizers and officials wrote praising the men for their organizational aid. A recent union recruit wrote: "our little handful of girls" was brought together "aided by our brother bartenders, our International officers and a degree of progressiveness ourselves." The prospects for a "credible organization of waitresses" in Philadelphia appeared good, according to Delia Hurley in February 1918, "for we have the good fortune of having men in our craft here who are ready to rise to the situation. I can not say too much for these boys as they have given me every assistance possible." In a similar vein, a male officer bragged a month later, "When Sister Agnes Moran . . . came to our city . . . to organize the waitresses, the boys of Local 763 did everything possible to make her efforts a success. In a few days a splendid enthusiasm was created and a large number of girls joined."[43]

Even New York City, notorious for its underrepresentation of women in culinary organizations, showed signs of progress. R. E. Croskey, an International organizer steeped in western traditions of inclusive unionism from his early days in Colorado with the Western Federation of Miners, helped start a waitress branch of Waiters' Local 1 on September 29, 1919. Despite ensuing struggles with the employer during which many of the women were arrested and others "assaulted by hired sluggers," three months later, Croskey reported a growing membership and a separate headquarters for the waitresses. Local 1 showed such largesse toward its sister branch that despite having "spent . . . money generously for this organization," they "proposed to assist them in getting a charter for themselves as soon as they are able to stand one."[44]

But after the war this spirit of cooperation dissipated in the face of increased job competition between men and women and the virulent open-shop campaigns of the employer. Waiters in lucrative full-service restaurants and in hotel banquet work who had lost their jobs to women during the war found ready allies in their former union brothers when they attempted to reclaim their old positions. "After the war conditions will change," one male officer explained to his women members, "where you [women] are now working with a mixed crew, you will find that men will come back to their old jobs, and once again the girls will work where they used to work." Mixed locals not only failed to recruit new female members; they actively sought to replace their current women members with men. In addition, the open-shop assaults of the early 1920s pitted women and men against each other as women were hired to take the jobs of striking male workers. In most instances, instead of organizing the female recruits, male workers chose to exclude them.

The bitterness between men and women lingered into the twenties and beyond. A handful of male officers persisted in calling for the organization of the women as the only effective response to the circumstances, but the bulk of the organized male work force obstinately refused to commit themselves to this endeavor. Hugo Ernst, one of the few to call for "more time and energy . . . to be devoted to the organization of girls, noted that unless this [unorganized] condition is remedied, we will be confronted with the situation of unorganized girls taking the place of organized men."[45]

Female trade unionists admonished their brothers as well but to no avail. As Nina Osborn, a Denver delegate to the 1925 HERE convention observed: "judging from the sentiments expressed, they [the men] are not so greatly interested in the women workers of the industry. They are making a serious mistake," she continued, "for if they do not organize the women and aid them in securing wages and conditions, they will be faced by more and more competition from unorganized women." Agnes Quinn of Portland declared: "The reason you have been unable to induce the women of the catering industry to organize . . . is because you have no faith in one another and will not work with each other." A third delegate accused men of being "the most wilful [sic] constructors of impediments" to the organization of women and of acting hypocritically. "Unions composed of males disavow their intention to limit the employment of women at the trade, yet seldom do they engage in work that promotes the better organization of females."[46]

Reports trickled in from female organizers confirming these accusations. Men were not cooperating in organizing drives, and male locals fought female over the distribution of jobs. "The organized men of Atlantic City do not want the women of this town organized," a female organizer audaciously complained in the pages of the national journal. Hugo Ernst, reporting back to his local in San Francisco after a 1923 cross-country trip, focused attention on one of the worst competitive situations. In St. Louis he found that "the waitresses have an organization of about 300 members, but there is no cooperation whatsoever between the waiters and waitresses. When the girls organize a house the boys try to take it away from them and vice versa. The consequence is that no one has anything." The male officials of Waiters' Local 20 privately wrote Ernst and denied his charge, claiming that "such tactics are to [sic] low and degrading to be resorted to by our organization." On the other hand, they continued, "you would have been hitting the nail on the head . . . had you stated that Local 249 [the Waitresses' Local] tries to take away establishments under the jurisdiction of Local 20." Clearly, Ernst had uncovered a pocket of resentment and backbiting.[47]

As late as 1930, women had to defend the need for having any women organizers on the International staff. Jennie Philcox wrote to *Mixer and Server* attacking Brother Martel's suggestion to drop the women organizers.[48] Fortunately, the International officials ignored Brother Martel and continued employing female organizers. From 1925 to 1930, at least two women organizers, Bee Tumber and Madge Argo, traveled tirelessly across the country, organizing waitresses into mixed and separate organizations on behalf of the International.

Allies Outside the Culinary Ranks

Thwarted by their male co-workers, waitresses sought allies outside culinary ranks. As service workers, waitresses were in close contact with the consuming public and could forge alliances with their customers. In addition, as women, waitresses could call on middle-class female allies: the Women's Trade Union League, Women's Civic Clubs, the Young Women's Christian Association (YWCA), and even local Women's Republican clubs. Nonetheless, before the 1930s, these outside sources of support often proved unreliable or unresponsive. All too often, waitresses were left to rely solely on their own wit, ingenuity, and solidarity.

In heavily unionized communities or areas with strong traditions of working-class solidarity, waitresses turned to union-conscious patrons and to other trade union organizations for aid. Typically, customers would pressure recalcitrant employers by insisting on a union house card in the restaurant window or a union button pinned on those who served them. In such communities as Butte, Montana, or Harrisburg, Illinois, this approach resulted in the organization of the entire town. As International organizer Madge Argo said enthusiastically, in Harrisburg "the miners have been a great help in bringing about the organization of our people. Most all the workers in that town are organized." Similar accounts poured in from scattered lumbering and logging communities throughout the Pacific Northwest, mining towns up and down the Rockies, and to a lesser degree from anthracite mining communities in Pennsylvania, Ohio, and Illinois. Ida Peterson, a Pacific Northwest waitress organizer and official for more than forty years, remembered waiting tables in 1906 in a cafe where longshoremen and shingle weavers ate. They questioned her about her union affiliation and within two weeks coaxed her into joining the local waitress union. Later, when Peterson moved to a neighboring community, she set up her own waitress local, this time with the aid of the pile-drivers who "helped talk up the union idea wherever they went, and helped . . . plant signs and literature."[49]

Support from tight-knit, union-oriented immigrant communities also induced unionization. The kosher houses in New York City joined, Ernst disclosed in 1923, because the class of people patronizing these places has been educated "by the United Hebrew Trade and the *New York Call* [newspaper] and is more class-conscious"; outside the kosher houses, the HERE "had nothing." In Detroit during the 1920s waitress organizer Saraine Andrews signed up "all the Jewish restaurants in the city within 48 hours. Hardly a soul went through our picket lines."

In large, heterogeneous urban areas, especially those without a strong union tradition, organizing proved more difficult. With so few unionized workers before the 1930s, nonunion restaurants often stayed open through the patronage of the unorganized sector of the working-class or the public at large, which in the main was indifferent to unionism. Bonds between waitresses and customers, even middle-class ones, sometimes proved surprisingly resilient, however. In Boston, a stunned *New York Times* watched as "the smiles of striking waitresses induced" many of their former patrons—college youth and "men in tall hats"—to join the waitresses' picket line.[50]

Of the women's reform organizations existing in this era, waitresses forged the strongest ties with the WTUL, a national cross-class alliance of primarily middle- and upper-class women dedicated to improving the lives of wage-earning women. Support from the WTUL reached its peak in the pre-World War I years, but cooperative activities continued into the 1940s. In New York City, Waitresses' Local 769 affiliated with the New York WTUL in 1908, and its successor, Waiters' and Waitresses' Local 1, contributed financially to the league and was listed as a league supporter. On the West Coast, San Francisco's Local 48 maintained loose ties with the national WTUL organization and even convinced the Central Labor Council to pay for officer Louise La Rue's attendance at the 1909 WTUL convention in Chicago.[51] On the whole, however, West Coast cities lacked the active middle-class support a WTUL chapter required, while East Coast cities lacked separately organized waitress locals that were free to forge social and political ties with the league. The most productive and long-lasting relations between waitresses and league chapters existed in midwestern cities where strong waitress organizations reached out to an organized, active, middle-class female community.

Close cooperation developed between waitress unions and league chapters in Chicago, St. Louis, and Kansas City. Local waitress groups called on and received WTUL help in organizing, in strike situations, and in legislative campaigns. Waitress officials such as Elizabeth Maloney of Chicago and Sarah Green of Kansas City built local league organizations in their communities, attended WTUL conventions, and served on the national WTUL General Executive Board. Elizabeth Maloney sat on the executive board from 1907 to 1916; Sarah Green, first elected to the board in 1920, was reelected throughout the 1920s. Frequently, organizational ties were reinforced by strong personal bonds between waitress leaders and middle-class reformers. When Elizabeth Maloney died in October 1921, her "guard of honor" included such prominent social reformers as Hull-House co-founders Jane Addams and Ellen Gates Starr, University of Chicago professor of social economy Sophonisba Breckenridge, and journalist and WTUL activist Alice Henry. Their memorial tributes to her dwelt on the loss of her friendship as well as her unflagging political spirit.[52]

Support from women's organizations other than the league was rare and often misguided. Waitresses themselves distrusted middle-class female organizations that advocated Prohibition and moral reform. Alice Lord, not averse to taking positions unpopular with her union brothers, publicly proclaimed her solidarity with men in the fight against Prohibition and directed her righteous anger toward female reformers. Usually a defender of women's right to work outside the home, in this case, Lord argued that middle-class female reformers should stay at home. If that proved impossible, then their time should be devoted "to bettering the conditions of their suffering fellow beings, who have to toil for their daily bread. Were these individuals to pay one-half of their attention and direct their energies toward relieving suffering occasioned by merciless employers," Lord declared, "they would accomplish more for the uplifting and advancement of humanity than if they succeeded in closing every dram shop in the land." Lord felt the "fanaticism" of crusaders "made them blind to the needs of the waitresses."[53]

Other writers echoed Lord's anger at "so-called reformers" who attended
to moral reform and neglected the economic problems of the working class.
One report from Chicago praised the WTUL for its support during the 1914
waitress strike but lashed out at the other reformers who want to "close up
the dance halls, saloons, cabarets, bowling alleys, pool rooms, nickel shows
and amusements parks, so all the girls would have no place to go than to
church. If a bona fide step is taken . . . by the girls themselves to protect
their womanhood and characters by obtaining a reasonable wage and workday, these reformers line up with the plutocrats in order to prevent the girls
from helping themselves." In another case, unionists in St. Louis condemned
the "woman societies" for their lukewarm response during the waitress strike
of 1912. "Where was their so-often flaunted love for the uplift of the downtrodden?" one writer demanded.[54]

Although many groups like the YWCA supported trade unionism, they
also favored welfare or "uplift" work—an idea many waitresses found repug-
nant and associated with charity.[55] Referring to the fact that the YWCA was
planning to open two hostess houses in Kansas City soon, Sarah Green, chief
officer of Waitresses' Local 503, said, "I want to give the YWCA credit for
endorsing women's trade unionism, but we don't care for their welfare activities because they are patronizing and because they are charity. The working
woman . . . doesn't have to be told where she ought not to go evenings. . . .
Neither does she want to be coddled, or sung to, or preached to, or patronized, or taught pleasant indoor games by a lot of other young women who are
paid to make her contented. You can't patronize a coal miner's daughter who
has been a waitress for ten years, and I was elected to my present job because
thousands of other women feel the same as I do."[56]

At times, waitress activists approached middle-class reformers assuming
that because these women were "interested in social welfare and other uplifting influences," they would assist in organizing. To their chagrin, waitresses
often found reformers unwilling "to take any action along that line." Perhaps
because many middle-class women associated waitressing with prostitution
and alcohol, even those few club women who normally lent support to union
women during strikes were indifferent.

As public perceptions of waitresses improved in the 1920s, middle-class
women responded more favorably to overtures for aid. Waitress organizers
reported a number of fruitful cross-class alliances. Delia Hurley attended the
Women's Civic Club of Rochester and for the first time found members
interested in women in the catering industry. Buffalo waitresses thanked the
Industrial Branch of the League of Women Voters and the YWCA for their
cooperation in a 1929 organizing campaign. The financial secretary of the
union added that to ensure future cooperation twenty-three of the Buffalo
waitresses would join the League of Women Voters. In a third case, cross-

membership ties helped the Atlantic City waitresses, many of whom belonged to the Women's Auxiliary of the local Republican Club. The waitresses requested that a HERE International organizer address the club on the problems of the unemployed and "needless to say the request was granted. Our organizer . . . made a great hit with them all," the press secretary of the local exclaimed. "They had never had a woman employed . . . in organization work address them." [57]

Forging Solidarity Among Waitresses

In addition to facing the hostility of employers and the lackluster support of potential allies, waitress unionists contended with internal divisions among their own ranks. Before the New Deal, some white waitresses—fully 90 percent of the trade in this period—reached out to black and Asian women, but on the whole, their attitude was ambivalent and even hostile. Female culinary activists were neither more nor less progressive on this issue than their brother unionists.

In the case of blacks, International officers "firmly urged" local unions where there were "no restraining influences to accept the Negro worker into membership," but most locals followed the HERE Constitution which allowed for the admittance of Negro workers into white organizations where no "colored" locals existed. Moreover, if the local white union refused them admission, rather than challenge the local unions' exclusionary policy, the International offered blacks affiliation as "members at large"—a status without the full economic and fraternal benefits of unionism. Consequently, before the 1930s, most black culinary workers organized into separate locals, joined as "members at large," or remained unorganized. Few belonged to mixed-race locals. [58]

Most white waitress officials, like their male counterparts, encouraged black women either to form separate black waitress locals or to join mixed-gender all-black locals. Separate locals of black waitresses sprang up in Philadelphia in 1918 and in Atlantic City in 1919. [59] A small number of waitress locals also accepted black women, at least temporarily. The Chicago waitresses in their earliest days organized black women and white into the same local, and the Butte WPU prided itself in "not drawing the color line"—in 1907 three of their members were from "the colored race." But most, like San Francisco, restricted union membership to "white women only" until the 1930s. [60]

In contrast to the ambiguous policy toward blacks, culinary unionists preached a stridently unambivalent message to Asian workers: they were unwelcome in the industry and in the union. The stated International position was that "no member of our International be permitted to work with asiatics, and that no house card or bar card or union button be displayed in such a place." For years, the frontispiece of the national culinary magazine proclaimed, "Skilled, Well-paid Bartenders and Culinary Workers Wear Them [union buttons]. Chinks, Japs, and Incompetent Labor Don't." Indeed, one of the most promising organizing strategies in this period was to gain sympathy for union labor by advertising the link between union-made products and white labor. Local unions frequently reported successful boycotts of restaurants employing Asian help and the subsequent implementation of contracts requiring the discharge of all Asian workers. Restaurant owners simply were not allowed to bring their Asian employees into the union.[61]

White attitudes toward Chinese and Japanese workers differed substantially from those expressed toward blacks. As one International official exhorted, "I feel very strongly with regard to the Japanese. While I am an internationalist to a large extent, you will not get me to assimilate with the Japanese. I don't want you to confuse our colored brothers, who were born in this country with the Asiatics." Culinary workers firmly opposed integration or cooperation with "the yellow race." As the International General Executive Board declared: "it has always been generally assumed that that group of workers was not acceptable and could not be assimilated in our social and economic surroundings."[62]

Female culinary activists shared these prejudices against Asian workers. Delia Hurley spent a considerable amount of her time speaking to unionists in other trades, beseeching them to honor HERE boycotts of restaurants employing Chinese and Japanese help. "We laid special stress on the injury these people were doing our organization, and that the members of our local were being dispensed with . . . through the inability of proprietors . . . to compete with these chinks." In Butte, where in the 1890s a successful union-led boycott of establishments employing Chinese had reduced the numbers of Chinese in the service trades, the WPU still refused house cards to the popular Chinese "noodle parlours" in the 1920s and insisted that white girls seek employment only in non-Asian restaurants. Alice Lord and Sarah Green spoke fervently against a resolution introduced in the 1920s by San Francisco's Hugo Ernst that would have allowed admittance of Asians who were American citizens. Ernst's resolution was resoundingly defeated.[63]

Nonetheless, because only a small proportion of waitresses were black or Asian, the exclusionary policies practiced by most female locals did not interfere substantially with the successful organizing of white waitresses. Exclusionary waiter and cook unions suffered more from unorganized nonwhite competitors than did waitress locals because employers who hired black and Asian front-service personnel preferred men. In fact, in the short run, racial exclusionary policies may have solidified the ranks of white waitresses and hence facilitated their organizing.

In contrast to the substantial degree of racial tension that existed in the industry, ethnic differences created little dissension. Because most waitresses were of Northern European descent, they were less divergent culturally than other occupational groups populated by immigrants from Southern and Eastern Europe or by a mix of old and new immigrant groups. In addition, because most culinary employers desired some command of the English language and waitress work demanded constant public interaction, waitresses probably were more "Americanized" than factory workers, domestic servants, or women in other occupations in which verbal skills and social presentation were not as central.

Only in New York, and to a lesser extent in other large cities east of the Rockies, could the employer tactic of divide and conquer be used effectively against waitresses. The further west one traveled, the more homogeneous waitresses became. Thus, in Seattle, San Francisco, or Portland, except for (and in some ways because of) the poor relations between the dominant white population and the few Asian and black women working in the trade, waitress organizations were untroubled by the classic American working-class problem of uniting culturally and socially diverse workers.[64]

Divisions among waitresses based on marital status, economic circumstance, and age hampered the organization of white waitresses more than cultural or ethnic divisions. Time and again, veteran organizers complained of the antiunion attitudes of the part-time married workers, the young waitresses, and the summer-only workers. After years of organizing, Hurley realized "the injury being done our organization by a certain set of women workers, viz, the short day workers, of whom most are married women who pretend they are only using their spare time, and have no desire to do anything that would further the interest of women workers." Another waitress organizer defined the problem as the naiveté of younger women who, upon first entering the trade, considered their work outside the home to be temporary. The new workers are young and "don't feel much responsibility for what happens to other people, and they don't look far ahead. 'It isn't worthwhile to join the union,' they say, 'because we will soon get married and quit working.' That's what they think now. A lot of them come back later, and want a job, and then they see what it means to the older women who still must work." According to a waitress business agent in Atlantic City, two classes of women undermined standards there: the school teachers working temporarily over the summer and "the kind . . . very popular with the men folks" that she chose not to describe by name.[65]

Nevertheless, waitress organizations suffered less from this problem than women's locals in other trades. The majority of waitresses not only worked year-round and full-time[66] but also perceived their work status as permanent and their work as essential to their economic survival and that of their families. This economic stake in their work underlay their trade identification and made it one of the more significant allegiances in their lives. Moreover, the impact of part-time and summer workers was minimized by their peripheral status in the trade. Significantly, the short-hour girls were married or living at home, whereas the long-hour girls were self-supporting single or divorced women.[67] This segregation of the industry by family and economic status meant that waitresses with "problem attitudes" were concentrated in certain peripheral sectors and were not a factor in organizing campaigns involving year-round hotels or full-service restaurants in which the staff was predominantly long-hour employees. "One-meal girls" did not compete directly with the long-hour waitresses and rarely were used as replacements in strike situations; in large part, they were not available or did not desire full-time employment.

In sum, although waitress solidarity was strained and sometimes broken by internal dissension, waitresses succeeded in forging sufficient unity to sustain unionism. In some circumstances, the union-oriented majority ignored the dissenters in their ranks and organized despite the disinterest of their "problem" co-workers. In other situations, white waitresses chose to exclude their Asian and black co-workers and organized in opposition to their nonwhite sisters. Nevertheless, in some notable instances, the ties of craft and gender overcame the differences of race, ethnicity, age, and family status, uniting all the sisters in the craft.

Victories on the Political Front

Unlike their brother AFL unionists, waitresses devoted a considerable portion of their energies to the pursuit of protective legislation in the pre-New Deal era. Many actively lobbied for maximum hour legislation and minimum wage laws.[68] Thus, they were not adverse to parting ways with the larger labor movement and asserting what they perceived as the particular interests of their craft and of their sex. They were pragmatists, however, rather than ideologues. The survival of their organization took precedence over advancing the interests of working-class women as a whole. Moreover, their position on protective legislation was determined by the economic, political, and social circumstances in which they operated rather than deriving from an overarching, universal belief concerning the role of the state. Where they perceived the law as beneficial to their trade, their support held firm. In other less propitious instances, they condemned protective laws. In short, waitresses were neither voluntarist nor antivoluntarist in regard to legislative matters, but adjusted their philosophy to the exigencies of their particular situation. By winning victories in the legislative arena, waitress locals demonstrated their effectiveness as reform organizations and created among unorganized waitresses a new respect for the power of collective activity.

Waitresses needed little prompting to join the movement for maximum hour legislation that peaked in the decade before World War I. Indeed, although middle-class women's organizations spearheaded the campaign nation-wide, waitresses and their sisters in working-class female organizations took the lead in states such as Washington, California, and Illinois. Waitress activists initiated legislative reform, shepherded bills through their state legislatures, and in many cases celebrated ensuing victories.[69]

According to Alice Lord, the movement for an eight-hour bill in Washington started in 1903 when Seattle waitresses sent a resolution to their Central Labor Council endorsing protective legislation for women workers. They then presented an eight-hour bill to the state legislature and prodded the Washington State Labor Federation into support. "We really learned how to lobby in those days," recalled another of Seattle's early waitress leaders. "We'd button-hole those old legislators with their whiskers and long beards, and talk to them until they finally gave in." Interviewed shortly after the eight-hour bill passed in 1911, Lord claimed the waitresses deserved primary credit for passage. "It was the Waitress Union that started the ball rolling and kept it rolling until its size fairly scared our lawmakers." The impetus for the legislation lay in the long hours forced upon female service workers, explained Lord. Even unionized waitresses worked sixty hours a week or more.[70]

Waitresses were pivotal players in the passage of hours legislation in Chicago as well. Frustrated with a series of inconclusive conferences on protective legislation in 1909, the waitresses' union announced that "no matter what others did, they would have a straight 8-hour bill introduced into the legislature." During hearings on the bill, waitress activists—along with other trade union women such as International Glove Workers Union officials Agnes Nestor and Elizabeth Christman—testified before the senate in front of nearly a thousand curious spectators. Elizabeth Maloney, Local 484's principal officer and chair of the Chicago WTUL Legislative Committee, made a particularly effective advocate because she knew many of the legislators from her former waitress days in a popular downtown Chicago restaurant. Maximum hour advocates won an initial ten-hour bill. Over the next decade, Local 484 was instrumental in turning back employer challenges to the constitutionality of the legislation, extending the ten-hour law to a broader spectrum of workplaces. They also applied ongoing pressure for an eight-hour day and a forty-eight-hour week, and for a minimum wage.[71]

After the legislative victories in Washington and Illinois, other states picked up the banner. By 1911, with male and female trade unionists leading the fight, the legislature passed California's first eight-hour statute.[72] Waitresses in Minnesota, Colorado, and Wyoming lobbied for protective legislation alongside middle-class women's groups. Waitress locals also used the economic arena. In Toledo, when the Hotel Men's Association fired waitresses for refusing to sign petitions against the eight-hour day, Waitresses' Local 335, with the help of the bartenders union, struck the hotels where members had been discharged. "The women workers of Ohio have been downtrodden long enough," proclaimed their local secretary.[73]

The arguments used by working-class women in promoting protective legislation resembled those of their middle-class sisters in that both justified state intervention to protect the health of future mothers. Working-class women, however, stressed the effect of the legislation on their own economic well-being and rarely cited its impact on consumers or on the morals of workers. In New York, for example, during the campaign to extend coverage of New York's 54-Hour Law to women employed in restaurants in cities with populations of more than fifty thousand, Consumers' League women urged passage of the law to protect the health of the consuming public from sickly food service employees. New York trade union women focused strictly on the needs of workers themselves, defining those needs to include not only the general health of women and the protection of their child-bearing capacities, but the need for rest and leisure time to ensure mental and physical well-being. "Long hours are very bad for women in restaurants," one New York City waitress asserted. "Most of [us] . . . have varicose veins and flat feet, and a large number suffer from stomach trouble. Look at me, I am strong and healthy, but when I'm through at night, I am just all in. It's a dreadful nervous strain."[74]

Waitresses in Chicago and other cities shared these practical concerns. In California, working women such as Hannah Nolan of the Laundry Workers' Union, Margaret Seaman of the Garment Workers, and Louise LaRue of the Waitresses were the chief speakers in favor of passage of the 1911 hours bill. Their principal arguments centered on preserving the health of working women, reducing the percentage of workers with tuberculosis, and protecting women's child-bearing functions. When the hotel proprietors challenged the law in court, winning a victory in the California lower courts, Louise LaRue responded: "We are sorry he [the lower court judge] isn't a woman and had to walk 10 to 12 hours a day and carry several pounds . . . , then perhaps he would realize that not half of the women who work in dining rooms are in condition physically to become mothers of the future generation."[75]

In contrast to the enthusiasm shown over maximum hour laws, waitresses were less certain of the advantages of minimum wage legislation. The majority of locals supported it, but some of the most actively involved vacillated, dramatically shifting their stance toward wage legislation in the course of their activities.[76] The twists and turns in the positions taken by waitresses in Washington and California clearly reveal how economic concerns undergirded waitress union policy.

After the passage of the Washington eight-hour law in 1911, Alice Lord turned her abundant energies to minimum wage legislation. "We may not be successful, but it will be a start," she vowed. Like the eight-hour law, "we will keep right after it until we accomplish our task and give to our working women a living wage." The law passed in 1913 and covered female service workers and other working women across the state. Yet ten years later, Lord urged the passage of a resolution at the 1923 HERE Convention condemning the attainment of minimum standards through law. She came armed with years of disillusioning experience in attempting enforcement of the Washington law. To convince her fellow delegates of the evils of minimum wage legislation, Lord argued that the laws were poorly written, rarely enforced, and flagrantly violated by employers, especially where women dominated the industry. Moreover, women workers were afraid to complain or testify against the employer for fear of losing their positions. As a result, actual wages remained below the legislative standards. Worse, by giving women the illusion of protection, minimum wage inhibited organizational impulses and weakened unions. Lord conceded that minimum wage had some validity where few women were employed and economic organization impossible, but overall it was "a menace and a detriment to the organization of women workers." In short, minimum wage benefited neither organized nor unorganized workers, Lord pronounced.[77]

On the other hand, after initially opposing the concept, California waitresses came to favor minimum wage laws by the 1920s. When the San Francisco Labor Council voted against the minimum wage in 1913, the loudest opposition came from delegates representing women workers: garment workers, waitresses, and laundry workers. San Francisco waitresses did not dispute the arguments of minimum wage proponents that the health of working women and their competency as future mothers would be enhanced; they simply found the protection of their own trade union organization more compelling. Joining in the general negative consensus of male unionists from AFL president Samuel Gompers to local AFL officials, they argued that "any minimum established by law would certainly be lower than that established by the unions, thus tending to undermine the union scales." Such legislation, they reasoned, "would prove a detriment to the only practical method of improving the conditions of the working women, namely organization." Significantly, waitresses also feared that a minimum wage for women would mean female job loss because women "are fitted to perform, without previous experience and study, but very few avocations" and must rely on situations where "job training is provided, but little in the way of cash compensation."[78]

Ignoring the objections raised by both unions and employers, the California public voted in favor of the legislation in a 1913 referendum election, and soon thereafter organized labor began vying with employers over the control of the Industrial Welfare Commission (IWC)—the five-person board given jurisdiction over maximum hours, minimum wages, and working conditions. Waitresses' Local 48 joined with the San Francisco Labor Council, Millinery Workers, Laundry Workers, Bakery Workers, League of Women Voters, and the YWCA to form the Committee for Enforcement of the Minimum Wage. Much to their surprise, they found they could obtain acceptable standards and that the commission was committed to aggressive enforcement of those standards. They also discovered that state regulation of minimum standards neither inhibited organizing sentiments nor depressed union wage scales. In fact, after the IWC passed its first wage order governing hotel and restaurant employees in 1919, organized labor negotiated one of its better contracts. The first IWC minimum, set higher than the current union wage scale, could be used effectively as a public indictment of the low wage rates in the service trades.[79]

Union support of protective legislation enhanced labor's appeal among its own members as well as among the unorganized. Because wage-and-hour orders were less frequently violated by union employers, that fact became one more argument in favor of organizing. In houses that employed members of the Waitresses' Union the law was never violated, Bee Tumber, a prominent Southern California waitress officer, pointed out in 1924. "The girls receive their wages in real money instead of 'charge offs' for meals [and] laundry." They have "good food served them," and above all it is "possible to have improper conditions remedied by the representative of the union." Organized workers received the protection of the collective bargaining agreement and the advantage of an outside organization that would ensure legislative standards were met.[80]

Although the majority of California organized labor continued to oppose the minimum wage, by the mid-1920s the waitress organizations broke publicly with their brother unionists. When the state supreme court heard arguments concerning the constitutionality of the legislation, Waitresses' Local 639 in Los Angeles, along with other female wage-earner organizations, filed briefs in support of the law. Waitresses had seen how government regulation could work for them, not against them. They moved from being leading opponents of government interference with wages to being staunch defenders.[81] In short, rather than relying on abstract principles in forming their positions, waitresses stayed close to the lessons taught by experience. In the case of the Washington and California waitresses, these divergent experiences with the enforcement and impact of minimum wage legislation resulted in diametrically opposed positions, yet both derived from pragmatic bases.

Before the 1930s, then, waitress unionists made limited but significant breakthroughs in both the collective bargaining and legislative arenas. Relying primarily on their own tenacity, ingenuity, and organizational strength, their accomplishments were piecemeal in scope and were often lost in bitter strikes or hostile court decisions. But unlike women in many other trades, waitresses established permanent institutions dedicated to the uplift of their craft. And as the next chapter will recount, after 1930, assisted by a radically different social climate and a labor movement aggressively extending its organizational sway, waitresses finally wrested a decent standard of living from their employers and extended those standards to large numbers of female service workers.

CHAPTER FOUR

The Flush of Victory, 1930–55

We are all working as we never did before, and our days and hours are forgotten. Our feet are sore, our bones ache, our throats are tired, but we feel great because we are getting something done.[1]
—Gertrude Sweet, International organizer, HERE, April 13, 1937

Described in 1930 as little more than "an association of coffin societies," the labor movement confounded critics by its unprecedented expansion over the next two decades, adding fifteen million members by the early 1950s.[2] Culinary workers were not immune to the union fever: HERE nearly doubled its membership in 1933, the first heady year of New Deal legislation favoring unionization. Membership spurted ahead during the sit-downs of 1936 and 1937, and again during the war years. By the end of the decade HERE membership topped four hundred thousand, with a quarter of all hotel and restaurant workers organized.[3]

As the International union matured into a substantial power within the hotel and restaurant industry, its membership became increasingly female. The percentage of women within the union doubled after 1930, climbing to 45 percent by 1950. Waitress locals aggressively reached out to unorganized waitresses in hotels, cafeterias, drugstores, and department stores; many waiters' locals opened their doors to female servers for the first time; and the new industrial hotel locals swept in large numbers of waitresses, chambermaids, female cashiers, checkers, and kitchen workers. By the late 1940s, more than two hundred thousand female culinary workers were organized, with close to a quarter of these within separate waitress organizations.[4]

The upsurge of unionism among waitresses undoubtedly was linked to larger societal forces that affected all workers: the more favorable public policy toward labor, the breakthroughs in organizing tactics and strategy on the part of the Congress of Industrial Organization (CIO), and the enhanced bargaining leverage of workers during World War II. But this general picture can not fully explain the growth of waitress unionism. After all, other groups of women workers, notably from the clerical and retail sector, failed in bringing permanent, widespread unionization to their industry.

In earlier chapters, the particular affinity of waitresses for self-organization
—rooted in their work experiences as well as their family status—has been
shown to underlie their achievements in unionization. Moreover, their separate organizational structures facilitated cohesion based on gender as well as
craft while also providing an institutional impetus for the extension of organization. The uneven course of union expansion among waitresses, however,
calls for another set of explanatory variables. Some communities reached close
to 100 percent organization, others remained virtually union-free. By analyzing waitress unionization in four key cities—San Francisco, Detroit, New York
City, and Washington—this chapter attempts to understand not simply the
phenomenon of waitress unionization, but its variation over time and place.

Early Stirrings

The recovery of organized strength among culinary workers occurred first
among male workers, primarily bartenders, and waiters. The repeal of Prohibition in December 1933 boosted male membership as restaurants added the
serving of hard liquor and soda fountains, creameries, and lunch stands meta-
morphosed into taverns and cocktail lounges. *Catering Industry Employee*,
HERE's national journal, proudly announced that union house and bar cards
"swing in perfect rhythm with the ceiling revolving fans of local beer gardens.
Banned during prohibition days because their presence would uncover the
close links between speakeasies and the Bartenders' Union, the displays . . .
now hold prominent places."[5]

HERE organizing campaigns also benefited from the passage of the National
Industrial Recovery Act in 1933. Like the mining and garment unions, HERE
sought to influence New Deal legislation and exploit the situation for organizing purposes. In the case of the restaurant code, HERE lobbied National
Recovery Administration (NRA) chief Hugh Johnson, threatened a strike
if the codes were not revised upward, and testified at hearing after hearing
along with the Amalgamated Food Workers (AFW), the Food Workers Industrial Union (FWIU), the Women's Trade Union League (WTUL), and the
Women's Bureau.[6]

The NRA codes sparked organization in the culinary industry because they
raised hopes of improved wages and working conditions, yet failed miserably in
delivering on these promises. The problem was twofold: the codes themselves,
largely determined by employers, were substandard; and employers violated
even these barest of employee protections because the government gave little
evidence of either having the will or the ability to uphold code standards. According to San Francisco waiter official Hugo Ernst, if employers in that city
adopted the governmental standards, working conditions would be "as bad as
those thirty years ago."[7]

By the early 1930s, at least on the national level, organizing had become a
top priority for HERE. By 1927, Edward Flore, a "wry, taciturn, and honest"

Alsatian-Catholic bartender from Buffalo, had taken over as principal officer from Jere Sullivan. Together with Ernst, who had run on the Socialist ticket for Congress in the 1920s while building an influential progressive faction within the union, Flore implemented far-reaching structural and philosophical changes within HERE. The 1929 convention required locals to honor the picket lines of other locals and to affiliate with the Local Joint Executive Board (LJEB) within each community. Three years later, the convention urged the adoption of industrial locals where useful. Where size warranted separate craft rather than industrial locals, organizing campaigns should be conducted by the LJEBs—the amalgamated body that "represents craft unionism molded into industrial operation." By 1941, no union house or bar card could be issued unless all crafts in the establishment were organized.[8]

Flore instituted annual spring organizing campaigns, lobbied energetically for the commitment of International resources to organizing, and attempted to educate the membership about the importance of unionizing all the catering crafts. In a typical editorial in *Catering Industry Employee*, Flore revealed his vision of an inclusive broad-based organization. "The strength of a union," he declared, "is measured by the percentage of workers that are organized." Only through massive organization could HERE sustain its "right to speak for and in the name of [culinary] workers."[9]

Encouraged by the reforms within their own International and the new receptivity among workers toward collective bargaining, waitress locals revived their organizing activities in the early 1930s. Some began campaigns even before the passage of the NIRA legislation and the repeal of Prohibition. In 1932, Butte, Montana, waitresses claimed 100 percent organization, including the food-counter workers in the 5 and 10 cent stores. In Chicago, after more than a decade of fruitless merger negotiations with the Chicago Waitress League and the Chicago Waitress Club, Waitresses' Local 484 reported success in bringing the two competing waitress associations into the union. Local 484 also assisted black waitresses on Chicago's South Side in organizing. Once recruited, however, black waitresses joined their brothers in Local 444, originally established in 1926 as a "colored waiters" local.[10]

The spirit of the times was infectious. Waitresses in Rochester, New York, reorganized, reporting "keen interest" in collective activity following "the repeal of the 18th Amendment and the introduction of the final NRA code." After the Cleveland local braved a strike in the bitter cold, Gertrude Sweet found her Portland members volunteering for picket duty. "When those boys and girls in Cleveland could stand on the picket line in the cold and the snow back there, then we surely can do as much for our union out here," one member explained.[11] The early victories required enormous sacrifice. "I took 78 trips in the patrol wagon in 1932 and would be glad to take that many in

1933," Kitty Amsler of St. Louis declared. Her waitress local won union recognition from the Eldridge Cafe in 1932 after three years of picketing and also reported "signing up new eating houses here and there—not merely holding our own, but making progress."[12]

San Francisco: The Fruits of Solidarity

In San Francisco, waitresses enjoyed not only a long tradition of separate-sex organizing among workers and city residents, but also a solid union-consciousness that resurfaced with a vengeance in the 1930s.[13] Waitresses' Local 48 organized first in restaurants patronized by union clientele, spread its drives to restaurants outside working-class neighborhoods, swept up cafeteria, drugstore, and tea-room waitresses, and then embraced waitresses employed in the large downtown hotels and department stores. By 1941, waitresses in San Francisco had achieved almost complete organization of their trade, and Local 48 became the largest waitress local in the country. Their success resulted from a combination of factors: an exceptionally powerful local labor movement, sympathetic, fair-minded male co-workers within the LJEB, and the existence of a waitress organization committed first and foremost to organizing and representing female servers.

In the early 1930s, Local 48 confronted unrelenting employer pressure for wage reductions and lowered standards. Delighted by the meager standards set by the NRA codes, restaurateurs replaced their union house cards with the Blue Eagle insignia (indicating compliance with government recommendations), lowered wages, and reverted to the fifty-four-hour week.[14]

In response, Local 48 informed the owners that the five-day, forty-hour week was the union standard, and, in conjunction with the other culinary crafts, they picketed some 284 restaurants in 1933 alone. They side-stepped restrictive local picketing ordinances by "selling" labor newspapers in front of targeted eating establishments during peak business hours. The attorney for one distraught employer complained to the judge that "the women walked back and forth in front of the plaintiff's restaurant, and prominently displayed newspapers bearing the headline in large black letters 'Organized Labor' and 'Labor Clarion,' and each of said women called out repeatedly in a loud, shrill, penetrating voice, at the rate of 30 to 40 times a minute, 'organized labor' 'organized labor.' "[15]

Culinary workers also resisted wage cuts in the hotels. After two years of reductions totaling 20 percent, the cooks struck the leading hotels in April 1934. The San Francisco LJEB considered calling a general strike of all culinary workers in San Francisco, but Edward Flore, assisted by federal mediators, convinced employers to submit the cooks' dispute to an arbitration board.[16]

Less than two months after the first discussion of an industrywide strike, culinary union members voted 1,991 to 52 to join the emerging citywide shutdown on behalf of striking maritime workers. Outraged over the death of two workers—one of whom was a cook and member of Local 44—during a bloody clash between police and picketers who had gathered in support of striking longshoremen, the San Francisco labor movement brought business to a standstill for three days. In the end, they secured collective bargaining in the maritime industry. The solidarity and militancy displayed by the culinary locals was typical. The International union wired sanction for an industry-wide sympathy strike, and culinary crews walked out 100 percent at midnight on Sunday, July 15. The few nonunion houses that dared open the following Monday morning closed their doors after "a little persuasion." Only two restaurants on Third Street where strikers ate—operated by people "apparently very close to the labor movement"—were in operation.[17]

Relying on the labor unity that prevailed among San Francisco unions in the aftermath of the 1934 General Strike, the waitresses' local doubled its membership over the next four years. They received general assistance from the Teamsters, the needle-trades workers pressured the kosher bars into compliance, and the printers, streetcarmen, longshoremen, and maritime trades organized the restaurants and bars adjacent to their work sites. Culinary spokespeople acknowledged their dependence: "There is a much better spirit of cooperation than formerly and the Culinary Workers have profited from it. We are indebted to the Maritime Unions and . . . in fact all the unions pull with us whenever we go to them with our troubles, thus our brothers did not give their lives for nothing."[18]

During the heady days of 1936 and 1937, organizing reached a fever pitch stimulated by the successful sit-down strikes in auto and other industries and the Supreme Court's favorable ruling on the constitutionality of the Wagner Act. San Francisco waitresses moved from their base in small independent restaurants to tackle campaigns in drug and 5 and 10 cent store lunch counters; in cafeterias and self-service chains; and in department store restaurants and the dining rooms of the major San Francisco hotels. The most significant break-through came as a result of the San Francisco hotel strike of 1937. The strike, which brought union recognition and a written contract covering workers in fifty-five hotels, inaugurated a new chapter in culinary unionism in San Francisco. With the backing of the San Francisco Labor Council (SFLC) and the promise from such pivotal unions as the butchers, bakers, teamsters, musicians, and stationary engineers not to cross the lines, three thousand hotel employees, one-third of whom were women, walked out on May 1, shutting down fifteen San Francisco hotels simultaneously.[19]

From the outset, the strikers were exceptionally well organized. "The union moved with military precision," wrote the federal mediator, "set up their strike headquarters [and] organized their picket squads, each squad consisting of one representative of each of the unions involved." As workers came off the job, they were handed printed cards bearing strike and picket instructions. Picket duty lasted for four continuous hours; failure to picket meant loss of one's job once the strike was settled. Margaret Werth, the waitress business agent assigned to the hotels, organized militant waitress picket lines and achieved notable results with her waitress parade and beauty contest. After eighty-nine days of effective mass picketing that closed off the hotels to food delivery and arriving guests, a back-to-work settlement was signed involving fifty-five San Francisco hotels. The unions gained wage increases of 20 percent for most employees, equal pay for waiters and waitresses, preferential hiring with maintenance of membership, the eight-hour day, and union work rules for all crafts. For a generation of food service workers, the curtain rang down on the open-shop era with resounding finality.[20]

After this victory, the union soon reached a separate four-year agreement with the majority of small hotels in the city. Next they secured recognition from the Owl Drug Company chain, operating eleven stores in San Francisco with culinary departments; the major resident clubs of San Francisco; the Clinton's Cafeteria chain; and, after fourteen years on the union's unfair list, the Foster System, which consisted of thirty-two luncheon restaurants. "Please rush fifty house cards," Hugo Ernst, president of the San Francisco LJEB wrote the International in 1937. "All Foster new houses will open up with a display of the house cards and other places too . . . demand the cards."[21]

The unionization of San Francisco's large downtown department stores also meant new members for Local 48. In October 1934, the LJEB moved into action against the Woolworth and Kress's 5 and 10 cent stores, placing them on the "We Don't Patronize" list, picketing, and distributing thousands of handbills house-to-house in working-class districts "to acquaint workers with the slave conditions that prevail." The Retail Clerk officials warned the LJEB that "it costs too much money to organize these national chains" and that they "would not consider wasting money on them," but the culinary workers continued picketing.[22]

Victory came in the spring of 1937 when Woolworth and twenty-five other department and specialty stores signed on with the newly chartered Department Store Employees, Local 1100, Retail Clerks International Union, AFL.[23] Initially, the retail local represented the food service workers in the stores as well as the sales employees because Ernst, supporting an industrial approach to organizing, had waived jurisdiction over the lunchroom employees. In 1940, however, Local 48 successfully demanded that the food service workers in department stores be part of their union.[24]

The infant department store and hotel unions faced major trials in their first few years such as the department store strike of 1938 and the hotel strike of 1941, but unionization had come to stay. Every eating establishment of any consequence had a union agreement. The Retail Creamery Association,

comprised of fifty ice cream and fountain stores, signed on with the waitresses in 1940, granting a wage scale and working conditions on a par with
the waiters. A year later, the union negotiated an agreement with the Tea
Room Guild (some twenty employers), winning the closed shop, a forty-hour,
five-day week, vacations with pay, and employer responsibility for providing
and laundering uniforms.[25] By 1941, culinary union membership in San Francisco approached eighteen thousand. A majority of the hotels and motels were
operating as union houses, and 95 percent of the estimated 2,500 restaurants
in San Francisco were organized.[26]

Tactics: Reason, Humor, and Muscle

The organizing and bargaining tactics employed by San Francisco culinary
unionists from the late 1930s to the 1950s represent the apogee of union power
and creativity. With the majority of the industry union, many shop owners
now voluntarily recognized the union. In 1941 alone, seventy-three restaurant
owners sent the LJEB requests for union cards. Evidently, many employers
judged the house or bar card announcing their union status essential to a steady
flow of customers in union-conscious San Francisco. To promote patronage in
unionized eateries, the culinary unions fined members for eating in nonunion
restaurants and bought "a steady ad in the [San Francisco] *Chronicle* advertising the various union labels." They also appointed a committee specifically to
devise "ways and means to advertise our Union House Card."[27]

In some cases, unionization appealed to employers who desired stability in
an industry characterized by extreme open entry and a high rate of business
failures. Citywide equalization of wage rates protected establishments from
cut-throat competitors and chain restaurants that could slash wages and prices
in one location until the independent competition capitulated. Employers
recognized this function of culinary unionism and on more than one occasion
approached the LJEB with names of nonunion houses that should be organized. "We, the undersigned, respectfully request your assistance" began one
employer plea to the LJEB. "Attempts have been made to get [unfair] places to
join us . . . these attempts have failed completely. We understand that union
houses are protected against cut-throats and we wonder why we have been
neglected."

Culinary unionists also realized that thorough organization was necessary
to protect the competitive position of union houses. In the union campaign
to organize tea rooms, for example, all but a few had signed up by the summer
of 1939. The union pursued those recalcitrants, insisting they were "unfair
competition for the others." Reasoning along similar lines, the LJEB refused
to issue house cards to employee-owned, cooperative enterprises although
they met wage scales and working conditions. Their lower prices, the LJEB
pointed out, were "a menace" to the union restaurants of the city. From 1937
through the 1950s, when organization among San Francisco restaurants re-

mained close to 100 percent, many employers willingly complied with this system of union-sponsored industry stabilization and cooperation.[28]

Employers who failed to recognize the good business sense of unionization were asked to justify their refusal before the united board of culinary crafts. If this interrogation proved fruitless, the employer was reprimanded to a higher body: the executive council of the SFLC or a conference of retail and service unions including the Bakery Drivers, Milk Wagon Drivers, Bakers, and other involved parties. When these oral persuasions went unheeded, the restaurant faced increasing pressure through the council's "We Don't Patronize" list. Few employers could withstand the business losses of withdrawn union patronage when approximately one-fifth of San Francisco's entire population belonged to a labor organization. The Duchess Sandwich Company, for instance, explained that they refused to "force unionism" on their employees and declined to recognize the culinary workers. After less than a month on the council's unfair list, the co-owners of the company wrote that "we have given further consideration to your request that we take the initiative in bringing our employees into the Culinary Workers Organization. . . . We will be glad . . . to work out ways of bringing our plant into complete union membership . . . [and] to get away from the penalties which have piled up on us as a result of your putting us on the unfair list."[29]

When necessary, culinary unionists turned to picketing, creative harassment of shop owners and their clientele, and innovative strike tactics. Traditional strikes, whether by skilled or semiskilled culinary workers, rarely had much impact on businesses that could use family members or find at least one or two temporary replacements. In response, locals often picketed without pulling the crew inside. In these cases, picketing could be successful even if the potential union members working inside were indifferent or hostile to unionism. If picketing persuaded customers to bypass the struck restaurant or halted delivery of supplies, the employer usually relented. With the unity prevailing among San Francisco labor following the 1934 General Strike, culinary unionists experienced few problems stopping deliveries. Influencing customers was a far more difficult proposition.

Mass picketing intimidated prospective customers, but even in the heyday of union rank-and-file activism the LJEB had trouble generating large groups of pickets for so many scattered, isolated locations.[30] To supplement and reinforce weak picket lines, the San Francisco culinary unions devised masterful public relations techniques. The 1941 department and variety store pickets, for instance, attended the Stanford-UCLA football game and passed out "score cards" asking the captive public to help them "hold that line." Using the extended metaphor of football, the leaflets explained that "when Hi prices and Hi taxes throw their full power against left tackle—that's where the pocketbook is kept—only higher wages can plug the hole, and stop the play."[31]

Other attention-grabbing devices used by the same strikers in 1938 and again in 1941 included "Don't-Gum-up-the-Works gum" given out up and down Market Street, boats cruising the Bay during the Columbus Day celebration to advise "Do Not Patronize," and costumed picket lines. The costume variations were endless: Halloween pickets, women on skates, and even Kiddie Day picket lines. One picketer engaged a horse and buggy and trotted around San Francisco carrying a large placard that read "this vehicle is from the same era as the Emporium's labor policy." During the 1941 department store strike when a prize was offered for the picketer with the best costume, a young lunch counter striker won with a dress covered entirely with spoons; on her back she carried a sign reading "Local 1100 can dish it out but can the Emporium take it?" The 1938 dimestore strikers called themselves "the million dollar babies from the 5 & 10 cent stores." Carmen Lucia, an organizer for the Capmakers International Union who assisted the strikes, recalled "I had them dressed up in white bathing suits, beautiful, with red ribbons around them, and [they'd] bring their babies on their shoulders." Strikers' children handed out leaflets reading "Take our mothers off the streets. Little Children Like to Eat." [32]

A community contingent reinforced the continuous flow of propaganda from the strikers. One group, developed out of the 1938 strike, called itself the Women's Trade Union Committee. Open to union women and wives of union men, the committee, chaired by waitress Frances Stafford, devoted itself to "educating women who have union-earned dollars to spend, as to where and how to spend them." During strikes, the committees escalated their "educational tactics." One devised a tactic called the "button game": shoppers were to go to stores in the busy hours, fill their carts with merchandise, and then demand a clerk wearing the union button. In eating places, supporters relied on somewhat different tactics. Helen Jaye, a San Francisco waitress in the 1930s, recalled one approach: "The people who came into the cafeteria . . . were members of the ILGWU and they . . . gave him [the owner] the very dickens. I remember a couple of men [took] their trays up to the cash register and just dumped them on the floor." [33]

The Compromise of Collective Bargaining

Faced by this intimidating array of union tactics and the more favorable legal and political climate for labor, employers revised their approach to unions in the 1930s and in the process profoundly reshaped labor relation practices in the hotel and restaurant industry. Small and large employers now formed employer associations whose primary goal was the establishment of formal industrywide collective bargaining. In addition to stabilizing the industry and reducing competition, they hoped to end once and for all the insidious union "whip-saw technique" whereby the union insisted on dealing with each employer separately, playing one against the other. They also sought an end to the system in which union workers unilaterally determined their wages and working conditions and then struck for employer compliance. In other words, rather than oppose unionization altogether, employers banded together to contain the power of unions through institutionalized collective bargaining.[34]

The union, on the other hand, desired the extension of its old system of unilaterally determined wage scales and enforcement of standards on a house-by-house basis. Before 1937, individual culinary locals met and voted on the conditions that would govern their craft. These wage scales and working rules were not discussed with the employer; they were arrived at by the mutual consent of the members of each separate local. The individual crafts then submitted their proposals to the LJEB for approval (if a LJEB existed). The board, on behalf of its member trades, presented the standards to individual employers. Employers agreeing to the union wage scales and working conditions earned the privilege of displaying a union house card. A single-page "Union Labor License Agreement," signed by both the union and the employer, bound the "union card employer" to hire only union "members in good standing dispatched from the office of each respective union" and to pay employees "not less than the rate of wages . . . adopted by the LJEB." It was "expressly understood" that the LJEB reserved "the right to alter or modify or change the said scales from time to time." Wages and conditions of employment, then, were determined by the union "on a unilaterial non-bargaining basis" and could be changed overnight at the whim of the unions.[35]

In 1937, the employers banded together and began organizing to subvert the old system. At a mass meeting of the restaurateurs, called by attorney David Rubenstein, they empowered the Golden Gate Restaurant Association (GGRA) to act as their negotiating body. The majority of small luncheonettes and cafeterias formed a separate but similarly inclined organization, the Dairy Lunch and Cafeteria Owners Association (DLCOA). Rubenstein, chosen to head both organizations, needled apathetic owners still outside the associations by constant warnings of the dire consequences of inaction. "They are picking us off one by one," he railed. "If you fail to attend [association meetings] and are squeezed to the wall like a soft tomato, blame none but yourself."[36]

For three years, neither the GGRA nor the DLCOA made headway in moving the LJEB toward industrywide collective bargaining.[37] Desperate, the restaurant employers turned for assistance to Almon Roth, president of the San Francisco Employer's Council. The council had solidified its reputation during the 1938 department store strike, helping the employers win a single master agreement on an open-shop basis.[38] When the culinary unions issued their 1941 wage cards, directing significant wage increases for the first time since the 1920s, Roth responded, "the terms and conditions set forth in the cards which you have presented . . . are not satisfactory." Sixty-seven of the larger downtown restaurants instituted a 25 percent wage cut and reverted to the six-day week, eight-hour day.[39]

In the end, after a two month lock-out in the summer of 1941, the employers gained their primary objective, a signed master agreement, but at the cost of acceding to union wage demands and a closed-shop clause. The LJEB compromised by signing one standard five-year contract covering the sixty-seven downtown restaurants, the tea rooms, dairy lunches, and cafeterias "with the right each year to re-open the contract and strike on wages but not on working conditions." The house card system continued, but the agreements signed by employers no longer required them to abide by wage scales determined solely by the LJEB. At the insistence of the employers, bilateral bargaining had come to San Francisco's restaurant industry.[40]

Association bargaining on a bilateral basis was more easily achieved in the hotel than in the restaurant industry. The few large hotel owners could coordinate and agree much more readily than could an unwieldy group of some hundred small restaurant entrepreneurs, some renowned for their flamboyance and boundless egos. Hotel employers also had no prior history of union-dominated unilateral bargaining to overcome. The hotel owners established industrywide association bargaining in their first encounter with the unions in 1937. In a second round of negotiations in 1941, the Hotel Employers Association and the union deadlocked over the union proposal for closed shop and preferential hiring through the union hiring hall. The ensuing hotel strike, called on August 30, 1941, convinced hotel employers that the open-shop era was an irretrievable heirloom of history. When back-to-work orders were finally issued by the National War Labor Board in April 1942, after eight grueling months, the union had proven itself a formidable opponent.[41]

Thus, by the early 1940s, an accord was achieved in the San Francisco hotel and restaurant industry that opened a new era of surprising stability and cooperation.[42] Union power had been extended over a wider terrain, yet at the same time employers had modified and diluted that power by forging a new bilateral bargaining system. The next major strike was not to occur until the 1980s, when the carefully crafted system of the 1930s began unraveling.

Sit-ins and Sip-ins: Detroit Sisters Take Over

By the mid-thirties, mixed-gender culinary locals began aggressive organizing as well. Few matched the 100 percent organization achieved in San Francisco, but in a large number of cities, locals secured contracts with a majority of hotel owners, extended their inroads among independent eating and drinking establishments, and opened their ranks to women for the first time. In fact, during the New Deal and after, the majority of new HERE female members entered sexually mixed units: hotel service worker locals (miscellaneous locals composed of cooks, waiters, waitresses, and bartenders) or mixed-craft organizations of waiters and waitresses.[43]

Next to San Francisco, Detroit culinary unionists came closest to achieving the thorough organization of a large heterogeneous community, building an organization with the help of the local labor movement that by the early 1940s was the second-largest local on the International union roster. Unlike San Francisco, however, no separate local for waitresses existed by the 1930s: the few organized female servers belonged to Waiters' Local 705. The lack of a separate organization and the ambivalence among waiters toward organizing women slowed the growth of waitress unionism in the early 1930s. But the desire for organization among Detroit's female servers was not to be contained.[44]

Local 705, led by Louis Koenig, an Austrian waiter who claimed to have been fired from one lucrative job "because of my sober face," reached out first to male cooks, waiters, and bartenders. The dominant sentiment among the waiters was that "the girls were their competition," and as such should be eliminated from the industry (or at least contained) rather than brought in on an equal footing with the men.[45] In 1932, however, Myra Wolfgang (nee Mira Komaroff), an outspoken young dynamo of an organizer, committed her energy to rebuilding the local, and the sexual balance began to change. Wolfgang, born into an upwardly mobile Russian-Jewish immigrant family, spent a few years in college pursuing art studies before being drawn ineluctably into the political and intellectual currents surrounding her. She quickly moved from being Koenig's office assistant to taking on full-time organizing and bargaining responsibilities. Male members reacted, complaining of the "new emphasis placed on recruiting women" and the "dominant role young Mira was assuming." The old-timers in particular protested "what they called 'the sisters' taking over their domain."[46]

Yet as the sit-down fever spread through Detroit, Local 705 jumped in to organize women as well as men. In the fall and winter of 1936 and 1937, after nearly five years of bitter unemployment punctuated by marches, demonstrations, and clashes with police, Detroit's workplaces blazed up under the spark of this new confrontational tactic. In February and March of 1937, sit-down strikes in Detroit involved close to thirty-five thousand workers. "Sit-downs have replaced baseball as the national pastime," one Detroit news reporter quipped. The eruption in the hotel and restaurant industry commenced when twenty-three-year-old organizer Wolfgang strode to the center of Detroit's main Woolworth store and blew her strike whistle, the union's prearranged signal for workers to sit-down. After Woolworth capitulated, signing an agreement covering 1,400 employees, the union toppled department stores, candy and soda shops, and eateries of every description "like nine pins in a bowling alley." Union inroads into the hotel sector began with a "terrific uproar" at the Barlum Hotel: two days after serving the Woolworth strikers a victory dinner, the hotel's coffee shop waitresses occupied their own workplace. After union activists barricaded themselves inside other key hotels, the Detroit Hotel Association granted union recognition and raises of 10 to 15 percent.[47]

Detroit waitresses responded en masse to the strike actions called by Local 705. They also initiated job actions independently of the local. "I'd be in the local union office," Wolfgang once disclosed, "and a girl would call up suddenly, saying, 'Is this Mira? Someone told me to call you. I'm Mamie, over at Liggett's Drug Store. We threw out the manager and . . . are sitting in. What should we do now?' "[48]

By 1941, Detroit culinary unionists had obtained collective bargaining agreements with most first-class restaurants, at least forty Woolworth stores, the Stouffer chain, numerous cafeterias and lunch counters, and all leading department stores and hotels. The union membership quadrupled, with women making up the preponderance of new members.[49] Although these victories rested on the militancy and enthusiasm of the food service workers themselves, the inclusive organizing posture of Local 705 by 1937, the openness of the International to unorthodox organizing tactics, and the support of the surrounding labor community all proved critical.

Once Local 705 committed itself to organizing all workers regardless of sex, race, or craft, they proceeded aggressively, using the latest techniques pioneered by the CIO. Strikes and sit-downs were rehearsed, planned in advance, and showily executed. "We walked in there right at 12 o'clock," organizer and cook Charles Paulsen recalled, "blew the whistle, and the waiters and waitresses and the rest of the help had been geared to answer . . . they all stopped and walked out." At the Woolworth stores and other retail outlets where the local chose the sit-down tactic, the challenge was to buoy the spirits of the sit-downers. (Since the premises were shut down from within, the customer's decision to shop or not became irrelevant.) The women inside were assigned committee responsibilities—food, finance, entertainment, and security—with an equal number of unionists setting up parallel support groups on the outside. From morning to night, the organizers scheduled meetings, singing, and calisthenics for the strikers. At the main Woolworth store, guest musicians visited for special evening concerts; a victrola was smuggled in for late-night dancing; and several women set up a beauty parlor where strikers received hairwaves and manicures. Workers occupying the Crowley-Milner Department Store danced to the music of two orchestras after viewing a floor show staged by the Woolworth strikers. Not all the needs of the sit-downers could be met, however. During one department store siege, two pregnant women were taken out of the store just before going into labor.[50]

The culinary local in Detroit also maintained a close cooperative relationship with the Detroit CIO affiliates, notably the United Auto Workers (UAW), and key AFL unions such as the Teamsters (IBT). Auto workers joined HERE-called "sip-ins" or "customer strikes" in which union sympathizers would keep out better-paying customers by ordering a single cup of coffee and remaining through the lunch or dinner rush. In some cases, Local 705 looked to Teamster muscle in applying economic pressure. The IBT refusal to deliver linens, fresh bread, vegetables, and other catering essentials to wayward employers usually brought quick resolutions to disputes. Although some initial joint ventures turned sour, by the late 1940s, Wolfgang and Jimmy Hoffa of the Teamsters settled into a fruitful working partnership.[51]

The International defended Local 705's militant actions even when the criticism came from William Green, president of the AFL. Green publicly disavowed the sit-down and sip-in tactics during a Detroit rally in Cadillac Square and later wrote HERE President Flore complaining of Local 705's adoption of these confrontational methods. Responding, Flore bluntly declared that if such tactics were necessary to break the open-shop hold in Detroit, they were good enough for him. Rather than disciplining Local 705's officers as Green suggested, Flore concluded his letter by praising them: "God bless 'em and full speed ahead."[52]

On other occasions, Local 705's close relationship with the CIO came under scrutiny. Yet in 1938, after hearing a stirring rebuttal from Wolfgang, delegates to the HERE convention voted down a resolution endorsing the AFL's competitive organizing posture toward the CIO. The delegates advocated the reopening of peace negotiations with the CIO and praised the CIO for helping organize thousands of culinary unionists. Referring to cities like Detroit, Harry Reich, a delegate, reminded the convention: "It must be borne in mind, that one of the reasons for the rapid growth of our International Union was the effects of the intensive organizing campaign of the CIO unions in the mass production industries."[53]

New York and Washington: Unrealized Potential

The organization of New York City waitresses lagged behind that of San Francisco and Detroit. New York City culinary workers lacked the full support of a united local labor movement, and the rifts between men and women in the industry were never bridged completely. This situation persisted despite the New York Women's Trade Union League promotion of female service worker interests and the existence of prominent New York City culinary unionists who identified with the left-wing movements of the day, as represented by the syndicalist-leaning Amalgamated Food Workers (AFW) and the Communist party-affiliated Food Workers Industrial Union (FWIU).[54] The neglect of female service workers would have been more severe, however, had not these two countervailing progressive forces been present.

The historic indifference of New York City male culinary workers to organizing their female co-workers derived from a number of circumstances. First, in other industries where men and women competed for employment, male culinary workers resisted the entry of women into their trade until women demonstrated by sheer force of numbers that they were an inevitable fixture

of the craft and could not be blocked from entry. Because the feminization of New York's food service industry occurred more slowly than in major
cities of the West and Midwest, male culinary workers in New York City had
not concluded by the 1930s that women food servers were an inexorable fact
of life.

Second, New York City employers used divide and conquer tactics that
aggravated the tensions between men and women. Food employers in hotels
and first-class restaurants had hired women as scabs during the culinary strikes
of the Progressive Era, effectively breaking the union's momentum. Practices
in the 1930s were no different. In May 1931, the Thompson's cafeteria chain
replaced its male day crews with young girls brought over from Ireland, England, and from rural areas in the United States, paying them half what the
men had been earning. Other employers followed suit, especially when they
sensed rising union sentiment among their male work force.[55] Instead of inten-
sifying organizing drives among their female competitors and forging a unified
front, New York City's male leadership defended the privileges and jobs of
the few organized male workers. Unionized waiters, cooks, and bartenders
also ignored the unorganized busboys, dishwashers, and cooks' helpers working alongside them in the same establishment. They feared their "chances
of holding their own would [be] hampered by further expansion," one male
official later lamented. "Such a thing as placing a union waitress or a union
helper in a union house was done with great difficulty," he added, since "our
organized craftsmen . . . preferred non-union help."[56]

To make matters worse, by the early 1930s, a number of New York City's
culinary locals ceased any genuine trade union functions at all. Under the
leadership of the infamous Dutch Schultz, gangsters assaulted their way into
positions of power within Locals 16 and 302, two of the major food service
unions with jurisdiction over women's occupations. To compensate for the
prospective loss of bootleg revenue, the New York City mob had captured the
moribund locals in 1932 and used them to milk restaurant owners and employees. Ostensibly signing "union agreements" with employers represented
by the Metropolitan Restaurant and Cafeteria Association, union business
agents spent more time strong-arming restaurateurs into protection pay-offs
than representing member grievances or negotiating pay raises.[57]

Without a separate citywide waitress local to bring together union women
scattered among the male-dominated culinary locals, no vehicle existed within
the labor movement that could rally waitresses to collective activity and challenge the limited perspective of the existing leadership. The WTUL, almost
by default, filled this organizational vacuum. In 1933, after receiving numerous requests from tea-room waitresses and other female food service workers
"anxious to organize," the league's Organizational Committee sent an investigator to discuss the situation with Local 1 and Local 16 and "see how the

League can cooperate in organizing waitresses." Finding that "neither of these locals show[ed] any great interest in organizing the women in restaurant work nor in representing the interests of their current women members," the league devised its own organizing scheme. The plan was two-pronged: the league petitioned for a separate charter for the women, and, after holding a series of conferences with the workers, they proposed starting a "Minimum Wage Club." The separate charter request failed when Local 16 objected, ignoring its earlier promise to support waitress autonomy in return for WTUL organizing assistance.[58]

Undeterred, the league promoted the Minimum Wage Club idea. The clubs linked union women isolated in male-dominated locals and proved to be an excellent tool for drawing in unorganized women. Meeting fortnightly during 1934 and 1935, club members disseminated information about various labor code provisions affecting waitresses and helped prepare waitress testimonies before the newly constituted Minimum Wage Board (MWB). The WTUL believed that the clubs would help both organized and unorganized waitresses "realize the necessity of cooperative action and trade unionism."[59]

The Minimum Wage clubs disbanded momentarily in early 1936 when the New York Court of Appeals ruled the MWB orders unconstitutional, but they reorganized in April 1937 with the passage of new minimum wage protection. Ironically, it was Local 16—now convinced by the WTUL experience of the viability of the clubs as a preliminary to trade union organizing—that pressured the league to "re-open and re-establish the minimum wage club with a view to organization of waitresses." The league complied, appointing Childs waitress Helen Blanchard as chair of an organizing committee composed primarily of Local 16 members. The league also assisted with organizing campaigns instigated by other AFL locals. These campaigns were the first since World War I that had the potential for successful execution, because by 1937 the old HERE craft unions had been thoroughly transformed.[60]

The rebuilding of New York City's culinary unions began with the absorption of the hotel and restaurant section of the AFW by the FWIU in February of 1935. Shortly thereafter, the FWIU—now numbering twelve thousand members—and the HERE International office began discussing amalgamation plans in New York City. Unity sentiments on both sides were prompted by the inescapable conclusion after decades of fruitless agitation that a single, unified labor movement was a necessary precondition to any expansion. In addition, the FWIU members affiliated with the Communist party were influenced by the shift in party policy away from dual unionism.[61]

The International approved the merger immediately, but the corrupt leadership of Locals 16 and 302 blocked local implementation for almost a year. The first break came in November of 1935, when FWIU members moved into the AFL locals. The racketeering elements subsequently crumbled, facing opposition from a loose coalition of progressives now operating from within the old craft locals as well as from New York State's aggressive antiracketeering prosecutions directed by special prosecutor and future governor Thomas E. Dewey. On April 6, 1937, a Local 16 committee—set up by the International and a newly formed Local 16 Executive Board with strong left-wing representation—brought charges against six former officials, suspending three from office. The committee's official report left little room for doubt about the sordid past of the local: "Money belonging to the union was paid out to gangsters more or less regularly from March of 1933 up to October of 1936," they concluded; and officials of Local 16, in league with Schultz and other mobsters, accepted huge sums of money from restaurant owners "for immunity from labor trouble. Honest officials had been physically abused and driven out of office." [62]

With the leadership vacuum created by the ouster of the gangsters, former FWIU and AFW activists came to power. The International hired such talented and experienced left-wing organizers as Jay Rubin, Gertrude Lane, and Michael Obermeier; within six months, the two unions doubled their paid-up membership and secured wage increases totaling more than a million dollars. Aided by financial support from the International, monetary assessments voted by the local membership, and the fortuitous passage of the New York State "Baby Wagner Act" in April 1937, the organizing campaigns of the late 1930s were spectacular successes. [63]

The first breakthrough occurred at Childs restaurant chain, adding 3,200 new members to the union rosters. WTUL members contributed financially and lent their considerable organizing and public relations expertise. Well-known league members such as Pauline Newman of the International Ladies Garment Workers Union (ILGWU) addressed mass meetings, and the city-wide organizing committee hired WTUL organizer Helen Blanchard. The organizing moved into high gear in late 1937, relying on foreign-language as well as English radio broadcasts, a full-time publicity director, and a corps of paid and volunteer organizers. Some male officials feared that the waitresses— the group, according to their projections, who "had shown the least interest in unionization"—would vote against the union, but the election, conducted under the auspices of New York's State Labor Board, resulted in a resounding union victory, with 2,181 voting for the union and 493 against. On September 25, 1937, the organizing committee signed a contract covering all fifty-two Childs stores in the greater New York City area and any additional stores Childs might open in the future. [64] Over the next three years, other major restaurant chains and numerous independents were brought under union contracts with Locals 302 and 42, the newly chartered chain-store local.

Attention now turned to New York City's hotel industry, an open-shop bulwark for sixty years. At the outset, the hotel organizing drive floundered, plagued by lukewarm cooperation from some of the craft locals. Fearing that workers would defect to the CIO, Flore chartered a new industrial union, Hotel Service Workers' Local 6, in February 1938. HERE also formed the Hotel Trades Council (HTC) to create unity with other nonculinary unions operating in the hotels. The HTC—representing Local 6 workers as well as the various AFL locals of engineers, printers, telephone operators, and electricians—would act as the organizing and bargaining agency in the hotel industry.[65]

With the structural issues resolved and craft hesitancy bypassed, the leaders tackled the problem of forging racial and sexual unity. To appeal to the large bloc of black hotel workers, the HTC established a "Negro division" under the direction of a black organizer. Determined to avoid "a defect characteristic of such drives in the past," the organizing committee also paid "special attention to the women workers, who form such a large group of hotel employees, . . . by having women organizers on the staff, by issuing leaflets to the women on their specific problems, but also by a directed campaign aimed at overcoming the great prejudice existing between many of the men and many of the women hotel workers." Committee members prepared themselves to "logically meet the arguments of so many men workers that women take their jobs away from them."[66]

For help, the committee turned once again to the New York WTUL, adopting league personnel and their organizing tactics and philosophy. The general organizer for Local 6, Gertrude Lane, served as an important link with the WTUL. After emerging with a master's degree from Hunter College at the age of twenty-one, the idealistic Lane was drawn into organizing department store and clerical workers through the Office Workers' Union (a Trade Union Unity League affiliate). Moving into restaurant organizing in 1937, Lane's eloquence and dedication quickly marked her as a leader. In Local 6's first election, Lane was chosen general organizer, a post she filled until 1947 when she became secretary-treasurer.[67] Lane joined the WTUL herself and sent Local 6 business agents, organizers, and rank and file to its general meetings, classes for new officers, and its training sessions for apprentice service worker organizers. (Sensitive to the needs of women in female-dominated industries, the league had developed a training curriculum geared specifically to service workers.[68]) Local 6 also secured the loan of Helen Blanchard for the hotel campaign, the league agreeing to pay half of Blanchard's wages, and Local 6 the other half.[69]

In addition to adopting the classic WTUL emphasis on women organizers, separate women's committees, and a sensitivity to the special needs of women workers, Gertrude Lane and other Local 6 women threw themselves into the campaign for minimum-wage legislation. Eventually, Lane sat on the New York State Hotel Wage Board, and Blanchard served on the Restaurant Wage Board. Local 6 waitress leaders viewed the minimum-wage struggle as inseparable from organizing. "We use minimum-wage legislation to extend organization," Blanchard lectured the 1946 Conference for Trade Union Women sponsored by the Women's Bureau. "We became the enforcement agency. We checked restaurants and hotels and we turned in complaints, and we fought through to see to it that the minimum wage was paid, and from there on the story was, 'If you want this security, you must become a member of our union.' "[70]

The unity achieved through such tactics, coupled with the favorable social and legislative climate and the vulnerable economic position of New York City's hotels on the eve of a world's fair, inaugurated dramatic gains in hotel unionization. In 1938 the New York Hotel Association signed the "status quo agreement" recognizing the Hotel Trades Council as the bargaining agent of hotel workers, and by 1941, seventy hotels, including many of New York City's finest, signed union contracts covering some fifteen thousand employees.[71]

With thirty thousand food service employees organized, the culinary unions stood on the threshold of enormous power. Yet they never crossed over. The fear expressed by the daily press that "soon the 3,500,000 New Yorkers who eat out would find sections of mid-town Manhattan with unbroken picket lines running for blocks, and few sections of the greater city without a quota of marchers" proved unfounded. Although union organizers drew on the creativity and commitment of rank-and-file workers, the league, and other community groups, organizing drives stymied without the backing of male workers in the industry and the full cooperation of the local labor movement. By the mid-fifties, the unions claimed food chains such as Longchamps, Savarin, Huylers, and Union News, but close to two hundred thousand culinary workers in greater New York remained outside the union fold. Successive attempts to unionize Horn and Hardart's forty-four restaurants met defeat, and the union lost elections at the Shanty chain and Schrafft's.[72]

In the campaign for Horn and Hardart's thousands of employees, Chain Store Local 42 used the entire membership of the league's New York chapter as volunteer organizers. Horn and Hardart immediately raised wages 15 percent above those paid at comparable enterprises, and when the first strike call sounded, only a third of the fluctuating work force walked out. Strikers and their supporters organized "lie-downs," mass picketing, and handcuffed themselves to Automat doors, all to no avail. With the Teamsters, Bakers, and Retail Clerks failing to honor their picket lines, with funds exhausted, and seventy-three members facing ninety-day jail sentences, the strike collapsed.

Subsequent Horn and Hardart campaigns in 1939, 1941, 1943, 1948, and 1953 met the same fate despite the aid of black community leaders such as the future congressman Adam Clayton Powell, Jr., and the use of imaginative theater skits, student organizing interns, and persuasive newspaper, radio, and bus-line advertising. Because the first female organizer was not hired until

1943, it is not surprising that union officers complained that the women were "the most backward section of the Automat workers. It is they who overwhelmingly voted against the union. Most of them are new . . . [and] the company scared them by threatening to fire them or take away their bonus if they voted for the union."[73]

Employers also triumphed in the drive against Shanty's twenty-eight Manhattan stores and staved off organization at Schrafft's until the early 1950s.[74] Helen Blanchard and Margaret Sweeney, Local 42's new female business agent and a WTUL member, put together an "Organizational Committee of 100" from among Childs waitresses to assist in organizing the young women employed by the Shanty chain, but the company fired the core organizing committee and harassed other union activists into quitting. One novel intimidation technique, the spotter tactic, involved hiring male customers who would purposely "date-up" a waitress and then report her reactions to the management. Any waitress found accepting dates with customers would be fired. Blanchard concluded in her final organizing report that "one of the major difficulties in the organization of Shanty workers . . . is the fear complex."[75]

Thus, without the full support of the local labor movement and their male co-workers, the move to extend unionization to the female-dominated sectors of the industry could not be sustained. Male culinary workers in New York fought for the organization of women in hotels and first-class restaurants because they realized that the unionization of male employees depended on the unity of all workers, men and women, black and white. Assisting the organization of tea rooms, cafeterias, and lunch counters, in which women predominated, was another matter altogether. Because of the rigid barriers of occupational segregation, the jobs of male waiters were not threatened by unorganized women waitresses in this sector of the industry. These non-union eateries posed little competitive threat to the higher-priced restaurants; they occupied two entirely different consumer markets. Moreover, so many female members coming into the union would undermine the character of the existing locals and the stability of the current officers. Good unionists knew that the hand of culinary fellowship should be extended, but these generous impulses rarely overcame male unionists' fear and indifference.[76]

The campaigns conducted in Washington, D.C. in the late 1930s serve as a final illustration of the difficulty of fully organizing waitresses without the support of the larger male-dominated labor movement or the local culinary leadership. The Washington waiters' union, Local 781, formed in January 1918, took in only male culinary workers—waiters, busboys, and countermen—until the mid-thirties. In 1936, the local petitioned the International for help in starting an organizing campaign among waitresses, but the language of the proposal revealed their self-oriented motivation: "The waitresses are coming into our business, with an ever increasing number, working in competition with our waiters in the Hotels, Cafes, Clubs, Restaurants, and other eating places, and . . . may be used against our men in case of trouble."

A waitress branch of Local 781 was initiated in late 1936 under the leadership of Beulah Carter, an International HERE organizer assigned to Washington and a veteran of North Carolina hosiery mill strikes. Almost immediately, Local 781's business agent claimed "splendid progress in organizing waitresses" and predicted the unionizing of "the majority of the girls in the best places in town within a short time." Four months later, the *Washington Evening Star* reported the fulfillment of his prophecy: "Today there is 100% organization in all first-class houses." The waiters could announce with relief that "employers of Washington will no longer be able to replace union men with non-union waitresses. Waitresses are fighting side by side with the men."[77]

In part, the early successes resulted from the general climate of the 1930s and the changed attitudes of male workers, but Beulah Carter's unorthodox use of Washington's middle- and upper-class female community also helped secure employer compliance. Before opening a drive on a particular house, "I get several persons to ask for union waitresses," Carter revealed. "When customers walk out because they can't get union service, the manager isn't likely to fire [a] . . . worker when she joins the union." Once the organizing campaign was underway, Carter had WTUL members draw up leaflets, visit waitresses individually, call on employers as a group to discuss the benefits of organization, and keep community organizations and unions from holding banquets in targeted houses. Her basic strategy involved block by block organizing, singling out employers who had been most unfair to the union. "This method has proven very successful," the May 1937 issue of the Washington *WTUL News* noted. In one week, ten restaurants, seven on a small stretch of H Street, N.E., signed closed-shop agreements with the union.[78]

Carter leaned heavily on the community in the drives against Washington hotels. Inspired by a spontaneous twenty-four-hour sit-in staged by hotel waitresses and cleaning workers at the prestigious Willard Hotel, a stone's throw from the White House, Washington's hotel work force began clamoring for organization. Faced with evidence of prounion sentiment in the hotels, Flore directed Carter to organize hotels as well as restaurants.[79] When sixteen waitresses were fired from the Harrington Hotel in the summer of 1938 because management claimed inability to pay the new minimum wage of $8.65 per day, Carter knocked out 80 percent of the hotel's dining-room trade by calling on her community network. The *Catering Industry Employee* reported that the public was reached through picket lines, notices circulated by union cab drivers, and through the aid of the WTUL and the Washington League of Women Shoppers. "The latter organization staged a picket line in evening dress that made headlines; the former enlisted the aid of Marion Hepburn, sister of the movie star, whose picture on the picket line in *Life Magazine* went to a million homes across the country." This assistance, reinforced by radio appeals, mass picket lines, and "the solid determination of the 16 waitresses throughout the 6 weeks of picketing, forced a complete victory in the Harrington Hotel," proclaimed Local 781's press secretary.[80]

Throughout the 1939 Washington hotel strike affecting thirteen of Washington's largest hotels, Carter enjoyed the backing of a similar configuration of community and women's groups. The WTUL newsletter summed up WTUL contributions: "For three weeks, our members were in charge of picket duty assistance; we assisted in setting up the relief and strike kitchen; we contacted all congressmen stopping at the struck hotels, inducing many to leave; we contacted every organization which contemplated holding an affair at one of the hotels and persuaded many of them to switch their parties or postpone them; we issued leaflets and arranged special publicity stunts on the picket lines and we rejoiced with the strikers when victory came." Mrs. William O. Douglas (whose husband, later to be Supreme Court Justice, was then chair of the Securities and Exchange Commission) and other prominent women could be found serving food in the union strike kitchen, the *Washington Post* observed with amazement. The Washington branch of the National Negro Congress also "conducted a powerful campaign among the Negro workers."[81] In the end, the employers agreed to a union shop clause and preferential hiring of union members.[82] By 1939, a scant two years after the Willard Hotel sit-in, the Washington LJEB—established as the culinary bargaining agent in 1937—boasted union shop contracts with the majority of Washington's hotels.[83]

Having unionized close to a 100 percent of Washington's first-class restaurants and major downtown hotels, Beulah Carter and her WTUL colleagues pushed to extend the campaign into tea rooms, small cafes, and lower-priced restaurants. But the priorities of the craft locals and the newly chartered hotel service local lay elsewhere. "The bartenders," Carter complained to Flore, "will not allow a picket line on houses in which they have contracts."[84] The International reprimanded the bartenders and other craft locals that acted in such flagrant fashion against the interest of the larger community of culinary workers, but indifference could not be eradicated through resolutions. Many waiters' locals, having organized the few women threatening their jobs, decided to rest on their organizing laurels. As was true in New York, most eateries in the female-dominated sector of Washington's culinary industry remained nonunion.

The Heyday of Waitress Unionism: The 1940s and 1950s

With the advent of World War II, women's position within the labor force and the union changed significantly. Their rosters swelled by the rapid feminization of the work force, the older established waitress locals in San Francisco,

Chicago, Seattle, and Portland moved ahead of all other crafts in size and influence. San Francisco's union doubled its ranks during World War II and by 1946 was the fourth largest local on the International roster, claiming more than six thousand members. In contrast, the San Francisco waiters' local dropped to less than four thousand. Female locals, eager for increased membership, negotiated jurisdiction over department store and variety store workers and asserted claims to female cashiers and checkers in hotels and cafeteria employees in schools and hospitals.[85]

In some cases, large, mixed locals experienced a similar surge in female membership during the 1940s. Local 6 in New York, the largest local in the International by the end of the war, had close to seven thousand women, one-third of its total. Detroit's 705, claiming 60 percent female membership, targeted carhops in drive-ins, workers in plant and school cafeterias, and expanded their membership among drugstore food servers. By 1947, after weathering a strike against the Detroit Restaurant Guild which involved some sixty restaurants, they reported a membership of eleven thousand. Hotel locals feminized as they organized cloak and hat checkers, female cashiers, and other white-collar employees.[86]

Unionism in smaller communities, particularly in the West where women service workers now thoroughly dominated the industry, reached a saturation point. Tacoma, Washington, Pittsburg, California, and other scattered towns across the western region reported 100 percent organization. The union secretary in Watsonville, California sent in a typical account: "This week in Santa Cruz County, we have placed cards in six restaurants, and believe me there are others asking to . . . sign them up, but I don't have cards enough." In Butte, Montana, Lena Mattausch complained that, having organized janitors and other non-food service women, "no more women could be found." The WPU turned its attention to bargaining, conducting a model strike in 1948 with the support of the Teamsters, the building trades, musicians, and virtually the entire citizenry. The strike secured labor peace and union control over wages and working conditions—a situation that lasted for the next twenty-five years.[87]

Waitresses' Local 639 in Los Angeles leapt into prominence by adding three thousand new members between 1941 and 1948. Established in the World War I era, Local 639 barely sustained its charter in the face of the open-shop, antiunion drives by Los Angeles employers in the 1920s. As late as 1939, the local told of "almost complete cessation of organizing activity" in part because of the city ordinance limiting strikes, picketing, and other concerted actions by labor. Los Angeles waitresses also confronted organized opposition from consumer groups, such as the Women of the Pacific financed by antilabor employers. These women picketed stores displaying the union card and campaigned against union organization.[88]

During the war years, however, with nine hundred or more restaurants on the verge of closing because of the shortage of help, desperate employers agreed to union standards for the first time. Sustained by staunch activists like Bee Tumber, Nora Saxton, and Mae Stoneman, Local 639 pressed its advantage, organizing house after house. Oklahoma-born Stoneman began her waitress career at thirteen and, following in her mother's footsteps, acceded to union office shortly thereafter. Stoneman was elected vice president of Denver's Local 14 in 1921; six years later she moved into the top position in Local 639, a perch she maintained until the 1950s. The War Labor Board also helped boost the union's prestige by granting substantial wage increases during wartime. By 1945, Class A houses were almost completely organized with new wage scales of 50 cents to $1 an hour. From this base, the union moved to organize table, counter, and cafeteria servers; hotel waitresses, hostesses, cashiers, and busgirls; carhops at the drive-ins, and commissary employees in the large Hollywood movie studios.[89]

Buoyed by the example of the Los Angeles local, culinary workers in such Southern California cities as San Diego, Long Beach, San Pedro, San Bernardino, and Bakersfield joined the fray, pressuring countless new houses into union agreements. And, although many of the locals were short-lived, unionism also blossomed in communities across the Southwest and South—communities like Kingman, Arizona, Chattanooga, Tennessee, New Orleans, and Houston. In 1944, the culinary local in Kingman reported 100 percent organization when the last nonunion cafe succumbed after three years of picketing—the employer finding it impossible to locate workers who weren't "either union members or union-minded."[90]

In this era, culinary locals also achieved notable successes among minority workers. During the 1930s, for example, Detroit's 705 had set up separate "colored sections" within the local and hired black organizers. But by the end of the 1940s, the colored divisions were gone, and black workers and white had picketed together successfully on behalf of black waiters in Detroit's Athletic Club, black cocktail waitresses serving in Detroit's East Side night clubs, and black hotel maids, bellboys, and food handlers.[91] And, when Hugo Ernst, a long-term socialist with firm ties to interracial equality, acceded to the International presidency in 1945, the union even appointed its first black organizer for the Deep South. In contrast to their success elsewhere, however, HERE made few inroads among southern minority workers. The notable exception was in Miami Beach, where by the late 1950s, the entire strip of oceanfront hotels had unionized.[92]

A few western locals even expanded their organizing among Chinese and Filipino workers.[93] Before the war, locals organizing Asian workers usually set up separate "Oriental locals," and those that bargained with Asian employers usually insisted on white workers being hired.[94] Although these traditions remained in many locals, others opened their doors to both Asian employers and workers. The San Francisco LJEB initiated its first negotiations with the Downtown Chinese Restaurant Association in the early 1940s, adding a large number of unionized Chinese workers. By the end of the war, Oakland and Berkeley reported the addition of thirty members to the Chinese Restaurant Association of Alameda County and the complete organization of their jurisdiction.[95] The WPU of Butte reversed its historic hostility toward Chinese restaurants in 1944: they voted in early January "to organize the girls working in the Chinese Parlours and . . . take copies of our agreements and conditions down to the [Chinese] bosses to sign." A month later, the Pekin Noodle Parlour signed; others soon followed.[96]

Yet by the early 1950s the flood of organizing victories had subsided. The union's proportion of hotel and restaurant workers began a slow decline from which it never recovered. Although organizing victories among hotel workers in Miami Beach and other cities were still to come, these gains were offset by losses among culinary workers outside of hotels. In 1953, HERE claimed a quarter of the work force; by the mid-seventies less than one worker in ten had the protection of a union contract. The burgeoning new food service work force of the 1960s and 1970s remained resolutely outside the union fold.[97]

Thus, for women food service workers, high levels of organization depended not only on a general climate receptive to unionism but also on the support of allies. Of course, in certain circumstances—notably in those few towns, generally in the West and Midwest, where the numerical dominance of female servers and their separate organizational structures allowed them to control the supply of labor through their own self-organization—waitresses could organize relying on their own strength. But these situations were rare. In most circumstances, the extent of unionism among waitresses was determined by the attitudes and actions of supporters outside the waitress community.

In New York, Washington, and other eastern cities, waitresses enjoyed the enthusiastic backing of the WTUL and middle-class women's groups. These female allies provided critical support in many campaigns and their work certainly helped extend union organization. Nonetheless, the most effective economic allies proved to be working-class men, not sympathetic middle-class women. Elite women often lacked the economic leverage possessed by working-class men such as teamsters or longshoremen. When the aid of working-class men was forthcoming, such as in San Francisco and Detroit, waitresses achieved close to 100 percent organization of their trade. Working-class men, then—often depicted as universally hostile or indifferent to female organization by feminist scholars—proved instrumental in extending unionization among female food servers.[98]

Significantly however, waitresses found that their own union brothers responded in a more ambiguous fashion than did male workers outside their union. Male cooks, bartenders, and waiters organized waitresses only after pressure from waitresses themselves or from interested women's groups. And, even then, the men often were more committed to reducing the competitive threat from women than in thoroughly organizing the trade. In New York and Washington, for example, where waitresses were in a minority position within their union, the organization of female food servers lagged behind that of their male co-workers, especially in the female-dominated sectors of the industry which seemingly posed little threat to male standards.

Men outside the culinary industry, however, saw female servers in a different light. Men from many different well-organized trades—longshoremen, logging, and mining—for example, frequented local cafes and restaurants, knew the waitresses personally, and saw the unionization of the eating establishments they patronized as a logical extension of the organizing of their own workplaces. Others, like the teamsters, delivered such daily necessities as fresh bread, milk, and vegetables to restaurants. These men—men for whom the enhanced power of waitresses would threaten neither their male privilege at the workplace nor in the union—proved reliable and quite effective allies, especially in the 1930s and 1940s. In short, the cross-craft, cross-sex ties between waitresses and male workers in other trades provided more crucial organizing support than did either same-sex or same-craft bonds.[99]

Detroit Woolworth waitresses take over the soda fountain in February 1937, demanding union recognition, wage increases, vacation with pay, and free laundering of uniforms. (*Detroit News*, 27 February 1937)

Mira Komaroff (Myra Wolfgang) with Michigan Governor Frank Murphy, around 1938. Wolfgang served as an International vice president (1952–76), secretary-treasurer of Local 705, and secretary of the Detroit Joint Executive Board. (Archives of Labor and Urban Affairs, Wayne State University)

Serving beer at a tavern on Chicago's South Side, April 1941. (Library of Congress)

Local 61, Tacoma's Unionized Drive-in. (*Catering Industry Employee*, January 1939)

In the dining room of a large hotel, a waitress receives instructions on "table-setting" from the waitress captain as the dining-room supervisor observes. World War II opened up "public housekeeping jobs" to black women, as well as jobs in manufacturing and other sectors of the economy. (Women's Bureau, Working Women in Industry, 1940–45, National Archives and Records Service)

"Curb Service from a Battery of Rolling Food Bars has cut the meal-time period to 20 minutes," according to the original government agency caption. Certain sectors of the food industry aspired toward factorylike precision, whether food was served in-plant or off the work premises. (Women's Bureau, Working Women in Industry, 1940–45, National Archives and Records Service)

Striking San Francisco hotel workers stage a fashion show outside the Mark Hopkins Hotel to parody the annual Junior League event inside, September 1941. (San Francisco Archives, San Francisco Public Library)

Soldiers being served dinner at a Fred Harvey restaurant at Washington, D.C.'s Union Station, February 1943. (Library of Congress)

Judy Garland as a "Fred Harvey girl" in the 1944 MGM film, *The Harvey Girls*. The film heralds "these winsome waitresses" as "symbols of civilization" who conquered the West "not with powder horn and rifle but with a beefsteak and a cup of coffee." (c. 1945 Loew's Inc., Ren 1973 Metro-Goldwyn-Mayer, Inc.; photo courtesy of Special Collections Department, University of Arizona Library)

Kartsen's Cafeteria Strike, 1946, Detroit. (Archives of Labor and Urban Affairs, Wayne State University)

Local 705 passes in review, 1947 Labor Day Parade down Woodward Avenue, Detroit. (Local 24, HERE)

In 1949, waitresses at a giant tourist and truck stop near Allentown, Pennsylvania, responded to the "driving demands" of their new manager and his bonus system of payments by walking off the job. Using a local firehouse to serve meals, the workers set up a rival enterprise, serving 343 dinners their first Sunday in business. (*Catering Industry Employee*, September 1949)

A TYPICAL DAY OF MAE STONEMAN AS OUR HARD WORKING SECY-TREASURER.

A dissident faction within the Los Angeles Waitresses' Local 639 used the artistic talent of an anonymous waitress-cartoonist in an attempt to discredit the incumbent secretary on the eve of election day, January 4, 1949.

San Francisco Waitresses' Local 48 Executive Board, August 1950. The homogeneity of age and appearance suggest a sisterhood based, in part, on close personal identity. (*Catering Industry Employee*)

PART III

The Waitress as Craft Unionist

The following section reconstructs the goals, achievements, and internal practices of the unionism created by waitresses. Chapter 5 focuses on the accomplishments of waitress labor organizations, and Chapter 6 analyzes the organizational dilemmas waitresses faced in structuring an institution suited for their particular workplace and industry. In what ways did their unionism resemble the unionism dominant among men? In what ways did it diverge? Of equal importance, what does their unionism reveal about differences among women? To what degree was their vision and practice a racial and class-based one?

CHAPTER FIVE

Uplifting the Sisters
in the Craft

At first we were a little timid about coming in, but after learning more about the benefits of unionism, we soon became convinced that it should be the one grand effort of our lives to elevate ourselves from the low financial, social, and mental standard
that is at present most predominant amongst the waitresses of this
locality. . . . We will soon have a majority of the cream of the craft.

—Louise Downing LaRue,
founding member, Waitresses'
Local 249, St. Louis, and
Waitresses' Local 48,
San Francisco, 1900[1]

Since I'm old enough to remember those rudderless days before the
Union, let me tell you about it. There was no pride or interest in
work, no security, no future, and most important no social standing. We polished pie cases and swept the floor. We cleaned silver
and glasses. We worked ten and twelve hour days. For this we were
paid a munificent $7 dollars a week—for seven days that is.

—Jane Morgan, Detroit Local 705
waitress, recounting her
nonunion days in the 1920s
and 1930s[2]

The goals waitresses enumerated in their union bylaws and constitutions often
began with the classic sentiments so often voiced by male craft unionists.[3]
"The object of this organization," the St. Louis waitresses announced in their
turn-of-the-century bylaws, "shall be to elevate the moral, social and intellectual standing" of our members and "to establish better wages, hours and
working conditions."[4] From these class concerns, waitresses typically moved
on to more explicitly gendered territory. The constitutions of the Boston and
the Buffalo waitresses—from the era before World War I to the 1960s—resembled that of St. Louis almost word for word, with the exception that they
pledged "to inculcate justice and good will amongst women." The Women's

Protective Union of Butte (WPU) justified their goals of economic and political equality for women by claiming these as the inherent rights of potential
mothers. The organization of women, the improvement of their working conditions, and their need for "an equal voice with men in saying what industrial
conditions will prevail" are of "vital importance," the WPU proclaimed, "for
our women are the members of posterity and on them revolves the responsibility for a perfect or degenerate race."[5] In its reliance on the power and
rhetoric of motherhood, the WPU preamble reveals the cross-class ties of gender and the ways in which working-class activists resembled their more elite
sisters; the language also suggests the limited nature of waitress sisterhood: for
waitresses—as well as for the dominant culture—*race* could often mean the
white race.[6]

Over the course of the twentieth century, waitress unionists came close to
achieving many of their stated aims. Unionization resulted in significant economic reforms and enhanced control over the working environment. Waitress
locals also responded effectively to the emotional and social needs of their
members—women who frequently lived outside the traditional family setting
and who looked to the union for comfort, friendship, and protection. They
initiated health and welfare funds, arranged social events, and set up their own
retirement and recreation centers. Persuading others that they were skilled
craftswomen and morally upstanding members of the community proved to be
more elusive. However, through the collective voice of their union, they did
gain an impressive measure of the power, privileges, and respect associated
with craft unionism.[7]

Less Hours and More Pay

Because twelve- and fourteen-hour days and seven-day weeks were common for turn-of-the-century food servers, reduced hours emerged as one of the
most important early demands. The first agreement obtained by Cleveland
waitresses in 1907 *reduced* hours to seventy a week. After Seattle waitresses
won a seventy-hour work week in 1902, they began campaigning for one day's
rest in seven, or a sixty-hour week. Employers reluctantly granted the six-day
week in return for the Seattle local's promise to furnish reliable substitutes
through the union hall. Chicago, Denver, San Francisco, and Butte waitresses
claimed similar victories, with Butte women enjoying the ten-hour workday
as early as 1903.[8]

Over the next two decades, waitresses secured further reductions in hours—
some by economic action, others through legislative enactment—but progress
was slow. By the 1920s, only a handful of states limited daily or weekly hours
for female service workers, the maximums varying from eight hours in California and Washington to ten or twelve in other states. And although the
best union agreements specified eight-hour days and six-day weeks, some still
allowed for a seven-day week.[9]

During the 1930s and the decades following, the five-day, forty-hour week remained a dream for most culinary workers. Excluded from the 1938 Federal Wage and Hour Law until the 1960s, unorganized hotel and restaurant employees relied on what little state protective legislation existed. By 1942, fourteen states had laws applying to food servers, but many of these allowed for a forty-eight-hour work week or longer. Not until the early sixties, the peak of state protective coverage, did a majority of states have laws setting a forty-hour week for hotel and restaurant workers.[10]

Through bargaining, most unionized servers in the 1940s achieved the minimum conditions recommended by the International—a six-day, forty-eight-hour week—and some even won contract language ahead of the recommended industry standards.[11] But as late as 1947, the HERE Officers' Report revealed that the five-day week was enjoyed by only one-fourth of its membership; three hundred thousand members still worked six or seven days a week. In 1953, the HERE convention adopted a strong resolution on the subject, which, according to *Catering Industry Employee*, resulted in a noticeable increase in the number of locals demanding and obtaining the five-day, forty-hour week.[12]

The strain of long hours was alleviated in part by improved clauses covering split shifts, meal and rest breaks, and holiday time. Early locals secured a limit on the number of "splits" per shift; by the 1950s, the majority of union contracts forbade splits altogether. Contracts also extended meal breaks from twenty to thirty minutes, and rest-break clauses were added.[13] Many unions negotiated holiday pay (including May Day for cafeteria employees in New York's Local 302) and paid vacations in the late 1930s and 1940s; they then upgraded these provisions, stretching vacations into five and six weeks for older employees. By 1960, a survey of organized culinary workers in California revealed that close to 100 percent of the ninety-seven thousand workers received paid vacations, and 50 percent received paid holidays.[14]

Forced overtime remained a problem for waitresses, however, especially those with family responsibilities. Historically, like other unionists, waitresses had sought reductions of overtime by levying a higher hourly rate for overtime work.[15] But in the 1940s and 1950s, as hourly wages occupied a shrinking proportion of labor costs, these financial disincentives declined in effectiveness. Some locals negotiated clauses forbidding compulsory overtime. Others protected members through creative grievance appeals: New York's Local 1 won back pay and reinstatement for two waitresses discharged for refusing to work a sixth day by claiming their responsibility for small children made them a special "hardship case." A few relied on state legislation to set maximum hours for women. Indeed, in the late 1960s, Detroit's Myra Wolfgang still cited the potential elimination of state protective laws, in particular the loss of regulations forbidding involuntary overtime, as one of the principle reasons for her opposition to the Equal Rights Amendment. She advocated amending the overtime provisions to allow for exceptions where needed "to effectuate equal opportunity with males" without losing the overall protections against involuntary overtime for women. Women have been "released to work," she declared, "but they have not been released from home and family responsibilities." Wolfgang argued that excessive overtime endangered women's health and safety and disrupted the entire family relationship.[16]

In addition to reasonable working hours, waitresses sought a living wage. They agitated for higher cash wages and the elimination of deductions for meals, lodging, uniforms, and employee "mistakes" such as breakage or runaway customers. According to a 1908 survey measuring the economic impact of the largest waitress unions in that period, 78 percent of waitress locals nationwide reported having increased the cash wages of unorganized waitresses by more than 10 percent; the other 22 percent reported increases but were unable to estimate the percentage gained. In 1920, Seattle, Butte, San Francisco, and other strong locals boasted cash wages of $17 to $18 weekly, significantly above the $14 a week estimated as the necessary minimum for a single woman. Weaker locals trailed behind—Boston reported $10 a week; New York, $12 to $15; and St. Louis, $12.50—but even the weaker unions reported wages above the waitress average of $8 to $10 a week.[17]

Unionized wages fell in the late twenties and early thirties, but with the recovery of union strength in the late 1930s, they climbed upward. San Francisco waitresses, the most thoroughly organized group nationwide, earned $3.25 a day in the late thirties, $9.35 in the mid-fifties, and $11.44 by 1961, the highest in the country.[18] In contrast, in 1935, the average wage for all waitresses nationwide barely topped $1 a day; in 1953, it totaled $3 a day. By the 1950s, unionized waitresses also enjoyed clauses requiring extra pay for night work, overtime, travel time, short shifts, and broken shifts.[19]

State and local minimum wage orders advocated by waitress unions helped lift cash wages for organized *and* unorganized waitresses. Despite the low hourly minimums promulgated by many of the wage boards, employers objected because their wage rates were even lower. In 1935, when the first New York hotel and restaurant wage board set a scale of 16 to 18 cents an hour for service workers, the employer members of the board objected and refused to sign the wage recommendation. Again, in 1940, New York chains such as Woolworth, Kresge's, and Green's went to court to challenge the restaurant board rates of 20 cents for service workers. Even in the 1950s, employers harped incessantly about the unreasonably high minimum rates.[20]

Waitresses also gradually gained protection from employer abuses in regard to room and board deductions. Many contracts specified the maximum deductions allowable; a few eliminated deductions altogether and set slightly lower wage scales for employees provided with room or board. Other language gave employees discretion over where to eat and live. "No employee shall be required . . . to eat or lodge at the hotel where . . . employed, or to accept food or lodging as part of . . . wages," one 1947 contract read.[21] Local and state statutes also limited deductions for housing and meals.[22]

To a surprisingly exacting degree, waitress contracts spelled out the quality and quantity of food that employers were to supply. The 1909 Chicago waitresses' agreement obliged employers to furnish wholesome food; the Cleveland waitresses preferred a more elaborate section that required a variety of palatable food served in a sanitary place. Negligent Cleveland employers faced an arbitrator's possible fines or, upon the presentation of a petition signed by two-thirds of the waitresses, the payment of 75 cents in lieu of every meal that did not pass muster. New York City cafeteria employers agreed in 1938 that each worker would have a "choice of all ready dishes, excluding steaks, chops and poultry." A stronger clause negotiated in 1950 stated: "Any employee working 7½ hours shall receive three meals of food comparable to that served to the customers in bona fide restaurants or one dollar and one-half in lieu thereof."[23]

Locals secured legislative and contract remedies for the exorbitant costs of uniform purchase and upkeep. One Buffalo waitress lamented that restaurant proprietors desired a wide "array of color and design in uniform," and that every time a new fancy struck—which was frequently—she lost at least a week's wages. She proposed that employers pay for such decorative touches.[24] Other waitresses agreed. Unionized servers in California secured a 1919 Industrial Welfare Commission (IWC) order mandating extra pay of 50 cents a week for the laundering of uniforms. Later, they won passage of a uniform bill requiring employers to pay for "special dress or uniform where the employee works for less than six months."[25] By 1961, with the exception of certain locales, predominantly in the South, employers furnished and cleaned the uniforms of a majority of hotel and restaurant employees.[26]

Union contracts limited employee responsibility for customer walk-outs and breakage, and forbade kickbacks to supervisors, head waiters and waitresses, wine stewards, and busboys. San Francisco's 1937 hotel contract, for instance, pledged that waiters and waitresses were "not to be charged for a guest's failure to pay." Others read: "no employee shall be required or permitted to contribute to the captain, headwaiter, or head waitress, or anyone in charge."[27] Breakage charges at first were restricted to the "wholesale price" of the item or the "cost price only"; later, charges were eliminated altogether.[28]

Calls for eliminating tips and demanding a compensatory raise in cash wages issued forth frequently from culinary union spokespersons, especially during the Progressive Era.[29] Food servers themselves, however, were divided over the issue, with the ranks of those interested in reforming the system thinning as tip income increased and public condemnation of tipping diminished. By 1945, according to the national union journal, most culinary workers did "not like the tipping system and freely complain[ed] about it . . . but many would not say a word lest it should be replaced by another system that would mean a financial loss to them."[30]

It is not surprising, then, that HERE locals proposed a variety of contract language in regard to tipping, ranging from demands for the elimination of the system to calls for its reinstatement.[31] In the 1940s, the New York Hotel Trades Council requested that "a fixed service charge be collected and distributed by the hotels for services rendered." The Hotel Association rejected their offer outright as did the San Francisco employers when the unions there offered in 1942 to "do away with the practice of tipping entirely in favor of a guaranteed fair minimum wage."[32] In contrast, Waiters and Waitresses' Local 1 in New York City signed a first contract for employees at Mary Elizabeth's Tea Room and Restaurant in 1950 that raised wages 233 percent, provided six holidays, vacations with pay, and "abolished the old system of 'service charges' tacked onto the customer's checks in lieu of tipping." The tipping system, they proudly noted, would increase earnings.[33]

Culinary unionists did seek legislative limits on the reduction of cash wages because of tips, but these efforts fell short. Union lobbyists convinced only a handful of state wage commissions in the 1920s that minimum wages should be set irrespective of tip considerations and that the employer should pay "a living wage exclusive of any additional pay the workers may receive from the public."[34] By World War II, the majority of state statutes clearly followed the National Recovery Act precedent of tipped and non-tipped categories, with lower minimums set for those receiving tips.[35]

Making Waitressing "A Real Trade"

Waitresses desired to raise their moral and social status by establishing their work as a distinct craft and themselves as skilled craftswomen. Their union would be the "authority whose seal [would] . . . constitute a certificate of character, intelligence, and skill."[36] Although society at large and their fellow union "brothers" thought otherwise, waitresses argued that their work required skill and was worthy of being considered, in the words of Elizabeth Maloney, "a real trade by which any girl might be proud to earn her living." To elevate waitress work and achieve the dignity they felt was rightfully theirs, waitresses developed extensive "craft rules" that were designed in part to define the boundaries of their occupation and secure employer recognition of table service as a specialized trade. They also restricted union membership to those deemed competent, took responsibility for training new entrants into the industry, and monitored work performance through fines and removal of unacceptable workers from the job.[37] Because women's work was often devalued and its skills rendered invisible, waitresses had more trouble raising the societal estimation of their worth than did their male co-workers.[38] Nevertheless, through unionization, waitresses gained many of the privileges reserved for "skilled" workers. Their achievements demonstrate, as Anne Phillips and Barbara Taylor have pointed out, that "skill" is a flexible concept and varies according to the balance of power between employers and labor organizations.[39]

Craft Specialization and Job Control

The concern for defining their work as a distinctive craft and hence a respectable, skilled occupation was shared by male members of the industry. One of the early goals of culinary workers was to distinguish themselves from "victualler's servants" and domestic service laborers. In the late nineteenth century, culinary locals, along with employers, expected members to be adept in many different skills, including food preparation, cleaning, and table service. Locals dispatched members to jobs indiscriminately, paying little heed to the particular specialties required. Gradually, however, intent on raising the standards of the work and differentiating it from mere generalized domestic service, local unions proclaimed that each member should choose a single craft and that workers would be dispatched according to their declared specialty.[40]

To limit the employer's discretion in task assignment and enforce craft specialization, waitress locals issued detailed work rules. Waitresses defined themselves as food servers; any work that hinted of food preparation, pantry duties, or cleaning was outlawed. The Cleveland local specified in the 1920s that waitresses should not "make coffee, sweep or mop floors, wash silver or dishes, mirrors, windows or coffee urns, clean fruit, vegetables or make salads, put away or count silver." In this same period, San Francisco waitresses revealed their disdain for menial labor and clean-up or kitchen-helper tasks in their rule that "steady or lunch girls can not shell peas, string rhubarb, peel apples; must not clean coffee urns, windows or ice boxes, . . . scrub chairs . . . sweep, clean catsup or mustard bottles or polish silver; not allowed to pick strawberries." Waitress organizers spoke pityingly of the poor unorganized waitresses who, without the union, were reduced to being "scrub women." Bee Tumber, an International organizer in the late twenties, reported the deplorable conditions in Pittsburgh, where one could find waitresses scrubbing with rag and dish pan.[41]

Union negotiators of the 1930s and 1940s incorporated the earlier union-determined craft rules into their contracts and increased the complexity and specificity of these clauses.[42] Negotiated agreements in San Francisco, bargained in the 1940s, stated that employees "shall perform only such services as are customarily performed by their crafts." A detailed list of forbidden tasks followed.[43] Similar clauses appeared in contracts across the country. San Jose's local forbade women to clean ice boxes, while Sacramento's local found it necessary to mention no washing of outside windows. In New York, waiters and waitresses gained relief from the onerous duty of opening oysters and clams as well as the more typical side-work task of polishing silver.[44]

Concern for the social meaning of the work was not the only motivating force behind the development of work rules, of course. Union rules delineating job classifications allowed waitresses to avoid some of the more disagreeable aspects of restaurant work—"peeling spuds or cleaning out the toilet,"—protected free time, and slowed the work pace.[45] Work speed, often determined by customer ebb and flow, proved resistant to contract control, but clauses allowing the union to "decide the size of the worker's station," or limiting the number of guests assigned to each banquet waitress, did provide noticeable relief from overwork. One local even decided to require "double wages . . . wherever 25 or more children [were] to be served" at a banquet.[46]

Craft rules, then, enhanced workplace control and elevated the status of food servers. Nonetheless, they proved to be a mixed blessing. Restaurant work became less varied, and the ability to pitch in and help workers outside your craft was restricted.[47] Of equal importance, although most unionized culinary workers, whether dishwasher or "vegetable girl," benefited from craft rules, these same rules set up a hierarchy of job categories within the restaurant that often aided those at the top—whether bartender, cook, or waitress—at the expense of those at the bottom—busgirl, kitchen helper, or dishwasher—who were stuck with doing the lowliest tasks. These hierarchies were gendered in that separate ladders existed for the male and the female jobs (and few employees crossed from one ladder to another); they were also racially and ethnically constructed. White men and white women occupied the top rungs of food preparation and service; black, Latin, Asian, and other minorities either acted as assistants or performed the most "menial" tasks, principally that of cleaning.[48] And, as will be discussed, the craft character of waitress unionism reinforced the racial and ethnic segregation of hotel and restaurant work in other ways as well.

"The Cream of the Craft"

Waitresses wanted not only to establish themselves as skilled, but also as respectable. As has been argued for male craftsmen, waitresses viewed the union as "a vehicle to achieve a more complete acceptance from the larger community. They wished to be understood as responsible moral members of the community."[49] Larger societal changes—the loosening of Victorian structures concerning female sexuality and propriety, the entry of native white women into the trade, and the advent of Prohibition—probably elevated the social and moral status of waitressing as much if not more than workplace reforms instituted by waitresses themselves. Nevertheless, the object of respectability remained central to the mission of waitress unions.

Their desire to be viewed as respectable and competent craftswomen is demonstrated clearly in the membership criteria devised by waitress locals. The bylaws of waitress organizations from the Progressive Era into the 1960s resembled the 1941 language of the Los Angeles local: membership was limited to "female persons . . . working at the craft, of good moral character and qualifications." Some locals also restricted membership to white women only, ensuring that "the creme of the craft" retained its multiple meaning.[50] Waitresses debated and continuously redefined the meaning of these standard barriers to admission—competence, race, and morality—revealing not only the differences among working-class women but also the ways in which their definitions of "respectability" and "moral womanhood" diverged from middle-class women.

Waitress locals took craft and occupational competency seriously.[51] Only experienced waitresses should bother applying for union membership in New York, one journalist turned "amateur waitress" reported in *McClure's Magazine* in 1907. Prospective candidates for membership in San Francisco's Local 48 were not only expected to have prior experience, but from at least the 1930s to the 1950s, the local also required a six-month probationary period. Applicants who proved "qualified and acceptable" were then taken in as full-fledged members. Not everyone succeeded. After working three weeks, one aspirant stated "she was ill and to [sic] nervous to be a waitress." Another completed her six months but was rejected because "she was not a capable craftswoman."[52]

By the 1940s, few clauses remained in waitress union bylaws or constitutions prohibiting the admission of nonwhite women,[53] but the issue of racial and ethnic integration persisted. The attitudes of most waitress locals resembled the decided ambivalence of Local 48. San Francisco waitresses had voted in 1938 that the word *white* be stricken from their admission criteria, but at subsequent membership meetings only a few Chinese and black applicants were admitted.[54] When black migration to the San Francisco Bay Area began in earnest during World War II, "the question of colered [sic] girls all over [the] district and the two [union] cafeterias at Hunters Point employing all colored help" resurfaced. The Executive Board voted to take in these new black workers, but there was a clear concern that the number of blacks be held to a minimum. In fact, when San Francisco's new Local 110 (representing "miscellaneous" culinary employees) applied to the International for permission to organize "Negro busgirls"—presumably because of Local 48's laxness in this regard—a contingent within Local 48 supported the idea of transferring "all colored women" to Local 110. Only after a scolding from general president Edward Flore did they vote to retain their right to organize and represent black women.[55]

White waitresses in San Francisco resisted equality for minority women in the workplace as well as in the union's admission policies. White waitresses filed complaints over their restaurant's policy of having "black bus girls . . . use the same dressing room as white girls." In another case, a Chinese woman, given a job as a checker, left her job after being harassed by unemployed white women who had observed her being dispatched from the union hall.[56] By the 1950s, Local 48 claimed a total membership of five thousand food servers, but only twenty-five black women, working primarily as busgirls, and a handful of Chinese and Filipina waitresses in "oriental type restaurants" belonged to the union.[57] Local 48 had neither organized the few black and Asian-owned restaurants where most minorities worked nor had they challenged the racist preferences of white employers.

Local 48's record was not exceptional. In 1949, Flore castigated the Buffalo waitresses for failing to admit black waitresses, yet despite the International's action, the number of black waitresses and busgirls in the local remained low. Membership in Los Angeles's Local 639 topped four thousand in 1950 but was predominantly white, with only a few Negroes, some Mexican and Chinese, Women's Bureau agent Ethel Erickson reported. During the 1950s, under pressure from the new HERE International president Hugo Ernst—a former socialist waiter who prided himself on his ties with the NAACP and his championing of racial equality—Seattle's local and others adopted more progressive policies, but many waitress locals remained essentially all white until the early 1970s when federal antidiscrimination laws forced changes in union admission practices as well as employer hiring policies.[58]

To what degree was the low proportion of nonwhite women a result of the racism of white waitresses and their fear that associating with minorities would lower their social status? Racist and elitist attitudes certainly appear to be part of the explanation, and craft traditions with their emphasis on social bonding and homogeneity fostered such categorization. Indeed, as Michael Kazin and others have argued, racism has been a pervasive and integral part of the craft tradition in the United States.[59] Yet, employers also must share responsibility for the lack of minority women. Historically, employers preferred white service personnel and shut out many capable minority applicants. They also refused minority candidates sent out from union hiring halls. Given such prejudice and the practice of many locals of taking responsibility for finding employment for whomever they admitted, the racial exclusiveness of locals stemmed in part from racism and in part from a realistic fear that minority women would not be hired and would thus become a financial burden to the organization.

Nevertheless, the actions of local unions could have made a difference, and few of the older craft-based locals took steps against the racial prejudices of employers. Tellingly, the membership policies of the large mixed-industrial locals—many of which were newly established in the 1930s and tied more closely to the progressive racial and inclusive traditions of the left and the CIO—were more open than those of the older waitress locals. Indeed, the large industrial locals in New York and Detroit took pioneering stances against racial discrimination in the 1940s that increased minority hiring and lessened job segregation by race. They continued the battle into the next decades, working closely with black community groups and the early civil rights movement.[60]

"To Raise the Moral Status of Women Toilers"

In order "to raise the moral status of women toilers," waitress locals concerned themselves over the morality of applicants as well, with most bylaws limiting membership to women of "good moral character." Yet little consensus existed over what that meant. At times, it could mean simply being white. In most cases, however, moral distinctions were made between white women, separating the "respectable" from the "rough," as well as between white and nonwhite.[61] Moreover, definitions of respectable behavior evolved over the course of the century and were influenced by the economic realities of a particular situation as well as by ideological predilections. Some locals pushed for greater conformity to acceptable middle-class gender ideals; others desired respect on their own terms and were unwilling to modify their behavior to secure outside approval.[62] For waitresses, as for other working-class groups, "respectability was not a filtered-down version of its bourgeois forms, but a fluid and variable idea."[63]

The early Chicago local prided itself on its commitment to fostering high standards of morality among its members. The local bought a reproduction of the Sistine Madonna for their headquarters, explaining that it represented woman on her highest plane and would serve as "the ideal woman for the girls to emulate." Their bylaws forbade the use of profane language, and waitresses caught uttering such language could not wear their union buttons publicly. "If she is going to disgrace it by bad words, she must wear it out of sight," one officer explained.[64]

Chicago waitresses also took steps to disassociate themselves from prostitutes or women who used waitressing "as a blind for the 'sad profession.'" Once waitresses organized, one observer noted approvingly, "women of such tendencies" could not survive. "The fellowship of the union, the protection it affords innocent girls against insult and injustice is just what cannot be risked by those whose deeds are shady."[65] Nevertheless, although most waitresses wanted to distinguish themselves from prostitutes, many viewed prostitution and prostitutes in a less judgmental fashion than the culture at large and the leadership of Chicago's 484. At times, prostitutes were deemed legitimate working women and hence worthy of respect simply because they paid their tab like everyone else. Waitress Kathryn Dewing defended the prostitutes who frequented her late-night cafe when interviewed in 1986: "They were all ladies," she insisted. Like the working-class Appalachian women described by historian Jacquelyn Dowd Hall, Dewing had her own definition of what being a lady meant. "They acted like ladies," she continued, "They weren't rowdy."[66]

The proper stance toward "b-girls" or "bargirls" was even less clear-cut than that toward prostitutes. Bargirls, employed by tavern owners or working independently, socialized with men in bars and were available to male patrons who bought them drinks for conversation, solace, and perhaps sexual interactions. Some bargirls also worked as waitresses, and although they often presented waitress membership books when harassed by the police, most did not serve food or liquor while working as bargirls. San Francisco's local, for example, initially admitted bargirls, but following a general public condemnation of bargirls in the late 1930s, the local appointed a committee to investigate the situation. At the committee's recommendation, the local sent a letter to the mayor asking that he close all places hiring such women. They also kept up a steady stream of complaint letters to the chief of police asking that he refrain from describing the women as waitress union members or at least make it clear that not all bargirls arrested were members of Local 48. At first, the bargirls who actually were members of the union escaped the direct wrath of their sisters—a motion to bring the known b-girls before the executive board lost and "Sister Cordes [was instructed] to destroy the list of girls' names at this time." But eventually, the local collected the union books of identified bargirls and barred future membership.[67]

Waitress locals, of course, were at odds with conventional definitions of female respectability simply by defending their own work as waitresses. By insisting on the respectability of waitressing, they were asserting the right of women—married and unmarried—to work in the public sphere and to mingle with men publicly, serving them food and liquor. Numerous locals also flaunted genteel morality by speaking out against Prohibition. In the years before World War I, Local 48 insisted on serving alcohol at annual fundraising affairs for their sick and death benefit fund, even though this behavior shocked polite society.[68] Indeed, waitresses supported the public availability of liquor and, as will be discussed more fully in chapter 7, argued for their right as waitresses to serve liquor.[69] They desired respectability, but wanted it on their own terms.

As with their defense of prostitutes as working women, waitresses at times displayed an alternative definition of female morality that revolved largely around the fulfillment of their responsibilities as mothers and as heads of households. The ability of unions to gain a living wage for women, one early waitress official argued, made them "a moral influence at least as good, if not better, than that of the women's clubs and snoopy old ladies societies."[70] How frustrating that waitresses continue "to be considered trollops" just because they wait tables, Local 705's president Florence Farr sighed, "don't people realize that a lot of these women are mothers?" [71]

The Double-Edged Sword of Sexuality

In the post-World War I period, tension lessened between the moral standards of the larger culture and those of waitresses. Waitresses who desired respectability on middle-class terms found their goal more achievable as attitudes relaxed toward public employment for women and strict sexual segregation. Moreover, the sexual expressiveness of some female servers that earlier had been frowned upon by middle-class society was less at odds with the dominant ideology. As Lois Banner has argued in her book *American Beauty*, by the 1920s "fashion culture" triumphed over "feminist culture" in that the majority of women accepted the public's newfound delight with such explicit displays of female sexuality as beauty contests and movie star vamps. [72]

Many waitresses had always assented to sexual display and flirtation as an integral aspect of their work. Their acceptance of the sexual character of their work was rooted in their distinctive mores, but it also derived from their situation as service workers in an occupation in which their livelihood depended on attractiveness and allure. Denial was largely foreclosed as an option because, for many, their work took place in an increasingly sexualized environment. Waitresses walked a fine line: unlike middle-class women, they wanted to express their sexuality, but they sought to do so without losing control over the uses of that sexuality. They wanted to determine by whom and for what ends it was to be used.

Waitresses saw attractiveness, in part, as an achievement and a confirmation of their femininity. The avid support among waitresses for beauty contests is one demonstration of this attitude. Detroit's local was typical: forty-two women competed for the title of Queen of Detroit's Waitresses for the first time in 1939; these union-sponsored contests continued unabated into the 1960s. Mae Stoneman, long-time business manager for Waitresses' Local 639 in Los Angeles, frequently described her local as "the one with the most beautiful waitresses of any local in the International." In an employee bathing beauty contest appropriately sponsored by the Rose Royal Cheese Cake Company, four of the six winners were Local 639 members. "Local 639 has always cooperated with community interests that afford some recreational benefits to our members," Stoneman maintained. Cafeteria Local 302 Women's Committee devoted a number of columns in the union paper to bathing beauty contests. In announcing the contest for Queen of the Trade Unions at the New York World's Fair, the committee exhorted, "C'mon, let's show them some of our 302 beauties." The Women's Committee savored the subsequent triumph of 302 members: "This will silence forever those who say that the only girls that get active in trade unions are cranks or old maids." [73]

Concern was expressed, however, over who would define attractiveness, the employer or the union. Locals also objected to the overemphasis on appearance by employers seeking help. Waitress locals argued with employers who fired or refused to hire waitresses for being too old, too fat, or too ugly. Waitress locals found employers most receptive in the early decades of the twentieth century, before the ascent of the "youthful ideal" and again in the 1970s, when the courts began stricter enforcement of the sexual discrimination prohibitions in the Civil Rights Act of 1964.

Elizabeth Maloney, the formidable Chicago official, was eulogized at her funeral in the 1920s as the champion of homely waitresses. One co-worker explained: "She stood up for us homely girls. She told the restaurant proprietors that they couldn't have just the peaches—that the other girls wanted the work, too."[74] Another early waitress business agent called her members off the job during the lunchtime rush rather than comply with the boss's demand for "four girls, g-i-r-l-s, . . . send me chicken, we are tired of old hens." The members hesitated until one waitress argued that their reluctance was an assent to employment based on "youthfulness and personal attractions" not "skill, capability, and knowledge of table service."[75]

Yet few locals effectively controlled employer preferences through such job actions. Protecting "unattractive" waitresses through the formal grievance procedures in place by the 1930s proved equally difficult. Most waitress agreements lacked strong language protecting a worker's job rights with an individual employer, and where stronger clauses were negotiated—theoretically safeguarding all employees from arbitrary employer personnel decisions—arbitrators and employers interpreted these "just cause" provisions as excluding older and "unattractive" women. In New York City, for example, where the large mixed-gender hotel local was active in taking up discharge and discipline cases, the union rarely won cases involving appearance. Management at the Bristol Hotel successfully discharged two waitresses, explaining that one, weighing 155 pounds was "too fat."[76] At a second hotel, management fired a salad girl, claiming "she was too old to serve any longer in that capacity." The entire union shop committee held a conference with management but were "unable to prevent her discharge." Grudgingly, they accepted a cash bonus for her and two weeks' severance pay. All too often, waitress leaders found themselves in the position of Local 639's Ruth Compagnon, who, according to the *Los Angeles Times*, had to fall back on "feminine persuasion" when managers refused older waitresses. The reporter quoted one of Compagnon's typical ploys: "Oh, you'll love this gal," she informed the restaurant owner, "She's 45 but she looks 35."[77]

The longest-running battle over the definition of attractiveness and its relation to work performance was fought between various HERE locals and the Playboy Club management in the 1960s and 1970s. Myra Wolfgang led the charge, attacking the whole Playboy philosophy as "a gross perpetuation of the idea that women should be obscene and not heard." After winning a contract with the Detroit Club in August 1964, Local 705 appeared proud of its unionized bunnies, featuring them in newspaper articles that commented favorably on their looks and their career plans. Yet the local was acutely sensitive to how an emphasis on looks could backfire. Their first bargaining demand had involved abolishing the employer's "no wage" policy—the bunnies had been expected to live solely on tip income.[78] Attention soon turned to the question of the employer's right to discharge waitresses who had lost their "bunny image."

According to a Playboy Club spokesman, bunny image was "as essential to being a bunny . . . as meeting deadlines is . . . to a reporter." The Playboy Club publicly defined bunny image as having "a trim youthful figure . . . and a vibrant and charming look," but bunnies claimed that defects cited in the Playboy literature included "crinkling eyelids, sagging breasts, varicose veins, stretch marks, crepey necks, and drooping derrieres." When management fired bunnies in New York, Detroit, and other cities because of their fading image, the women contested the charge using the various state commissions on human rights, the EEOC, and the union grievance procedures. The rulings were mixed, in part because of bargaining agreements allowing the employer wide discretion in judging the suitability of bunnies.[79] One New York arbitrator, for example, sided with the club in 1974 and mocked the vanity of the four bunny plaintiffs. "While a freshness of youth is manifestly transitory and evanescent, it is not always easy for a Bunny to accept the inevitable—that it has finally happened to her."[80] The widest publicity accompanied Myra Wolfgang's victory in Detroit, however, which involved the reinstatement of a bunny who was a shop steward and union militant. Claiming that Hugh Hefner had been "displaced as the sole qualified beholder of bunny beauty," Wolfgang quipped that the Playboy Clubs "didn't want a bunny that bit back."[81]

What waitresses would wear at work was another contested issue. As with the jousts over who would determine employee selection, the conflicts over uniforms were muted until the 1970s. The early amicability resulted in part from the conservative garb chosen by most employers before the 1920s. It also stemmed from a working-class sensibility that differed from the second-wave feminist sensibility of the 1970s in its attitude toward female sexual expression and its definition of what constituted male exploitation.

Most employers before the 1920s followed convention, outfitting their waitresses in prim black dresses with white cap, apron, and cuffs. Unlike department store women, who preferred to dress like their customers and refused to wear uniforms that in their minds denoted working-class status, waitresses apparently were not humiliated by their black and white uniforms.[82] Not one local proposed doing away with the uniform, and many took pride in their neat, starched appearance. "Your collar better be stiff and standing and you had your side towel on your arm," said Clela Sullivan, her body straightening as she savored the memory. Similar dress also resonated well with waitresses' own sense of belonging to a corps of workers all in the same trade.[83] Moreover, waitresses indicated little concern over the alternate uniforms employers chose. Some contracts limited dress to the standard black and white, but most allowed employers to choose the cut or style of the uniform as long as they were willing to pay.[84] Rank-and-file waitresses appeared satisfied with this emphasis and often remarked on the economic savings gained from these contract provisions.[85]

As employers began opting for more explicitly sexual outfits, a few waitresses objected, but the issue essentially remained dormant until the 1970s. Members of Local 48 spoke up in 1938, pointing out that they preferred to buy their own uniforms and thus have more control over their choice of dress style, but they were overruled by a membership vote to continue having employers choose, pay for, and launder the uniforms.[86] Waitresses also indicated a preference for functional uniforms with large pockets and plenty of room to move, a national survey found in 1948, but "less than 2 percent of the waitresses expressed any thought on trick or novel uniforms sometimes seen in night clubs." Indeed, union newspapers from the 1930s to the 1960s, including newsletters edited and produced by separate waitress locals, ran photographs of waitresses in explicitly sexual uniforms without comment or complaint.[87]

Significantly, the major grumbling about waitress uniforms in this period came from male waiters. Whether prompted by moral scruples or envy of the ability of waitresses to earn tips, one man argued that the union should see to it that waitresses were provided with "decent uniforms." Another wrote his union newspaper in disgust after it published a photograph of a corps of female dining staff in sexually revealing dress. Instead of plastering photos of waitresses exhibiting their "naked limbs in public places just to draw customers to a joint," he wrote, "our union [should] step in and stop that form of degrading exploitation." His was the only letter of complaint printed.[88]

Were waitresses too intimidated to speak out, or too desperate for tips to protest? Probably both factors affected the attitudes of many. Nonetheless, waitresses did not object to flaunting their charms. At one restaurant in New York City, the manager instructed the hostess "to tell the girls they shouldn't swing their hips so much when they walk." The waitresses protested, demanding that their union representative intercede with management. They stood by "their inalienable right as females to walk as females have walked through the ages."[89] Like the flight attendants who organized in 1960s in response to the management rule prohibiting hair coloring and requiring short hair, waitresses resisted any management interference with their "female identity." And not unlike their male craft brothers, they organized quickly when management actions affronted their gender identity as well as their workplace autonomy.[90]

Waitresses, however, did not accept the idea that their sexual expression gave men license to be disrespectful or to demand sexual favors. Rather than simply circumscribe the expression of their own sexuality, waitresses asked men to meet them halfway by taking responsibility for their own responses. They expected their bosses and their male co-workers and patrons to exercise self-control and to treat them with decency. Butte's Valentine Webster identified "the bosses getting smart with some of the girls," as one of the most important and typical grievances brought to the Butte local. In San Francisco, when a waitress complained in 1938 that the actions of the boss were "unbecoming to a gentleman," Local 48 instructed the union representative to see that the boss mended his ways. Two years later, the union filed charges of "immorality" and "abuse of girls on the job" against another boss and gained his pledge to "cease in all abuse hereafter."[91] Where contract language offered insufficient protection, rank-and-file waitresses took matters into their own hands. Newly hired waitresses in Dartmouth College Freshman Commons walked off the job in 1924 when the permanent student workers greeted them with whistles of approval and delight. After delivering some caustic remarks, the offended waitresses removed their caps and aprons and declared their intention never to return to the college.[92]

By the 1970s, waitresses objected publicly to seductive waitress uniforms. Although not all waitresses agreed, many now considered certain sexually revealing uniforms as exploitative and demeaning,[93] and many believed that the wearing of these outfits should be restricted as well as the aggressive behavior they evoked in men. The "short bunny outfits" introduced by Butte's Burger King disappeared after business representative Clela Sullivan "jumped down their throat and chewed them out good."[94] Other locals such as Detroit's 705 forced employers to provide "uniforms that fit—[some employers refused to buy uniforms over a size 12]—and adequately covered all parts of the body normally covered by personal clothing."[95] But other cases involving uniform choice were lost due to legal opinion granting employers broad discretion in setting employee dress codes and to the murkiness of legal definitions of sexual harassment. Whether a waitress like the Sizzleboard countergirl who refused to don the "little red apron and hat, with the nameplate that read, 'I'm Your Sizzle-Girl'" can be fired legally has yet to be resolved.[96]

Waitress Unions as "Next-of-Kin"

In 1909, when waitress Laura MacDonald's lover deserted her and her two-year-old son, she attempted suicide and shot her child. Throughout the long and lurid trial, the San Francisco Waitresses' Union stood by their member.

They packed the courtroom, held a benefit ball for her court costs and living expenses, and when MacDonald ultimately was acquitted, she convalesced at Maud Younger's home. MacDonald expected no less: in the hospital recovering from her suicide attempt, she had listed the Waitresses' Union as her next-of-kin.[97]

The San Francisco local was not alone in acting as a surrogate family for its members. Because many waitresses lacked strong family bonds and lived outside the traditional family setting, they needed union institutions that would provide emotional and social sustenance as well as economic. In response, locals adopted the standard union practice of setting up sick and death benefit funds for its members. They also organized social events, concerned themselves with family problems such as child care, and even attempted to establish rest and recreational homes.[98]

As early as 1905, the International union constitution encouraged locals to set up sick and death benefit funds even if it meant raising dues. Waitress locals embraced the idea, and by 1909 many of the major locals had both sick and death benefit funds. Chicago waitresses inaugurated their sick benefit fund "to save the girls from the dangers of the nobody to know and nobody to care feeling"—all too common a feeling for the many waitresses who roomed apart from families in the early twentieth century. In 1913, Seattle waitresses reported having paid out more than $3,000 in sick benefits and about $1,500 in death benefits since 1900. Waitresses interviewed by one investigator in that same year dwelt upon these benefits as among the chief advantages of unionism. The waitresses accepted this mutual aid from one another, the investigator observed, "where it would be resented or attended with humiliation if it came from outside."[99]

The benefit funds provided some very basic necessities, such as financial assistance during illness. When their sick benefits ran out, workers could borrow money from the union treasury. The bylaws of Local 249 in St. Louis promised money to an ill member until she was once again "able to follow her vocation."[100] In addition, upon a member's death, waitress unions offered a lump-sum payment to the closest surviving relative. If burial benefits were insufficient, locals took up collections or made donations from the treasury to cover "whatever amount" was needed. They also made funeral arrangements when no family member was forthcoming. Without the union, many a waitress would have been "buried in potters field" and her death uncommemorated, one secretary declared.[101]

In most locals, health and welfare assistance meant something beyond the mere monetary. Many locals had active sick committees that not only oversaw the disbursement of union funds, but also screened and hired a physician for union members to consult free of charge. "If a waitress got sick," an official from Portland explained, "there was often real problems without somebody looking after her kids, or getting her bills paid. I remember even picking up radios [from] the repair shop . . . or getting the laundry done for them. . . . There was never a person that we knew about on the sick list that we didn't look after." [102]

Waitress locals, however, were unable to adopt as extensive a benefit structure as their brother locals, and they were unable to pay benefits equaling what their male counterparts received.[103] Women workers simply had less money available for dues and benefit payments. Moreover, like many male-dominated organizations, they denied sick benefits to pregnant women, to those whose illness was chronic, or a "direct result of personal vice, intemperance, narcotics, illegal or immoral conduct." [104] Clauses replicating this sentiment were adopted by waitresses in Butte, Boston, Washington, Buffalo, and elsewhere.[105]

At first glance these provisions seem punitive and heartless in their denial of care to pregnant women and "immoral" women, but upon closer scrutiny a different evaluation emerges. In a situation of limited resources, waitresses balanced the needs of certain individuals against the needs of the majority of members. The restriction on illness resulting from personal vice suggests that individuals were expected to meet certain standards of personal morality and responsible behavior before being entitled to group support. Because those suffering from chronic illness were also excluded from benefits, one must conclude that even women of pristine morality faced loss of group support when their needs exceeded the resources available from the group.

The exclusion of pregnant women also may have derived more from a pragmatic evaluation of group resources than a moral judgment condemning pregnant women to self-reliance and community ostracism. Perhaps waitresses reasoned that pregnant women were more likely to be younger, married, and have family resources; thus, limited sick funds would be better preserved for the use of waitresses facing illness in their old age and waitresses without family support. Moreover, unlike male trade unionists, waitresses actively lobbied for state-derived pregnancy benefits. Thus, where funds to support pregnancy were not to be gained at the expense of other female health needs, waitresses demanded consideration for pregnant women. Beginning in the late 1940s, the San Francisco local repeatedly passed resolutions advocating monetary benefits during pregnancy through the California Unemployment Insurance Act. In 1973, the section of the act denying benefits to pregnant women was finally ruled unconstitutional.[106]

Waitresses also pressed for improved contract coverage for pregnancy and childbirth once employer-paid health-care plans took hold in the 1950s. Extending health coverage to pregnant women took priority over closing the gap between the amount of sick leave benefits paid men and women in the mixed locals. As a result of pressure from female members, the first industrywide employer-paid health plan, negotiated by New York City's hotel local in 1945, "provided for two groups of workers who are ordinarily discriminated against—namely women and Negroes," according to *Hotel and Club Voice*. In the case of women, the editors added, "the plan makes proper provisions for furnishing maternity benefits and for providing benefits for both female members and wives of male members." [107]

Although child care must have been a problem for some waitresses, it was never a top priority for waitress locals. Waitress locals, however, did depart from the general union culture in identifying child care as a legitimate union issue and in agitating for state support. Concern over the issue surfaced primarily in the 1940s and 1950s. Local 48, for example, helped instigate a Labor Council Committee on the Care of Children of Working Mothers in 1942. Through this group and others, they urged the state financing of child-care centers in 1943 and created such a furor over the discontinuation of federal funding for child care after the war that San Francisco's city government became one of the few in the country to provide municipal funds for child-care centers. [108] A few locals offered child-care assistance through the union office as well. Seattle's Beulah Compton won election in 1953 on a platform promising a union-sponsored nursery for children during afternoon and evening union meetings. The "experiment in baby-sitting" began in 1954 with "free play, story-telling, and fruit juice and cookies." Compton also arranged for an older, former waitress to be on call through the union when working waitresses needed emergency child care. Local 6 in New York set up a welfare department where women could receive help with child care, adoption, and divorce. In other cases, locals made accommodations for child-care responsibilities in their organizational rules. Members who missed meetings because of sick children, for example, were not fined. When a few members in one local complained about the presence of children at union meetings, they were overruled. [109]

Waitresses wanted their unions to function as social organizations. Chicago's local held open house three times a week, providing light refreshments and entertainment. A New York City waitress, interviewed in 1907, volunteered that the best thing about her union were the "sociables. Sometimes they have lectures with magic lantern pictures and it gives a girl somewhere to go evenings." [110] Female locals instituted annual balls as soon as they were chartered. San Francisco waitresses held yearly dances into the 1950s and used the money they raised for their sick and death benefit funds. These affairs brought a "a better feeling among the girls," a Los Angeles waitress organizer reported, and they forged ties between waitress locals and the local labor movement. One female organizer relied on the annual waitress dance as a wedge to gain entry into male union meetings and garner support for organizing. Social events also helped engage the uncommitted rank and file and attract unorganized waitresses. [111]

Labor Day parades offered another chance to build social bonds between members. San Francisco waitresses frequently captured prizes for their large turnouts and their elaborate floats in that city's Labor Day parades. In 1941, they hired an all-women's band for the parade and extended "an invitation to any women who wish to parade and do not have a Division [to] parade with us." On another occasion, they expended funds for the purchase of "old-fashioned uniforms" and asked their "members' daughters to parade as waitresses of the future in uniform." [112]

Female unionists reinforced social ties among members by developing attractive headquarters and meeting rooms. In contrast to the somewhat boisterous and unruly activities in male headquarters, waitress locals used their halls for social and intellectual stimulation and as places of rest. In 1905, the Chicago waitresses' union, with the help of the local Women's Label League, moved into its own suite in the Chicago Labor Temple and set up a rest area and library for waitresses caught downtown between shifts. Later, they secured a large two-story building. There, they opened a bright new employment office decorated with pictures of conventions and union parades, and furnished the upstairs club rooms with a piano, a sewing machine, and beds for women desiring rest and quiet. The Philadelphia waitresses' local offered its headquarters as a place for waitresses to congregate between shifts and after work. Their complex included a reading room, a library, and a free employment referral service for union waitresses. [113]

A few locals even built recreation and rest homes for their members. Here, through a single institution, unions could act as a surrogate family in caring for the waitress when she was ill, in offering a setting for social interaction, and in being a solace from the cares of the work world. Seattle waitresses set up the only permanent waitress home in 1913, but many locals attempted to duplicate their accomplishments in the years before World War I. The Seattle waitresses worked for four years raising funds for a home and had almost given up hope when a wealthy local lumberman offered to buy them property and help remodel the building. The resulting home contained large kitchen and parlor areas, a reception hall with a piano, a library, and upstairs bedrooms where "girls will come when they are tired out and in need of vacations or when they are convalescent after illness." As Alice Lord explained, "many of the members of the waitress union have no other home than the little room in which they sleep at night among strangers." The Seattle waitresses held social functions at the home and in general enjoyed "the advantages of club life." Thus, through the union the women would be given the social and home life many of them lacked. [114]

Thus, waitress unionists achieved many of the goals they enumerated so precisely in their union bylaws and constitutions. Collective activity aimed at securing both legislative and contract protections raised workers' living standards, shortened their working day, and provided for greater control over their work environment. In addition, waitresses sought the moral and social advancement of their craft and of their sex. In so doing, they revealed their allegiance to many tenets and practices common among male unionists, particularly those associated with craft unionism: they emphasized the skilled nature of their work, their competence and morality as workers and as women, and the sororal aspects of unionism. At the same time, however, they modified these concepts and adopted others to meet their particular needs as wage-earning women.

CHAPTER SIX

Waitress Unionism:
Rethinking Categories

I never missed a meeting. We loved to go. . . . We'd have three
hundred or four hundred people at a meeting. It was wonderful.
It was just a joy to go and hear the business agent, Bridget Shea
and Lena Mattausch, the secretary, get up and tell you what they'd
done, how they'd go around and how our girls was abused by this
one and how they'd take it up, and how they'd pick up a broom
and chase the boss with the broom.

> —Valentine Webster, speaking of
> her days as a union official in the
> Butte, Montana, Women's
> Protective Union (Local 457)
> in the 1940s and 1950s[1]

When workers organize, they face collective choices about how to proceed
organizationally. Practices must be developed to govern the day-to-day interaction with employers, and rules must be devised to oversee the union's
relationship with its members. For union organizations—described by A. J.
Muste as "part town meeting and part army"[2]—the regulations must allow
for member participation and dissent without unduly jeopardizing the union's
strength in bargaining. In response to these challenges, waitresses devised a
form of unionism that for nearly a half a century fostered worker loyalty to
the organization and enabled them to exert control over their occupation and
their work lives.

The unionism developed by waitresses shared many of the craft features
common to labor organizations built before the New Deal; it differed, however, in fundamental ways from the unionism that first came to prominence
among mass-production workers in the 1930s. I have termed their unionism
occupational unionism to distinguish it from the worksite unionism that arose
among mass-production workers, and I argue that it was the dominant form of
unionism among waitresses from the turn of the century to the 1960s. Occupational unionism emphasized the occupational identity of the worker and
tied union power to control over those within the occupation; in contrast,

worksite unionism focused on the worksite identity of the worker and devised rights and protections linked to a particular employer or jobsite.

Control over the Labor Supply

At the heart of occupational unionism lay a reliance on union-run hiring halls and the closed shop.[3] Hiring halls provided unions with a regular means of access to the mobile population that comprised the hotel and restaurant work force. Job-seekers went first to the hiring hall, where, through the use of a rotation system, they were dispatched according to the time they registered. Those desiring work had to meet the approval of the union dispatcher and were required to be fully qualified union members "in good standing." Unlike the employment agencies against which the union hiring halls competed, union-run agencies prided themselves on offering free services to workers and employers.

For example, in 1904, the Butte Women's Protective Union recognized the importance of the hiring hall in building union loyalty and in offering a needed service for members and employers. They launched a virulent campaign against the non-WPU employment agencies, claiming the agencies "carried on a straight-out, shameless, holdup system by requiring high fees from employers, garnishing wages, and supplying scabs." When the dust settled, the WPU had established itself as the single employment source for female servers; they maintained that monopoly for the next half century.[4] The Los Angeles local had a thriving hiring hall as late as 1967, where according to the *Los Angeles Times*, 350 "extras" were sent out on a typical weekend. The local's secretary likened the hiring hall to a Travelers Aid, where transient and impoverished waitresses came in search of help. "Some of them come to town with children in the car, no money, and somebody here comes up with money for a hotel room and a job."[5]

Many locals secured "100 percent" closed-shop agreements requiring that all employees join the union *before* being hired and that employers obtain all personnel through the union hiring hall.[6] Hiring halls flourished when backed by such contracts. Most functioned smoothly under the less restrictive union shop and preferential hiring arrangements, in part because culinary employers relied on the hiring hall for "good and reliable" full-time workers as well as for the extras needed in emergencies.[7] Under these other typical clauses, employers relied on union hiring halls for referrals, but different workers could be requested or, if "suitable" union members could not be located, an employer could hire off the street. Those hired, however, had to be approved by the union and were required to maintain their membership in good standing.[8] Workers who violated union bylaws and work rules were not considered in good standing and could be removed from the job.

Hiring halls also were sustained by the control of the union over its work force. In some cases, waitress locals persuaded the majority of the occupation to seek work first through the union hall, thus making it difficult for employers to hire from any other source. Worker loyalty was achieved through appeals to the employee's self-interest in avoiding "the vampire system" of high-fee employment agencies and through the union's internal disciplinary system whereby a worker would be fined and denied future use of the hiring hall if she solicited work on her own.[9] In addition, some food servers may have supported the hiring hall concept because it gave them, rather than the employer, control over when and how much they worked. As long as they maintained their union standing, waitresses could quit a job and "lay off" for however long they chose; they could also work on a regular part-time basis by relying on extra jobs coming into the hall.[10]

Through these negotiated provisions, then, the union exercised control over the labor supply in the industry, offered employers a vital service, and provided members employment security and flexibility in a highly transitory, unstable sector of the economy. In addition, strong union security clauses provided membership stability (and hence financial stability) for the union as an institution and protected workers from employer harassment and favoritism on account of union membership.

Occupational as Opposed to Job-based Rights

Unions relying on the closed shop and the hiring hall typically paid little attention to the individual employee's right to a particular job. Rather, they emphasized expanding the union's control over work in the industry and keeping union shops viable. They rarely battled employers who fired an individual member unless they suspected discrimination based on union activities; laid-off or fired individuals simply returned to the union hall and were sent out to another job. During times of economic adversity, locals abided by work-sharing principles in which all members cut back equally on their employment time rather than relying on seniority. Thus, in contrast with the system developed primarily by mass-production workers in the 1930s, occupationally based unions offered employment security, not job security.[11]

The emphasis on employment security is evident in the response of waitress unions to unemployment. Rather than have a few members work full schedules while others were unemployed (as typically would occur where layoffs were governed by seniority), culinary locals distributed the available work among all union members. As Chicago's local secretary explained, "in slack seasons . . . in place of putting any [waitresses] . . . off the payroll . . . [we would have] each girl leave off one or two meals a week." No matter what the age of the employee or her longevity with the company, every worker, once a union member, had the same right to work as every other union member. Adversity was shared equally, and as long as the union had shops under contract, some employment would be available.[12]

Work sharing and employment security were enforced through work rules giving the union the right to determine what constituted a week's work and how overtime would be divided. Waitress locals routinely fined members who were caught working extra hours or moonlighting, that is, taking on more than one job. "Any member working on the sixth day when a substitute can be furnished," San Francisco's 1921 work rules read, "shall be fined the sum of ten dollars for each offense, and . . . suspended . . . until said fine is paid." The local also passed resolutions limiting work to eight hours a day and prohibiting double shifts. "Girls working breakfast and lunch can't work dinner at any time," the executive board proclaimed, and in 1938 they added: "any member working over 8 hours shall be fined, suspended, or expelled as the union sees fit." Employers who needed overtime from their employees sought the permission of the business agent or the executive board of the union, and unless a labor shortage existed, most locals refused to allow it, preferring instead to pass on the extra work to an unemployed or underemployed union member.[13]

Paralleling their emphasis on employment security over job security, most waitress unions allowed employers wide discretion in discharging employees. New York's Cafeteria Local 305, for example, mandated that an employer who discharged a worker in the middle of a shift must pay her at least a half day's pay, however, the employer was not required to demonstrate the justice of the decision or show "just cause."[14] Indeed, in an ironic twist, some agreements contained a "just cause" clause that protected the employer not the employee: "Any member walking out without 'just cause,'" one 1921 agreement read, "shall be subject to a fine by the local." Instead of requiring the employer to present legitimate reasons for his actions, the contract asked the *member* to justify her behavior. In the instances where the union suspected discrimination on the basis of union activities, business agents or local officers would intervene, demanding the employer rehire the aggrieved party or face union sanctions.[15] These interventions, however, were seen as justified in order to protect the union as an institution. The individual job rights of the employee were not the motivating factor.[16]

Traditions of Self-regulation and Peer Discipline

Waitresses also conceived of their organizations as vehicles for setting and regulating occupational standards. Like a "professional" association, the union would not only be the source of work, but also would set the standards of competence in the trade and would determine appropriate discipline for those who violated group norms. Indeed, waitress locals assumed responsibility for such "management" tasks as the hiring and discharge of members, the mediation of on-the-job disputes, and the assurance of fair first-line supervisory practices. In a sense, workers in the culinary industry had instituted a form of self-management.

To ensure the competence and reliability of their members, many locals screened prospective members carefully, weeding out the inexperienced and inept. They also invested in training programs to upgrade and maintain the skill level of members and hence the reputation and appeal of the union. One training brochure pledged through its program to "establish better relations between employer and employee" and to help those "who wish to get ahead in their craft."[17]

Portland waitresses pioneered in this undertaking. Gertrude Sweet reported in 1925 that they had instituted "a training school for waitresses—one that will teach the girls who have gained their experience in the smaller places the finer points of service work." In the Seattle local's program, employers in the 1950s released certain waitresses for classroom training and paid them full wages during their absence. The "personalized dining service" training included wine appreciation, service styles, personality, sales techniques, courtesy, menu terminology, grooming, and teamwork. In Long Beach, California, waitresses opened a free school in 1939 "to create a higher type of service." The Culinary Arts School evidently thrived, with a full curriculum on waitress training in place by 1947. As late as 1966, sixteen graduates completed the "waitress apprenticeship courses," by then offered in conjunction with Long Beach City College.[18]

The apprenticeship model of combining classroom and on-the-job training caught on in other locals as well. Locals in the 1920s and 1930s negotiated an apprentice or starter rate for inexperienced waitresses; trainees were entitled to union scale after satisfactorily completing their apprenticeship.[19] Wage gradations could exist between journey-level waitresses as well, thus fostering occupational competency by pegging wage rates to skill level. For Butte, Montana, waitresses in the 1940s, the union scale acted as "a minimum" and did not "prevent a superior . . . craftswoman from receiving more." Waitresses in Dallas agreed: their wage scale specified that "nothing contained herein shall prohibit first class help from receiving higher wages."[20]

Once on the job, union waitresses were expected to conform to the craft standards devised by their fellow members; noncomplying waitresses faced discipline from other waitresses, not the employer. Penalties for infraction of the group-devised codes ranged from minimal fines or loss of a few days' pay to union blacklisting in the industry and social ostracism.[21] These measures against individual waitresses were deemed necessary to protect the jobs and working conditions of the group. After having told one "sister" to solicit her own work because of "the way she acted on a job," one Local 48 business agent justified her action before the membership by explaining that she did not want to deprive anyone of work, but "there will be less [work] if the jobs are not taken care of and worked proper."[22]

The first responsibility of waitresses was regular attendance and punctuality. Working rules in Chicago, in force from 1909 to 1962, fined waitresses for absences and for "walking out during meals." Proper behavior meant arriving for work "at least 15 minutes before the hour called for" and not leaving "during working hours except in case of sickness." Employees arranged their own substitutes, and, if overtime was necessitated by the failure of a co-worker to appear, "the wages for the overtime must be paid by the one causing the extra labor." Maintaining staffing levels was, then, the responsibility of the union and of individual employees, not the employer. The culinary local in Tacoma even allowed the employer to file charges against the union and collect the day's pay of a member who quit without notification.[23]

Locals guaranteed the honesty and sobriety of their members. To establish their credibility with employers, Local 484's 1909 agreement reimbursed "proprietors for all losses caused through dishonesty on the part of the members, provided the report is made in writing to the organization and accusations substantiated before the grievance committee." Waitresses in Rochester in 1952 required that members not "smoke or drink while on duty." Portland waitresses and others devised and maintained similar rules from the turn of the century into the 1960s.[24]

Proper attention to duty and civil behavior with customers were essential. One local promised that its members would "care for . . . the business of our employer with courtesy"; another agreed "to discipline members for incivility to customers." Locals held trials in which members accused by employers of inattention to duty were prosecuted. One such trial, held before the executive board of the San Francisco local in 1951, involved "the trouble at Jeanettes with a customer." The waitress, appearing in her own defense, said she had been "very busy working her station . . . and [only] threw her tray at the customer . . . after he called her a slob." As it was her first offense, the waitress escaped with a warning and a lecture on handling offensive customers.[25]

At times, waitresses in the newly established, semi-industrial locals of the 1930s engaged in self-regulation and peer discipline, but usually they did so through informal means because their locals lacked the extensive web of by-laws and work rules governing employee behavior developed by the older craft locals. After a series of weekly meetings, Local 6 coffee-shop waitresses decided to punish any woman who was late repeatedly by giving her a back station. One justified her action for the union newspaper: "It is usually regarded as the function of the management to take disciplinary action," she said, "but if we undertake to discipline ourselves we will be in a much better position when we want to ask for something."[26]

When personality problems and other disputes between members interfered with job performance, the union, not the employer, stepped in to resolve them. One waitress, summoned to the union executive board "on a complaint she was making life miserable for other girls," received instructions from the president of the local about "her duties as a member" and was told to "refrain from interfering with other members on the job." Another local prosecuted "any sister who abused, called vile names, or in any way . . . mistreat[ed] another sister while on duty."[27] Butte officers rebuked union members for their treatment of each other at work and asked "girls with experience to consider the less experienced girls and help them out instead of mocking them."[28]

Because adequate job performance as a food server involved the cooperation of cooks, busboys, and sometimes bartenders, waitress locals mediated disputes between their members and co-workers belonging to other locals. When a Local 48 waitress claimed she walked off the job because the cook slapped her in the face, Local 48 demanded the cook be brought up on charges before his own local. After hearing complaints from waiters and bartenders that a certain cocktail waitress was impossible to work with, Local 48's president scolded her and threatened to remove her from the job if complaints persisted. When the lounge manager attempted to find out why the waitress was cited, the local made it clear that "this was our business, not his."[29]

In locals without strong bylaws governing such problems, good business agents sometimes intervened and resolved differences informally. In 1944, Local 6 hotel and club coffee-shop waitresses, with the help of their business agent, thrashed out the ill feeling existing among them because of haggling over tips and customers. They agreed "not to let tips come between them again," and "with the air cleared, went back to work in a friendly and cooperative spirit." In fact, some employers relied upon the judgment of respected union representatives for advice about employee morale and supervision; the opinion of a business agent might prevail even without specific written contract protection, especially if the local union had established basic control over the labor supply in the area.[30]

Waitress locals took responsibility for fair first-line supervisory techniques. Because supervisors—hostesses, head waiters, and waitresses—belonged to the union, they were subject to certain union bylaws forbidding "conduct unbecoming a union member" and could be brought before the union upon a complaint by their subordinates. Unions heard accusations ranging from uneven tip distribution, unfair station and shift assignment, and unjust firings, to what boiled down to poor supervisory techniques and simple unpleasantness. One waitress supervisor faced the wrath of the Butte executive board for "slapping a sister across the face," with "nagging and abusing" five other sisters, and with holding up the orders of waitresses she did not like. In a second case, San Francisco's officers removed a head hostess after finding her guilty of discharging women without reason, failing to notify the union for replacements, engaging in "conduct unbecoming to the union," and "making conditions miserable for the crew."[31]

Some unions mandated that the hiring of captains and hostesses "be taken up" with the union; others prevented abuse by determining ahead of time what constituted good supervisory behavior. One contract stipulated that waitresses "not be reprimanded in the presence of guests." Another decreed that all stations be rotated. The advantages of rotation were obvious to one union official: "it enables all workers to share in the benefits of preferred stations; it does away with favoritism and eliminates the possibilities of friction among the workers."[32]

Certain employers could be disciplined by the union for bylaw infractions as well. Many owners, especially those who had worked in the trade formerly, kept their membership in the union—they were passive or nonvoting members—to maintain their health and welfare benefits. One owner, for example, was summoned before the executive board of Local 48 in 1942 because she "wasn't civil to union girls in her shop." She changed her ways because the alternative was expulsion from the union.[33]

Ensuring Group Loyalty

In general, however, proper union wage scales, working conditions, and craft rules were maintained as much through self-regulation as through actions taken against employers. Occupational unionism was effective in part because the union expected a certain level of loyalty and commitment from its members. The union made its expectations known explicitly. The union constitutions, bylaws, and work rules delineated the responsibilities of members toward co-workers and the union as an institution. Penalties for infraction of these group-devised codes were meted out routinely, despite the anger it provoked on the part of individual workers. The union existed for the good of the whole; individual rights were subordinate to the advancement of the collective.

The first duty of a union member on the job was to insist on proper union wage scales and working conditions. St. Louis waitresses, like the majority of locals, explicitly stated their expectations: "any employee not receiving correct wages, overtime, or working conditions, shall, upon conviction thereof, be suspended from the local."[34] Members were expected to uphold union craft rules as well. In 1941, Local 457 found a "sister guilty of washing dishes" and forbid her to work at that house for a year. From at least the 1920s into the 1960s, Local 48 repeatedly brought sisters up on such craft rule infractions as "sweeping the floor," "cleaning waffle irons," and "scrubbing anything at anytime." Most were fined, but those who violated such craft rules a second time were "pulled off the job and replaced."[35]

Members were responsible for making sure their fellow employees honored the standards. Those failing to do so, according to bylaws enforced by the Washington, D.C., local as late as 1962, "were subject to charges and such penalties as may be imposed by the membership." In some cases, locals removed whole crews when individual offenders were found—the theory being that the others knew of the violation and were thus equally guilty.[36]

Honoring union standards meant never working with a nonunion co-worker. As a result, union members were ever alert in organizing new workers on the job. Beulah Compton recalled how she first joined the union in the 1930s. "I'd never heard of the union. And the way I joined, one of the girls asked me why I wasn't a union member. So I wanted to know what a union was and she told me; and very sweetly said they wouldn't work with a non-union girl. So I just marched myself down to the union and joined. Otherwise, I just had no idea what a union was all about. I've always loved those spirited girls, giving me the word." Membership was also sustained by the practice begun in pre-World War I days of requiring every member to wear a union button "in a conspicuous place" at all times while on the job.[37]

Unions regulated member behavior off the job too. Members either took their turn picketing every month or faced stiff fines; attendance at union meetings was mandatory; and members honored the organization's unfair list and strike calls or risked rebuke from their fellow workers. Local 48 fined one member $100 and then expelled her for going through a picket line although she lived in the hotel being picketed. Another member who crossed picket lines during the 1938 Department Store Strike was "suspended from headquarters for 60 days" and required to "read the history of the Labor Movement and report to the education committee."[38] Butte waitresses decreed "patronizing nonunion establishments, employing non-union labor or buying nonunion goods in preference to union" all worthy of fines.[39]

Broad clauses bound members to conduct themselves in such a manner that they would bring credit to their organization. From Butte waitresses in the Progressive Era to Buffalo waitresses in the late 1950s, union members accused of a "disreputable act" that would "bring disgrace on the Union or a Sister member" drew the righteous anger of a waitress grievance committee and a stiff fine. Local bylaw provisions forbidding "conduct unbecoming a union member" justified fines for "disorderly conduct at meetings, parades, or the Labor Council," for "loud talking or swearing," for "cursing the union to the Secretary," and for signing an affidavit against another union sister. The standards for conduct "unbecoming a union member" differed, of course, depending on the particular morals of the officials in charge. Gertrude Sweet wrote President Flore in 1938, chagrined that a recent change in leadership in the Portland local brought in women with low standards of personal conduct. "Several of those elected as executive board members," Sweet complained, "were so drunk after the election that they went down into the recreation room and bar of the Labor Temple and did disgraceful things and it hurts so badly after Agnes and I worked for years to build for the local a good reputation and never permitted any lewd happenings around the offices."[40]

The seriousness with which locals took their role in regulating member behavior is suggested by the number of members actually cited and the enormous amount of time spent in investigating and prosecuting offenders. Single hearings could require hours of testimony, witness preparation, and transcripts. Locals also allowed members reconsideration privileges. Local 240, for example, reheard the case of an expelled member in 1901 and decided to "give her another chance to be good." Members who felt unjustly charged could appeal their cases to the area Local Joint Executive Board (LJEB). Although LJEBs rarely overturned an individual local's decision, many members did exercise their appeal rights.[41] Cases could also be remanded to "a lower court" as a form of public punishment. One irate executive board in 1938 sentenced the defendant to endure the wrath of the membership. The fact that guilty members could be punished sufficiently by being humiliated in front of their sisters suggests the operation of a powerful group norm.[42]

The Appeal of Occupational Unionism for Employers

Why did employers tolerate the union's control over work standards and work performance? At times, as in the heyday of culinary unionism in the 1940s and 1950s, locals called the shots because of their economic and political clout. At other times, however, locals secured cooperation because they offered employers concrete services and assistance. Indeed, although unionization could mean a loss of flexibility and authority, some employers tolerated that loss because, as noted earlier, they relied on the union to provide trained, competent labor and to oversee employee job performance. As Elizabeth Maloney summarized in 1914 when questioned before the U.S. Commission on Industrial Relations on the advantages unionization held for employers: "they get steadier help, girls whose actions are responsible to their [union] organization." The system of employee responsibility to the union, she continued, "had so many advantages . . . that the people who have contracts with us have no hesitancy at all in saying that they are well satisfied with the help we send them."[43]

The union's willingness to shoulder responsibility for the economic viability of unionized enterprises enticed others. In an industry renowned for its high percentage of business failures, unionization could enhance business stability and ensure the success of an individual enterprise. Once employers adopted union standards and hired only union help, the union protected their business interests by attacking "unfair" competition and by encouraging patronage of union houses. Numerous culinary contracts bound unionists to help "stabilize business" and to maintain the efficiency and profitability of the establishment where they worked. Locals agreed to use their "influence with organized labor and its friends to patronize only such places as display the Union House Card" and "to distribute printed matter, visit various labor groups and advise them to patronize union houses." Applicants for membership into the Los Angeles waitresses' union pledged to "interest themselves individually and collectively in protecting the trade, and the business of the employers."[44]

At times culinary unionists promised more general kinds of business assistance. Union bylaws from the turn of the century to the 1960s vowed to "assist employers in all legitimate ways" and to "look after the boss's interests." The bylaws of one waitress local summarized these sentiments: to "promote friendly relations between the employer and the union; to establish fair, equitable, and profitable . . . working conditions and to achieve . . . a high standard of service to the public."[45]

The recognition of mutual interests and obligations between unions and employers often precluded the necessity of a formal grievance procedure ending in binding arbitration. Because occupational unionists placed less emphasis on the protection of individual members and more on the mutual interests of the overall industry and the occupation, disputes were less frequent and common ground more easily found than in worker representation systems in which the union was reacting continually to employer discipline and in which its identity and appeal were based largely on a day-to-day adversarial stance.

Occupational Unionism under Siege

The occupational unionism of waitresses was not a static, unchanging entity, nor did every HERE local follow these practices unswervingly. The hotel locals, in particular, were influenced by the mass production unionism that rose to prominence during the 1930s and 1940s.[46] Hotel locals organized along industrial lines and tended to develop employer or worksite-centered protections and rights: they stressed individual job security through just-cause protections and relied upon seniority provisions to govern lay-offs and re-hires. They deemphasized work-sharing approaches and union formulation of performance standards and proper job discipline.[47]

In addition, during World War II and after, some locals began allowing more employer discretion over the scheduling and working hours of individual employees. Given the war labor shortage and the employers' willingness to pay time-and-a-half, some locals waived the five-day work week, allowing their members to keep up with wartime inflation by working overtime. The practice continued after the war, with more contracts allowing work "performed in excess of a week's work [to] . . . be compensated at the rate of time and one half."[48] Moreover, the first employer-paid health-care plans took hold in the 1940s. New York City's hotel local led the way by negotiating an industry-wide, employer-paid plan in 1945 that included hospitalization and maternity benefits, weekly sick-leave pay, life insurance, and death benefits. Similar plans soon appeared across the country.[49]

The impact of these changes was paradoxical. When unions began recognizing the employee's right to retain an individual job, they took less responsibility for providing full employment for all their members. The principle of a worker's right to a particular job came to predominate over the principle of union members' collective claim to all work in their craft jurisdiction. As locals concentrated on protection against unjust firings and lay-offs, they expended less energy on organizing the industry and upholding occupational standards at the workplace. Individual employees benefited from the more extensive financial reimbursements available through employer-paid health and welfare plans and from overtime pay, but the union as an institution was no longer the source of income or benefits. The ties binding members together and to the union were loosening.

Despite the new practices instituted by the hotel locals and the dilution of the older traditions under the influence of mass-production unionism, the majority of culinary locals retained their allegiance to the basic tenets of occupational unionism into the early 1960s. Throughout the 1950s, waitress bylaws continued to mandate work-sharing and the equal division of overtime hours.[50] A few even kept control over the funding and disbursement of benefits. Most significant, however, was the continuing commitment to craft structures, to employment security rather than individual job rights, and to setting and regulating occupational standards.[51] Thus, occupational unionism dominated the daily life of the majority of culinary locals into the 1960s. Only then, as later chapters will document, did a changing legal, social, and political climate force the abandonment of their model.

PART IV

Controversies over Gender

Reflecting the realities of their lives as women who were often self-supporting and outside the traditional family unit, waitresses rejected arguments that assumed their economic or emotional reliance on a primary male wage earner. They fought tenaciously for their share of waiting jobs, they pushed for equal pay once they perceived it as no longer a threat to their basic livelihood, and they demanded the right to self-representation in the political life of their union. The idea of giving up their jobs to a male breadwinner or their political independence to a male protector were options they discarded. In other words, they resisted paternalism in the political governance of their union in much the same way as they fought against it in the work world.

Yet while waitress unionists defied the dominant mores concerning gender in some circumstances; in others, they clung to "traditional" interpretations. The following two chapters look at the controversies over "women's place" at work and in the union. Not only did men and women confront each other over such issues as equal pay, night work legislation, and the right of women to mix and serve liquor, but waitresses themselves often failed to reach agreement. Black waitresses in particular formulated and acted upon different notions of "gender equality" and "economic advancement" than did white waitresses. Chapter 7 dissects these quarrels and attempts to understand how men and women themselves constructed the gendered labor force of which they were a part. Chapter 8 documents the efforts of waitresses to gain political power within their union and explores both the reasons for their unusual propensity for union leadership as well as the circumstances surrounding their failure to achieve real political power within the International.

This final section extends and refines earlier themes as well. What affect did the specific form of unionism fashioned by waitresses have on their economic and political advancement? In what ways did their craft traditions and practices shape their choices? How did their sex separatism, that is, their organization into separate-sex locals, facilitate or inhibit the advancement of their gender and class interests?

CHAPTER SEVEN

"Women's Place" in the Industry

How come that the Bartenders and Waiters are looking after the morals of the waitresses? Who says I can't work after 9 at night and that I will be disgraced if I serve a glass of beer? [They're] trying to legislate someone out of a job. Why not try another method: organize the Waitresses and then go into a meeting and fight it out?

— Bee Tumber, waitress official, Los Angeles Local 639 and Santa Barbara Local 498, International vice-president HERE, June 1935 [1]

We who want equal opportunity, equal pay for equal work and equal status for women, know that frequently we obtain real equality through a difference in treatment rather than identity in treatment. . . . We are different and remember, different does not mean deficient. We do want our cake and eat it too.

— Myra Wolfgang, organizer and officer, Local 705, International vice-president HERE, 1971 [2]

In 1959, entering her third decade of leadership in the Los Angeles waitress local, Mae Stoneman wrote the International "in desperation," complaining that "over a long period of time" her members had "been handicapped, harassed, maligned, and abused by officers and employees of the waiters' union." Most recently, the waiters' local forbade busboys to assist waitresses with heavy trays, claiming that "it would place the waiters in an unfair position if waitresses [were] . . . permitted to replace them and receive the same pay for lighter duties." Two years earlier, waiters had set up a picket line at the Coconut Grove when managers assigned male and female servers similar duties in response to waitress demands for "full participation in all services to the guests" and an "[equal] share in any and all gratuities." The local Joint Culinary Board coaxed the waiters back to work, but they refused "to work in harmony" with their new equals, resorting to "pushing and tripping the waitresses." Despite Stoneman's plea, International president Ed Miller decided against intervention. Perhaps he had been persuaded by the advice of the local LJEB official who judged that "Matters of this kind, where a fair decision is difficult, are best left to employees on the job to work them out amicably." Yet that was just what the waiters and waitresses seemed incapable of doing.[3]

Acrimonious disputes between men and women food servers such as the one in Los Angeles were not isolated phenomena. Beneath the seemingly unchanging sexual hierarchy of labor in the hotel and restaurant industry, the distribution of work between locals, the gender-labeling of particular jobs, and the proper compensation for men and women were continually being contested. The policies waitresses advocated and the point at which they "drew the line" separating "men's" jobs from "women's" reveal their priorities as wage-earning women and how they attempted to reconcile their gender and class interests.

The Struggle for Equal Pay

The issue of equal pay received minimal attention among culinary unionists until World War I. As increasing numbers of women entered the industry, male unionists hoisted the banner of equal pay, hoping to prevent the loss of their jobs or the decline of their wages.[4] Male culinary workers "must be afflicted with astigmatism and shy on mental balance if they can not see women steadily taking the places of men sent to the front," scoffed the editor of *Mixer and Server*. "The slogan 'equal pay for equal work' should be heeded now . . . organize the women, insist on equal wages for equal work, and prevent industrial slavery," he proclaimed. Heeding his advice, delegates to the 1919 HERE convention adopted a nonbinding resolution calling for the organization of women and equal pay for "women doing the same work as men."[5] Although an important indicator of sentiment, the convention resolution failed to equalize wages or to reduce competitive tension between waiters and waitresses.[6] In frustration, San Francisco's Hugo Ernst presented a revised equal pay proposal to the General Executive Board (GEB) meeting of 1923, touching off a debate that erupted repeatedly for the next two decades.

Male culinary workers divided over the issue throughout the 1920s and 1930s. Proponents put forth a variety of rationales. Some argued that equal pay would check the tide of women workers into the industry; others assured the convention that women would not suffer job loss. A handful saw equal pay as not only just but also empowering for both sexes. With the passage of equal pay, "restaurant owners won't have the club always of threatening boys with girls."

Those opposed to equal pay often cited their concern for preserving the jobs of female servers. The GEB, for example, rejected Ernst's 1923 equal-pay proposal, concluding that it would mean dismissal for women. Unlike female servers, however, most men opposed to equal pay reasoned that women would lose their jobs because they were inferior employees. The board's recording secretary summarized the thinking of the GEB: employers "sensed an advantage" in hiring women because of the smaller wage scale and female "attractiveness," but faced with having to pay the sexes the same wage, employers would prefer men since they could "stand the daily grind better." Most male convention delegates agreed. "Girls can not render similar service as the men," one declared. Another noted that women were incapable of lifting heavy trays and of equaling men in the amount of work they performed. Only a few men valued the service of women equally with that of men and favored the principle of women being rewarded equitably for their work. Nevertheless, they opposed mandating equal wage scales because they feared the prejudices of employers and saw women at a competitive disadvantage.[7]

Female delegates, on the other hand, overwhelmingly opposed equal pay in these early debates.[8] They, too, believed women would lose their jobs and that employers, if required to pay men and women equally, would hire men. But the female delegates had different explanations for why substitution would occur. Instead of noting male superiority in skill and ability, they emphasized that women's coverage under protective legislation put them at a competitive disadvantage. To compensate, women needed to offer their services for less. Kitty Amsler voiced the sentiments of her nine-hundred-member St. Louis local at the 1927 HERE Convention. Equal pay "would put the Waitress Union out of business," Amsler argued, because her home state of Missouri had a law which restricted the hours women could work while permitting extra hours for men.[9] A second female delegate insisted that although the resolution was introduced "ostensibly to help women, . . . this does not fit" when waiters work ten hours and waitresses work eight. Other female unionists questioned whether women could compete successfully against men when they had childbearing and child-rearing responsibilities. One maintained that women were "just as good workers as the men, but can not always be on the job like the men. Their physical condition won't permit it." In the end, the delegates rejected equal pay in 1925 and 1927, but in 1929 passed a watered-down version urging "wherever possible, the achievement of the principle."[10]

Strong language favoring strict equal pay rates was not adopted by the convention until 1936, when a majority of women backed the resolution for the first time.[11] By the late 1930s, a different economic assessment was in order, and waitresses adjusted accordingly. Waitress leaders—once "so hesitant to take a stand for its recognition," according to Catering Industry Employee—now reversed their position on equal pay.[12] Their realistic concern that employers would prefer male workers over female workers (who were restricted to eight hours a day and covered by various other legal protections) faded as limitations on hours and other improvements in working conditions were extended to male workers via collective bargaining and amended protective legislation.[13]

Nevertheless, some rank-and-file waitresses remained convinced that equal pay could cost them their jobs. When the culinary negotiating team submitted an equal-pay proposal to the San Francisco Hotel Employers Association in 1936, a number of hotel waitresses objected. According to Margaret Werth, waitress representative on the Hotel Negotiating Committee, the protesters were "inspired with fear . . . that they would loose [sic] their jobs in the hotels and be supplanted by waiters." To allay their concerns, she recommended that the LJEB reaffirm "its former declaration . . . that we will not permit . . . any replacement by members of the opposite sex or different race—unless for good cause and that the LJEB shall be the judge of the cause in such matters." San Francisco employers rejected equal pay in the 1936 negotiations and prevailed, but they faced a local increasingly united and persistent in support of equal pay.[14]

During the 1940s, the majority of rank-and-file culinary workers, both male and female, embraced the equal-pay concept. The consensus among male culinary workers derived from many sources. Some saw the justice in the idea; others continued to hope that equal pay would dampen the ardor of employers for hiring women. Some simply relented in the face of the increased legitimacy of the concept on a societal level and the unity of women behind the idea.

The reasons given by waitresses indicate that their position was determined as much by a realistic appraisal of their own economic needs and opportunities as by a commitment to a particular ideological perspective. As waiting work sexualized and men gained protections and such benefits as rest breaks and controls over overtime, waitresses observed the reality of the service job market—employers increasingly preferred female service workers to male even when required to pay men and women the same. Indeed, some employers preferred women even where state law continued to provide benefits and protections to women only. The expanding service economy in the postwar decades undercut any remaining fears of job loss. Moreover, the experience of receiving equal pay during World War II (as a result of National War Labor Board rulings, new state laws, and contract provisions) made many waitresses loathe to return to inequality.[15]

Waitresses were prime candidates for conversion to the equal-pay principle once they deemed it economically feasible because they never fully embraced either the "family wage" concept or the idea of male superiority in skill. At few points in the extensive debates over equal pay did waitresses argue that male culinary workers deserved greater wages because of their family responsibilities.[16] In fact, they used their own family roles as primary breadwinners to support their position on equal pay—whether pro or con. Even when HERE women voted on the same side as male delegates, they rejected the assessment of their male colleagues who spoke of women's inferior capabilities and the unskilled nature of waitressing. In the 1960s, Gertrude Sweet defended equal pay not according to the liberal notion that workers should be judged as individuals, but because "women worked harder than men."[17]

Once convinced of the advantages of equal pay, waitresses pushed for it through bargaining and legislation. In part because of pressure from female members, local unions and LJEBs in many cities established identical hourly rates for waiters and waitresses. In California, every single culinary contract examined by the State Department of Industrial Relations had adopted the same wage scales for waiters and waitresses by the late 1950s.[18] Where equal pay was not a possibility, locals at least attempted to narrow the wage gap. Local 61 in Tacoma, for example, opened its equal-pay campaign by nego- tiating a 14 percent raise for waitresses and a 2.5 percent raise for waiters in 1941.[19]

In the postwar period, waitresses also joined with the Women's Bureau and other women's groups in lobbying for the passage of equal-pay laws on the federal and state level.[20] The Women's Equal Pay Act was introduced in 1945; it was reintroduced every succeeding year until a version passed in 1963 as the Federal Equal Pay Act. Breakthroughs on the state level occurred more quickly: only two states had enacted equal-pay laws before World War II. By the end of the decade close to half of all wage-earning women were covered by state legislation.[21]

Although the laws eventually enacted were referred to generically as "equal pay legislation," women active in the movement actually had a much broader concept in mind: they argued for fair "rates for the job irrespective of the sex of the worker." As Mary Anderson, the immigrant shoeworker who rose to be head of the Women's Bureau, explained in 1944, "equal pay for equal work is a catchy slogan," but its effect is limited to situations where women "take the place of men in the same work that men have been doing." The "rate for the job" idea, remarkably similar to the comparable worth argument of the 1980s, questioned the very basis by which most women's jobs were evaluated and assigned pay grades. The potential for upgrading women's pay relative to men was thus vastly improved; not only those jobs where women did exactly the same work as men, but also female-dominated job categories could theoretically be affected.[22]

The legislative campaigns for equal pay, however, fell short of the goals of their backers. Many equal-pay laws were watered down before passage and once on the statute books interpreted narrowly by the courts. Moreover, de- spite the best efforts of equal-pay advocates, often the laws protected only a small slice of the female labor force. Most waitresses in New York, for example, fell outside the scope of the law. The New York Department of Labor inter- preted the statute as allowing differentials in wages where men and women had "different duties," where men had more seniority and were "able to work nights," or where men and women "did the same thing almost exactly, [but] for a short time men did some heavy work such as packing ice."[23]

In the end, both legislative and collective bargaining action on behalf of equal pay failed to alter the secondary economic status of women workers. Not only were the legislative victories piecemeal and limited in scope, but advocates of equal pay also faced a labor force so segmented that limiting equal pay to those few situations when women and men worked at the same jobs proved to have a negligible effect. Even in such jobs as table service, where men and women did virtually identical work and where the union backed and secured equal-pay provisions, female workers found their economic ambitions stymied. The sexual division of labor in the industry—waiters predominated in dinner houses; waitresses in breakfast and lunch establishments—undercut equal-pay requirements.[24] Moreover, even though the *hourly* wage differential narrowed, men retained their advantage; a much larger proportion of waiting income derived from tips than from hourly wages, and men predominated where the tips were better—supper work in the costlier restaurants, night club work, and liquor service.[25]

Finally, once male food service workers could no longer command a higher hourly wage than their female counterparts, they became more firmly committed to preserving the sexual division of labor and monopolizing the higher-tipped brackets of the industry. As Ruth Milkman has pointed out, equal-pay demands certainly are compatible with sex segregation and in some cases may have "helped consolidate the general structure of gender inequality."[26] In the period from the 1930s to the 1970s, male food service workers turned increasingly to legislation prohibiting women from serving liquor or working at night and to contract clauses specifically negotiated to protect male employment in certain jobs and in certain "male" restaurants.[27]

Shall Waitresses Serve Liquor?

In the late nineteenth and early twentieth centuries, numerous ordinances forbade women either to serve liquor or to work in establishments where liquor was available. A turn-of-the-century law in Missouri, for instance, made it "a felony for a female to be employed in a dram shop, bar or concert hall, as barmaid, bartender or in any capacity where intoxicating beverages are sold or dispensed." A similar 1898 ordinance in Butte threatened to arrest and fine any woman who engaged "as a waitress . . . in a dance house, hurdy-gurdy house" or any place "in which beer, wine, or spirituous liquor is sold or drunk."[28]

Although it is unclear whether waitress opposition to such legislation was widespread before the 1930s, in California at least, waitresses argued successfully against restrictions on female liquor service in 1906 and again in 1911. According to Louise LaRue, secretary for Waitresses' Local 48, the local's opposition to the statewide legislation proposed in 1911 reflected their realization of the potential negative economic impact of the legislation. After a similar ordinance passed in Los Angeles, the women lost several good "female houses," LaRue noted. Indeed, the law had the potential to "injure girls all over the state and particularly in this city [San Francisco], as nearly all the restaurants serve liquor." LaRue concluded by pointing to the conflict of interest between men and women on this issue. "We have heard that Brother Wiseman urged the passage of the Los Angeles ordinance; of course we don't censure him for that, as he is working for [Waiters'] Local 17 and must get the best he can for them." [29]

In the early 1930s, when the repeal of Prohibition revived not only liquor service but also sentiment for legislation prohibiting women servers, waiters saw an opportunity to resuscitate the old web of restrictions surrounding women and liquor and preserve at least one high-paying stratum of the occupation for waiters. [30] Using both the legislative and internal union arenas, they submitted resolutions to exclude women from liquor service to LJEBs, HERE International conventions, and state and municipal politicians.

Waitresses objected vehemently to such proposals. They blocked convention resolutions that included blanket restrictions on liquor service by women, and their active lobbying halted similar bills in state legislatures. The Boston waitresses' local, for instance, reported in 1934 that the bill before the Massachusetts legislature banning women from liquor service in taverns "would have passed but for the efforts put forth by Sister [Eva] Rankin and a committee chosen by the organization. Our girls stormed the legislature; obtained a lot of publicity, and won." [31]

Waitresses drew on their belief in women's right to employment and on certain notions of gender equity to counter arguments against their serving liquor. Kitty Donnelly, who served Waitresses' Local 107 of Cleveland for close to thirty years as business agent and who had been widowed at an early age with three sons to support, expanded the family wage concept to include women. Donnelly wondered whether the "brothers" supporting such restrictive proposals "realize [that] there are a lot of self-supporting women who head families?" Equally strong outrage was directed at the seeming paternalism of these resolutions. "How come . . . the Bartenders and Waiters are looking after the morals of the Waitresses? Who says I will be disgraced if I serve a glass of beer?" Southern California organizer Bee Tumber queried. Such legislation "would throw 5,000 waitresses out of work," veteran officer Kitty Amster of Missouri argued. "Women are equal to men, [and] such distinctions shouldn't be made between the sexes." [32]

Waitresses also stressed their rights as unionists and their jurisdictional claim to any work that fell within the purview of the waiting craft. Drawing attention to the impact of such legislation on their union, the members of Chicago Local 484 proclaimed that "such legislation would eliminate the waitresses as a majority of eating places have retail licenses to sell liquor." San

Francisco waitresses held that any resolution that banned women from liquor service or that "used the words served or serving" was discriminating against "bona fide waitresses."[33]

By 1936 waitress unionists had persuaded their union brothers to drop such blanket prohibitions, but they opened the way for the success of prohibitions on female bartenders by conceding the legitimacy of male claims to "ownership" of certain kinds of work. The allegiance of white waitresses to their craft heritage and to deeply held notions of gender separatism prompted Kitty Donnelly, like many other waitress unionists, to narrow her protest to the restrictions on women *serving* liquor, not *mixing* liquor.

Moreover, a long-standing concern over preserving the respectability of waitressing and a reluctance to invade male-defined terrain led many waitresses to specify the kinds of establishments in which it would be acceptable for women to serve liquor. Generally, those establishments that served *only* liquor were seen as the domain of men. There, male culture reigned and women not only were interlopers but also without protection or power. Donnelly, for example, hoped that "the girls will get work in serving it [liquor] on a 50-50 basis with the boys," but she added that she drew "a line to beer being served by girls in beer halls unless there is food served with it." She even allowed that cocktail waitresses should be banned unless they also were serving food.[34]

Local 48 waitresses "drew the line" at exactly the same spot as Donnelly. They voted in 1942 to "take no application from any girl who works in a tavern" or in any establishment that did not serve food and to instruct the secretary "to write to Lt. Governor De Witt protesting the employment of women in bars." The waitresses' local also supported the LJEB policy discouraging "employment of women in cocktail lounges and bars." Facing a flurry of protest letters from waitress locals in Chicago, Buffalo, Seattle, and Santa Barbara, Chicago Bartenders' Local 376 amended its resolution "prohibiting the employment of women in premises licensed for retail sales of liquor" to "except establishments where the serving of food is the principal part of business." The complaining letters ceased.[35]

Black waitresses in Chicago, however, fought to preserve liquor service and to have their work as cocktail waitresses accepted as legitimate. In 1934, Chicago's all-male "colored" waiters' Local 444 applied to the International for reinstatement.[36] Concerned with rebuilding their organization and aware of the large number of taverns on Chicago's South Side, the waiters' local seized upon the recent introduction of alcohol as the propitious moment to assert an exclusive claim to cocktail work. Rather than appeal to the black women workers in the taverns to join the union, Local 444, under the leadership of Livert "St. Louis" Kelly, picketed the bars and threatened the owners with violence if women were not replaced with men from Local 444. As a result, some two to three hundred black cocktail waitresses lost their jobs.[37]

In reaction, black cocktail waitresses organized and requested that the International charter a separate local. Having a union, they hoped, would help them "recover their jobs" and prevent interference "on the part of pickets and union leaders . . . with their efforts to earn a livelihood as waitresses." When Kelly accused them of immorality and demanded they be "sent back home and to school," the waitresses proudly claimed that they were not schoolgirls, but mature women who supported themselves and their husbands and children. Moreover, there was "nothing indecent" or dangerous about the work; it was "better than industry in many ways." As for the alleged danger in serving drunken men, they argued that men were more of a threat "in the streets [and] in public hallways than in taverns."[38]

When both George McLane, a pivotal Chicago culinary official,[39] and the International refused their charter request—in part because of protests from Local 444—the women hired a Chicago attorney, Georgia Jones Ellis, and sought the backing of the Women's Bureau. Obtaining a letter of introduction from the black congressman Oscar De Priest, Ellis traveled to Washington and met with Women's Bureau chief Mary Anderson to plead her case. Anderson dispatched Ethel Erickson, a Women's Bureau field agent, to Chicago with instructions to "get the facts" regarding the "displacement of the colored waitresses," and she wrote to John Fitzpatrick, president of the Chicago Federation of Labor, asking his cooperation. In her letter to Fitzpatrick, Anderson stressed the gravity of the situation: "As there are about 300 women employed, the loss of the jobs is a very serious question, not only to the individual women, but to them as a group."[40]

Erickson's report from Chicago revealed a dismal situation. On the basis of interviews with tavern owners, waitresses, union officials, newspaper reporters, attorneys, and the Chicago Urban League, Erickson accused the black waiters' local of requiring kickbacks from the men it dispatched and of planning to put the newly unemployed waitresses "on the street to hustle," thus setting up in one stroke two illegal sources of revenue. The justifications put forward by the male union officials regarding the need to protect the morals of the women obviously were disingenuous, she contended. "If this were an actual issue," why wasn't the union "as considerate in protecting the morals of the white women . . . serving as waitresses in taverns in other sections of the city?" Removing the black women from their cocktail jobs made them more vulnerable, it appeared, especially because these taverns were not yet operating as brothels. Equally important, none of the women complained of "any special problem of morality"; and, because most were older, married women with dependents, in Erickson's view they were quite capable of protecting their own morals.[41]

The situation was finally "resolved" when the International, under pressure from the Women's Bureau and tavern owners who continued to resist hiring male waiters, decided "that these colored waitresses [will] be invited to join our present colored local in Chicago, Local 444." After Fitzpatrick advised them that "the door of the union had been closed against them and now it was opened and they should go in and secure membership and the future would take care of itself," the black waitresses accepted. "I regard this as a very happy ending to a nasty situation," Fitzgerald wrote Erickson. "If they put 50 or 60 women into that union, I imagine they will have the balance of power, that is, if I know women." Attempting to close on a jocular note, Fitzpatrick inadvertently touched the core of a potentially serious problem for the black waitresses: the power imbalance within the local union.[42]

Once inside the local, the women continued to push for the expansion of their job rights and their power with respect to their male union brothers. It appears that black women held their own under extremely inhospitable circumstances. By 1935, Local 444 had at least one female business agent, Kathleen Slate, who, with the backing of women within the local, successfully organized a considerable number of cocktail waitresses.[43]

By the late 1930s, the dispute over whether women should serve liquor receded into the background. Tension over the distribution of jobs between men and women and the sex-labeling of specific job categories, however, continued to plague the industry. With the rise of union power in the 1930s and 1940s, the collective bargaining arena became increasingly important in determining the sexual division of labor. Waiter locals interpreted existing contract language to favor the retention of jobs by men and negotiated new language requiring employers to hire or retain male workers. Waitresses pushed for quite different agreements with employers and brought their own distinct interpretations to bear on union texts.

Slowing Feminization through Collective Bargaining

In New York, San Francisco, and other key urban areas where the balance of power lay with the men, waiter locals succeeded in slowing—but not halting—the feminization of the industry. New York City's Local 302 obtained a clear-cut promise from employers in their 1934 contract that the number of female counter personnel would be kept to less than one-third. Later, employers demanded "the right to replace men by women" and even considered enduring a strike for this prerogative, but the clause remained.[44] Waiters and Waitresses' Local 1 in New York City negotiated a similar clause in the 1930s, freezing the sex ratio of crews during the life of the contract. They retained the clause into the 1950s.[45] Of course, these clauses protected women as well as men—and at times women used them to prevent job loss[46]—but overall, contract language slowed the entry of women into food service work.

In San Francisco, the LJEB exerted a critical influence on the sexual composition of the industry; from the 1930s through the early 1960s, no San

Francisco employer could "replace waiters by waitresses or vice versa, without having the consent of both unions involved, or the approval of the LJEB." Initially, in the 1930s, the LJEB sought to strike a balance between preserving the status quo and accommodating employer requests for change. Generally, they held employers to past practice but allowed deviations where "extenuating circumstances warranted" and contract language was not violated.[47]

In the forties, as requests for waitresses flooded the LJEB, new policies were developed—ones which explicitly favored waiters. During the war, the LJEB permitted the replacement of men because of the extreme shortage of male labor, but at the war's close, they amended the written policy governing substitution to allow employers to rehire men regardless of female seniority. They also consistently denied employer requests for female help, even in cases involving newly opened restaurants.[48] The waitress representatives on the LJEB (along with the female delegates from the local representing hotel maids) voted against these decisions, but to no avail.[49] By 1948, despite the continuing employer preference for females, the waiters had gained almost two thousand members *above* its prewar record, while the waitresses declined in membership. Jackie Walsh, president of the waitresses' union, wrote International president Hugo Ernst in 1949, requesting a shorter work week for officials and staff of Local 48 to prevent lay-offs. The local's problems, she noted, were due to "a general decline in business and the fact that the Waiters' Union has been taking back the jobs that were given to us during the war." Ten years later, female restaurant workers outnumbered men in every county in California except San Francisco; there, due to union power, market forces had not had free rein.[50]

In the few communities in which waitresses dominated the industry, the situation was quite different; employers faced few if any impediments to feminization. Butte Waiters' Local 22 threatened repeatedly "to fight [Waitresses'] Local 457 to a finish" over retaining certain houses, but despite their offer to work for less pay and their complaints to the International about past jurisdictional claims, they lost every battle. The Women's Protective League (WPU) in Butte, which took in janitresses, maids, candy-store employees, and women factory workers who handled food,[51] enjoyed a decisive numerical advantage over the waiters' local as well as over the larger culinary work force of cooks, bartenders, and busboys. With the unabashed support of the WPU, Butte employers ignored the objections of the waiters and replaced men with women. According to the waitresses of Local 457, the traditions of union solidarity necessitated only one slight concession; they decided that if the waiters walked out in a body, then waitresses would not replace them. But after "the employers had a signed contract and decided to lay them off gradually, a waitress could take their place without violating any union rule."[52]

Lifting the Hours Curfew on Waitresses

From the late 1920s to the 1960s, waiter and waitress locals also were embroiled in bitter disputes over the issue of night work restrictions for women. Night work restrictions typically forbade work between the hours of midnight and 6 A.M., but a few statutes banned work between 10 P.M. and 7 A.M. Neither waiters nor waitresses were active in the early Progressive Era campaigns which secured passage of such restrictions,[53] but they were prominent in the second round of battles that began in the late 1920s. In New York, for instance, the National Woman's party bill, which proposed that waitresses be exempted from state laws restricting night work, met resistance from Waiters' Local 171 and the State Federation of Labor as well as from such traditional opponents as the National Consumers' League and the Women's Trade Union League. Emanuel Koveleski, secretary of Local 171, told "the boys that they had better watch out . . . if the [current] law is repealed look out for your banquet work."[54]

The majority of waitresses who spoke publicly in these initial forays sided with their union brothers. In the 1920s and again in the 1930s, waitresses from New York City, Buffalo, Syracuse, and even Kansas City joined with other trade unionists in testifying on behalf of retaining New York's night work prohibitions. Some spoke against night work because there would be "no one to care for the children at night" but most spoke against repeal of the restrictions, one spokeswoman explained, "to help our Brother Locals, for we do know that if the bill had been passed a great many of the men would be out of work now."[55]

Waitress spokeswomen who opposed restrictions on night work before the 1940s often adapted the "family wage" argument to support women's claims to better jobs and higher wages. One waitress leader declared: "A great many of our women are working to support themselves and their children, the same as the men, and are certainly entitled to do so." A second insisted that many women worked at night because they had "a family to support where there is no husband to depend on. I do think they should be consulted as to their wishes in the matter."[56]

Some also stressed their own desire for increased earnings and opportunity. The *New York Times* reported that some waitresses testified on behalf of repeal in 1930 because "they could make more money in night work and wanted to be able to take advantage of this opportunity."[57] A few defended a woman's right to independence as well as a living wage. "We do not wish to be dictated where we should work or what hours of the day we should work," one activist proclaimed. Another defiantly questioned the authority of the men who were so eager to protect women. "Who says I can't work after 9 at night?" she asked. Their notions of gender equity included individual autonomy and personal freedom for women wage earners equal to those of men.[58]

By the 1940s, the majority of waitresses unequivocally opposed restrictions on night work. A variety of factors prompted this shift. As a result of the growth of women in cocktail service during the 1930s and the widespread use of women in waiting jobs traditionally held by men during World War II,[59] a large number of waitresses now actually worked at night. Thus, the economic issues involved were now more pressing; the retention of union jobs for women was at stake as well as the distribution of future work. Moreover, the prominence of male culinary workers in the postwar campaigns clarified the basic adversarial relation between the sexes on this issue and undercut the loyalty of waitresses to their brother unionists.[60]

In the postwar campaigns, waiters and waitresses fought bitterly for what each perceived as their own self-interest, their rhetoric revealing the clear economic and gendered nature of their concerns. Male culinary officials frequently relied on the family wage concept, narrowing it to apply to men only. "Night work for women would take away jobs from men, particularly during the period of highest earnings which rightfully should be reserved for men who support families," one wrote. Underneath the plea for higher wages lay a concern for maintaining traditional gender relations. "A man begins to lose faith in himself" when he becomes "dependent upon his wife as a wage-earner," reasoned one Cleveland unionist. "When this happens the woman will become domineering and independent."[61]

Night work would also protect the "weaker sex" and preserve the ever-vulnerable female moral character. Extensive night work was detrimental to the health and well-being of future mothers, and it subjected them to dangerous nighttime travel. Male culinary workers warned of moral decay when "glamour replace[s] craftsmanship as illustrated in one leading Manhattan hotel where their waitresses are garbed in transparent skirts and in another Manhattan hotel where the [low-cut] Faye Emerson neckline is the fad."[62] In briefs submitted to the state legislature in 1950, the New York State Culinary Alliance, a state federation of culinary locals, claimed that the moral reasons to prohibit night work were "as valid today as they were 25 years ago." Drawing on the 1908 Brandeis brief submitted in defense of an Oregon statute limiting the daily hours of female laundry workers to ten a day, the HERE wrapped up its case as if forty-two years had changed nothing. "Medically, physically, socially, and morally there is a difference between men and women, and the difference is one that the State has the right and indeed the duty to recognize and protect."[63]

The position of the State Culinary Alliance clashed with the postwar views of most waitresses. Where previously the majority had agreed with their male colleagues, they now argued for the retention of the jobs they currently held as well as the right to a portion of the new jobs appearing daily. They fought for their own economic interests as they defined those interests. At the 1945 Culinary Alliance meeting, "there was practically an open fight on the floor," according to Gertrude Lane, secretary of Local 6. The waitresses "became very voluble," pointing out that night work restrictions would keep them from working the supper jobs, typically the best-paid waiting work. New York City waitresses agitated "to work Broadway 'hot spots' at night because there [were] . . . greater tips there and greater opportunities." In upstate New York, according to waitress organizer Helen Blanchard, waitresses wanted "particularly to work . . . where the tips are higher," and to have their share of lucrative banquet and night club work.[64] A sympathetic culinary business agent, Charles Darling, interviewed by the Women's Bureau that same year, revealed that the attitudes of waitresses in Connecticut differed little from those in New York.[65]

Waitress locals in Buffalo and Rochester—two separate-sex locals that broke with the State Culinary Alliance position and lobbied for repeal—voiced their economic concerns first but also attempted to refute the gender-based objections raised by their opponents. They agreed in 1949 on a variety of propositions: night work restrictions kept women out of the most lucrative work (dinner shifts and cocktail service); night work had no ill effect on women's health or morals; night work prohibitions did not keep women from being molested; and women should be able to choose the hours of work best suited to their particular needs.[66] Thus, they rejected the notion of women's fragile health and moral character and questioned the logic of protecting women from male aggression by keeping them home at night. They asserted the right of women themselves to determine when they worked and how best to meet the demands of work and family,[67] repudiating the concept of a paternalistic state that adjusted the workplace to ensure that women would not shirk their family duties.

Waitresses and waiters in the postwar period appear to have perceived the economic consequences of night work legislation correctly.[68] Waitress locals such as Rochester's Local 227 reported declining membership in the late 1940s as a direct result of revived night work legislation. Women's Bureau investigators ran across concerned HERE officials who explained that "the men, particularly the waiters, don't like what has happened now that the women's night work law has been abolished" and "men are losing their jobs." In New York, an official state study surmised that since "one-half of all restaurants stay open past 12, it is estimated that 7,500 to 8,000 women might be employed in restaurants if the law were repealed." These economic considerations, in addition to the fact that working-class women themselves preferred to make their own decisions in the matter, lend validity to the opinion of contemporary scholars that the disadvantages of night work prohibition (more than almost any other protective statute) outweighed its advantages.[69]

Unfortunately, waitresses who advocated repeal never acquired full support from their historic allies, the WTUL and the Women's Bureau. Both organizations reviewed their stance toward night work in the years after World War II, but by 1948 they reaffirmed their allegiance to protective legislation, including night work prohibitions.[70] Without the backing of these key organizations, the movement for repeal was only partially successful. No new states adopted night work legislation after the war and by 1949, eight states had relaxed their regulations, continued their wartime suspension of the laws, or, as in the case of Pennsylvania, repealed their restrictive night work statutes altogether. But in a handful of states, legislation specifically regulating night work for adult women in restaurants remained on the books until the 1960s.[71]

Thus, as in the disputes over equal pay, women serving liquor, and job distribution, in some circumstances waitresses defied both the dominant gender ideology and the "class" arguments put forward by their union brothers to push for what they perceived as the interests of their craft. In the case of night work, economic necessity and a changing assessment of economic opportunity prompted their challenge. Indeed, protest against night work prohibitions swelled over the course of the twentieth century as increasing numbers of waitresses—swept into such nontraditional areas as dinner and banquet work, evening cocktail service, and late-night café jobs by the unrelenting demands for female service labor—realized that their own night-time jobs were at risk. Moreover, the promise that night work would open up "opportunities" for waitresses gained legitimacy as the hiring practices of employers indicated that in fact jobs for women in night work positions actually existed.

And, as with other disputes, the economic motivations of waitresses were buttressed by cultural resources peculiar to their situation as wage-earning women. They drew on such working-class concepts such as the "family wage" and "craft interest," but they reinterpreted these ideas to their advantage. Thus, they contended that single and divorced women deserved a family wage just like male heads of households. And because most night jobs could be encompassed within the generally accepted parameters of the waitress craft, the jurisdictional traditions of their various locals in conjunction with their craft heritage as waitresses helped legitimize their claims. Yet, as the controversy over female bartenders will reveal, the craft mentality left waitresses an ambiguous legacy; it encouraged them to claim certain jobs as their own—those that fell within the purview of the waitress craft—but undercut their ability and desire to question their exclusion from other kinds of work.

The Closed Priesthood: Barmaids and Mixologists

Like the waiters, bartenders evolved a shifting set of strategies for deterring female aspirants to their craft. Before the 1930s, bartender locals were relatively untroubled by female competition; societal mores backed by legislative and contract exclusion of women effectively kept women from the craft.[72] Following the repeal of Prohibition, however, the possibility of women encroaching on the newly reestablished craft aroused widespread fear among male bartenders. Bartender locals revived their constitutional curbs on female membership, and in New York, Illinois, Massachusetts, Rhode Island, California, and elsewhere they pursued local and statewide ordinances excluding females from their craft. Where legislation failed, they instituted economic action, setting up picket lines and initiating boycotts against bars that hired women. Local 41 of San Francisco distributed pocket-sized boycott cards in the late 1930s with this message: "Union Men! Do not patronize taverns that have WOMEN behind the bar. These places are all UNFAIR to organized labor. Demand the Union Button from the bartender that serves you."[73]

These tactics sufficed until World War II when the increasing number of "barmaids,"[74] provoked bartenders to experiment with limited organizing campaigns among women coupled with demands for equal pay. Faced with the shortage of male labor, the International "bowed to the inevitable" and recommended that locals dispatch women as bartenders and sommeliers.[75] Strong contract clauses, however, guaranteed that "female work will be only temporary and that women can be replaced by men during and after the war." And, at the war's end, bartender locals ensured that women lost their jobs en masse. They threatened to picket and boycott recalcitrant employers who kept on barmaids, pushed for the restoration of the prohibitive laws that had lapsed during the war-time crisis, and introduced new legislation.[76]

Buoyed by the 1948 U.S. Supreme Court decision upholding the Michigan law that forbade women to work as bartenders, the legislative crusade reached its height in the late 1940s and early 1950s.[77] The International issued a pamphlet featuring successful local campaigns to date—some seventeen states prohibited barmaids by 1948—and encouraged similar drives in other states. Five years later, the International's officers proudly reported new state laws and local ordinances in places "such as Ohio (1949), Oregon (1952), Washington (1952), Michigan (1950) and Illinois (1951) to cite a few." By the 1960s, twenty-six states prohibited women from working in mining, bartending, or other occupations.[78]

The motivations of bartenders were clearly economic, but deep-seated beliefs about gender lent additional force to the economic. "The dispensing of Alcoholic Beverages [should] be restricted to men only, to enable our members to get back to work," Bartenders' Local 503 explained. Bartenders contended that barmaids lowered the standards of the craft by working for less, were incapable of being "proficient mixologists," and were not "emotionally or temperamentally suited for the job." They maintained that women could not handle unruly customers without male support; that female "moral and physical well-being" was endangered by exposure to alcohol;[79] and that a woman behind the bar would give critical ammunition to the prohibitionists' efforts to create "dry" districts. One union official went so far as to argue that "a bartender must be a good conversationalist or know when or when not to talk, and you show me the woman who knows that."[80]

The push for restrictive legislation also drew on an emotional commitment to preserving what one Michigan official described in 1942 as "the sacred professional realms of the male." Bartending "should remain a cloister for men," the International GEB intoned.[81] For generations, bartenders had prided themselves on being the priestly overseers of exclusively male drinking "societies" that were entrenched in particular taverns and bars. The tavern "functioned as the poor man's counterpart to the private social club." These establishments, "bastions of male fellowship and independence," had been and were to remain a public space reserved solely for the expression of male culture—a space "unrestrained by feminine social conventions" where men did not "have to work at being gentlemen." At times, a woman might enter if escorted by a man or if in a subordinate, thoroughly feminized role, such as that of the female stripper or bargirl who solicited drinks with the implicit assumption of sexual favors to follow. A woman behind the bar, however, undercut the strict segregation between the sexes and challenged the traditional hierarchical gender relations that reigned in tavern society.[82]

The aversion of male bartenders to opening their ranks to women was shared by the American public. "The tavern hostess or barmaid . . . is a disgrace," one Chicago columnist wrote, "one step away from the lowest form of livelihood. It's a very sordid situation." The American public had long condemned women who handled liquor and publicly mingled with men, and now they deemed women eminently corruptible by liquor and incapable of exerting the authority over customers required of the bartender.[83]

Although waitresses had balked at legislation restricting them from serving liquor, they raised few objections to legislation banning women bartenders, despite the numbers of female servers who had moved into bartending during the wartime shortage.[84] When Flore announced in 1941 that "we are secure in the conviction that service at public or private bars is exclusively the employment of male employees" and that "this thought has been generously concurred in by the female members of our International Union," he apparently spoke the truth. Portland waitresses refused to dispatch women as bartenders because "this is not proper employment for women," and they joined with bartenders in picketing a place where two women dispensed beer. The members of the Los Angeles local, according to their business manager Mae Stoneman, had "strict instructions not to pour, open, [or] mix [liquor], or even pick up a piece of garnish on penalty of a stiff fine, suspension, or even expulsion."[85]

Reports from Ohio, where waitresses lobbied on behalf of a law "forbidding the employment of women, except owners and or owners' wives, as bartenders," reveal some of the explanations voiced by those waitresses who publicly favored the legislation. According to *Catering Industry Employee*, waitresses testified that "tending bar is a man's job, and that handling kegs, beer cases, packing coolers and similar work . . . [was] unsuited to women." The union brief claimed that waitresses favored restrictive legislation because a woman serving liquor "can turn away from an unruly or uncivil customer and refuse to approach his table while the girl tending bar must remain near at hand"; and because many "felt more secure working where a male bartender was on duty" and preferred having "a man to back up" their decisions. The brief also noted that waitresses supported the crusade because plenty of jobs existed for them as waitresses.[86]

Kitty Amsler, a St. Louis waitress official since 1917, along with a few other waitresses, raised the only feeble exceptions to the arguments advanced by the bartenders. In a letter to the International, Amsler first took pains to voice her "complete accord with the opinion that women have no place behind the bar." Only then, did she question certain aspects of their logic: "If women bartenders are grist for the Dry Mill why aren't the wives and daughters of the licensee who appear to be excepted by most of the state laws you exhibit?" Amsler's mild letter provoked a terse and irritated reply from Hugo Ernst. Ernst reprimanded her for "passing judgment" and in a veiled threat commented that he didn't like to see women *in front* of the bar either.[87]

The decision of waitresses to claim the serving of liquor as their own while allowing the mixing to be done by men is best understood within the context of competing economic and ideological (class and gender) considerations. As the Ohio waitresses noted, the retention of jobs was not so pressing an issue in the postwar years as it had been in the 1930s. Indeed, white waitresses were enjoying a surplus of jobs in the 1940s and 1950s. Those few who had moved into bartending during the war found it easy to transfer back into waitressing.

Moreover, the restrictive policies advocated by bartender locals were legitimized by strongly held societal proscriptions against women invading the sacred male space of the bar—proscriptions that many waitresses accepted.[88] When pressed to explain why barmaids for so long were not accepted in the union, Gertrude Sweet finally pointed to certain gender concerns. "Men . . . women as well . . . simply felt that it was not the place for a woman to work in a bar." The self-defined feminist leader Florence Farr of Detroit's Local 705 revealed the deep-seated, almost unconscious nature of these gendered assumptions when she confided in an 1989 interview that it "simply never dawned on me to demand to go behind a bar."[89]

Finally, for many waitresses, to be a bartender was not only unladylike, but also unwaitresslike. In disputes with the waiters, the proud craft traditions of waitresses fueled their protests. Waiters were attempting to claim aspects of waiting work that to a skilled waitress properly fell within the boundaries of her craft. With the bartenders, the opposite was true: the craft heritage shared by food service workers lent credence to the bartenders' claim that the work "belonged" to them. As San Francisco's veteran waitress leader Jackie Walsh explained some years later in regard to the admission of bargirls: "There wasn't anything really wrong with having them in except that they weren't bonafide waitresses nor did they do waitress work. . . . In other words they were not qualified craftsmen."[90]

Significantly, the single organized protest came from black women bartenders in Chicago. In 1951, when the Chicago city council adopted an ordinance forbidding women "to dispense alcoholic beverages," three hundred barmaids belonging to the all-black Waitresses, Bartenders, and Cooks' Local 444 refused "to pay dues until the matter [was] cleared up." The officers of Local 444 contemplated replacing the female bartenders with men but in the end decided they were "not in a position to force the issue." Women continued to be dispatched from the hiring hall, and the local even included women in their bartender training program, hiring Lilli Belle Curry, a former Local 444 officer, and two other black women as instructors.[91]

In 1961, however, the old city ordinance was finally enforced, and some four hundred black female bartenders lost their jobs. With few equally lucrative options open to them, they were outraged at this discrimination. Because their local refused to help—despite having collected dues from them for years—the barmaids organized community support. They picketed City Hall and demanded repeal of the ordinance. Basing their claim on their rights as individuals, as mothers, and as family providers, they advertised their economic plight through placards reading "City Fathers Unfair to Working Mothers," "Help Us Keep Our Children Educated," and "The Right to Work Is the Right to Live."[92] Black community newspapers carried their story, stressing the lack of concern shown by the city council and the union as to whether "these Negro women, many of them mothers" were employed or were to be "thrown on ADC's Relief Rolls. Unlike white girls," the *New Crusader* continued, "these women . . . have little or no recourse except to apply for relief." Those who have been able to find jobs are largely working as baby sitters, housemaids, 'day workers,' part-time waitresses . . . and mail order house employees."[93]

In desperation, the women wrote the International for assistance, stating that their local officers "told us there is nothing they can do" and pointing out that "many of us have families to raise and are not experienced in any other field." Ed Miller's curt reply offered little consolation and in fact was rather disingenuous in view of the active support of the International for state and local barmaid ordinances. "Please be advised that the International Union had nothing to do with the law in Chicago, Illinois, and the matter is entirely up to the local union in Chicago." Without the backing of either their International or local union, many black barmaids permanently lost their "career union jobs"—as the *New Crusader* dubbed them—even though eventually the ordinance was overturned.[94]

These protests by black women erupted precisely because of their more extreme economic situation and their distinct cultural inheritance as black women and black trade unionists. Because of the discrimination against black women in the food service industry, their economic alternatives were more limited than those of white women. In addition, because their daily experience largely conflicted with the reigning ideology of "separate spheres," black women were less encumbered with the desire to conform to these gender prescriptions, especially when "moral protection" conflicted with economic need. Finally, because of the history of discrimination against them from their International and at times even from their co-workers, black waitresses did not fully embrace the white craft traditions so firmly revered by their white union brothers and sisters. They had never been thoroughly accepted as either "ladies" or "sisters in the craft." Thus, unlike white waitresses, black women boldly proclaimed their right to serve liquor in taverns even where no food was available as well as their right to mix drinks.

The bartender campaign ultimately was a losing one, but the policies advocated by male unionists and tolerated by their union sisters did slow the feminization of bartending considerably. Less than 3 percent of bartenders were female in 1940 and twenty years later women still comprised less than 11 percent of the craft, despite the continued demand by employers for female barmaids.[95] In the 1960s, female bartenders became more common as the percentage of unionized bars declined and societal prohibitions on female mixers lessened with the proliferation of "family-style" bars attached to restaurants.[96] It was not until the 1970s, however, when lawsuits charging sex discrimination under Title VII overturned the legislative and contract restrictions on women, that the female tide surged forward. The *San Francisco Chronicle* announced the overturning of the state's 1935 law forbidding female bartenders in May 1971, and the "city's first female bartender and member of Bartender's Local 41," Jacklyne Warren, began mixing drinks in June 1971.[97] Bartending feminized more rapidly in the next two decades than virtually any other occupation; by the end of the 1980s, a majority of bartenders were women.[98] After close to a century of resistance, the union opened its doors to women mixologists.

The policies pursued by male and female culinary workers not only determined the gender boundaries within the industry but also critically affected the rate of feminization of certain categories of work. The contract clauses and protective legislation put forward by male culinary unionists retarded the movement of women into food service jobs and restricted them to the least lucrative waiting jobs. Nevertheless, waiters were never as successful as bartenders in implementing restrictive measures. The reasons are manifold. First, women entered waitressing earlier, that is, before unionization, and in greater numbers. Second, although their entry was slowed by moral judgments from the public at large, the public never felt strongly enough against waitresses *serving* liquor to countenance widespread restrictive legislation. In contrast, female bartenders were rare until World War II, and societal proscriptions against barmaids were deeply felt.

Third, as members of a classic male preserve, bartenders supported exclusionary policies almost unanimously. Male waiters, on the other hand, were divided in their response to female co-workers. Instead of excluding women from the union entirely, from the earliest days, a sizable number had argued for their organization, had admitted them into their locals, and, in fact, had even recognized them as sister craftswomen. Thus, waiters who advocated restrictive policies never had the complete and enthusiastic backing from their fellow craftsmen which the bartenders enjoyed. Moreover, waiter officials of mixed-sex locals faced opposition from women members within their own union. The vast majority of bartender officials were free of such political and organizational hindrances.

Of course, where and when unionized waitresses "drew the line" between men and women's jobs also played a critical role in determining the *patterns* of sex segregation in the industry. The elite position of men within the industry was sustained in part by the reluctance of unionized waitresses to challenge men's claim to own the coveted work of pouring drinks and the prestigious, lucrative waiting work in formal dinner restaurants. Yet when external forces such as Prohibition, World War II, and the unremitting demand for female service work over the course of the twentieth century opened up *new* categories of waiting work, waitresses ensured the institutionalization of these changes. Organized into craft-based, sex-segregated locals, they effectively *defended* against attempts to deprive them of liquor service and night work. They permanently extended the boundaries of the territory labeled as "female" and facilitated the feminization of their craft.

The policies pursued by waitresses reveal the complexity of working-class female consciousness. The process by which waitresses formulated their stance on these issues was not simple or straightforward; they delicately juggled economic, gender, and class considerations. Their desire for higher wages and increased employment options had to be balanced against their desire for economic security for themselves and their families. They also weighed the economic advantages of moving into male-dominated jobs against the loss of female community, societal approval, and the sometime pleasure of the "emotional labor" associated with women's jobs.[99]

Equally important, waitresses operated within the parameters of their craft union traditions and structure. These class loyalties shaped their positions on gender issues just as did their family status and the economic and social realities of the workplace. As active women unionists, they partook of a class culture which included elements of the craft traditions of the AFL and a communitarian "moral economy" perspective.[100] Collective advancement of their craft and the preservation of their union organizations were of utmost importance.

Their shifting definitions of gender equality affected their ultimate position. At times, these considerations reinforced each other, as with the issue of liquor service and ultimately with night work: their defense of their historic craft jurisdiction, their desire for economic advance, and their repudiation of the particular conceptions of gender advocated by their male counterparts all combined to lead them into sharp conflict with their union brothers. At other points, such as during the bartender campaigns, the concerns of waitresses competed, forcing them to pursue one allegiance at the expense of another. Their desire for economic opportunity and gender equality was circumscribed by their loyalty to craft traditions and their notion of gender separatism.

Viewed from within this context, the decisions of waitresses emerge as realistic, suited to advancing their needs as they perceived those needs. Although waiting work transformed into a female-dominated occupation over the course of the twentieth century, waitresses rightly perceived themselves in competition with men, although this competition was tempered by the preference of most restaurants for either an all-male or an all-female waiting staff. Thus, their rejection of equal pay was premised not on a view of women's work as inferior or less skilled but on an assessment of their market position. Likewise, their position on night work was based as much on a judgment about the economic impact of the legislation on their own particular craft or occupation as a commitment to a more traditional view of women's capacities or a belief in the appropriateness of restricting women's participation in the labor force to accommodate family needs. As more waitresses worked in lucrative evening jobs and others felt more optimistic about the real possibility of being hired into such jobs, the economic reasons for repealing the legislation became more compelling for waitresses. Thus, by the 1940s, waitresses perceived night work laws as taking away tangible economic benefits without offering anything in return.[101]

Ironically, although waitress unionists were in the forefront of equal pay campaigns and had fought tenaciously for their share of wait work in the industry, by the mid-1960s, they were out of step with the majority of feminists, and at times with the needs of the majority of unorganized waitresses. As later chapters will show, the craft traditions and notions of gender that initially had sustained waitress leaders in their battles with their male co-workers by the 1960s brought them into conflict with middle-class feminists and with a new generation of wage-earning women—women with decidedly different ideas about unions and different strategies for achieving equality between men and women.

CHAPTER EIGHT

"Women's Place" in
the Union

Born in Youngstown . . . and widowed more than thirty years ago, Kitty Donnelly came to Cleveland with her three sons . . . and got a job as a waitress. Donnelly was a dominant personality. Determined and outspoken, she was probably as widely known here as anyone in the labor movement. Her courage was widely acknowledged. Typically Irish, Mrs. Donnelly was frequently heard at Cleveland Federation of Labor meetings. In particularly bitter fights and in the midst of confusion she would often get to her feet, square her jaw and demand recognition in a loud voice, continuing until she had gained the attention of the chair. Twenty-three years ago she was elected business representative and secretary [of Waitresses' Local 107] and she held the job continuously until her death.

> —Obituary for Kitty Donnelly,
> *Cleveland Plain Dealer*,
> 17 February 1936[1]

The underrepresentation of women in the activities and leadership of the labor movement has been a long-standing problem shared by virtually all unions. In the early decades of the twentieth century, men were even officers of organizations such as the International Ladies' Garment Workers' Union (ILGWU) that boasted a majority of female members.[2] The patterns of male dominance survived the rise of the industrial union movement in the 1930s and 1940s and the influx of women into unions during World War II.[3] In 1986, researchers could still report that despite the growing ranks of women in unions, the number in the highest national offices (both elective and appointive) had increased only slightly.[4]

The participation of waitress unionists in their International union, however, contrasts with this overall picture. Among those unions in which female leadership have been documented, HERE ranks at the top in the proportion of women among its leaders although women were a minority of its membership. HERE waitresses also evidenced a high degree of participation in union activities, and, in marked contrast to the traditional portrait of intense but short-lived mobilization among women workers, they maintained their heightened level of activity from the early decades of the twentieth century into the post-World War II period.[5] Yet the achievements of HERE women have gone unrecognized. Manufacturing unions, such as the ILGWU or the United Auto Workers, have received the preponderance of attention from scholars.[6] The few reports that include service workers have focused solely on the national level—thus bypassing the activism of HERE women on the local level—or on unions with a majority of female members.[7]

To explain this extensive record of waitress activism previous researchers have credited separate female locals and other structures, such as women's departments and women's committees, with a key role in augmenting the participation of women in the labor movement. Separatism has not been viewed uncritically, however. These same writers acknowledge that separatism has been a problematic long-range strategy for women, capable of sustaining women's leadership in some situations, yet undermining female equality and authority in others.[8] In addition to the central role reserved for separate female structures, scholars have also pointed to the importance of a visible and active middle-class women's movement in giving legitimacy to the demands of women inside the labor movement.[9]

But how crucial were these factors for waitress unionists? The feminist movement, as represented by the Women's Trade Union League and the Women's Bureau, aided HERE women, but certainly not more than other wage-earning women. On the contrary, because of the perceived "immoral" character of waitress work before the 1920s and the decentralized nature of restaurant service (which produced numerous local unions scattered in small towns throughout the country) the cross-class ties between waitresses and the larger middle-class reform community were weaker than for women in many other trades.

Separate female structures, on the other hand, played a critical role in stimulating leadership among waitresses. As this chapter will detail, the participation of waitresses within their International union reached its peak in the 1920s when the greatest number of waitresses belonged to separate-sex locals; similarly, the decrease in waitress activity from the 1930s onward closely paralleled the decline of female locals.

Yet separatism alone can not fully explain the remarkable extent of waitress activism. After all, women garment workers, laundresses, and bookbinders, among others, set up separate female structures,[10] and waitress leaders rose from thoroughly integrated culinary organizations as well as from separate locals and women's divisions. An adequate explanation must move beyond separatism per se to recognize the particular character of sex separatism in the food service industry.

Unlike women's locals in other industries that included women from many different trades, waitress locals had an "occupational homogeneity" and a legitimacy as craft-based organizations.[11] Because the sexual divisions were also perceived as craft divisions, waitress locals received the same treatment and were accorded the same benefits as any other craft-based local. They had equal voting rights with waiter or bartender locals on the Joint Culinary Boards, and, like every other local, they elected delegates to HERE conventions based on the size of their membership. Their institutional legitimacy as craft organizations also helped waitress locals sustain their gender-based structures.

Thus, in contrast to the situation of "Ladies Branches" or "Women's Committees," the craft locals created by waitresses enjoyed an autonomy and a separate institutional status that augmented their political power. Yet because the locals were all-female, they could increase gender consciousness, build leadership skills among women, and voice the special concerns of women workers. In short, for waitresses, the "ghettoizing" imput that can accompany separatism was minimized, whereas the positive aspects of female institution-building were maximized.

To fully understand the proclivity for activism among waitresses, however, one must examine the particularities of their work and family lives. The occupational community and work culture of waitressing nurtured female leadership in much the same way as it had facilitated waitress unionism. Waitresses also shared certain family demographics, such as an economic and psychological independence from their family of origin and a relative freedom from home and child-care responsibilities, that have been associated with high rates of female activism.[12] The case of waitresses confirms these linkages. It also suggests certain revisions to the standard portrait of the working-class female activist and the ways in which these female leaders resolved the tensions between their work and family commitments.

The Extent of Waitress Activism

Women were never a majority of HERE membership nationally, but their numbers jumped from approximately 2,000 (5 percent of the total) in 1908 to about 181,000 (45 percent) in 1950 (Table 7). Despite this persistent minority status, however, female food servers sat on the General Executive Board (GEB) of their International from 1909 on and participated vigorously in its conventions, state bodies, LJEBs, and local unions. Waitress activists also took on paid work as full-time labor officials, and many became lifetime "career" labor leaders. Although their dynamism did not always secure favorable policy decisions, they played a decisive role in shaping the character of their union.

After the first female delegate broke the ice at the HERE convention of 1901, women attended every succeeding convention. Significantly, female participation in convention life was greatest from World War I to the early thirties, coincident with the flowering of the movement for separate female locals. In 1919, when women were approximately one-tenth of the total membership, one-tenth, or 231, of the delegates to the HERE convention were women. And in the late twenties and early thirties, when women represented one-fifth of the membership, they occupied between 21 and 26 percent of the delegate slots (Tables 7 and 9).[13] Female representation at HERE conventions dipped in the 1930s and 1940s as more female culinary workers joined mixed organizations, but even in this later period, waitress activity was disproportionately high when compared with women in other unions.[14]

HERE women were also elected to convention committees in disproportionately high numbers,[15] and beginning with the 1911 convention, they secured representation on the GEB and maintained it throughout the twentieth century. At various periods in the history of the union, women actually occupied two and sometimes three seats on the GEB, a board whose total membership averaged fifteen. Of the women serving on the GEB, only one, Detroit's Myra Wolfgang, was from a mixed local. The other women—Elizabeth Maloney, Kitty Donnelly, Kitty Amsler, Bee Tumber, Olivia Moore, Gertrude Sweet, and Fay Rothring—were all from separate waitress locals.[16] Indeed, most waitresses who rose to prominence came from separate locals. In a 1940 tribute to significant women culinary leaders of the past and present, the *Catering Industry Employee* editor listed twenty-six outstanding women; twenty were from separate locals.[17]

Nonetheless, waitress leadership in male-dominated mixed locals and LJEBs was impressive as well. Cooks and Waiters' Local 550 in Bakersfield, California, survived the depression because of the "inestimable fortitude and perseverance" of its secretary-treasurer, Josephine Perry Rankin. Originally a member of Los Angeles Waitresses' Local 639, Rankin "loaned her guiding influence" to Bartenders' Local 378 and was "so effective" that Bakersfield bartenders achieved 100 percent organization. Women like Myra Wolfgang— "A fearless exponent of trade unions, who can emphatically demonstrate her principles on the platform, on the stump, or any place; an orator of ability"— also took leadership positions in mixed locals. As one male officer from Local 31 in Oakland wrote in 1938, "Many of our highest offices, both International and local, are held by our women members. They hold these offices with honor and credit—credit to themselves and honor to the office."[18]

These were not isolated cases. Teresa Wolfson, writing in 1926, estimated that nationally forty-three culinary locals had female "secretaries." Although she thought that more women should have been elected president instead of secretary—a position she considered stereotypically female—in reality, labor organizations often deemed the secretary-treasurer as their chief officer. Beulah Johnson, secretary-treasurer of Local 324 in Glendale, California, proudly told of her research on California female culinary leaders in the March 1944 *Catering Industry Employee*; twenty-one of the seventy-five local unions in California had women secretaries. Only three of these were composed exclusively of women, Johnson added, the rest were mixed locals.[19] Gertrude Sweet, a carpenter's daughter who became International vice-president for the Northwest Region, recalled that "in Oregon, Washington, and Montana, we had more women officers in the union than we had men [officers]. I find that the women did work and talk and did as good a job as did the men."[20]

From heading up mixed and separate-sex locals, waitresses moved into prominence on male-dominated joint culinary boards. Amanda Keleher took over the top slot of the Salt Lake City LJEB in 1923; in 1946 she still maintained a firm hold. In Oakland, California, Ruby Hall, secretary-treasurer of Culinary and Bartenders' Local 832, acceded to the presidency of the LJEB in 1947; and across the Bay, Jackie Walsh, elected president of Local 48 in 1942, captured the San Francisco LJEB presidency in 1950 after a bitter struggle. She retained her power for more than two decades. In 1940, *Catering Industry Employee* reported that nationwide approximately nineteen LJEBs had women as their chief officers.[21]

Waitresses held their own in the state culinary alliances as well. At the sixth annual convention of the California State Council of Culinary Workers, Bartenders, and Hotel Service Employees, held in 1949, about 30 percent of the 185 delegates, 37 percent of the committee members, and 25 percent of the Executive Board were female. The president of the council, Frankie Behan, was a San Francisco waitress from Local 48. In the 1930s, the council had also been led by a waitress, Bee Tumber of Santa Barbara. The picture in Oregon, Washington, and other states with strong separate-sex locals was no different.[22]

Local Strategies for Representation

Accomplishments grew in part out of waitresses' own keen sense of the importance of equitable female representation. The way to achieve this equality was not so self-evident, however, and waitresses debated the proper strategies for enhancing female participation and power. On a local level, the majority of waitresses clearly favored sex separatism, at least until the 1930s. After that, most newly organized waitresses adjusted to the new industrial structures of the union. Even in these mixed locals, however, waitresses sought a sphere of autonomy by creating women's committees and councils. Both strategies proved problematic, each in their own way, but clearly, the separate-sex route granted a degree of organizational power that the women's committees could not duplicate.

Waitresses who preferred separate locals gave many reasons, but one recurring rationale involved the effect such organizations had in developing

Ten finalists for the Miss or Mrs. Local 705 Contest, 50th Anniversary Ball, 1965, Detroit. Front row: union secretary-treasurer Myra Wolfgang with Mary Beck, Detroit Common Council Woman. (Local 24, HERE)

Yvonne Tiffany (in bunny outfit) pickets with Ann Juzuman in October 1963, protesting the Detroit Playboy Club's policy of scanty costumes and no wages. Detroit's Playboy Club, the first to unionize nationally, signed with Local 705 in 1964. A national master agreement between the International and the Playboy Clubs International covering more than five hundred Playboy bunnies in eight cities was negotiated in 1969. (Local 24, HERE)

Hotel Employee and Restaurant Employee delegates caucus at the Founding Convention of the Coalition of Labor Union Women, Chicago, March 1974. At center, in black jacket, is Myra Wolfgang. Jackie Walsh, former executive officer of San Francisco Waitresses' Local 48, sits to Wolfgang's left. (Local 24, HERE)

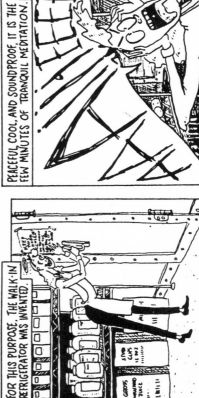

Mimi Pond's Famous Waitress School cartoon, reproduced from the Women's Legal Defense Fund, *Waitress Handbook* (1986), originally appeared in *Tables* magazine, October 1985. (c. 1990 by Mimi Pond)

women's leadership. Separate locals ensured that women would hold responsible positions within the union and learn what was required to run a local—from grievance handling, negotiating contracts, to public relations and parliamentary procedure. Female participation was neither expected nor encouraged in mixed organizations, but in separate locals, women had no choice but to participate, even if the activities struck them as unappealing and unfeminine. Alice Lord of the Seattle waitresses understood this principle. "In a mixed local," she wrote to the editor of the January 1906 *Mixer and Server*, "the girls do not take the interest that they should; they always leave the work to the boys, . . . but if the girls know that the success of the local depends on their efforts, they will put their shoulders to the wheel, and most invariably they will come out ahead, as the few waitresses' locals which are in existence prove that such is the case." [23]

Waitresses also recognized the role of separate locals in creating the proud history of waitress representation. "A great deal has been said about having one local union for waiters and waitresses," Carrie Alexander of Chicago's Local 484 began, when the issue of merging the waiter and waitress locals at the 1927 HERE convention was raised, but "if the waiters and waitresses were in a local union, we would not have 51 delegates at this convention." After the applause died down, she underscored her point: "What is the matter with the local union there? They have waitresses in their local union, but there are no women here." She closed her speech with a final appeal for separate locals. "Let me tell you that the women will have to get up and fight for their own and stay in their own local. I hope no delegation here will consider amalgamating with the men because I believe it would be the elimination of the waitresses." Rank-and-file waitresses in Butte had voiced similar sentiments a year earlier when despite pressure from the International and the local organization of cooks and waiters, they voted 177 to 26 against amalgamation with the male culinary workers. [24]

Separate organizations ensured staff positions for women. Waitresses were not satisfied with having men as "their champions and protectors," they wanted to represent and speak for themselves. [25] Many waitress locals resisted merger pressures, for example, because they feared losing female staff. In 1962, the *Chicago Tribune* reported that Waitresses' Local 484 was fighting the proposed merger with Waiters' Local 25 and 256 because "they want their union representatives to be women, not men." Four Executive Board members from Local 484 confirmed the newspaper account in a letter to General President Miller: "The rank and file are strongly opposed to a merger and feel that, if Mr. Madison [the male candidate for business agent] is hired, it will not be long before the other female business representatives are replaced by male. This, to the rank and file, is the beginning of the end. The waitresses have had a charter for 61 years and do not wish to surrender it." Even though the business agent in question was a black man, the women insisted that the issue was one of sex, not race. "We are not segregationist because we opposed the hiring of a Negro male business agent, but we felt that a Negro woman should be considered for the job. (At least three wanted it.)" The International pressed for merger and for sexual integration of the staff. Two other female locals now had male staff, Miller reminded the local, and he "heartily" supported such assignments "especially at night, and in districts where it would not be safe for a girl to be." [26]

Waitresses took pride in the accomplishments of their all female organizations and in their ability to take on jobs that the culture deemed inappropriate or too difficult for women. Lord encouraged the press secretaries of female locals across the country to write letters for the opinion column of the national journal by pointing out the similarity between writing for the public audience—an unfamiliar task—and talking with each other in private—a common, everyday activity. "Now, girls, I would like to see an article every month in the Forum from one of our number. Do not be afraid, or imagine you cannot do so. Write just as you would talk to one another, even if it is not just correct. I am sure our broad-minded editor will find space for it." [27]

Local 48 of San Francisco bragged of being "completely officered by women and [of constituting] an outstanding example of women's ability both as executives and administrators." The Los Angeles waitresses' local printed the following slogan on the back cover of their bylaws: "Who Says 'Women are the Weaker Sex?' We are the largest culinary craft union in the World." [28]

Women's Committees and Female Participation

By the 1930s, the majority of new waitresses were entering mixed-gender locals. For these women, new strategies were required. The story of the women's committees they created—their brief organizational life and frustratingly piecemeal accomplishments—contrasts markedly with the longevity and achievements of the separate locals. The comparison demonstrates that separatism in and of itself could not always guarantee increased power and participation for women: the form in which separate organizing occurred was critical.

Of the culinary locals in New York City, at least four—Locals 1, 42, 302, and 6—had large functioning women's committees at various times between the 1930s and the 1950s. Women were never the majority in any of these locals, but they comprised between 30 and 40 percent of the membership in Locals 302 and 6.[29] The failure of these committees is noteworthy in light of their numerical potential, persistence, and creativity.

Although the committees defined their first task as promoting female leadership, they made little headway. The Executive Board of Hotel and Club Workers' Local 6 generally had two women out of approximately fifteen to twenty members; the staff ratio of women to men was similar.[30] Ironically, Local 6 prided itself on its progressive democratic character, but because one-third of the union throughout the 1940s and 1950s was female, clearly a major portion of their rank and file was not represented. The records of other New York City locals were worse. Cafeteria Workers' Local 302 did not have a female business agent representing its three thousand women members until 1942. Fifteen years later the picture was remarkably stable: only one of the fifty Executive Board members was female.[31] The New York LJEB reflected the dearth of female leadership in its affiliate locals: Gertrude Lane was frequently the sole woman in a delegate body of thirty to fifty members.[32]

Women's committees aimed to increase women's participation in the life of the union, but the barriers were numerous and ultimately impossible to surmount. Ida Brown, a Local 1 waitress, explained the source of the problem: "Many of us who can talk the legs off an 'iron pot' when in our shops are smitten with stage fright at general membership meetings—and to tell the truth, we do not receive any particular encouragement from our brothers." A Local 302 cafeteria server admitted that "too many of us have qualms about going before a General Membership meeting and stating our opinions, but we wouldn't have any stage fright if we were part of a Council for women. Men just don't understand these things."[33]

Women's committees initiated various programs to foster women's participation. In conjunction with the New York WTUL, Local 6 held leadership training classes for "women only" in organizing techniques and public speaking. Local 1 organized a parliamentary procedure class. Other committees organized social and sporting events to draw "women members closer to the union." Bingo parties, swimming and bicycling clubs, dancing events, and softball teams were commonplace. A women's dramatics class held through Local 302 helped create a musical, *Sunny Side Up*, about the lives of cafeteria workers.[34]

Women's columns in the union newspaper were begun. Even the women's committee of Local 6, which carefully pointed out that they "were not segregating" themselves "from the men . . . far from it . . . [because] men and women are dependent on cooperation with each other for the success of the trade unions," started a "women's corner" in the *Hotel and Club Voice*. "Yes, this is something new, a little corner all to ourselves" to get "by ourselves and let our hair down." The *Voice of Local 1* encouraged women to write letters for the "Woman's View" column and to attend their union meetings. Local 302's *Cafeteria Call* had a "Hello Sister" column for a number of years and later a "Our Sisters Talk It Over" column.[35]

Early on, the columns emphasized the needs of women on the job, but as the committees lost steam, the columns shifted, appealing to women as housewives and mothers. Local 302's column changed tone in 1943, concomitant with a change in the local's administration. After five years of broadsides directed toward workplace issues, a new columnist appeared who urged women to "join union activities to make this a better world for [their] children." In 1954, the "Woman's View" column in the Local 1 newspaper became the "Ladies' Corner" with articles on preserves, fashions, and household hints.[36]

Significantly, women's home responsibilities rarely were mentioned as a potential source of conflict for women activists, nor were home responsibilities perceived as a duty from which women should be relieved. The chair of the Women's Committee of Local 6 reminded women that they had a duty to participate in their union even though they had household responsibilities and had to "go home, clean house and prepare meals." Remember the pioneer women, she exhorted. When the Indians attacked, they "didn't say 'excuse me, I have to bake a cake' . . . they came to the front and helped their men." Instead of attempting to rectify the problem of women's dual responsibilities in the workplace and in the home, women were expected to do both.[37]

Determined to gain representation, women's committees pressured male-dominated locals for quotas regarding women and minorities. Local 6 passed a bylaw provision in the 1940s requiring that one black officer and one female officer be appointed "in the event that no Negro . . . or no woman has been elected to serve either as a General Officer of the union or the Board of Vice-Presidents." Local 1 women pushed through a resolution early in 1936 that at least two women would be elected to the Executive Board of the union. In the late 1940s, they amended the local bylaws to "provide that both the delegates to the WTUL must be women in addition to the mandatory two executive board members."[38]

The most ambitious activities devised by women's committees, however, involved organizing semi-independent all-female councils that functioned almost as separate branches within the main locals. The women of Local 302 started a Women's Council composed of representatives from each shop where women were employed. The Women's Council formulated bylaws and collective bargaining demands, and "other matters effecting [sic] women more than men."[39] Similarly, under the auspices of the New York LJEB, Gertrude Lane set up a Woman's Advisory Committee consisting of five women from each local with female membership. This all-woman group paralleled the male joint committee structurally but differed ideologically. As opposed to the collective bargaining thrust of the virtually all-male LJEB, the female group was committed primarily to legislative and organizing activity concerning minimum wages and maximum hours.[40]

Ironically, success could create problems for committees. Indeed, women's committees were in something of a double bind. The male leadership saw the principal function of women's committees as attracting women to the work of building the general union organization, yet the most effective way of involving women was by appealing to their special interests. Because the gender concerns of women were often at odds with the priorities of a male-dominated union, the committees were stifled at precisely the point at which they developed a strong following among the women members of the local.

The demise of Local 302's committee is a case in point. From its inception, the committee defined broad and bold concerns. Besides the traditional entreaties for women's involvement in ongoing union activities, they wanted equal pay, a portion of the best jobs, and "important positions" in the union. They were tired of taking a "backseat" to the men. When the committee ran a letter-writing contest on "What do you want the Union to do for you as a woman member?" the winning essayist wanted a forty-hour week with no reduction in pay—clearly a useful demand for women with family responsibilities—and the runner-up opted for the union "to create equal opportunity for women to earn equal money for equal work with men." During the 1941 negotiations, the Women's Committee distributed "7-hour day for women" buttons and made other suggestions to the negotiating team "such as having cots in the dressing room for emergencies . . . and having sanitary dressing rooms." The committee members elaborated further objectives, including a veiled reference to the problem of sexual harassment: "We felt that not enough girls in the union . . . [knew] their rights and that sometimes they are laid off, or bothered, or something else like that." [41]

During the early years of World War II, the committee toned down its feminist orientation in the actual activities they pursued, but their sassy rhetoric continued. One 1942 column grabbed attention with this opening: "What do you say to the wise guy who tells you that women belong at home in the kitchen? Or the bright boy who tells you women are taking men's jobs? Or the know-it-all who says girls are not as capable as men? Do you feel a slow burn creeping all over you while you want to tell him off—but good! Well, we have all the answers to those very short-sighted males who strut around this earth feeling that all things begin and end with them." [42]

Nevertheless, although the committee elicited enthusiastic response from women, the male-dominated Executive Board withdrew its support after a few years, effectively crippling the committee. Few lasting changes had occurred. The number of women in leadership remained small, and glaring wage inequalities persisted between women and men. [43]

On the other hand, those committees advancing only goals that complemented the interests of male co-workers found they lost the support of the very constituency they were trying to reach. The committees within Locals 6 and 1, for example, steered clear of "divisive issues" and in the end died from lack of female support. Although they agitated for more female staff for Local 6 and exhorted women to get more involved in the life of their union, the calls for women "to pitch in" and "shoulder the load" were directed at involving women in activities that did not challenge the ongoing traditional priorities of the union.[44] In Local 1's women's column in the *Voice of Local 1*— begun in 1948 for "the gentler sex . . . our waitresses, and the wives of our male members"—committee members addressed the problems of discrimination based on race not sex: the grievants were all black men.[45] Despite the urging of the local, few rank-and-file women members wrote for the women's column; there was "a deathly silence from our women," the editor admitted. A union administrator told women to visit the union office if they needed help writing, but to no avail.[46]

In the end, without the autonomy, power, and institutional legitimacy enjoyed by the separate female locals, the impact of women's committees was episodic and ephemeral. Even the strongest committees—those dedicated to advancing the cause of women workers and supported by such groups as the WTUL—sustained their activities only briefly. In contrast to the experience of waitresses in separate locals, the on-going participation of women rank-and-filers was minimal, and only a handful of exceptional women such as Gertrude Lane and Myra Wolfgang managed to sustain careers as labor officials in these mixed, male-dominated unions.

Without a majority vote within the local or a separate institutional base of power, women could neither change the priorities of the male leadership nor act independently. Moreover, the basic legitimacy of women's committees was always in question. The separate waitress locals had to overcome male (and female) skepticism toward their sex-segregated structure before they gained separate charters, but once their locals were established, their basic right to exist was not challenged. The committee form, however, was not an organizational structure recognized by the International union constitution. Waitress locals garnered credibility because they represented not just the women of the union but also the waitress craft; in contrast, women's committees justified their existence through establishing the special needs and interests of women. Waitress locals forged unity through combining craft and organizational loyalty with gender concerns; in the case of women's committees, organizational and craft loyalties often were at odds with gender.

Strategic Dilemmas on the National Level

Waitresses also experimented with various schemes for enhancing female power on the national level, relying on arguments for both equal treatment and special protection. Before the 1930s, for instance, female delegates to union conventions agitated against HERE's policy, instituted in 1909, "That one member of the Board shall be a woman to represent the women workers of our craft." The four female delegates in attendance in 1909 did not participate in the convention debate, but Alice Lord later made her opposition known, arguing that women did not need such motions to win GEB seats. In 1921, women delegates, all from separate locals, submitted a resolution to abolish the special seat reserved for women. During the floor fight that ensued, women objected to the quota system as a "protective" measure that set a maximum for female representation rather than a minimum. Others saw it as demeaning and encouraging the view of women as the weaker sex in need of special treatment. "You must get away from the idea that women are less able than men," one delegate said. "We don't want to be patronized and that is what the present law produces." Male delegates opposed the motion and prevailed.[47]

Unable to do away with the quota or elect more women to the board, female delegates switched tactics. In 1938, they embraced a recommendation that backed special protection for both women and dining-car workers and increased the female quota from one to two. In these debates, waitresses now argued that women needed protection from the prejudices of their male colleagues and that, although the quota system at times seemed to limit the number of women board members, at least it ensured some female participation. Women delegates also expressed less optimism about their chances in open elections and appeared less sensitive to being categorized as a distinct constituency. In part, this shift may have been due to the increasing number of women entering mixed locals, the corresponding decline in female delegate proportions, and the general perception that chances were slim for increasing female representation by abolishing the quota system.[48] The resolution requiring two seats for women passed, and in the election following, waitresses secured three of the fifteen elected seats on the board.[49]

Dissatisfied with the new policy, the general officers of HERE backed a resolution at the next convention eliminating one of the female vice-presidential slots. In contrast to previous conventions, male delegates now argued against paternalistic treatment of women, using the rhetoric of impartiality and equal treatment of the sexes. How can you support equal wages, GEB member Hugo Ernst asked the women delegates, yet desire differential treatment when it comes to elections? "If you are entitled to the same wage on the job, which you no doubt are, you are also entitled to take your same chances with the representation for the women on the General Executive Board." But Ernst showed signs of not being as fair-minded and consistent as he was exhorting the female delegates to be. "I believe you good sisters are clannish," he began, "when you insist that there should be more representation, proportionately speaking, than the number would warrant." Vice-president John Kearney also begrudged the female delegates their two seats on the board, denouncing those who "in the disguise of equality ask for more than they are entitled to have." In reality, of course, because women were at least one-third of the membership, two board seats were hardly overrepresentation.

Despite pressure from male colleagues, not one of the 150 women delegates spoke in favor of the amendment. They stressed their numbers and their entitlement to proportionate representation. As Anna Farkas, a delegate, succinctly put it: "We have probably one-half females in this Hotel and Restaurant International Alliance, and I think we are entitled to female representatives." Taking a different tack, Gertrude Lane of New York City admitted that "women had very little chance to be elected on a district basis and that was one of the reasons it would be a fatal error for the organization to take away any of the women representation." Besides, she added, in organizing she found that "one of the best arguments . . . [was] the fact that our International recognized the importance of women in the industry."[50] Despite "sharp debate from many different quarters," the quota requiring two female vice-presidents met defeat, and, as a result, HERE women lost one of the three women on the board. Nevertheless, waitresses retained two vice-presidential seats on the GEB throughout the 1950s and 1960s even though they competed against men for those positions.[51]

Thus, many waitresses supported sex-segregated policies on a local level, but they rejected the full implications of the "separate-sphere ideology" at the national level. Initially, they argued against quotas for female representation on the highest body of the International and when they shifted their tactics and argued for special seats for women in the late 1930s, they never followed the logic of separatism to its ultimate conclusion by asking for their own national division or considering the formation of their own International union.[52] Waitresses never devised a system to ensure proportionate representation for women, but they did manage to maintain and even increase their presence at the top levels of decision making. Ultimately, of course, whether waitresses advocated special quotas or open elections, or whether they chose to organize separately or in mixed locals, as long as they remained a numerical minority within the International, they could advance only with the support of men.

Work Culture and Family Life

To fully explain the activism of women within HERE, one must look beyond the strategies devised by waitresses, even those as effective as separate locals. One must look to the particularities of their work experience and family backgrounds. As was argued in Part 1, the close-knit occupational community and the worldly, unromantic work culture of waitresses helped promote collective action and unionization. This same activist-oriented community nourished the waitress representatives who braved the masculine world of union conventions and high-level Executive Boards.

Other aspects of the work experience of waitresses fostered women's leadership in subtle but powerful ways. The craft and sex segregation of work, for instance, solidified the occupational ties among waitresses while mitigating their identity with male workers in the craft. The strict categorizing of waiting jobs by sex meant that waitresses and waiters rarely worked together in the same house. This internal segregation of waiting work physically separated women and men food servers and created the basis for a collective identity among waitresses. Yet unlike women in many other sex-segregated workplaces, waitresses continuously interacted with male cooks, bartenders, and busboys, as well as male customers. These exchanges were often fraught with conflict that derived in large part from the structure and demands of the workplace itself. In order to survive, waitresses developed ways of manipulating these interactions and asserting their own ends. The daily adversarial maneuverings with men prepared waitresses for the conflicts that emerged in their own union. Indeed, the arguments between waitresses and their male co-workers on the shopfloor influenced their readiness to engage in conflict with these same union brothers in the union hall. How could they accept paternalism in the union when they so firmly rejected it in the workplace?

The kinds of skills acquired by waitresses in their daily work life transferred directly to union leadership. At work, waitresses learned to take charge verbally with customers, to deflect criticism and sarcasm by developing their own quick-witted retorts, and to be persuasive in their interactions so that their needs as waitresses would be met. Practice in "thinking on your feet" and in sharpening sparring skills came in handy during union debates, grievance meetings, and negotiation sessions. The women who survived as waitresses were the ones who learned to control situations by initiating action rather than those who let the customer define the interaction.[53] This boldness became a habit with some waitresses and aided them in their union activities. They were not intimidated by men, nor were they accustomed to following the male lead. Unlike the office environment, for example, waiting work discouraged traditional female behavior.[54]

Their ability to size up individuals and predict their behavior in regard to tips and manners became a resource that waitresses could draw upon in their labor activities. The best defense for a waitress was a good offense—but to know which offense to pursue the waitress had to be able "to read" the customer. Expert waitresses were keen judges of human character. They could assess an individual quickly by reading nonverbal cues, and adjust their behavior to the mood of the other person. This grasp of character allowed the waitress to interpret the best approach with the particular customer—the one which would enhance the tip as well as protect the waitress from potentially abusive behavior. A customer perceived as a bully or a pest could be put in his or her place before having the chance to launch an offensive. The work of waiting encouraged the development of the very qualities that women needed in order to survive in the fast-talking, person-oriented, conflictual world of labor relations.

Waitressing may also have attracted more unconventional women than other occupations such as clerical or sales or even factory labor. Certainly, before the 1920s waitressing was looked upon as a disreputable trade; and even later in the century, waitressing retained a somewhat unsavory cast. The "intemperate" personal qualities that waitresses exhibited on the job were noticed by the public and frowned upon. The stereotype of the bold, free-talking, aggressive waitress was partially based in reality. For these women then, already working in a "unladylike" job, becoming a labor activist—clearly nontraditional behavior for women—did not seem like much of a change of pace.

Finally, for waitresses, as for other groups of women workers, their particular household arrangements affected their level of workplace activism.[55] Ronald Schatz, for example, argues that the distinctive factor shared by the women union pioneers in the electrical industry was their nontraditional family home life: many were divorced, living alone, or living with sisters or peers. These women rose to leadership, Schatz maintains, because they had either broken the patriarchal ties of their past family or challenged the authority structures in their current family.[56] Waitresses conform to Schatz's schema because they, like the women organizers in the electrical industry, also diverged from other women in their propensity to shun conventional family life. Waitresses more than women in many other occupations tended to be divorced, separated, or widowed, or if single, living apart from their family of origin (chapter 1).

Equally important, the nontraditional family status of waitresses meant that a disproportionate number were the primary support of themselves and their family and, at least until the 1950s, were attached to the workplace in a permanent fashion as full-time, long-tenure workers. The implications of these particular attributes for female mobilization are profound, as Louise Tilly and Carole Turbin point out. Women who were primary wage earners were more likely to take the lead in labor struggles; they had a greater stake in improving their wages and enjoyed more independence from male authority. Older women with more years in the labor force were more committed to workplace struggles. They perceived their work as continuous and permanent, had developed more extensive workplace networks of support, and hence were more willing to invest in long-term union-building.[57]

The Waitress Official: A Group Portrait

Kitty Donnelly (1876–1936) and Florence Farr, born in 1929, were born more than a half century apart, but their life histories reveal remarkable similarities. Donnelly and Farr, both with native-born, working-class roots, turned to waitressing early to support themselves and their children. Donnelly's husband died when she was thirty; Farr divorced at twenty-five. After years working in the trade and volunteering time on union projects, at mid-life—Donnelly at thirty-seven and Farr at forty—they became full-time paid waitress officials. Donnelly held her job as secretary and business agent of Cleveland Waitresses' Local 107 continuously until her death at age sixty and was the second woman to serve as a HERE International vice-president. Farr, an official of Detroit's Local 24 (formerly Local 705) since 1969, became the local's principal officer in 1982 and an International vice-president in 1985 and shows no sign of loosening her hold on the reins of leadership.[58] The portrait of the typical waitress official that emerges from an analysis of the life histories of Donnelly and Farr plus some forty other waitress leaders[59] confirms the linkages between family characteristics and a propensity for collective action.

Although the characteristics of women workers, including waitresses, underwent tremendous change in this period—the young, single woman workers who dominated the workplace before the 1930s being gradually replaced by older, married workers—the qualities and backgrounds of waitress labor leaders remained stable. In both generations of waitress officials, only 6 percent—were single. Although some four-fifths of the women had been married, close to a third were divorced, separated, or widowed (Table 10A). Thus, despite the fact that a large number of younger, single women were available in the earlier era and many married women with husbands worked in both periods, those who rose to positions of leadership were consistently older and often lived apart from a male breadwinner.

Many leaders began their labor careers after years of working as waitresses. More than 50 percent of the women started their full-time union work in their thirties. Of the remaining women, roughly half began in their twenties and the rest in their forties and fifties (Figure 2). Of course, this phenomenon was in part due to the absorption of women's energies in child-rearing in their early years—a surprisingly large number of waitress leaders had children, the average being 2.1 for the earlier generation and 1.8 for the later cohort—but many waitress leaders turned to full-time union careers as their waiting work dropped in income and status (Table 10A). Waitresses who earlier enjoyed table service resented the work as the downward slant of their lives became apparent. Many of these women were rescued from a bitter and frustrating decline by their entry into work as labor officials. As one official wrote upon coming into leadership after years as a waitress, "I am very happy in my new work . . . and find it so very interesting that I look forward to each day with zest, instead of the job I had . . . which had become drudgery for me."[60] Charles Paulsen, a life-long HERE official, noted the phenomenon of the older waitress leader in an interview in 1983. "You go to the Pacific Northwest and . . . the Mountain States, it was always the older women who ran the show, the motherly type, the matronly type." Older women, he explained, went into union work because they simply could not get as well-paying a job as a younger waitress.[61]

Predictably, these midlife labor officials demonstrated remarkable longevity and success in their new work. Their careers as union leaders often lasted twenty, thirty, and sometimes forty years, with many working full time into their sixties and seventies. They succeeded because they were well prepared by their years of waitressing and relatively unencumbered with home and child-care responsibilities. They may not have had supportive spouses by their thirties, but neither did they have the full demands of marriage and family.

The foregoing profile of waitress leaders also suggests certain revisions in the conventional portrait of the kinds of women who organized and led unions. All too often the typical woman union activist has been presented as young, single, and childless.[62] Although young women without family responsibilities often took leading roles in building labor organizations and some later served as officials for brief periods, older divorced, separated, or widowed mothers were just as significant.[63] In fact, the older, formerly married waitress leader may be more representative of female labor officials than the frequently studied single ILGWU women of the Progressive Era, the young electrical women of the CIO, or even the portrait of the "typical" female labor leader sketched by Gary Fink (Table 10B).[64]

Not surprisingly, given the number of waitress activists who were married and had children, reconciling family life with a full-time career was as problematic for them as it was for other female activists (Tables 10A, 10B). Waitress officials resolved the conflict in a different fashion, however, than many of the female activists who emerge in other historical portraits. Unlike the female ILGWU leaders who chose to remain single or the many other middle-class women who found marriage and children almost insurmountable barriers to a full-time commitment in the public realm,[65] waitresses typically resolved the conflict between family and work by taking on the tasks serially rather than choosing one or the other or attempting both simultaneously. Child-raising and marriage occurred early and were curtailed, then waitresses entered their labor careers in midlife (Figure 2).

Of course, a few waitress officials had dual responsibilities at work and at home.[66] And, despite the difficulties of combining marriage, children, and labor work, many waitress leaders maintained that combination as the ideal. In 1955, Fay Rothring, business manager of Waitresses' Local 276, held up this ideal, although as a divorced mother she knew intimately the weight of these multiple burdens. In a message published for the silver anniversary ball of her local, Rothring threw out her challenge. "Women workers in our industry have a threefold duty to perform: first, they are usually mothers and house-wives; second, they have the obligation, as women, to advance the economic position of their sex to an equality with the best that men have attained; third, they have the duty to advance the interests of all workers." She concluded, martyrlike, "We accept the challenge, and shoulder the responsibility, placed upon us by the labor movement, with a smile."[67]

Finally, the data on waitress officials reveal a group overwhelmingly from working-class backgrounds (Table 10D) and suggest the need for further documentation for assertions that female labor leaders were more frequently from middle-class and upper-class backgrounds, while male labor leaders had working-class or lower-middle-class roots.[68] In part, the discrepancy may be explained by the reliance of many studies on the more abundant historical sources available on middle-class women reformers. Obtaining reliable data on the roles of working-class women and their contributions to the labor movement has been much more problematic.[69] Although it is possible that more middle-class women than middle-class men chose labor careers, working-class women certainly were not as underrepresented as has been portrayed.

Thus, data on waitress leaders suggest that female labor leaders may have resembled their male counterparts more closely than formerly suspected. The representative male labor leader was married with children, spent time in his trade before embarking on a union career, held his position for a number of years, and came from a working-class or a lower-middle-class background—an apt description of the majority of waitress leaders. Of course, many waitress leaders, unlike their brethren, survived the demands of union work without the support of a spouse whose full-time concern was caring for the needs of the family, including those of the wage-earning partner. In other words, while working-class female labor leaders diverged from their middle-class sisters in how they reconciled work and family demands, they also faced problems unknown to their brothers in the labor movement. As always, for working-class women, the path lay somewhere in between those trod by working-class men and by middle-class women.

The Decline of Waitress Unionism

[In 1959] . . . oh, yes, Butte and Anaconda were strictly union. . . . and *nobody* but nobody dared do anything against the union, because then you were labeled a scab for the rest of your life. . . . [getting] that label on you, that was worse than hell itself. . . . We had a dandy [business] agent . . . and if you didn't put your union button on . . . it was a fifty-cent fine. And you didn't work unless you were union. Now . . . girls working at the Park [Cafe] they don't even know we have a union. You know, I had a twenty-five year union button . . . and it had little diamonds around the edge and Restaurant Hotel Employees on it, see? And I wore it on my uniform one day just for the fun of it. And everybody was telling me, "Well, isn't that pretty, what is that?" All those girls down there in the last, say, three years, not one of 'em recognized it.

—Kathryn Wetzel Dewing,
waitress for forty years at
the Park Cafe, Anaconda,
Montana[1]

Last week we said goodbye to a waitress who'd been here for years. We took her into the alley out back and burned her skirt so she'd never have to wear it or wash it again. It was polyester, and instead of burning it just melted away kind of sad. Waitresses can be so good to each other.

—Susan Montanye, 1980s cocktail
waitress[2]

When the new owner of the West Hollywood coffee shop fired the "granny waitresses" in 1984, he also fired the union. The courts placed few obstacles in his path: with new employees and a slight change in "business orientation," his legal obligation to "bargain in good faith" had ended. The granny waitresses responded as so many others of their trade had done in the past: they picketed; they reached out to customers and to women's organizations; they turned to the larger male-dominated labor movement for backup. Their close-knit occupational community and their sense of pride in providing "good, loyal service" reinforced their determination. Yet in the 1980s, these tactics no longer sufficed. The union could neither mount enough economic pressure to force the rehiring of the "grannies" nor could it organize the younger replacements. The restaurant, like many other established union houses in Los Angeles, fell by the wayside. Local 11 retained strength in the hotel sector (some 60 percent of area hotels were still organized in 1990), but the proportion of unionized restaurants plummeted. A mere handful—perhaps 5 percent—remained with the union.[3]

The spectacle of decline was not limited to Los Angeles. Seattle had close to four thousand union waitresses in 1956, waitress official Beulah Compton recalled, and was 90 percent organized. Twenty years later, the membership dropped to 2,600, and only one in four female servers belonged to the union.[4] Nationwide, barely one-tenth of the culinary work force was covered by a collective bargaining agreement by the 1970s, and the total number of unionized waitresses was less than in 1950 (Tables 5A–5C). Waitress power within the International suffered setbacks as well. Only one woman sat on the GEB, the same as in 1909, female representation at conventions lagged despite the feminization of union membership, and local leadership appeared to be increasingly in the hands of male-dominated LJEBs and mixed-sex industrial locals.[5] What happened? How can the unraveling of waitress unionism and its loss of influence be explained?

On the broadest level, waitress unionists confronted obstacles common to all unions after World War II: the backlash against unionism as evident in the passage of the Taft-Hartley Act in 1947, the general conservatism of the McCarthy period that dampened any challenge to the status quo,[6] and the growing power of capital. In addition, dramatic changes specific to their own industry made organizing more difficult.

The hotel and restaurant industry was shifting geographically. In the 1940s and 1950s, the center of the industry moved away from its traditional urbanized core to new unorganized, hostile territories: the Deep South, the Southwest, and into the suburbs.[7] With the lower and middle classes relying as never before on eating out, the restaurant sector also burgeoned at a dizzying rate. Low-priced, quick-style eateries opened by the thousands, scattered haphazardly over the new decentralized landscape and drawing in a rash of young new recruits with little experience or understanding of unionism. The union found it virtually impossible to keep control over such a rapidly expanding, geographically dispersed work force.

Perhaps the most significant structural change, however, was the transformation of countless small independent proprietorships into chain outlets under the control of national and international conglomerates.[8] In 1931, fewer than 3 percent of the nation's restaurants were chain-operated; in the 1980s, McDonald's alone accounted for 17 percent of all restaurant visits. From the family-style chains (Howard Johnson's, Denny's, Sambo's) to the fast-food empires (McDonald's, Burger King, and Pizza Hut), the species proved almost invulnerable to organizing.[9]

As nonunion competition proliferated, skepticism about the benefits of unionism spread among organized employers. When enterprising young applicants appeared daily at their kitchen doors seeking work, union employers resented having to hire through the union. Although inexperienced, these fresh-faced workers, so flexible and eager to please, seemed preferable to seasoned, union-conscious workers who were accustomed to strict craft classifications and other contract protections. Moreover, as the unionized work force aged, employers had to call the hiring hall three or four times before a young attractive woman would be sent.[10]

Once a few nonunion restaurants established themselves in a community, they became visible evidence to unionized employers of the ability of unorganized restaurants to attract an adequate labor supply and a loyal clientele. As working-class communities dispersed, and the union house card lost its power to attract customers, signing up with the union no longer meant a reliable base of patronage.

Unorganized restaurants with their lower labor costs also enjoyed a higher profit margin. Master contracts had once stabilized labor costs and reduced competition because the majority of employers in a community were providing similar wages and working conditions. Now they hobbled the minority of union employers who were bound to union labor, union work rules, and high wages and benefits while their nonunion competitors hired compliant young workers, paid minimum wages, and disregarded health and welfare benefits—all without suffering a loss in patronage.

To make matters worse, the union rules and regulations, which at one point relieved the burden of managing and disciplining employees, now constricted the employer's authority at every turn—not just in setting economic compensation but in demanding reliability and competence. Many culinary locals, partially in response to the growing dominance of the hotel sector, had adopted worksite union practices such as just cause and seniority provisions. Rather than bring recalcitrant employees up on union charges of incompetence, HERE locals now demanded that problem workers be retained. And under seniority provisions, younger workers were the first to be laid off.

With the extension of the Taft-Hartley Act to the hotel and restaurant industry in 1955, and the passage of the Landrum-Griffin Act in 1959, the ability of waitress unions to exert control over their occupation was severely hampered.[11] Closed shops, the removal of members from the job for noncompliance with union bylaws and work rules, union membership for supervisors, top-down organizing, long-term recognitional picketing, and secondary boycotts all became illegal. Locals lost their ability to set entrance requirements for the trade, to oversee job performance, and to punish recalcitrant members.[12] And once the fining system lost its teeth, "you couldn't enforce the contract, you couldn't even get a quorum" for union meetings, recalled waitress official Clela Sullivan. Union-sponsored training programs declined; hiring halls fell into disrepair and neglect.[13] By the late 1960s, the key tenets of occupational unionism lived only in the minds of an aging waitress membership.

Centrifugal forces pulled at the craft sisterhood from every direction, undermining member loyalty and consensus. Sororal ties broke down, for example, as the unions moved from member-funded sick and benefit funds to employer-paid health plans in the decades after World War II.[14] Members no longer were bound together through their mutual commitment of funds once unions stopped being responsible for collection and disbursement of benefit funds. Without the monetary commitment, the emotional commitment slackened as well. Committees for the sick stopped functioning; retired members went their own ways independent of the union.

Of equal importance was the breakup of the occupational community of waitressing that had nourished union sentiment and activist inclinations. A new generation of waitresses arose after World War II—a generation with less commitment to their craft and to advancing that craft collectively. Part-time and temporary waitresses had always been a significant sector of the trade but definitely a minority faction. In the postwar era, the retail food industry became a primary employer of part-timers—teenagers, college students, married mothers, and multiple job-holders or "moonlighters" flooded into the new part-time job openings.[15] In 1940, 21 percent of female servers were part-time; thirty years later the figure had skyrocketed to 63 percent. The rise of male part-timers was just as phenomenal: from roughly one in ten in 1940 to a majority of the trade by 1970 (Table 4). By 1980, the Department of Labor estimated that only one-fifth of food service workers were employed year-round and full-time, the lowest of any occupational category except private household. The average age of food servers dropped as well as employers turned to teenage and student help.[16]

Changes in technology and consumer tastes accompanied the shift toward a younger, part-time work force.[17] A larger proportion of restaurants depended on delivering quick and inexpensive meals to an anonymous public. "Between 1967 and 1977, fast-food outlets increased their market share of all eating places from 19 percent to 37 percent."[18] In these restaurants, convenience and speed took priority; personal service was neither expected nor desired. Younger, inexperienced minimum-wage workers floated in and out, with the turnover rate estimated at 300 percent. The typical interaction between server and customer was routinized and of short duration; regular customers were few and far between. In these settings, the server's relation with the customer was marginal to the successful "service encounter." In cases where self-service was implemented, food servers were bypassed altogether; customers gave food orders directly to preparers and gathered up their own food and table settings from the counter. Cashiers totaled the check.[19] The abbreviated nature of food service work in fast-food emporiums inhibited the development of an identity with the craft of waiting and with other food servers.

Not surprisingly, many among the growing ranks of part-timers and fast-food workers thought of their jobs as temporary. The temporary worker mentality even predominated among many of the younger servers who worked full-time, would have long-term stints in the occupation, or had landed the plum jobs in the better full-service restaurants. Many had attended college and believed they would soon leave the "blue-collar" restaurant world far behind. Few saw their primary commitment as being to the culinary workplace; their identity and interests resided elsewhere. They considered themselves actresses or students or some other label—but not food servers. Waiting, said one, "is like the way station of life. You can't have your dream now, so you work in a restaurant." Most took the advice of the waitress-writer in *Glamour Magazine*: when the "waitressing blues strike . . . bear firmly in mind that this is only temporary."[20]

Building union sentiment among this new work force of part-timers, students, and fast-food workers proved difficult indeed. In addition, in family-style and elite restaurants where service was still personalized—still estimated to be a little more than half of all establishments[21]—and an older, more permanent work force predominated, employer-controlled training programs encouraged food servers to think of themselves as individual entrepreneurs or salespeople who could "determine their own income" through "upselling" or "suggestive selling." By recommending the more expensive entré or the pricier wine or even the consumption of an unwanted appetizer or dessert, the server's tips and the restaurant's revenues could be upped.[22] The group sense among servers was tested further as tips comprised an ever-larger proportion of the server's income. Although some new entrants to the occupation could still enthuse that "being a waitress is like being part of some big sisterhood," others complained of a prevailing "air of competition."[23]

Generational tensions could be felt inside the waitress unions as well. An aging waitress leadership—a leadership who came to power primarily in the late 1920s and early 1930s—faced a rapidly expanding younger membership with new and different perceptions about work and unionism. Younger waitresses flaunted the craft rules so lovingly developed by their predecessors. Waitress business agents lamented the lack of allegiance to the union and the willingness of younger workers to cooperate with the employer in bending union rules. "The girls won't stand on their own feet [anymore]," Valentine Webster complained. "They do everything they are not supposed to, such as scrape and wash dishes."[24] Younger women also defied the power and the craft principles of the older generation of waitress officialdom in more organized ways.

In the postwar era, dissension and factional fights split many waitress locals into warring camps for the first time.[25] A certain amount of dissension was inherent in the practices of occupational unionism—a system in which individual rights were sometimes sacrificed for the good of the whole, and officials held a large degree of unchecked power. Moreover, in any organization, chronic complainers and frustrated attention-seekers absorb an inordinate amount of energy.[26] Yet the sheer volume of accusation and counteraccusation and the organized nature of the dissent suggests that serious ideological divisions underlay the sometimes vitriolic, personalized attacks. A breach between the waitress leadership and the rank and file had emerged. Indeed, in many locals the fissures widened to such an extent that the International sent in special officers to investigate and manage the situation. The International even ordered three waitress locals into trusteeship—a rarely exercised option in which the local turned over its governance and finances to the International—noting an inability to maintain operations because of factional struggles, failure to service the membership, organize the jurisdiction, and improper actions on the part of the officers.[27]

Thus, generational and philosophical differences exacerbated institutional tensions. The San Francisco local, for instance, avoided trusteeship in the postwar period, but a bitter generational struggle raged within the organization for years. Most reformers were younger women, many of whom sympathized with the more class-conscious, industrial union movement. As reformer Helen Jaye explained, "the older waitresses dominated the union floor. . . . The Secretary . . . had quite a little group around her of really die-hard waitresses." These "die-hard" waitresses would back whatever "the administration brought up . . . regardless of what it was. I guess it was age against youth or something like that; but they didn't like us young people in there because we were a little bit too radical."[28]

The reformers offered a comprehensive critique of the existing methods and philosophy of the union leadership. They advocated just cause provisions and job security at an individual worksite, an elected steward system that would enforce the contract more aggressively than the employer-oriented business agents, less officer and executive board discretion in job dispatching, a fair employment practices committee, and increased concern with the problems of members off the job such as unemployment, housing, and child care.[29]

Moreover, their critique of occupational unionism involved a subtle mocking of the craft standards and pride of the older generation. One waitress activist recalled issuing a little publication called the *Hasher's Herald* that older officials "didn't like one bit." Tellingly, what officials "resented the most," she remembered, "was the use of the word 'hasher.'" They found the term demeaning; to them waitressing was a profession—a craft through which one derived identity and pride.[30]

The incumbent waitress leaders defeated the rebels in San Francisco in the 1950s (as did leaders under assault in other locals across the country), but their tactics widened the gulf separating them from the younger rank and file. Instead of incorporating the new generation of activists into the leadership, the older officials shunned alliances with the newcomers and shut them out. Instead of adopting some of their ideas, they clung rigidly to older approaches. Instead of seeking to smooth over the rifts, unify the organization, and address the underlying issues, the incumbent leadership ensured lingering bitterness by personalizing the conflict. Rivals were personally attacked and vilified.[31] One Los Angeles official denounced her opponent as a certain man's mistress, not his wife. Another labeled her rivals "bitches" and "black SOBS."[32]

The factionalism and decline of craft consciousness in the 1950s and 1960s weakened the old style of waitress unionism but did not end it. In the 1970s, however, waitress unionism unraveled further as the younger waitress activists challenged the gender separatism of the older generation. Younger waitresses embraced alternative routes to achieving gender equality. Rather than expand the number of jobs defined as "female," they sought an end to the separation of the work world into "men's jobs" and "women's jobs." Rather than support sex-based protective statutes, they sought equal treatment under the law for men and women. Separate sex-based institutions and work divisions appeared outmoded. A paradigm had shifted.

With the 1964 passage of Title VII of the Civil Rights Act prohibiting employment discrimination based on sex, race, or national origin, the discriminatory hiring practices of hotel and restaurant employers were subject to legal challenge for the first time. The new legal climate meshed well with the sense of entitlement and possibility voiced by many younger, college-educated women. In the early 1970s, lawsuits flew fast and furious, prompted in part by the more aggressive stance against sexual discrimination taken by the Equal Employment Opportunity Commission (EEOC), the federal agency responsible for interpreting and enforcing Title VII.[33]

Women seeking entrance into the elite echelons of food service, such as formal dinner service and hotel banquet work, did not meet the stiff resistance from the union and the public that greeted female bartenders. Yet, on the whole, the initiative rested with the women, not with the union. At times, HERE locals *defended* the rights of women where contract violations occurred, but they failed to institute court actions against sexual discrimination or to negotiate strong affirmative action clauses. Significantly, the bulk of the lawsuits that helped open new categories of work for women were instigated by younger, college-aged women, and frequently, the union was named as a defendant along with the employer. In 1976, for example, twenty-nine-year-old waitress and college graduate Jeanne King opened formal dining service to women in New York City through her American Civil Liberties Union-sponsored suit against the Four Seasons, the 21 Club, La Caravelle, and other elite establishments. HERE Local 1, named in the suit, claimed they had no control over hiring. Technically, they were correct—by the 1970s they had lost much of their influence over hiring—but clearly, eradicating sexual discrimination in hiring for formal waiting jobs had never been a priority for the union.[34]

Even the more sympathetic culinary locals relied on contract protections rather than the courts. Detroit's local moved airport cocktail waitresses into bartending jobs under broad housewide seniority provisions. Seattle's Joint Board used the grievance procedure to retain the jobs of three dinner waitresses who, according to management, had been replaced by male waiters in order "to upgrade the quality of service." The arbitrator remained unimpressed by management claims that waitresses "could not be scheduled efficiently, [were] unduly quarrelsome, could not open wine bottles, and were inferior salesmen." Some of the large mixed locals defended their new pioneering female members against discharge and harassment; the San Francisco local joined forces with Bay Area feminist groups in 1980 to protest the rape of a hotel room-service waitress and to demand effective safeguards against sexual assault.[35]

The union's reputation in the eyes of the younger feminists suffered, however, because of what was perceived as a lack of leadership on issues of sexual discrimination and job segregation. The stance taken by many waitress leaders in the legislative battles to overturn certain sex-based protective laws further tarnished the "feminist" credentials of HERE. In the 1950s and even into the 1960s, waitress locals advocating special protections for women had the support of their membership and the larger labor community although they met resistance from groups like the Business and Professional Women, the National Organization of Women, and other Equal Rights Amendment (ERA) advocates.[36] By the 1970s, however, the "equal treatment" viewpoint enjoyed a wide consensus, not only among middle-class women, but also, increasingly, among female union officials.[37] As noted in chapter 7, waitresses themselves had altered their position on certain sex-based statutes by World War II, judging night work restrictions, for example, as more debilitating than protective. Yet waitress officials were not ready to make a blanket endorsement of equal treatment: the idea of differential treatment as a means to achieve equality was never wholly abandoned. As Myra Wolfgang argued in 1971, "We who want equal opportunity, equal pay for equal work and equal status for women, know that frequently we obtain real equality through a difference in treatment rather than identity in treatment." In the 1960s and 1970s, waitresses led the fight in California to defend the existing hours legislation, and

Wolfgang gained national notoriety for her opposition to the ERA, her clashes with Betty Freidan, and her obstinate refusal to back down on the need for overtime and other sex-based protections for working women.[38]

Nevertheless, the separate sex-based structures within the culinary unions eventually fell prey to the new paradigm as well. The actual suit, *Evans v. Sheraton Park Hotel*, that prompted the merger of sex-based culinary locals was initiated by a Washington, D.C., banquet waitress, Lorraine Evans, in the early 1970s. Evans, a member and union steward in Waitresses' Local 507, claimed that she and other women had suffered sexual discrimination in being denied access to the more lucrative banquet assignments. The suit named Waiters' Local 781, the Washington, D.C. Joint Board, and the International union as well as her own waitresses' local as defendants. The courts ruled in Evans's favor, noting that the banquet captain's practice of "favoring waiters over waitresses with respect to assignments to lucrative receptions" was illegal under Title VII. Moreover, the judge ventured an opinion on "the abuse inherent in maintaining and recognizing separate female and male locals: It is inevitable . . . that the more dominant group, in this case the males, will gain privileges of various kinds. The failure of Local 507 to support plaintiff's justifiable official complaints concerning uneven and unfair assignments demonstrates the inability of a Janus-headed union to safeguard sex equality." In the judge's view, the "maintenance of sex-segregated locals constituted a per se violation of the Act."[39] The death knell had sounded for waitress separatism.

The International had no choice but to merge the separate waiter and waitress locals nationwide. The older waitress officials objected vehemently. In Butte, Blanche Copenhaver, the local's principal officer, and others resisted, despite the merger's demonstrated positive impact on female wages and the International's guarantee "that Local 457 will be the absorbing local and that all female officers will continue." Clela Sullivan remembers having "her orders from Blanche . . . no merger. She wanted a female organization. . . . The men might take over and start bossing the women around."[40] In San Francisco, the "shotgun" marriage between the waiters and waitresses occurred only "under pressure of the Civil Rights Act of 1964 and their common international union" despite the admittance by union officers that the merger would open up a wider variety of jobs for both sexes. "Naturally, we'd rather be by ourselves," said Flo Douglas, president of the waitresses' local. Once the two locals were joined, the International initiated another round of mergers, uniting all crafts—cooks, bartenders, food servers, maids, and others—into one large industrial union.[41] By the late 1970s, every major city had a single amalgamated organization representing all hotel and restaurant employees. The separate craft and sex-based locals were a relic of history (Table 6).

Many of the older waitress officials stayed on as leaders in the merged locals, sometimes holding top positions, but often they were subsumed within the larger, male-dominated structures and out of step with the younger rank and file. By the 1970s and 1980s, even those unorganized waitresses who inclined toward collective solutions were now rejecting unionization by HERE. Some relied on informal group mechanisms to resolve such contentious problems as scheduling, station assignments, and task allocation. The union appeared as an alien institution that could impose disagreeable rules just as could the boss, not as a way of formalizing their own group-derived solutions.[42] Others did unionize but chose an independent union rather than affiliation with HERE. In Cambridge, Massachusetts, for example, waitresses formed an Independent Restaurant Workers Union in 1971 and organized four Harvard Square restaurants over the next few years. Madison, Wisconsin, food servers struck in 1978 over sexual harassment and later affiliated with the Madison Independent Workers' Union.[43]

Ironically, although they rejected HERE unionism, unorganized waitresses gave primary emphasis to some of the very issues—work autonomy, dignified treatment, and the revaluing and upgrading of service labor—that had united union waitresses historically. The Harvard Square Waitresses Union saw one of their main goals as "raising the status of service positions. People who work in service positions, such as waitressing, perform the natural function of helping to care for other people. . . . Many of us who felt that in our homes the preparing and serving of food to others was an act of love or friendship saw this same act degraded in a work situation. We began to ask why." Control over scheduling, equitable station assignments, improved supervisory behavior, benefits, and sexual harassment also emerged as important concerns.[44]

Yet food servers in the 1980s, rarely perceived union craft rules and strict job classifications as the mechanisms by which to achieve their goals. At least one waitress official argued that "you can't use a craft union approach in a restaurant when there are no longer any craft demarcations," but all too frequently HERE locals assumed a consensus on craft rules among younger workers that simply did not exist.[45] In 1984, for example, when the leadership of San Francisco's now-merged Local 2 struck the city's restaurant employers in part over retaining strict job classifications, they faced a divided and ambivalent membership. A surprising number of rank and file expressed sympathy with the employer argument that job rotation and the blurring of job classifications enhanced teamwork, work flexibility, and variety. Protection from employer abuse remained important to food servers, but certain craft rules now seemed to create as many problems as they solved.[46] And ironically, the very practices of the older craft unionism that would have been appropriate for this new work force—portable benefits, a hiring hall where workers determined when and how much they worked, training and upgrading, and peer management—had been voluntarily discarded or legally constrained.

Into the 1980s, the union continued to be viewed by younger waitresses as male-dominated and traditional in its attitudes toward women. A few locals conscientiously pursued instances of sex discrimination and sexual harassment, but their efforts remained invisible. The cases picked up by the media featured either harassed waitresses who turned to the courts after receiving the cold shoulder from their local union or solitary fighters who never considered the union a possible ally. Employers brazenly fired their aging waitforce and publicly claimed that "whether or not I hire women is my own goddamned business"; they also shunted nonwhite applicants into the lowest-paid kitchen and cleaning positions. Culinary unions appeared helpless and at times even complicit. When the newspaper headlines blared that Oakland, California's culinary union president faced indictment for offering jobs as prostitutes and call-girls to the prospective waitresses sitting in the union's hiring hall, the reputation of culinary unionism sank yet another notch.[47]

In the late 1980s, a new generation of female leadership emerged within HERE locals. Sherri Chiesa, secretary-treasurer of Local 2 in San Francisco, and Maria Elena Durazo, executive officer of Los Angeles's Local 11, are representative. Of necessity, their programs are based on advancing the interests of the mixed-sex, craft, ethnic, and racial membership of the large heterogeneous locals they govern; they did not rise to leadership as advocates for a female constituency. Yet perhaps with the union's continuing feminization, it will be possible for the new female leadership to represent the larger whole without losing sight of the needs of women. Chiesa, for example, began her tenure by returning to aggressive guerrilla tactics of the 1930s like the sip-ins and rolling strikes. She took on the sagging public image of the union by sponsoring "queen size" advertisements on city buses showing "72-year-old waitress Silvana Osuna with the caption '20 years on your feet and they treat you like leftovers.'" Local 2 also reinstituted a food server training program, geared in particular to upgrading waitress jobs and moving women into the formal hotel dining jobs still retained primarily by men.[48]

The task of creating a revitalized and relevant feminist unionism remains formidable, however. Organized labor continues to decline, and the heady days of second wave feminism have given way to the sobering reality of bitter clashes over strategy and of seemingly intractable sexual inequalities in the public and private sphere. A return to the form of union feminism practiced by waitresses in the past is not the solution; a new vision of unionism is needed that can claim the cooperation and tolerance of service-sector entrepreneurs while holding the allegiance of a membership with new definitions of worker power and gender equality.

Yet the historic concerns of female servers for recognition of the craft of food service and the skill of their "emotional labor" must remain at the center of the movement. Of equal importance, the "special needs" of women—their continuing exclusion from the better-paying jobs in the industry, the sexualized nature of their work, their relation to child-bearing and to the family—cannot be lost in the rush to integration and equal treatment. A new gender politics must be fashioned that recognizes difference and that creates opportunity and choice without sacrificing the historic needs of wage-earning women for economic security and a living wage. Contemporary attempts to advance the interests of wage-earning women would do well to consider the struggles, compromises, and victories of waitress unionists. The solutions they devised, although partial, have all too readily slipped from memory.

Tables and
Figures

Table 1. Emergence of Waiting Work as a Female-dominated Occupation, 1900–1970

Year	Total in Waiting Work	Number Women	Percent Women	Rank of Waiting as an Occupation for Women
1900	103,984	41,178	40	not in top 20
1910	188,293	85,798	46	not in top 20
1920	228,985	116,921	51	17
1930	393,288	231,973	59	14
1940	523,583	356,036	68	8
1950	708,600	579,810	82	6
1960	895,662	777,482	87	7
1970	1,230,434	1,132,000	92	6

Sources (all U.S. Department of Commerce, Bureau of the Census): A. M. Edwards, *Sixteenth Census of the U.S., 1940: Comparative Occupational Statistics for the U.S., 1870–1940* (Washington, D.C., 1943), Table 15, 172; Joseph A. Hill, *Women in Gainful Occupations, 1870–1920* (Washington, D.C., 1929), 83; *Statistical Abstract of the U.S., 1982–83*, 103 ed. (Washington, D.C., 1983), Table 621, 391; *Seventeenth Census of Population: 1950*, vol. 4: *Special Reports* (Washington, D.C., 1953), pt. 1, 1-21; *Eighteenth Census of Population: 1960, Subject Reports, Occupational Characteristics* (Washington, D.C., 1963), 9; *Nineteenth Census of the Population: 1970, Subject Reports, Occupational Characteristics* (Washington, D.C., 1973), 27; Special Reports of the Census Office, *Statistics of Women at Work, 1900* (Washington, D.C., 1907), 158; and U. S. Department of Labor, Women's Bureau, *The Occupational Progress of Women, 1910 to 1930*, Bulletin no. 104, by Mary V. Dempsey (Washington, D.C., 1930), 39, 73; *Women's Occupations Through Seven Decades*, Bulletin no. 218, by Janet M. Hooks (Washington, D.C., 1947), 141; and *Changes in Women's Occupations, 1940–50*, Bulletin no. 253 (Washington, D.C., 1954), 61.

Table 2A. Race and Nativity of Waitresses, 1900–1970 *

Year	Native White	White	Foreign-born White	Black	Other†
1900			42,839 Total		
1910	64% (55,047)		27% (23,069)	8.7% (7,434)	.29% (248)
1920	68% (77,507)		20% (23,039)	12.1% (13,836)	.1% (276)
1930	78% (180,363)		14% (31,989)	7.6% (17,628)	.86% (1,993)
1940		95% (338,956)		4% (17,080)	.9% (2,004)
1950	88% (510,705)		4.7% (27,415)	7% (40,410)	.22% (1,290)
1960		93% (723,727)		6% (46,797)	.89% (6,958)
1970		94% (923,285)		5% (52,439)	1% (10,417)

Sources (all U.S. Department of Commerce, Bureau of the Census): *Twelfth Census of the U.S., 1900, Population*, vol. 2: pt. 2 (Washington, D.C., 1902), 505; *Fifteenth Census of the U.S., 1930, Population*, vol. 5: *General Report on Occupations* (Washington, D.C., 1933), 76, 85; *Sixteenth Census of the U.S., 1940, Population*, vol. 3: *The Labor Force*, vol. 2: *Occupational Characteristics* (Washington, D.C., 1943), 69; A. M. Edwards, *Sixteenth Census of the U.S., 1940: Comparative Occupational Statistics for the U.S., 1870–1940* (Washington, D.C., 1943), 172; *Seventeenth Census of Population: 1950*, vol. 4: *Special Reports*, pt. 1, ch. B, *Occupational Characteristics* (Washington, D.C., 1953), 1b-35, 1b-27; *Eighteenth Census of Population: 1960, Subject Reports, Occupational Characteristics* (Washington, D.C., 1963), 29; *Nineteenth Census of Population: 1970, Subject Reports, Occupational Characteristics* (Washington, D.C., 1973), 27; *Statistical Abstract of the U.S., 1982–83*, 103d ed. (Washington, D.C., 1983), 391.

*No breakdown is available for 1900. Nativity was not specified for 1940, 1960, and 1970.

†Includes Indian, Japanese, Chinese, Filipino, Korean. Before 1930, Mexicans were included in the nonwhite category; after 1930, they were included with the white category.

Table 2B. Race and Nativity of Waiters, 1900–1970

Year	Native White	White	Foreign-born White	Black	Other
1900			64,591 Total		
1910	30% (29,893)		34% (33,493)	33% (32,676)	2% (2,503)
1920	30% (33,744)		38% (42,968)	28% (31,681)	3% (3,671)
1930	36% (58,552)		34% (54,305)	25% (39,750)	5% (8,708)
1940*		86% (241,943)		12% (33,851)	2% (5,560)
1950†		86% (293,169)		12% (42,490)	2% (5,760)
1960†		85% (263,414)		12% (37,527)	2% (7,358)
1970		77% (92,430)		16% (18,890)	7% (7,985)

Sources (all U.S. Department of Commerce, Bureau of the Census): *Twelfth Census of the U.S.*, *1900, Population*, vol. 2, pt. 2 (Washington, D.C., 1902), 505; *Thirteenth Census of the U.S.*, *1910, Population*, vol. 4: *Occupational Statistics* (Washington, D.C., 1913), 432–33; *Fourteenth Census of the U.S., 1920, Population*, vol. 4: *Occupations* (Washington, D.C., 1923), 358–59; *Fifteenth Census of the U.S., 1930, Population*, vol. 5: *Occupations* (Washington, D.C., 1933), 85; *Sixteenth Census of the U.S., 1940, Population*, vol. 3: *The Labor Force*, pt. 1 (Washington, D.C., 1943), 89; *Seventeenth Census of the Population: 1950*, vol. 2: *Characteristics of the Population*, pt. 1 (Washington, D.C., 1953), 1–277; *Eighteenth Census of the Population, 1960*, vol. 1: *Characteristics of the Population*, pt. 1 (Washington, D.C., 1963), 1–545; *Nineteenth Census of the Population: 1970, Subject Reports, Occupational Characteristics* (Washington, D.C., 1973), 27.
*Waiters and bartenders. No nativity was specified after 1930.
†Waiters, bartenders, counter workers

Table 2C. Black Waitress Employment by Region, 1910–70

Year	Northeast	North Central	South	West
1910	3,007	780	3,183	135
1920	3,926	2,429	7,397	225
1930	5,200	3,663	7,915	441
1940	2,855	3,001	9,042	395
1950	6,560	8,958	24,437	2,184
1960	9,589	10,919	30,532	3,083
1970	7,622	9,649	25,187	2,862

Sources (all U.S. Department of Commerce, Bureau of the Census): *Thirteenth Census of the U.S.*, *1910*, vol. 4: *Population* (Washington, D.C., 1913), 434–534; *Fourteenth Census of the U.S.*, *1920*, vol. 4: *Population* (Washington, D.C., 1923), 874–1048; *Fifteenth Census of the U.S.*, *1930*, *Population*, vol. 4: *Occupations, By States* (Washington, D.C., 1933), 123–1792; *Sixteenth Census of the U.S.*, *1940*, *Population*, vol. 3: *The Labor Force* (Washington, D.C., 1943), 95–96; *Seventeenth Census of Population*, *1950*, vol. 1: *Characteristics of the Population*, pt. 1 (Washington, D.C., 1953), 1–719; *Nineteenth Census of Population*, vol. 1: *Characteristics of the Population*, pt. 1 (Washington, D.C., 1973), 1–1272, 1–1279.

Table 3. Marital Status of Waitresses Compared to All Working Women, 1910–60*

Year	Percent Married Spouse Present/ Spouse Absent	Percent Widowed/Divorced	Percent Single
1910	16 (?)	—	84 (?)
	(24.7)	(15)	(60.2)
1920	27.1	†	72.9†
	(23)	†	(77)†
1930	34.2	16.4	49.4
	(28.9)	(17.2)	(53.9)
1940	—	—	—
	(30.1/5.8)	(15.1)	(49)
1950	48.5/9.8	5.7/12.2	23.8
	(46.5/5.7)	(16)	(31.9)
1960	54/8.9	6.1/9.7	21.4
	(55.2/5.5)	(15.7)	(23.6)

Sources (all U.S. Department of Commerce, Bureau of the Census): *Fifteenth Census of the U.S., 1930, Population*, vol. 5: *General Report on Occupations* (Washington, D.C., 1933), 290; Joseph A. Hill, *Women in Gainful Occupations, 1870–1920* (Washington, D.C., 1929), 83, 187; *Seventeenth Census of Population: 1950*, vol. 4: *Special Reports*, pt. I, ch. B, *Occupational Characteristics* (Washington, D.C., 1953), 1b-93, 1b-97; *Eighteenth Census of Population: 1960, Subject Reports, Occupational Characteristics* (Washington, D.C., 1963), 29; *Historical Statistics of the U.S. Colonial Times to 1970* (Washington, D.C., 1975), 133.
*Top figure: waitresses; bottom figure: all working women.
†Statistic for single includes widowed/divorced.

Table 4. Percentage of Waiters and Waitresses Working Full-time and Part-time, 1940–70

	Female		Male	
	Full-time	Part-time	Full-time	Part-time
1940	79	21	89	11
1950	71	29	77	23
1960	52	48	61	39
1970	37	63	49	51

Sources (all U.S. Department of Commerce, Bureau of the Census): *Sixteenth Census of the U.S., 1940, Occupational Characteristics* (Washington, D.C., 1943), 144–45; *Seventeenth Census of Population: 1950, Special Reports*, pt. 1, vol. 4 (Washington, D.C., 1953), 1B–151, 1B–157; *Eighteenth Census of Population: 1960, Occupational Characteristics* (Washington, D.C., 1963), 192–202; *Nineteenth Census of Population: 1970, Occupational Characteristics* (Washington, D.C., 1973), 774, 760.

Tables 5A–5C. Statistics on Union Organization in the Food Service Industry, 1891–1980

5A. Membership in the Hotel Employees and Restaurant Employees International Union: Selected Years, 1891–1980

1891	450	1935	55,965
1900	5,340	1940	210,934
1905	39,317	1945	283,857
1910	39,453	1950	403,702
1915	61,923	1955	411,724
1920	53,540	1960	439,690
1925	38,427	1970	461,000
1930	39,694	1980	400,000

Sources: *Proceedings*, HERE Convention, 1947, 8; *Proceedings*, HERE Convention, 1957, 15; U.S. Department of Commerce, Bureau of the Census, *Statistical Abstract of the U.S.*, *1982–83* (Washington, D.C., 1983), 409.

5B. Estimates of the Extent of Union Organization in Eating and Drinking Places, 1910–75

Year	Percent Organized
1910	5.8
1920	9.2
1930	4–7
1940	10–25
1949	24
1953	25
1954	22
1967	15–19
1975	9.7

Sources: Leo Wolman, *Ebb and Flow in Trade Unionism* (New York, 1926), 118–21; Philip Taft, "Brief Review of Other Industries," in *How Collective Bargaining Works*, ed. Harry A. Millis (New York, 1942), 924–25; *Catering Industry Employee*, May 1949, 8, January 1954, 2; *Officers' Report*, HERE, 1953, 48; U.S. Department of Labor, Bureau of Labor Statistics, *Industry Wage Survey: Eating and Drinking Places, October 1966 and April 1967* (Washington, D.C., 1968), 2; U.S. Department of Labor, Bureau of Labor Statistics, *Earning and Demographic Characteristics of Union Members* (Washington, D.C., 1980), 5.

5C. Regional Variations in Union Organization in Eating and Drinking Places, 1961

Region	Percent Organized
Oakland/San Francisco	80–90
Detroit, New York, St. Louis, Cincinnati	60–70
Los Angeles, Long Beach	50–60
Chicago, Philadelphia, Washington, D.C.	20–30
Pittsburgh, Denver, Boston	Less Than 10

Source: U.S. Department of Labor, Bureau of Labor Statistics, *Industry Wage Survey: Eating and Drinking Places, June 1961*, Bulletin 1329 (Washington, D.C., 1961), 9.

Table 6. Organizational Life of the Fifteen Largest Waitresses' Locals, 1900–1976[*]

	1900	1910	1920	1930	1940	1950	1960	1970
Local 240 Seattle	1900–1973							
Local 249 St. Louis	1900–1905	1910–74						
Local 107 Cleveland	1900–1905	1908–67						
Local 484 Chicago	1902–73							
Local 335 Toledo		(1904–22)			(1938–72)			
Local 276 Cincinnati		(1905–11)		1930–72				
Local 227 Rochester		(1905–9)	(1919–23)	1934–67				
Local 48 San Francisco	1906–72							
Local 457 Butte, Montana	1907–72							
Local 503 Kansas City		1914–74						
Local 112 Boston		1915–55						
Local 347 Buffalo		1917–74						
Local 639 Los Angeles		1919–73						
Local 305 Portland		1921–76						
Local 507 Washington						1954–72		

[*]All dates are based on the history and jurisdiction records for HERE locals, HERE Files. Charter and merger dates in parentheses are estimates. No separate waitress locals existed before 1900 o[r] after 1976.

Table 7. Female Membership in the Hotel Employees and Restaurant Employees International Union, 1908–68

Year	HERE Members Total	Number of Women	Percent Women	Percent in Separate Locals
1908[a]	37,000	1,928	5	—
1910	37,000[b]	2,015[b]	5.4	85[c]
1920	60,400[b]	5,600[b]	10.4	70[c]
1924	38,500[d]	4,000[e]	—	—
1927	39,880[d]	8,700[f]	21.8	60
1950	403,702[g]	181,000	45[h]	20–25[c]
1958	443,616[g]	179,664	40.5[i]	20–25[c]
1968	459,062	146,900[j]	32[j]	15–20[j]

Sources: a. John Andrews and W. D. P. Bliss, *A History of Women in Trade Unions*, vol. 10 of *Report on the Condition of Woman and Child Earners in the U.S.*, U.S. Senate Doc. 645, 61st Cong., 2d sess. (Washington, D.C., 1911; reprint New York, 1974), 136.

b. Leo Wolman, *Growth of American Trade Unions, 1880–1923* (New York, 1924), 98, 114–15.

c. Estimates based on totaling membership figures for the largest female locals supplied by the HERE office files.

d. *Proceedings*, 1947 Convention, HERE, 8. HERE Proceedings were published by the HERE International Union located in Cincinnati, Ohio. They are available in the Social Science Library Labor Collection, University of California, Berkeley.

e. Teresa Wolfson, *The Woman Worker and the Trade Unions* (New York, 1926), 126–27.

f. Teresa Wolfson, "Trade Union Activities of Women," *Annals of the American Academy* 143 (May 1929): 122.

g. John P. Henderson, *Labor Market Institutions* (East Lansing, 1965), 132.

h. R. L. Davis, Director, HERE Department of Research and Education, to Mary Pidgeon, 8 February 1950, Box 995, file "Correspondence on Bulletin #239," RG-86, National Archives.

i. Labor Research Association, *Labor Fact Book* No. 14 (New York, 1959), 80.

j. Lucretia Dewey, "Women in Labor Unions," *Monthly Labor Review* (February 1971), reprint 2713, Table 2, 43.

Table 8. Membership in Selected Waitresses' Locals, 1908–60*

	1908	1918	1929	1940	1945	1948	1955	1960
Local 48 San Francisco	320	449	1036	3035	5311	6325*	4783	4232
Local 240 Seattle	249	457	569	2200	3051	3390	3715*	3656
Local 305 Portland	—	—	474	1030	1825	2014*	1715	1781
Local 457 Butte	—	229	508	600	929	947	1149*	1065
Local 484 Chicago	420	342	331	1625	2086	2629*	2313	2108
Local 639 Los Angeles	—	—	452	800	3217	4198	5263	6257*

Source: Local union membership records, HERE Files.

*Indicates peak year for membership.

Table 9. Participation of Women HERE Members at Selected HERE Conventions, 1901–76

Year	Place	Number Delegates	Number Women Delegates	Women as Percent of Delegates	Percent of Women from Separate Locals
1901	St. Louis	62	1	1.6	100
1909	Minneapolis	187	4	2.1	75
1915	San Francisco	213	16	7.5	75
1919	Providence	231	22	9.5	77
1923	Chicago	152	25	16	68
1925	Quebec	118	21	18	81
1927	Portland	180	47	26	64
1929	Kansas City	162	40	25	60
1932	Boston	100	21	21	—
1934	Minneapolis	146	22	15	—
1936	Rochester	360	49	14	—
1941	Cincinnati	820	150	19	36
1947	Milwaukee	1159	273	24	—
1957	Chicago	868	194	22	—
1966	St. Louis	773	204	26	—
1976	Palm Springs	471	133	28	—

Source: HERE Conventions Records, 1901–76.

Tables 10A–10D. Summary Data on Waitress Union Officials*

10A. Family Characteristics of Waitress Leaders

	Cohort A (b. 1880–1901)	Cohort B (b. 1902–20)
Marital Status:		
married (husband present)	50%	55%
married (husband absent; divorced or widowed)	31	33
never married	6	6
unknown	13	6
Age at first marriage	25.3	22.7
Average number of children	2.1	1.8

10B. Family Characteristics of All Women Labor Leaders

	1925	1946	1976
Marital Status:			
married	21.8%	56%	57%
unmarried	78.2	44	43
Age at first marriage	N/A	24.8	23.7
Average number of children	N/A	.6	1.4

Source: Gary Fink, *Biographical Dictionary of American Labor* (Westport, 1984), Table 10, 32.

10C. Nativity of Waitress Leaders

	Cohort A (b. 1880–1901)	Cohort B (b. 1902–20)
Native-born	82%	82%
Foreign-born	0	9
Unknown	18	9

10D. Occupation of Fathers of Waitress Leaders

	Cohort A (b. 1880–1901)	Cohort B (b. 1902–20)
Professional/white-collar	0%	0%
Clerk/sales/small business	15	23
Union official	8	0
Skilled blue-collar	46	46
Farmer	23	16
Unskilled labor/factory	8	15

*Unless otherwise noted, all tables are based on the author's compilation of statistics on forty waitress officials. The sources did not always provide data in every category desired, thus, the samples used are sometimes less than forty, but in no case below thirty-two.

Figure 1. Hotel Employees and Restaurant Employees International
Union Membership, 1891-1961

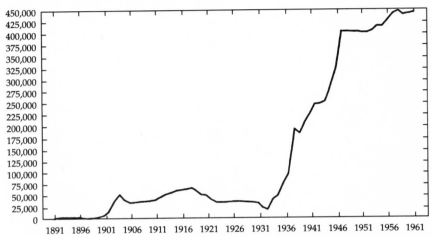

Source: John P. Henderson, *Labor Market Institutions and Wages in the Lodging
Industry* (East Lansing, 1965), 133.

Figure 2. Age at Which Full-Time Union Work Began for Waitress Leaders

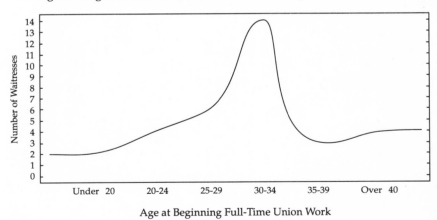

Abbreviations
Used in the Notes

Annals	Annals of the American Academy of Political and Social Science
AF	*American Federationist*
BL-UCB	Bancroft Library, University of California, Berkeley
SFLCR	San Francisco Labor Council Records
BSBA	Butte-Silver Bow Public Archives
WPU	Women's Protective Union Collection
HR	Hotel and Restaurant Union Files
CC	*Cafeteria Call*, official organ of the Cafeteria Employees Union, Local 302, New York, N.Y.
CHS	California Historical Society, San Francisco, California
BMC	Bertha Metro Collection
HREB	Hotel Restaurant Employees and Bartenders Union Records
CIE	*Catering Industry Employee*, official journal of the Hotel and Restaurant Employees International Alliance and the Bartender's International League of America, Cincinnati
DRE	*Dining Room Employee*, official publication of the Dining Room Employees, Local 1, New York, N.Y.
HCV	*Hotel and Club Voice*, official publication of the Hotel and Club Employees, Local 6, New York, N.Y.
HERE	Hotel and Restaurant Employees International Union
HERE Files	Hotel and Restaurant Employees International Union Files, Washington, D.C. (formerly Cincinnati)
DUR	Defunct Union Records
GOR	General Office Records
LUR	Local Union Records
JCR	Jurisdiction and Charter Records
MJM	Matthew Josephson Materials

HM	*Hotel Monthly Journal*, Chicago
JAH	*Journal of American History*
LJEB	Local Joint Executive Board
Local 1 Files	Files of Hotel Employees and Restaurant Employees, Local 1, Chicago (successor to Waitresses' Local 484)
Local 2 Files	Files of Hotel Employees and Restaurant Employees, Local 2, San Francisco (successor to Waitresses' Local 48)
EBM	Executive Board Minutes
MM	Membership Minutes
Local 6 Files	Files of Hotel Employees and Restaurant Employees, Local 6, New York, N.Y. (successor to Waiters and Waitresses' Local 1, Hotel and Club Employees' Local 6, and other New York City locals.)
Local 24 Files	Files of Hotel Employees and Restaurant Employees, Local 24, Detroit (successor to Waiters' and Waitresses' Local 705)
Local 457 Files	Files of Hotel Employees and Restaurant Employees, Local 457, Butte, Montana
LAT	*Los Angeles Times*
MLR	*Monthly Labor Review*
MS	*Mixer and Server*
MHBRR	*Michigan Hotel Bar Restaurant Review*, official journal of Local 705, Detroit
MHS	Montana Historical Society, Helena
WPUC-174	Women's Protective Union Records, Collection 174
NYT	*New York Times*
NA	National Archives and Records Service, Washington, D.C.
RG-9	National Recovery Administration Records
RG-86	Women's Bureau Records
RG-174	Francis Perkins Records
RG-257	Bureau of Labor Statistics, Collective Bargaining Agreements
RG-280	Federal Mediation and Conciliation Service
RWA-NYU	Robert F. Wagner Archives, Tamiment Library, New York University
Local 1-S	Local 1-S Collection, Department Store Workers Union
SDS C-2	Strikes and Department Store Organizing of the 1930s, Collection 2
SFLC	*San Francisco Labor Clarion*, official journal of the San Francisco Labor Council
SA	*Serving America: Hotel-Bar-Restaurant News*, Long Beach, California, official journal of the Culinary Alliance, Local 681

SW	*Southland Waitress*, published for the information and advancement of women culinary workers, Local 639, Los Angeles
SSLLC-UCB	Social Science Library Labor Collection, University of California, Berkeley
SLA-GSU	Southern Labor Archives, Georgia State University, Atlanta, Georgia
VOL	*Voice of Local 1*, official organ of Waiters and Waitresses' Local 1, New York, N.Y.
WRL-WSU	Walter Reuther Library, Wayne State University
IWW	Industrial Workers of the World Collection
JR	Jack Rugh Collection
MOW	Mary Ovington White Collection
MW	Myra Wolfgang Collection
VF-HR	Vertical Files-Hotel and Restaurant
WHS	Wisconsin State Historical Society, Madison
RCIA Records	Retail Clerks International Union Records
WTUL	Women's Trade Union League of America
WTUL Papers	Papers of the Women's Trade Union League and its principal leaders, Microfilm Edition
C-2	Collection 2, National WTUL Papers, Schlesinger Library
C-4	Collection 4, Records of the New York WTUL
C-9	Collection 9, WTUL Publications

Interviews

Beulah Compton interview, conducted by Elizabeth Case for the University of Michigan Institute of Industrial Relations-Wayne State University Oral History Project, Twentieth Century Trade Union Women, Vehicle for Social Change, 1978.

Blanche Copenhaver interview, conducted by Mary Murphy, 21 February 1980, Butte, Montana, BSBA.

Florence Douglas interview, conducted by the author, 4 August 1986, San Francisco.

Kathryn Wetzel Newton Dewing interview, conducted by Laurie Mercier for the Montana Historical Society, 11 August 1986, Anaconda, Montana.

Idoniea Golding Duntley interview, conducted by Laurie Mercier for the Montana Historical Society, 28 April 1982, Sunrise Bluff Estates, Fort Benton, Montana.

Florence Farr interview, conducted by the author, 28 June 1989, Detroit.

Lou Goldblatt interview, conducted by Lucy Kendall for the California Historical Society, n.d.

Helen Jaye interview, conducted by Lucy Kendall for the California Historical Society, 16 March 1981.

Sam Jaye interview, conducted by Lucy Kendall for the California Historical Society, 23 March 1981.

Nellie Stone Johnson interview, conducted by David V. Taylor for the Black History Project, Minnesota Historical Society, St. Paul, 1975.

Lucy Kendall interview, conducted by the author, 4 August 1986, San Francisco.

Carmen Lucia interview, conducted by Seth Wigderson and Bette Craig for the University of Michigan Institute of Industrial Relations-Wayne State University Oral History Project, Twentieth Century Trade Union Woman, Vehicle for Social Change, 1978.

Charles Paulsen interview, conducted by the author, 28 July 1983, Cincinnati.

Jeri Powell interview, conducted by the author, 7 August 1986, San Francisco.

Charlotte Stern interview, conducted by the author, June 1984, New York City.

William G. Storie interview, conducted by Corinne Gilb for the University of California, Berkeley, Institute of Industrial Relations Oral History Project, January–April 1959.

Clela Sullivan interview, conducted by the author, 1 August 1989, Butte, Montana.

Gertrude Sweet interview, conducted by Shirley Tanzer for the University of Michigan Institute of Industrial Relations-Wayne State University Oral History Project, Twentieth Century Trade Union Woman, Vehicle for Social Change, 1978.

Loretta Szeliga interview, conducted by Bea Lemisch for the Grandma Was an Activist Project, Tamiment Library, RWA-NYU, 1981.

Jackie Walsh interview, conducted by Lucy Kendall for the California Historical Society, March–November 1980, Larkspur, California.

Jackie Walsh interview, conducted by the author, 5 August 1986, Larkspur, California.

Valentine Catherine Kenney Webster interview, conducted by Mary Murphy, 24 February 1980, Butte, Montana, University of Montana at Missoula Oral History Collection.

Notes

Introduction

1. Ann Japenga, "Granny Waitresses Picket Restaurant to Reclaim Jobs," *LAT*, 23 February 1984, part 5, 1, 7.

2. The term *waitresses* may be seen as a pejorative feminization of the standard term, *waiter*, which commonly refers to male food servers. I have adopted it, however, because the women themselves used the term and because it is a less cumbersome way of distinguishing the male and female groups within the occupation. A similar decision was made with regard to *barmaid* and *bartender*.

3. The classic sociological treatments of waitresses are Frances Donovan, *The Woman Who Waits* (Boston, 1920) and William Foote Whyte, *Human Relations in the Restaurant Industry* (New York, 1948). For one of the few recent book-length studies, see James Spradley and Brenda Mann, *The Cocktail Waitress: Women's Work in a Man's World* (New York, 1975).

4. *Village Voice*, 8 December 1987, 116.

5. Rachael Migler, "The Philadelphia Waitress," *Philadelphia Magazine* 76 (April 1985): 108.

6. The dominant element of the postindustrial work force at first was perceived as "white-collar" professional and technical workers. Then, researchers noted the prominence of such low-paid, pink-collar occupations as sales and clerical. Statistics point to personal service jobs as the leading growth sector in the 1990s. See George Silvestri and John Lukasiewicz, "Occupational Employment Projections: The 1984–95 Outlook," *MLR* 108 (November 1985): 42–57.

7. Silvestri and Lukasiewicz, "Occupational Employment Projections," Table 5, 59.

8. Table 1 in the Appendix; U.S. Department of Labor, Employment and Training Administration, *Career Opportunities in the Hotel and Restaurant Industries* (Washington, D.C., 1982), 43; Richard Carnes and Horst Brand, "Productivity and New Technology in Eating and Drinking Places," *MLR* 100 (September 1977): 9–15.

9. For an overview of the gender biases in the sociological literature, see Myra Marx Ferree and Beth B. Hess, "Introduction," in *Analyzing Gender*, ed. Ferree and Hess (Beverly Hills, 1987). For the androcentric assumptions embedded in labor history, see Anne Philips and Barbara Taylor, "Sex and Skill: Notes Toward a Feminist Economics," *Feminist Review* 6 (October 1980): 79–88; Susan Porter Benson, " 'The Customers Ain't God': The Work Culture of Department Store Saleswomen, 1890–1940," in *Working-Class America: Essays on Labor, Community, and American Society*,

ed. Michael Frisch and Daniel Walkowitz (Urbana, 1983), 185–211; and Mary Blewett, *Men, Women, and Work: Class, Gender, and Protest in the New England Shoe Industry, 1780–1910* (Urbana, 1988), xiii–xxii. Even women's labor history has been dominated by what one review called "the industrial paradigm." See Lois Helmbold and Ann Schofield, "Women's Labor History, 1790–1945," *Reviews in American History* 17 (December 1989): 505.

10. The distinct character of service labor only now is being recognized, and the implications of these findings for basic sociological and economic theory have yet to be sorted out. For one of the best sociological treatments of service work, see Arlie Hochschild, *The Managed Heart: The Commercialization of Human Feeling* (Berkeley, 1983). Historians appear to be taking the lead in examining service occupations. Excellent analyses include David Katzman, *Seven Days a Week: Women and Domestic Service in Industrializing America* (New York, 1978); Barbara Melosh, *The Physician's Hand: Work Culture and Conflict in American Nursing* (Philadelphia: Temple University Press, 1982); Susan Reverby, *Ordered to Care: The Dilemma of American Nursing, 1850–1945* (Cambridge, 1987); and Susan Porter Benson, *Counter Cultures: Saleswomen, Managers and Customers in American Department Stores, 1890–1910* (Urbana, 1986).

11. For example, Benson, *Counter Cultures* and Barbara Melosh, *The Physician's Hand*. By focusing on waitress union activism, I do not mean to suggest that union-building represents the "quintessential form of worker resistance" (to use Ava Baron's phrase) or that militancy connected with the waged-work sphere is more important than collective responses occurring in other arenas. For further discussion of these points see Ava Baron, "Gender and Labor History: Learning from the Past, Looking to the Future," and Dana Frank, "Gender, Consumer Organizing, and the Seattle Labor Movement, 1919–1929," in *Work Engendered: Toward a New History of Men, Women, and Work*, ed. Baron (Ithaca, 1991).

12. For comparisons with other service trades, see Stephen Norwood, *Labor's Flaming Youth: Telephone Operators and Worker Militancy, 1878–1923* (Urbana, 1990); Sharon Strom, " 'We're No Kitty Foyles': Organizing Office Workers for the Congress of Industrial Organizations, 1937–50," in *Women Work, and Protest: A Century of U.S. Women's Labor History*, ed. Ruth Milkman (Boston, 1985); and George Kirstein, *Stores and Unions: A Study of the Growth of Unionism in Dry Goods and Department Stores* (New York, 1954).

13. See Tables 5–8 and Figure 1 in the Appendix.

14. For overviews of female union activity, see Alice Kessler-Harris, *Out to Work: A History of Wage-Earning Women in the United States* (New York, 1982), 152, 268, and Ruth Milkman, "Organizing the Sexual Division of Labor," *Socialist Review* 49 (January–February 1980): 95–150.

15. See Table 6 for the organizational life of the major waitress locals; Table 7 provides an overview of female membership in HERE. Because the union did not keep records by sex and by craft, the exact number of waitresses residing in separate locals has been impossible to calculate. Nevertheless, before the late 1930s, it is clear that the majority of waitresses resided in separate locals because almost all female HERE members were waitresses. During the industrial upsurge of the 1930s and 1940s, HERE increasingly organized hotel maids and female kitchen workers. Because most of these women joined mixed, industrial locals, the percent of HERE

women in separate locals drops sharply after the 1930s. The percent of waitresses in separate locals probably declined less precipitously, however, because a large percent of waitresses who organized in the 1930s and 1940s joined the already established, all-female waitress locals.

16. In contrast with the national bargaining structures that developed in auto or steel, culinary locals either bargained contracts themselves or participated through cross-craft culinary councils, known as Local Joint Executive Boards (LJEBs). Even in the latter case—which was the typical pattern after the 1930s—waitress locals still formulated their own demands and appointed their own representatives on the craftwide negotiating committees.

17. Specifically, I gained access to the voluminous archives of the Hotel Employees and Restaurant Employees International Union now located in Washington, D.C. The archive contained the records—correspondence, union newsletters, bylaws, work rules, and contracts—of hundreds of culinary locals across the country, including all the major female-dominated organizations. Individual HERE locals also allowed me to review their records. The holdings of locals in San Francisco, Butte, Montana, New York City, and Detroit proved to be the richest. Relevant public collections at the Walter Reuther Archives, the Butte-Silver Bow Public Archives, the Montana Historical Society, the Tamiment Library, the National Archives and Records Service, and the Bancroft Library yielded additional material.

18. For a discussion of the renewed interest among labor historians in the possibilities of institutional history see David Brody, "Labor History, Industrial Relations, and the Crisis of American Labor," *Industrial and Labor Relations Review* 43 (October 1988): 7–18.

19. In addition, questions concerning institutional structures and changing legislative and collective bargaining positions suggested the need for a national focus. Other works that take either a national or an institutional approach while also attempting to address questions of culture include, for example, Alan Derickson, *Workers' Health, Workers' Democracy: The Western Miners' Struggle, 1891–1925* (Ithaca, 1989), and Leon Fink and Brian Greenberg, *Upheaval in the Quiet Zone: A History of Hospital Workers' Union, Local 1199* (Urbana, 1989).

20. See, for example, Bylaws, Local 112, 1915–44, Reel 20, DUR, HERE Files; Bylaws, Local 457, 1946, 1964, Reel 970, LUR, HERE Files; Bylaws, Local 457, 1954, Box 13-8, WPUC-174, MHS.

21. The potential for militancy among working-class women has been thoroughly documented; the ways in which working-class female activism challenges conventional theory concerning the nature, sources, and periodization of women's activism less so. Much of that theory rests on the experiences of white middle-class women. For accounts of protest activity among working women see, Meredith Tax, *The Rising of the Women: Feminist Solidarity and Class Conflict, 1880–1917* (New York, 1980); and Milkman, ed., *Women, Work, and Protest.*

22. As labor historians have returned to questions of institutional arrangements, a number of good case studies of female workers and their unions have appeared. See, for example, Norwood, *Labor's Flaming Youth,* and Carole Turbin, *Working Women of Collar City: Gender, Class, and Community in Troy, 1864–1886* (Urbana, in press).

23. See, for example, Blewett, *Men, Women, and Work;* Joan Scott, "Work Identi-

ties for Men and Women: The Politics of Work and Family in the Parisian Garment Trades in 1848," in *Gender and the Politics of History* (New York, 1988), 93–112; Patricia Cooper, *Once a Cigar Maker: Men, Women, and Work Culture in American Cigar Factories, 1900–1919* (Urbana, 1987), and Cooper, "The Faces of Gender: Work and Work Relations at Philco, 1928–1938," in *Work Engendered*, ed. Baron. For overviews detailing the continuing lack of attention among labor historians to gender, see Baron, "Gender and Labor History," and Alice Kessler-Harris, "A New Agenda for American Labor History: A Gendered Analysis and the Question of Class," in *Perspectives on American Labor History: The Problems of Synthesis*, ed. J. Carroll Moody and Alice Kessler-Harris (DeKalb, 1989), in particular, 225–32.

24. The definition of family wage is from Alice Kessler-Harris, *A Woman's Wage: Historical Meanings and Social Consequences* (Lexington, Ky., 1990), 8. The impact of the "family wage" idea and the degree to which working-class women supported the concept have been intensely disputed; the meaning it held for working-class women has received less attention. See Jane Humphries, "The Working-class Family, Women's Liberation, and Class Struggle: The Case of Nineteenth-century British History," *Review of Radical Political Economics* 9 (Fall 1977): 25–42; and Martha May, "Bread Before Roses: American Workingmen, Labor Unions and the Family Wage," in *Women, Work, and Protest*, ed. Milkman, 1–21.

25. Hochschild, *Managed Heart*, 3–12, passim. Male culinary workers argued their claim for "skilled status" on a different basis, using terms denoting technical expertise and status differentials. Bartenders considered themselves "mixologists"; waiters called themselves "service experts," "service specialists," and "first-class waiters."

26. Waitresses' notions of "respectability," "sexual morality," and "equality" were class and gender-based. They also evolved over time. For an exploration of evolving female working-class conceptions of virtue, see Alice Kessler-Harris, "Independence and Virtue in the Lives of Wage-Earning Women: The U.S., 1870–1930," in *Women in Culture and Politics: A Century of Change*, ed. Judith Friedlander et al. (Bloomington, 1986).

27. Joanne Meyerowitz, *Women Adrift: Independent Wage Earners in Chicago, 1880–1930* (Chicago, 1988), 39–41.

28. For detailed discussions of the shopfloor practices of craft unionism, see Selig Perlman, *A Theory of the Labor Movement* (New York, 1928), 254–79; and Seymour Martin Lipset, *Union Democracy: The Internal Politics of the Typographical Union* (Glencoe, 1956), 25–32, passim.

29. Until the 1970s, a remarkable consensus existed among historians concerning the political nature of the AFL. Both the "Wisconsin school" and their critics agreed that the AFL represented the conservative perspective of a craft elite: broad social reform was suspect, the dominant business values of efficiency, profit, and laissez-faire controlling. See Perlman, *A Theory of the Labor Movement*, for the fullest theoretical statement of the Wisconsin school. For the assessment of later scholars, see Maurice Isserman, "God Bless Our American Institutions: The Labor History of John R. Commons," *Labor History* 17 (Summer 1976): 309–29.

30. Michael Kazin, *Barons of Labor: The San Francisco Building Trades and Union Power in the Progressive Era* (Urbana, 1987); David Montgomery, *The Fall of the House of Labor: The Workplace, the State, and American Labor Activism, 1865–1925* (Cam-

bridge, 1987); Christopher Tomlins, "AFL Unions in the 1930s: Their Performance in Historical Perspective, *JAH* 4 (March 1979): 1021–42, and Tomlins, *The State and the Unions: Labor Relations, Law, and the Organized Labor Movement in the US, 1880–1960* (Cambridge, 1985).

31. Montgomery, *Fall of the House of Labor*; Charles Sabel and Jonathan Zeitlin, "Historical Alternatives to Mass Production: Politics, Markets, and Technology in Nineteenth Century Industrialization," *Past and Present* 108 (August 1985): 133–76.

32. Benson, *Counter Cultures*, 286; Philip Scranton, "The Workplace, Technology, and Theory in American Labor History," *International Labor and Working-Class History* 35 (Spring 1989): 5–7.

33. Milkman, "Organizing the Sexual Division of Labor," 95–150, and Milkman, "Gender and Trade Unionism in Historical Perspective," in *Women, Politics, and Change*, ed. Louise A. Tilly and Patricia Gurin (New York, 1990), 87–107.

34. Thus, my reading of craft unionism on the shopfloor parallels the much-misinterpreted writings of the Wisconsin school. Although Perlman, for example, deemphasized the legislative involvement of craft unionists, he never argued that craft workers were "bread and butter" unionists concerned only with higher wages. In fact, Perlman specifically noted the "idealistic" nature of American workers' focus on shop-floor control. To see "job consciousness" as purely economistic and materialistic is a misreading not only of Perlman, but also of the history of craft union struggles on the shopfloor and at the bargaining table. See *A Theory of the Labor Movement*, especially 254–79.

35. See Sanford Jacoby, "American Exceptionalism Revisited: The Importance of Management," unpublished paper, UCLA Graduate School of Management, October 1987 for a comparative analysis that points to the unusual authoritarianism of U.S. managers.

36. My reconception of union forms has been influenced by industrial relations scholars. See, for example, Van Dusen Kennedy, *Nonfactory Unionism and Labor Relations* (Berkeley, 1955); Charles Sable and Michael Piore, *The Second Industrial Divide: Possibilities for Prosperity* (New York, 1984), 111–32; and Arthur Stinchcombe, "Bureaucratic and Craft Administration of Production," *Administrative Science Quarterly* 4 (September 1959): 168–87. The nonfactory-factory typology developed by Kennedy appeared feasible at first; nevertheless, I ultimately rejected Kennedy's terms because many of the features he associates with factory unionism—large employers, plant-centered activities, an elaborate seniority system—also characterize unions formed by such nonfactory workers as government employees, hospital workers, or even hotel employees. For a critique of Kennedy, see James Wallihan, *Union Government and Organization* (Washington, D.C., 1985), 76–79.

37. For a review of the trajectory of women's history and the breakdown of consensus, see Nancy Hewitt, "Beyond the Search for Sisterhood: American Women's History in the 1980s," *Social History* 10 (October 1985): 229–321. Ellen DuBois and Alice Kessler-Harris have urged new conceptual models based on incorporating the history and experience of working-class women. See DuBois, "Working Women, Class Relations, and Suffrage Militance: Harriot Stanton Blatch and the New York Woman Suffrage Movement, 1894–1909," *JAH* 74 (June 1987): 34–58, and Kessler-Harris, "Gender Ideology in Historical Reconstruction: A Case Study from the 1930s," *Gender*

and History 1 (Spring 1989): 31–37. For work focusing on working-class values, see the works cited in note 38.

38. Sarah Eisenstein, *Give Us Bread but Give Us Roses: Working Women's Consciousness in the U.S., 1890 to the First World War* (London, 1983); Jacquelyn Hall, "Disorderly Women: Gender and Labor Militancy in the Appalachian South," *JAH* 73 (September 1986): 354–82; Meyerowitz, *Women Adrift*; Christine Stansell, *City of Women: Sex and Class in New York, 1789–1860* (Urbana, 1987); Kathy Peiss, *Cheap Amusements: Working Women and Leisure in Turn-of-the-Century New York* (Philadelphia, 1986).

39. It is important to clarify that I am discussing dominant tendencies rather than reified and nonoverlapping oppositional categories. Not all waitresses nor all working-class women thought alike; neither did the middle-class second-wave feminists that I discuss later.

40. For the varieties of female activism, see, for example, Temma Kaplan, "Female Consciousness and Collective Action: The Case of Barcelona, 1910–1918," *Signs* 7 (Spring 1982): 545–66, and an unpublished essay by Deborah White, "Race, Class, and Gender: The Troublesome Alliance in Twentieth Century Black Female Organizations." In "What's in a Name? The Limits of 'Social Feminism': or, Expanding the Vocabulary of Women's History," *JAH* 76 (December 1989): 809–9, Nancy Cott calls for a mining of the "rich, historical vein" of female activism.

41. Although not all forms of female protest are necessarily "feminist," the definition of feminism has tended to be class-biased. I have chosen to call waitress unionists "feminists" because of their recognition and critique of sex-based hierarchies and their active engagement in challenging male power and authority. Nancy Cott's definition of feminism is similarly inclusive. See Cott, "What's in a Name?" 809. Karen Offen, "Defining Feminism: A Comparative Historical Approach," *Signs* 14 (Autumn 1988): 119–57; Daniel Scott Smith, "Family Limitation, Sexual Control, and Domestic Feminism in Victorian America," *Feminist Studies* 1 (Winter-Spring 1973): 40–57; and Eileen Boris, "The Power of Motherhood: Black and White Activist Women Redefine the 'Political,'" *Yale Journal of Law and Feminism* 2 (Fall 1989): 25–49 have also recognized that feminism is not necessarily incompatible with support for sex separatism and a commitment to family.

42. The emphasis on sex separatism in working-class culture is found in spheres other than the workplace. Sex separatism in leisure pursuits, for instance, appears to be more characteristic of adult working-class men and women than of middle-class. See the discussion by David Halle, *America's Working-Man: Work, Home and Politics Among Blue-Collar Property Owners* (Chicago, 1984), 34–73.

43. For other studies portraying the attempts of working women to reconcile class and gender see, for example, Maurine Greenwald, "Working-Class Feminism and the Family Wage Ideal: The Seattle Debate on Married Women's Right to Work, 1914–1920," *JAH* 76 (June 1989): 118–49.

44. For other critiques that note the tendency of scholarship to assume individual upward mobility at the workplace as the best choice for all classes, see James Henretta, "The Study of Social Mobility: Ideological Assumptions and Conceptual Bias," *Labor History* 18 (Spring 1977): 165–78; Myra Marx Ferree, "She Works Hard for a Living: Gender and Class on the Job," in *Analyzing Gender*, ed. Ferree and Hess, 322–47;

and Greta Foff Paules, "Behind the Lines: Strategies of Self-Perception and Protection Among Waitresses in New Jersey," Ph.D. diss., Princeton University, 1990.

45. For accounts of feminist activism that note its variegated ideology in these years, see Nancy Cott, *The Grounding of Modern Feminism* (New Haven, 1987); and Cynthia Harrison, *On Account of Sex: The Politics of Women's Issues, 1945–1968* (Berkeley, 1988).

46. For the consensus among middle-class feminists, see Harrison, *On Account of Sex*. Works in addition to my own that trace the evolution of working-class feminism include: Nancy Gabin, *Feminism in the Labor Movement* (Ithaca, 1990); Carol Kates, "Working-Class Feminism and Feminist Unions: Title VII, the UAW, and NOW," *Labor Studies Journal* 14 (Summer 1989): 28–45; and Ruth Milkman, "Union Responses to Workforce Feminization," unpublished paper in possession of the author.

47. Women who competed directly with men—often those working in male-dominated occupations—frequently assessed the economic impact of equal treatment strategies as beneficial: whereas women in female-dominated jobs, where direct competition was minimal, came to different conclusions. This division is clearest in relation to protective laws. In fact, the labor market position of a particular group of laboring women may be a more useful predictor of their position on protective legislation than assumptions about their gender consciousness. The correlation between labor market position and stance on protective legislation has been noted by Elizabeth Baker, *Protective Labor Legislation with Special Reference to Women in the State of New York* (New York, 1925), 425; Alice Cook, "Women and American Trade Unions," *Annals* 375 (January 1968): 127; and Nancy Schrom Dye, *As Equals and as Sisters: Feminism, Unionism and the WTUL of New York* (New York, 1980), 158.

48. Press Release, "Wolfgang Routs Friedan," 22 October 1970, Local 705 Files, Detroit; Bernard Rosenberg and Saul Weinman, "Young Women Who Work: An Interview with Myra Wolfgang," *Dissent* 86 (Winter 1972): 32–33; Myra Wolfgang, "Some of the Problems of Eve," presented to the AFL-CIO Conference Women at Work, 13 March 1971, Box 1, File 6, MW, WRL-WSU.

49. See, for example, Leonore Weitzman, *The Divorce Revolution: The Unexpected Social and Economic Consequences for Women and Children in America* (New York, 1985); and Tamar Lewin, "Maternity Leave: Is It Leave, Indeed?" *NYT*, 22 July 1984.

50. For one of the more influential analyses, see Carol Gilligan, *In a Different Voice: Psychological Theory and Women's Development* (Cambridge, 1982). For a penetrating application to historical scholarship, see Alice Kessler-Harris, "The Debate Over Equality for Women in the Workplace: Recognizing Differences," in *Women and Work: An Annual Review* 1, ed. Laurie Larwood et al. (Beverly Hills, 1985).

51. Ruth Milkman first crystalized the notion of a new gender politics rooted in the labor movement in "Union Responses to Workforce Feminization in the U.S."

52. The history of waitress unionism adds, then, to the growing recognition of the limited nature of sisterhood, especially in regard to race. See, for example, Dolores Janiewski, *Sisterhood Denied: Race, Gender, and Class in a New South Community* (Philadelphia, 1985); Bonnie Thornton Dill, "Race, Class and Gender: Prospects for an All-Inclusive Sisterhood," *Feminist Studies* 9 (Spring 1983): 131–50; Hewitt, "Beyond the Search for Sisterhood," and Ellen DuBois and Vicki Ruiz, "Introduction," to *Unequal Sisters: A Multicultural Reader in U.S. Women's History*, ed. DuBois and Ruiz (New York, 1990), xi–xvi.

53. My assumption is that consciousness derives from both the productive and the domestic realm. Labor historians have concentrated on the workplace, whereas historians of women typically root their analysis of women's culture in the home. For the need to look at the "point of production" as well as the domestic sphere, see Alan Dawley, "The Worker's Brain under the Historian's Cap," review of David Montgomery's *Fall of the House of Labor* in *Radical History Review* 40 (January 1988): 101–14, and Kessler-Harris, "Gender Ideology in Historical Reconstruction," 31–37.

54. Leslie Tentler, *Wage-earning Women* (New York, 1979), and Winifred Wandersee, *Women's Work and Family Values, 1920–40* (Cambridge, 1981) stress the traditionalism of working-class women.

55. For example, Louise A. Tilly, "Paths to Proletarianization: Organization of Production, Sexual Division of Labor, and Women's Collective Action," *Signs* 7 (Winter 1981): 400–417.

Chapter 1. The Rise of Waitressing

1. *MHBRR*, March–April 1942, 7.

2. See Table 1 for an overview of the feminization of waiting work in the twentieth century.

3. New York Hotel and Motel Trades Council, *Twenty-Fifth Anniversary of the First Contract* (New York, 1964), 12–13, 18; U.S. Department of Labor, Employment and Training Administration, *Career Opportunities in the Hotel and Restaurant Industries* (Washington, D.C., 1982), 1, 43; Norman Sylvester Hayner, *Hotel Life* (Chapel Hill, 1936), 20; Donald Lundberg, *The Hotel and Restaurant Business* (Boston, 1979), 20–27.

4. Jefferson Williamson, *The American Hotel: An Anecdotal History* (New York, 1930), 13–17, passim; Hayner, *Hotel Life*, 22, 98; Lundberg, *The Hotel and Restaurant Business*, 26–27.

5. Thomas E. Dabney, *The Man Who Bought the Waldorf* (New York, 1950), 158; Frances de Talavera Berger and John N. Parke Custis, *Sumptuous Dining in Gaslight San Francisco* (Garden City, 1985), 39; Lundberg, *The Hotel and Restaurant Business*, 32–33; Henry C. Barbour, "Wages, Hours, and Unionization in Year-round Hotels," unpublished study, School of Hotel Administration, Cornell University, 1948, 7; Connecticut (State of), *Report of the Bureau of Labor on the Conditions of Wage-earning Women and Girls* (Hartford, 1916), 98; Frances Strakosch, *Job Study of Waitresses: Opportunities for Waitresses in New York City* (New York, 1931), 18.

6. For the decline of black waiters, see Douglas Henry Daniels, *Pioneer Urbanite: A Social and Cultural History of Black San Franciscans* (Philadelphia, 1950), 40–43; Kenneth Kusmer, *A Ghetto Takes Shape: Black Cleveland, 1870–1930* (Urbana, 1976); and Mary White Ovington, "The Negro in the Trade Unions in New York," 95, Box 3, File 13, MOW, WRL-WSU; SFLC, 22 May 1903, 11.

7. Lundberg, *The Hotel and Restaurant Business*, 141, 326; Gerald Lattin, *Careers in Hotels and Restaurants* (New York, 1967), 8–11. For a fuller description of the early hotel industry, see Robert A. Beck, "A Study of Cooperative Collective Bargaining as Developed in the Hotel Industry of New York City," Ph.D. diss., Cornell University, 1954, 50–60, passim.

8. See Table 2A; the racial and ethnic composition of waitresses and how that changed over the course of the century will be more fully analyzed in a later section of this chapter.

9. Lundberg, *The Hotel and Restaurant Business*, 326; E. W. Weaver, *Profitable Vocations for Girls* (New York, 1915), 31; *NYT*, 27 January 1909, 1; Lorenzo Greene and Carter Woodson, *The Negro Wage Earner* (New York, 1930, rept. New York, 1969), 83, 90–96, 228–32; John Daniels, *In Freedom's Birthplace* (Boston, 1914, rept. New York, 1969), 324, 336; John Ragland, "Situation in Louisville," *Opportunity*, February 1926, 72; William A. Crossland, *Industrial Conditions Among Negroes in St. Louis* (St. Louis, 1914), 63, 69–70.

10. *NYT*, 13 July 1918; Lucius W. Boomer, *Hotel Management: Principles and Practice* (New York, 1931), 241–42; Helen C. Hoerle and Florence B. Saltzberg, *The Girl and the Job* (New York, 1919), 38.

11. Hoerle and Saltzberg, *The Girl and the Job*, 42; *NYT*, 16 December 1918, 22 December 1918; Lois Peirce-Hughes, "Opportunities for Women in the Modern Hotel," *HM*, August 1919, 6; Strakosch, *Job Study of Waitresses*, 18; *Hotel Worker*, 5 April 1919, 26 April 1919.

12. *NYT*, 22 December 1918, 16 December 1918; Boomer, *Hotel Management*, 241–42; *MS*, January 1919, 54.

13. Joseph O. Dahl, *The Efficient Waitress Manual* (New York, 1935), 2; George Stigler, *Trends in Employment in the Service Industries* (Princeton, 1956), 63; New York (State), Commission Against Discrimination, *Employment in the Hotel Industry* (New York, 1958), 1–2; *CIE*, April 1955, 25.

14. See, for example, *HM*, December 1925, 45, February 1927, 31, April 1927, 69, August 1920, 54; and Arnold Hill, "The Present Status of Negro Labor," *Opportunity*, May 1929, 143.

15. Mary Lee Spence, "They Also Serve Who Wait," *Western Historical Quarterly* 14 (January 1983): 9–13; *MHBRR*, May 1951, 4–5; James Marshall, *Sante Fe: The Railroad That Built an Empire* (New York, 1945), 97–113; Leon Elder, "How the Harvey Girls Won the West," in Leon Elder and Lin Rolens, *Waitress: America's Unsung Heroine* (Santa Barbara, 1985), 14–15; Fred Harvey, *The Alvarado: A New Hotel at Albuquerque, New Mexico* (promotional brochure from the Sante Fe Railroad, 1914), n.p.

16. Barbara Drake, "The Tea-shop Girl," *Women's Industrial News* 17 (April 1913): 115–34; Spence, "They Also Serve Who Wait," 6–8.

17. Jon M. Kingsdale, "The 'Poor Man's Club': Social Functions of the Urban Working-class Saloon," *American Quarterly* 25 (October 1973): 472–78; Berger and Custis, *Sumptuous Dining in Gaslight San Francisco*, 62.

18. U.S. Department of Labor, U.S. Employment Service, *Job Descriptions for Hotels and Restaurants* (Washington, D.C., 1938), xiii; San Francisco Board of Education, Attendance and Guidance Bureau, *The Restaurant Industry in San Francisco: Occupational Study No. 8* (San Francisco, August 1932), 10; U.S. National Youth Administration, *Restaurant Occupations*, Research Report no. 1 (Chicago, 15 September 1938), 4, 22–23, 48, 56.

19. Boomer, *Hotel Management*, 1, 5, 487; George S. Chappell, *The Restaurants of New York* (New York, 1925), 7, 99; Alice Foote MacDougall, *The Secret of Successful Restaurants* (New York, 1929), 14–15, 125–26; Daniel E. Sutherland, *Americans and Their Servants* (Baton Rouge, 1981), 182–99. See George J. Stigler, *Domestic Servants in the U.S., 1900–1940*, Occasional Paper no. 24 (New York, 1946), 3, 29 for the decline of domestic help.

20. Albert B. Wolfe, *The Lodging House Problem in Boston*, Harvard Economic Studies no. 2 (Cambridge, 1906), 5, 27, 38–48; Arnold M. Rose, "Living Arrangements of Unattached Persons," in *Social Problems in America*, ed. Elizabeth B. Lee and Alfred M. Lee (New York, 1949), 93–98; Mary S. Fergusson, "Boarding Homes and Clubs for Working Women," *Bulletin of the Department of Labor* (March 1989), 3: 142; Stanley C. Hollander, "A Historical Perspective on the Service Encounter," in *The Service Encounter: Managing Employee-Customer Interaction in Service Businesses*, ed. John Czepiel, Michael Solomon, and Carol Suprenant (Lexington, Mass., 1985), 54–55.

21. Generally, cafes and tea rooms offered complete meals served at tables (the tea room atmosphere being more subdued, private, and formal and the repast lighter because the clientele was predominantly female). "Hash houses," open day or night, served short orders to patrons seated primarily at counters. ("Short orders" were those dishes that could be prepared quickly using a grill or burner.) Lunchrooms and coffee shops typically were smaller than restaurants and served food at tables or at a counter. Cafeterias pioneered self-service and the viewing of precooked à la carte items before selection. See *Electrical Workers' Journal*, May 1951, 56–64 for one account of the introduction of the cafeteria concept to the United States. Philip Langdon, *Orange Roofs, Golden Arches: The Architecture of American Chain Restaurants* (New York, 1986) includes a superb discussion of restaurant types and the evolution of each.

22. U.S. Department of Commerce, Bureau of Foreign and Domestic Commerce, *The San Francisco Restaurant Industry* (Washington, D.C., 1930), 3; *Hotel Worker*, 12 April 1919; Rhode Island (State), *Women and Minors in the Restaurant Occupations of Rhode Island* (Department of Labor, Division of Women and Children, 1941); Joseph Dahl, *Soda Fountain and Luncheonette Management* (New York, 1930), xi–xvi, 10–14, 55–79; Ina Hamlin and Arthur Winakor, *Department Store Food Service Bulletin No. 46* (Urbana, 1933), 3.

23. Langdon, *Orange Roofs, Golden Arches*, 8–19; Lundberg, *The Hotel and Restaurant Business*, 60–61, 209–10; San Francisco Board of Education, Attendance and Guidance Bureau, *The Restaurant Industry in San Francisco*, 16; *Hotel Monthly*, November 1931, 42–48.

24. Joseph O. Dahl, *Dining Room Management for Head Waitresses and Hostesses* (New York, 1933), 2; HCV, 24 August 1946, 1; MS, January 1918, 63, May 1922, 52, May 1928, 69, December 1929, 48, June 1930, 35; MHBRR, March–April 1942, 7.

25. William Leach, "Transformations in a Culture of Consumption: Women and Department Stores, 1890–1925," *Journal of American History* 71 (September 1984): 319–42; MacDougall, *The Secret of Successful Restaurants*, 126; Langdon, *Orange Roofs, Golden Arches*, 24; *Hotel Monthly*, September 1929, 68. See Chappell, *The Restaurants of New York*, 78, 102–3, 164, for other examples of exotic restaurant interiors.

26. MacDougall, *The Secret of Successful Restaurants*, 126; Langdon, *Orange Roofs, Golden Arches*, 24; *Hotel Monthly*, September 1929, 68; Strakosch, *Job Study of Waitresses* 5, quoting an editorial in *Restaurant Management*, August 1930; Priscilla Boniface, *Hotels and Restaurants: 1830 to the Present Day* (London, 1981), n.p.

27. MS, April 1928, 64, July 1918, 39.

28. For the larger context see Mary P. Ryan's chapter on "The Sexy Saleslady," in *Womanhood in America: From Colonial Times to the Present* (New York, 1975), 253–

303, and Jacqueline Jones, *Labor of Love, Labor of Sorrow: Black Women, Work, and the Family* (New York, 1985), 178–79. Lois Banner, *American Beauty* (New York, 1983), 5, 15–16, discusses "fashion culture." For the situation in food service and for the quotes, see Strakosch, *Job Study of Waitresses*, 9; Ethel Smith, "The Union Waitress Interprets," 2, Reel 2, C-2, WTUL Papers; Dahl, *Dining Room Management for Head Waitresses and Hostesses*, 4; and MacDougall, *The Secret of Successful Restaurants*, 55, 72, 77, 184.

29. Elizabeth Ross Haynes, "Negroes in Domestic Service in the U.S.," *Journal of Negro History* 8 (October 1923): 384–442.

30. Jones, *Labor of Love, Labor of Sorrow*, 156.

31. Greene and Woodson, *The Negro Wage Earner*, 228.

32. Boomer, *Hotel Management*, 229–30; *Hotel Monthly*, April 1923, 23; U.S. Department of Commerce, Bureau of Census, *Statistical Abstract of the U.S.* (Washington, D.C., 1957), 867, as quoted in Morris A. Horowitz, *The New York Hotel Industry* (Cambridge, 1960), 5; Gladys L. Palmer, "Ten Overcrowded Occupations," *Occupations: The Vocational Guidance Magazine* 12 (February 1934): 48–56; Ruth Gordon, "The Forgotten Industry," *Survey*, 15 January 1923, 516.

33. See Sheila Rothman, *Woman's Proper Place: A History of Changing Ideals and Practices, 1870 to the Present* (New York, 1978), 114–38; and Sarah Eisenstein, *Give Us Bread but Give Us Roses: Working Women's Consciousness in the United States 1890 to the First World War* (London, 1983), 70–82 for discussions of the public disdain toward certain occupations in the Progressive Era.

34. Frances Donovan, *The Woman Who Waits* (Boston, 1920, rept. New York, 1974), 16, 26–27, 36, 63, 140, 221.

35. *Wage-Earning Women in Stores and Factories*, vol. 5 of *Report on the Conditions of Women and Children Wage-earners in the U.S.*, Senate Doc. 645, 61st Cong., 2d sess., 199, as quoted in Alice Kessler-Harris, *Out to Work: A History of Wage-Earning Women*, (New York, 1982), 136.

36. See the discussion of the issue by Spence, "They Also Serve Who Wait," 23–24.

37. For example, see Kathy Peiss, *Cheap Amusements: Working Women and Leisure in Turn-of-the-Century New York* (Philadelphia, 1986).

38. *Hotel Monthly*, March 1929, 51.

39. Strakosch, *Job Study of Waitresses*, 20–23, 26; Boomer, *Hotel Management*, 487–89; "No Hashers: Waitresses Now Must Have Tact and Charm," *Literary Digest*, 1 May 1937, 26–27; Hoerle and Saltzberg, *The Girl and Her Job*, 42; Walter I. Hamilton, *Employer-Employee Relations in Hotels* (Baltimore, 1925), 89–91; Emilie Josephine Hutchinson, *Women's Wages: A Study of the Wages of Industrial Women and Measures Suggested to Increase Them*, Studies in History, Economics and Public Law 89 (New York, 1919, rept. New York, 1968), 171–74; *Hotel Monthly*, June 1930, 83–84, March 1929, 51. Details about the union schools are presented in chapter 6 of this volume.

40. Anonymous waitress interviewed by Jacqueline D. Hall in 1983 quoted in Hall, "Disorderly Women: Gender and Labor Militancy in the Appalachian South," *Journal of American History* 73 (September 1986): 362; interview with Gertrude Sweet; William Whyte, *Human Relations in the Restaurant Industry* (New York, 1948), 369; William Whyte, E. L. Hamilton, and M. C. Wiley, *Action Research for Management* (Homewood, 1964), 44; Patricia Stoll, "Occupational Alienation: The Case of the

Cocktail Waitress," master's thesis in sociology, University of Missouri-Kansas City, 1973, 39–68, 80; *CIE*, August 1950, 28.

41. Table 1; *NYT*, 25 July 1935; "A Waitress Training Course in Pittsburgh," *Employment Service News* (June 1936): 3, 10–11; *NYT*, 2 July 1929, 4 July 1929, 5 January 1933; *CIE*, January 1930, 13; Palmer, "Ten Overcrowded Occupations," 56.

42. Evelyn Klugh, "Colored Girls at Work in Boston," *Opportunity* 6 (October 1928): 295–99; Lois Rita Helmbold, "Downward Occupational Mobility during the Great Depression: Urban Black and White Working-class Women," *Labor History* 29 (Spring 1988): 135–72.

43. As Table 2C indicates, between 1930 and 1940 the number of black waitresses declined in every region except the South. Julia Blackwelder, "Women in the Work Force: Atlanta, New Orleans, and San Antonio, 1930–1940," *Journal of Urban History* 4 (May 1978): 331–58; Helmbold, "Downward Occupational Mobility During the Great Depression," 165–69.

44. *NYT*, 17 June 1943; *CIE*, May 1940, 30; Lundberg, *The Hotel and Restaurant Business*, 61. The history of protective laws in the industry are discussed more fully in later chapters.

45. Lundberg, *The Hotel and Restaurant Business*, 206; *Electrical Workers Journal*, May 1951, 56; National Youth Administration, *Restaurant Occupations*, 2; Daryl Wyckoff and W. Earl Sasser, *The Chain Restaurant Industry* (Lexington, Mass., 1978), xxv–xxviii; Louisiana Department of Employment Security, Research and Statistics Unit, *Employment Trends: Eating and Beverage Establishments, 1958–1968* (August 1969), 1, 7; Stan Luxenberg, *Roadside Empires: How the Chains Franchised America* (New York, 1985), 71–72.

46. Table 1; USDL, *Career Opportunities in the Hotel and Restaurant Industries*, 43; Richard Carnes and Horst Brand, "Productivity and New Technology in Eating and Drinking Places," *MLR* 100 (September 1977): 9–15. For an overview of the growth of waitresses in relation to other female-dominated occupations, see the Appendix in *America's Working Women: A Documentary History—1600 to the Present*, ed. Rosalyn Baxandall, Linda Gordon, and Susan Reverby (New York, 1976), 406–7.

47. For changes in the 1960s and later, see Charles K. Sherck, "Changes in Food Consumption Patterns," *Food Technology* 25 (September 1971): 50–52; Thomas Powers, "Industry Dynamics: An Institutional View," in *The Future of Food Service: A Basis for Planning*, ed. Powers (University Park, 1974), 35–36, 45–49; and George Silvestri and John Lukasiewicz, "Occupational Employment Projections: The 1984–95 Outlook," *MLR* 108 (November 1985): 42–57. Research indicates that census data undercounts women's work in family enterprises and in the informal economy. Thus, many women who work in small, family-run eating and lodging establishments, whether as family members or outsiders, do not appear in the official statistics. One of the most thorough treatments is Penelope Ciancanelli, "Women's Transition to Wage Labor," Ph.D. diss., New School for Social Research, 1983.

48. For instance, in San Francisco, Class A hotels offered à la carte French service dining with male waiters only; Class B hotels had set (or table d'hôte) meals with a mixed crew; Class C hotels were on the American plan and used Chinese chefs and women food servers. See Transcript of the Arbitration Proceedings between the San Francisco Local Joint Executive Board and the Hotel Employer's Association of San

Francisco before Chairman Edgar Rowe, 18 August 1942, Local 2 Files; Boomer, *Hotel Management*, 487; U.S. Department of Commerce, *The San Francisco Restaurant Industry*, 10, 13; National Youth Administration, *Restaurant Occupations*, 2. The preference of employers for white women will be documented in a later section.

49. Eleanor LaPointe, "Waitressing: The Politics of the Labor Process," unpublished seminar paper in sociology, Rutgers University, September 1986, 2–6; Lydia Salisch and Emily Palmer, *An Analysis of the Waitress Trade*, State of California, Department of Education Bulletin, no. 21 [November 1932] (Sacramento, 1933), 4; Hugo Ernst to Coughlin, 16 July 1953, Reel 690, LUR, HERE Files. Joseph Dahl's manual for waiters deletes the section on breakfast and lunch work found in his waitress pamphlet; see *The Efficient Waiter* (New York, 1933) and *The Efficient Waitress Manual*, 18–31; Elaine Hall, "Serving Side by Side? The Organizational Stratification of Waiters and Waitresses Between and Within Restaurants," working paper, University of Connecticut, 1989.

50. Salisch and Palmer, *An Analysis of the Waitress Trade*, 6–7; USDL, BLS, *Industry Wage Survey: Eating and Drinking Places*, June 1961, Bulletin no. 1329 (Washington, D.C., 1962), 1. See Spence, "They Also Serve Who Wait," 13–14, for a discussion of early feminization of waiting in the West.

51. See, for example, Margery Davies, *Women's Place Is at the Typewriter* (Philadelphia, 1982); Samuel Cohn, *The Process of Occupational Sex-Typing: The Feminization of Clerical Labor in Great Britain* (Philadelphia, 1985); Sharon Hartman Strom, " 'Light Manufacturing': The Feminization of American Office Work, 1900–1930," *Industrial and Labor Relations Review* 43 (October 1989): 53–71; Myra Strober and Carolyn Arnold, "The Dynamics of Occupational Segregation among Bank Tellers" in *Gender in the Workplace*, ed. Clair Brown and Joseph Pechman (Washington, D.C., 1987), 107–58; and Barbara F. Reskin and Patricia A. Roos, *Job Queues, Gender Queues: Explaining Women's Inroads into Male Occupations* (Philadelphia, 1990).

52. Davies, *Women's Place Is at the Typewriter*; Patricia Roos, "Hot Metal to Electronic Composition: Gender, Technology, and Social Change," in Reskin and Roos, *Job Queues, Gender Queues*, 275–78.

53. Dee Garrison has also noted the important connection between the sexual composition of the patron base and the sex of those who serve them, see *Apostles of Culture: The Public Librarian and American Society, 1876–1920* (New York, 1979), pt. 4.

54. Strober and Arnold, "The Dynamics of Occupational Segregation among Bank Tellers," 110–19; Reskin and Roos, *Job Queues, Gender Queues*, ch. 1.

55. See, for example, Ruth Milkman, *Gender at Work: The Dynamics of Job Segregation by Sex During World War II* (Urbana, 1987); Susan Hirsch, "Rethinking the Sexual Division of Labor: Pullman Repair Shops, 1900–1969," *Radical History Review* 35 (April 1986): 26–48; and Ava Baron, "Women and the Making of the American Working Class: A Study of the Proletarianization of Printers," *Review of Radical Political Economics* 14 (Fall 1982): 23–42.

56. Many fascinating problems are simply beyond the scope of this study. Why, for example, was public food preparation and service done by men in the first place since women universally are responsible for this work in the domestic realm?

57. Rachel Migler, "The Philadelphia Waitress," *Philadelphia Magazine* 76 (April 1985): 108.

58. Louise de Koven Bowen, *The Girl Employed in Hotel and Restaurants* (Chicago, 1912), n.p.; Consumers' League of New York City, *Behind the Scenes in a Restaurant: A Study of 1,017 Women Restaurant Employees* (New York, 1916), 2, passim; New York Women's Trade Union League, "The Conditions of Women Workers in the Hotel and Restaurant Industry: Findings Submitted to the Minimum Wage Board For the Hotel and Restaurant Industry," n.d. [ca. 1933], Reel 2, C-2, WTUL Papers.

59. Joan Younger Dickinson, *The Role of the Immigrant Women in the U.S. Labor Force, 1890–1910* (New York, 1980), Table 15, 76–77, 80–81, 85, 107; Daniel Sutherland, *Americans and Their Servants* (Baton Rouge, 1981), 49–56. See also David Katzman, *Seven Days a Week* (New York, 1978), 56–73; Bowen, *The Girl Employed in Hotels and Restaurants*; Mary E. Trueblood, "Household Versus Shop and Factories," *Independent* 13 November 1902, 2693; MacDougall, *The Secret of Successful Restaurants*, 66; Eli Ginzberg and Hyman Berman, *The American Worker in the Twentieth Century: A History Through Autobiography* (New York, 1963), 311.

60. Donovan, *The Woman Who Waits*, 114, 133–36; Strakosch, *Job Study of Waitresses*, 8, 19–20. Biographical data that I compiled on the ethnicity of forty waitress union leaders who came to prominence in the period from 1900 to 1950 conforms to this general picture; 82 percent were native born. A sizable number were Lutheran (of Swedish and German ancestry) and Irish Catholic. In addition, 23 percent of those born between 1880 and 1901 and 16 percent of those born between 1902 and 1920 were the daughters of farmers; 46 percent of the officials came from a skilled blue-collar background—both backgrounds much more typical of "old" immigrant groups than the peasant and unskilled backgrounds typical of "new" immigrants (Tables 10C, 10D).

61. Strakosch, *Job Study of Waitresses*, 3, 9, 19–20.

62. For portraits of other female-dominated occupations, see Susan Porter Benson, *Counter Cultures: Saleswomen, Managers, and Customers in American Department Stores, 1890–1940* (Urbana, 1986); Davies, *Women's Place Is at the Typewriter*.

63. Consumers' League of New York City, *Behind the Scenes in a Restaurant*, 6; Donovan, *The Woman Who Waits*, 133; New York, Department of Labor, Bureau of Women in Industry, *Women Workers in Newburgh Industries* (Albany, December 1929), 73.

64. See San Francisco Board of Education, Attendance and Guidance Bureau, *The Restaurant Industry in San Francisco*, 11–12, and the New York Women's Trade Union League, "The Conditions of Women Workers in the Hotel and Restaurant Industry," 69, for the age of waitresses in the 1930s. Also see Strakosch, *Job Study of Waitresses*, 4; U.S. Department of Labor, Women's Bureau, *Training Mature Women for Employment: The Story of 23 Local Programs*, Bulletin no. 256 (Washington, D.C., 1955), 24; U.S. Department of Labor, Women's Bureau, *Part-time Jobs for Women: A Study in 10 Cities*, Bulletin no. 238 (Washington, D.C., 1951), 12–53; U.S. Department of Labor, Women's Bureau, *Changes in Women's Occupations 1940–50*, Bulletin no. 253 (Washington, D.C., 1954), 21–22; John D. Durand, *The Labor Force in the United States, 1890–1960* (New York, 1948), 38, as quoted in Ronald Schatz, *The Electrical Workers: A History of Labor at General Electric and Westinghouse, 1923–60* (Urbana, 1983), 109.

65. "Story of a Waitress," *Independent*, 18 June 1908, 1381; Consumers' League of New York City, *Behind the Scenes in a Restaurant*, 10; U.S. Department of Commerce, Bureau of the Census, *Historical Statistics of the United States: Colonial Times to 1970* (Washington, D.C., 1975), 133.

66. Consumers' League of New York City, *Behind the Scenes in a Restaurant*, 10; Donovan, *The Woman Who Waits*, 134; USDL, Women's Bureau, *Changes in Women's Occupations*, 30–31; New York Department of Labor, Bureau of Women in Industry, *Women Workers in Newburgh Industries*, 13; U.S. Department of Labor, Women's Bureau, *Women Workers and Their Dependents*, Bulletin no. 239, by Mary Elizabeth Pidgeon (Washington, D.C., 1952); Stoll, "Occupational Alienation," 11. See Table 3 of this volume for Census Bureau figures.

67. Bowen, *The Girl Employed in Hotels and Restaurants*, n.p., approx. 13; Consumers' League of New York City, *Behind the Scenes in a Restaurant*, 10; U.S. Department of Commerce, Bureau of the Census, *Women in Gainful Employment* by Joseph Hill (Washington, D.C., 1929), 124–25; U.S. Department of Labor, Women's Bureau, *Women Workers and Their Dependents*, 15, 32. Union groups surveyed included women from the needle trades, machinists, communication workers, railroad and airline clerks, and a miscellaneous group recruited from WTUL members.

68. Donovan, *The Woman Who Waits*, 132; State of Connecticut, *Report of the Bureau of Labor on the Conditions of Wage-Earning Women and Girls*, 104–5; U.S. Department of Labor, Women's Bureau, *Women Workers and Their Dependents*, 15, 32. See also, Joanne Meyerowitz, *Women Adrift: Independent Wage Earners in Chicago, 1880–1930* (Chicago, 1988); Benson, *Counter Cultures*, 208; and Leslie Woodcock Tentler, *Wage-Earning Women: Industrial Work and Family Life in the U.S., 1900–1930* (New York, 1979), 116.

69. See Table 4 of this volume; "Waitress Work in Summer Hotels by One Who Has Tried It," *American Kitchen Magazine*, June 1900, 85–86; Donald E. Lundberg, *Personnel Management in Hotels and Restaurants* (Minneapolis, 1949), 40; and Albert Leggett, *The Student Waiter and Waitress* (New York, 1956), 3–6.

70. Suellen Butler and James Skipper, "Working the Circuit: An Explanation of Employee Turnover in the Restaurant Industry," *Sociological Spectrum* 3 (1983): 19–33; *NYT*, 20 May 1928; Elder and Rolens, *Waitress*, 49, 51, 56.

71. Quote is from the Idoniea Duntley interview; see also interviews with Kathryn Dewing, Gertrude Sweet, Jackie Walsh, Florence Douglas, and Clela Sullivan; *CIE*, April 1952, 15, March 1923, 45, April 1931, 43; *NYT*, 12 May 1929; Lundberg, *The Hotel and Restaurant Business*, 140; Douglas Bauer, "The Prime of Miss Jean Brody," *Esquire*, June 1985, 116–23.

72. The literature here is immense. On the importance of racial and ethnic identity for other groups of workers, see, for example, Michael Kazin, *Barons of Labor* (Urbana, 1987), ch. 6; and Josh Freeman, "Catholics, Communists, and Republicans: Irish Workers and the Organization of the Transport Workers Union," in *Working Class America*, ed. Frisch and Walkowitz, 256–83. A strong cohesive work group, however, may nurture solidaristic tendencies, but not necessarily promote formal mechanisms of control such as unionization. For elaboration, see Micaela di Leonardo, "Women's Work, Work Culture, and Consciousness," *Feminist Studies* 11 (Fall 1985): 491–95; and Hannah Creighton, "Tied by Double Apron Strings: Female Work and Organization in a Restaurant," *Insurgent Sociologist* 11 (Fall 1982): 59–64.

73. As has been pointed out by scholars concerned with working-class female activism, the family status of women and whether they are primary wage earners are integrally related to their propensity to organize. See, for example, Ronald Schatz, "Union Pioneers: The Founders of Local Unions at GE and Westinghouse, 1933–37," *JAH* 66

(1979): 586–607, and Carole Turbin, "Beyond Conventional Wisdom: Women's Wage Work, Household Economic Contribution, and Labor Activism in a Mid-Nineteenth-Century Working-class Community," in *"To Toil the Livelong Day": America's Women at Work, 1780–1980,* ed. Carol Groneman and Mary Beth Norton (Ithaca, 1987), 47–67.

Chapter 2. Work Conditions and Work Culture

1. Consumers' League of New York City, *Behind the Scenes in a Restaurant: A Study of 1,017 Women Restaurant Employees* (New York, 1916), 13–14.

2. Interview with Valentine Webster.

3. "Waitress Work in Summer Hotels by One Who Has Tried It," *American Kitchen Magazine* 13 (June 1900): 85–86; New York WTUL, "The Conditions of Women Workers in the Hotel and Restaurant Industry," 18, Reel 2, C-2, WTUL Papers; U.S. Department of Labor, Women's Bureau, *The Woman Wage Earner: Her Situation Today,* Bulletin no. 172, by Elizabeth D. Benham (Washington, D.C., 1939), 24; Consumers' League of New York City, *Behind the Scenes in a Restaurant,* 12, 15–16; see Table 4 in the Appendix; U.S. Department of Labor, Women's Bureau, *Part-time Jobs for Women: A Study in Ten Cities,* Bulletin no. 238 (Washington, D.C., 1951), 63.

4. Lillian Ruth Matthews, *Women in Trade Unions in San Francisco,* U.C. Publications in Economics (Berkeley, 1913), 3:76–80; Consumers' League of New York City, *Behind the Scenes in a Restaurant,* 12; George Stigler, *Domestic Servants in the United States,* Occasional Paper no. 24 of the National Bureau of Economic Research (New York, 1946), 19; Mary Trueblood, "Household versus Shop and Factories," *Independent,* 13 November 1902, 2691–93.

5. L. S. Chumley, "Hotel, Restaurant, and Domestic Workers," 18, Box 163, IWW, WRL-WSU; Elizabeth Ross Haynes, "Negroes in Domestic Service in the U.S.," *Journal of Negro History* 8 (October 1923): 426; Frances Strakosch, *Job Study of Waitresses: Opportunities for Waitresses in New York City* (New York, 1931), 9; Dorothy Pope, "Hours of Labor of Hotel and Restaurant Employees, *MLR* 10 (March 1920): 91–108; Alice Foote McDougall, *The Secret of Successful Restaurants* (New York, 1929), 236–37; *Hotel Monthly,* August 1920, 29–30; Walter Hamilton, *Employer-Employee Relations in Hotels* (Baltimore, 1925), 16; Ruth Gordon, "The Forgotten Industry," *Survey* 15 January 1923, 514–15; Lorine Pruette, "The Married Woman and the Part-time Job," *Annals of the American Academy of Political and Social Sciences* 143 (May 1929): 301–14. The hotel industry was exempt from most state laws limiting hours, see *Survey,* 18 September 1922.

6. Anonymous to Frances Perkins, 15 May 1932, File-"HRE," Box 82, RG-174, NA; U.S. National Youth Administration, Illinois, *Restaurant Occupations* (Chicago, 1938), 18; Rhode Island Department of Labor, Division of Women and Children, *Women and Minors in the Restaurant Occupations of Rhode Island* (1941), 2–3; transcript of typed mss., "Speech by Mrs. Best at the Hotel Hearings," 1–2, n.d. [ca. 1931], Box 283, RG-86, NA; San Francisco Board of Education, Attendance and Guidance Bureau, *The Restaurant Industry in San Francisco* (San Francisco, 1932), 32; Henry C. Barbour, "Wages, Hours, and Unionization in Year-round Hotels," unpublished study, School of Hotel Administration, Cornell University, 1948, 46.

7. See NRA, Code of Fair Competition for the Restaurant Industry, approved 10 August 1933, and NRA, Code of Fair Competition for the Hotel Industry, Code 121, approved 17 November 1933 (Washington, 1933); *Free Voice*, December 1933, 3; G. G. Hinckley, NRA compliance officer, to Mary Anderson, 7 February 1935, file— "Complaint letters," Box 1731, RG-86, NA; Exhibit P, "Statement on Proposed Modification of Restaurant Industry Codes," Hearing by Mary Anderson, 20 August 1934, Box 283, RG-86, NA; *NYT*, 10 May 1935; *The Woman Worker*, 7; U.S. Department of Labor, Women's Bureau, *Women Employed under the NRA Codes*, Bulletin no. 130, by Mary Pidgeon (Washington, D.C., 1935), 8–9; New York WTUL, "The Conditions of Women Workers in the Hotel and Restaurant Industry," 15, 72; "Statement of the Joint Committee on National Recovery Concerning the Proposed Code of Fair Competition for the Hotel Industry," 5, attached to a letter from John P. Davis to Elizabeth Christman, 25 September 1933, Reel 2, C-2, WTUL Papers.

8. Hotel Code, Reel 2, C-2, WTUL Papers; San Francisco Hotel Arbitration Award, Fred Athearn, arbitrator, in the Arbitration between the San Francisco LJEB and the San Francisco Hotel Operators, 1937, 15, Local 2 Files; Gordon, "The Forgotten Industry," 514–17; 536–37; Hamilton, *Employer-Employee Relations in Hotels*, 33.

9. Stigler, *Domestic Servants in the United States*, 19–20; U.S. Department of Labor, Women's Bureau, in cooperation with the State of Maine, Department of Labor and Industry, *Earnings and Hours of Women Employed in the Retail Trade and Service Industries in the State of Maine*, miscellaneous pamphlet (Washington, D.C., 1952), 12–13; U.S. Department of Labor, Bureau of Labor Statistics, *Industry Wage Survey: Eating and Drinking Places, June 1961*, Bulletin no. 1329 (Washington, June 1962), 6. Before the 1966 amendments to the 1938 Fair Labor Standards Act, employees of eating and drinking places and hotels/motels were exempt from the minimum wage and overtime provisions of the act. See U.S. Department of Labor, Workplace Standards Administration, *Cash Wages and Value of Tips of Tipped Employees in Eating and Drinking Places and Motels and Hotels* (Washington, 1971), 4–5.

10. Albert Wolfe, *The Lodging House Problem in Boston*, Harvard Economic Studies no. 2 (Cambridge, 1906), 97–98; Trueblood, "Household versus Shop and Factories," 2691; Susan Porter Benson, *Counter Cultures: Saleswomen, Managers, and Customers in American Department Stores, 1890–1940* (Urbana, 1986), 190; Matthews, *Women in Trade Unions in San Francisco*, 44; MS, November 1918, 22; Emilie J. Hutchinson, *Women's Wages: A Study of the Wages of Industrial Women and Measures Suggested to Increase Them* (New York, 1919, rept., New York, 1968), 15; Connecticut (State), *Report of the Bureau of Labor on the Conditions of Wage-earning Women and Girls* (Hartford, 1916), 99–100; Haynes, "Negroes in Domestic Service in the U.S.," 416–21; "Waitress Work in Summer Hotels by One Who Has Tried It," 85–86; MLR (September 1919): 196; *NYT*, 20 May 1928; Dagny Hansen, "Don't Kid the Waitress," *Collier's*, 4 May 1929, 14, 67; Frances Donovan, *The Woman Who Waits* (Boston, 1920), 31–38, 126–27.

11. Transcript, "Minimum Wage Conference for Administrators," 11 October 1938, Box 904, RG-86, NA; "Speech by Mrs. Best at the Hotel Hearings," 1–2; New York WTUL, "The Conditions of Women Workers in the Hotel and Restaurant Industry,"

25–31; U.S. Department of Labor, Women's Bureau, *Women in the Economy of the U.S.: A Summary Report*, Bulletin no. 155, by Mary Pidgeon (Washington, D.C., 1937), 124; New York (State) Department of Labor, Division of Women in Industry and Minimum Wage, *Report of the Industrial Commissioner to the Restaurant Minimum Wage Board* (New York, October 1939), 92; *Women Worker*, January 1941, 9. For examples of some of the more destitute cases, see file—"Hotel/Restaurant," Box 866, RG-86, NA, and Lois Helmbold, "Downward Occupational Mobility During the Great Depression: Urban Black and White Working-class Women, *Labor History* 29 (Spring 1988): 135.

12. New York State Department of Labor, Bureau of Research and Statistics, *The Restaurant Workers and Unemployment Insurance* (New York, 1952), 7–22; CIE, June 1954, 11.

13. Anne F. Cole, *The Expert Waitress: A Manual for the Pantry, Kitchen, and Dining Room* (New York, 1911), 126; New York Hotel and Motel Trades Council, 35th Anniversary Committee, *The Story of the First Contract* (New York City, 1974), 11–13; New York WTUL, "Conditions of Women Workers in the Hotel and Restaurant Industry," 35, 52, 64; "The Story of a Waitress," SFLC, 6 September 1907, 12–13; *Electrical Workers Journal*, May 1951, 56–63; Suellen Butler and James Skipper, "Working the Circuit: An Explanation of Employee Turnover in the Restaurant Industry," *Sociological Spectrum* 3 (1983): 23.

14. "The Story of a Waitress," 56–63; U.S. Commission on Industrial Relations, "Industrial Conditions and Relations in Chicago," *Final Report and Testimony* (Washington, D.C., 1916), 3247; MacDougall, *The Secret of Successful Restaurants*, 82–83; New York (State) Department of Labor, *Report of the Industrial Commissioner*, 59, 92; Pennsylvania Bureau of Hours and Minimum Wages, Department of Labor and Industry, *Report to the Wage Board for Restaurants on Employment of Women and Minors in Restaurants and Other Eating Places* (December 1938), 44–46; Leslie Tentler, *Wage-earning Women: Industrial Work and Family Life in the United States, 1900–1930* (New York, 1979), 23; *Free Voice*, 1 February 1931, 4.

15. New York WTUL, "The Conditions of Women Workers in the Hotel and Restaurant Industry," 41–42.

16. Matthews, *Women in Trade Unions in San Francisco*, 33; Hamilton, *Employer-Employee Relations in Hotels*, 11; backup notes for Women's Bureau Bulletin no. 238, Box 696, RG-86, NA; typed excerpt from unidentified newspaper clipping, n.d., file—"DIW-Misc.," Box 4, SFLCR-UCB; Consumers' League of New York City, *Behind the Scenes in a Restaurant*, 12–13.

17. Ibid., 28; CIE, September 1954, 15–16; *Free Voice*, 1 August 1927, 2; U.S. Commission on Industrial Relations, "Industrial Conditions and Relations in Chicago," 3535–36; Leon Pescheret, *Gluttony and Lucre: A Great Social Evil Exposed or the Catering Industry under the Lime-light* (Chicago, 1913), 11; George Orwell, *Down and Out in Paris and London* (New York, 1933), 30; "The Henrici Strike," *City Club Bulletin* 7, 13 June 1944, 195; interview with Valentine Webster; New York Hotel and Motel Trades Council, *Story of the First Contract*, 9.

18. New York WTUL, "The Conditions of Women Workers in the Hotel and Restaurant Industry," 21–26; Barbour, "Wage, Hours, and Unionization in Year-round Hotels," 88; James Marshall, *Santa Fe: The Railroad that Built an Empire* (New York,

1945), 100–101; Connecticut (State), *Report of the Bureau of Labor on the Conditions of Wage-earning Women and Girls*, 91–93; Joanne Meyerowitz, *Women Adrift: Independent Wage Earners in Chicago, 1880–1930* (Chicago, 1988), 73–79; Albert Leggett, *The Student Waiter and Waitress* (New York, 1956), 7–8; Arthur Timmins, *Coming Sir: The Autobiography of a Waiter* (London, 1937), 83–92.

19. Ernest M. Porter, *Hotel and Restaurant Careers for Women* (London, 1931), 11; Hugo Ernst to Joseph Marino, 17 March 1938, Alice Condroy to the San Francisco LJEB, 4 February 1937, LJEB Correspondence Folder, Local 2 Files; Amy E. Tanner, "Glimpses at the Mind of a Waitress," *American Journal of Sociology* 13 (1907–8): 48–55.

20. *Food Worker*, March 1932, 3; HCV, 21 July 1945, 3; Sarah Comstock, "Miss Deaver and the Hotel Maid," *Harpers Weekly*, 17 January 1914, 8–11; "Story of a Summer Hotel Waitress," *Independent* 15 (June 1905): 1337–43; Mary Dewson, *The Unstandardized Industry, Hotels: How to Standardize It* (New York City, 1921).

21. U.S. Department of Labor, Bureau of Labor Statistics, *Industry Wage Survey: Eating and Drinking Places June 1961*, 5–6; U.S. Department of Labor, Bureau of Labor Statistics, *Industry Wage Survey: Eating and Drinking Places October 1966 and April 1967*, Bulletin no. 1588 (Washington, D.C., April 1967), 2; Transcript of the Ninth Minimum Wage Conference, 1939, 7, Box 904, RG-86, NA; MS, November 1918, 22; U.S. Department of Labor, Women's Bureau, *The Woman Wage Earner: Her Situation Today*, Bulletin no. 172 by Elizabeth Benham (Washington, 1939), 37.

22. New York WTUL, "The Conditions of Women Workers in the Hotel and Restaurant Industry," 26–32; "Address to Hotel and Restaurant Workers," *Industrial Union Bulletin*, 4 January 1908, Box 156, IWW, WRL-WSU; "Being a Waitress in a Broadway Hotel," *Scribners Magazine* 70 (September 1921): 324–25.

23. Pennsylvania Bureau of Hours and Minimum Wages, *Report to the Wage Board*, 36–37; New York WTUL, "The Conditions of Women Workers in the Hotel and Restaurant Industry," 26–29.

24. *Free Voice*, 1 August 1927, 2. See William Fisher's novel *The Waiters* (Cleveland, 1953) for a vivid description of the dank, unsanitary employee accommodations at one of Long Island's finest eateries.

25. Donovan, *The Woman Who Waits*, 15, 73, 131–32; Chicago Commission on Race Relations, *The Negro in Chicago: A Study of Race Relations and a Race Riot* (Chicago, 1922), pp. 367–68; Strakosch, *Job Study of Waitresses*, 20; interview with Clela Sullivan.

26. U.S. Commission on Industrial Relations, "Industrial Conditions and Relations in Chicago," 3256–57; *NYT*, 6 September 1935; New York Department of Labor, *Report of the Industrial Commissioner*, 93; Pennsylvania Bureau of Hours and Minimum Wages, *Report to the Wage Board*, 38–40; John P. Henderson, *Labor Market Institutions and Wages in the Lodging Industry* (East Lansing, 1965), 67.

27. Gordon, "The Forgotten Industry," 516; Charlotte Hughes, "Girl with a Tray," *NYT*, 30 March 1940, 8; Joanne Meyerowitz, "Holding Their Own: Working Women Apart from Family in Chicago, 1880–1930," Ph.D. diss., Stanford University, 1983, 54; Ludwig Bemelmans, *Hotel Bemelmans* (New York, 1946), 134–41.

28. U. S. Commission on Industrial Relations, "Industrial Conditions and Relations in Chicago," 3256–57; Lois Rita Helmbold, "Making Choices, Making Do:

Black and White Working Class Women's Lives and Work During the Depression,"
Ph.D. diss., Stanford University, 1982, 144–57; New York WTUL, "The Conditions
of Women Workers in the Hotel and Restaurant Industry," 6–7; interview with Beulah
Compton, 19; interview with Valentine Webster.

29. John E. Schein, Edwin Jablonski, and Barbara Wohlfahrt, *The Art of Tipping*
(Wausau, 1985), 21–23; William R. Scott, *The Itching Palm: A Study of the Habit of
Tipping in America* (Philadelphia, 1916), 33, 122–43; Edith Hilles, "Who Pays the
Waiter?" *Survey*, 18 February 1922, 795–76; "Tipping as a Factor in Wages," *MLR* 45
(December 1937): 1304–22; Lydia Salisch and Emily Palmer, *An Analysis of the Wait-
ress Trade* (Sacramento, 1933), 8; Ira Hamlin and Arthur Winakor, *Department Store
Food Service*, Bulletin no. 46 (Urbana, 1933), 26. See also Mabel M. Smythe, "Tip-
ping Occupations as a Problem in the Administration of Protective Labor Legislation,"
Ph.D. diss., University of Wisconsin, 1942.

30. *NYT*, 25 April 1909; *SFLC*, 6 September 1907, 13 March 1914, 11 November
1927; *Hotel Worker*, 3 May 1919; Consumers' League of New York City, *Behind the
Scenes in a Restaurant*, 2–7; New York WTUL, "The Conditions of Women Workers
in the Hotel and Restaurant Industry," 70; Louise Bowen, *The Girl Employed in Hotels
and Restaurants* (Chicago, 1912), n.p., approx. 20; U.S. Commission on Industrial
Relations, "Industrial Conditions and Relations in Chicago," 3254, 3257–58.

31. Chumley, "Hotel, Restaurant and Domestic Workers"; Louis Melis, "Hotel,
Restaurant, and Domestic Workers," *One Big Union Monthly*, April 1919, 59–62;
"Wake Up! Hotel, Restaurant and Cafeteria Workers," Box 177, IWW, WRL-WSU.

32. *CIE*, February 1932, 11; February 1940, 28.

33. Transcript of the Eighth Minimum Wage Conference, 10 November 1938, 15–
16, 19–21, Box 904, RG-86, NA; Minutes of the Minimum Wage Conference, 1 October 1934, 2, File "Minimum Wage Conferences," Box 906, RG-86, NA; Smythe,
"Tipping Occupations as a Problem in the Administration of Protective Labor Legislation," 4; *MHBRR*, May 1942, 6; "Fifty Years of Progress: A Brief History of Our
Union, 1891–1941" (Cincinnati, 1941), 37; Alvin F. Harlow, "Our Daily Bribe: The
Degrading Practice of Tipping," *Forum* 5 (April 1938): 231–35; Clyde Brion Davis,
"Tips," *Atlantic Monthly*, September 1946, 126–27; Leo P. Crespi, "The Implications
of Tipping in America," *Public Opinion Quarterly* (Fall 1947): 424–35; *CIE*, June 1951,
12–13.

34. Scott, *The Itching Palm*, 5; Crespi, "The Implications of Tipping in America,"
430; *NYT*, 20 May 1928; Hughes, "Girl with a Tray," 8; *Dining Room Employee*, November 1957, 3; interview with Clela Sullivan; William Foote Whyte, *Human Relations
in the Restaurant Industry* (New York, 1948) 98; Charles O'Connor, "Wages and Tips
in Restaurants and Hotels," *MLR* 94 (July 1971): 47–50; Suellen Butler and James
Skipper, "Waitressing, Vulnerability, and Job Autonomy: The Case of the Risky Tip,"
Sociology of Work and Occupations 7 (November 1980): 487–502; "Wages and Tips
in Hotels and Motels," *MLR* 103 (December 1980): 60; Donald Schmitt, "Tips: The
Mainstay of Many Hotel Workers' Pay," *MLR* 108 (July 1985): 50–51.

35. Claudia Goldin, "The Work and Wages of Single Women, 1870–1920," *Journal
of Economic History* 40 (March 1980): 86; Benson, *Counter Cultures*, 190.

36. John Henderson, *Labor Market Institutions and Wages in the Lodging Industry*,
69–97; *NYT*, 10 May 1935, 20; U.S. Department of Labor, Bureau of Labor Statistics,
Industry Wage Survey: Eating and Drinking Places June 1961, 5.

37. Hannah Creighton, "Tied by Double Apron Strings: Female Work Culture and Organization in a Restaurant," *Insurgent Sociologist* 11 (Fall 1982): 62; Eleonor LaPointe, "Waitressing: The Politics of the Labor Process," seminar paper, Sociology Department, Rutgers University, 1986, 10; Gerald Mars and Michael Nicod, *The World of Waiters* (London, 1984), 75–76. George Orwell held the tip exchange responsible for why waiters were seldom socialists; see *Down and Out in Paris and London*, 77. Susan Woods, "Waitressing: Taking Control of Our Work," *Quest* 5 (Summer 1979): 82–94; Butler and Skipper, "Working the Circuit," 24; Butler and Skipper, "Waitressing, Vulnerability, and Job Autonomy," 487–502.

38. LaPointe, "Waitressing," 15–16.

39. Whyte, *Human Relations in the Restaurant Industry*, 171–88.

40. Interview with Loretta Szeliga. For other examples of sexual harassment, see "Story of a Summer Hotel Waitress," 1342; Pescheret, *Gluttony and Lucre*, 13–14; Cornelia Stratton Parker, *Working with the Working Woman* (New York, 1922), 212–13; MHBRR, January 1936, 6; interview with Beulah Compton.

41. Interview with Loretta Szeliga.

42. CIE, August 1950, 28; see also Liza Bingham, Meredith Golden, and Holly Newman, "Harvard Square Waitresses Strike," *Second Wave* 1 (1972): 3–5; Leon Elder and Lin Rolens, *Waitress: America's Unsung Heroine* (Santa Barbara, 1985); and Louise Kapp Howe, *Pink-collar Workers: Inside the World of Women's Work* (New York, 1977), 103–42.

43. CIE, August 1950, 15–6; HCV, 11 January 1947, 5; Howe, *Pink-collar Workers*, 119.

44. Maurice Zolotov, *Never Whistle in a Dressing Room* (New York, 1944), 173; Whyte, *Human Relations in the Restaurant Industry*, 95–96, 369; William F. Whyte, E. L. Hamilton, and M. C. Wiley, *Action Research for Management* (Homewood, 1964), 44.

45. "The Essentials of Good Table Service," Cornell Hotel and Restaurant Administration Quarterly Pamphlet, 1960, 48; *NYT*, 29 October 1985; Rachel Migler, "The Philadelphia Waitress," *Philadelphia Magazine* 76 (April 1985): 108; Bea Pixa, "Wait Training," *San Francisco Examiner*, 7 January 1986; Jack Smith, "In Praise of Waitresses: In Diners and Restaurants Across the Land, They Serve Their Country Well," *Los Angeles Times Magazine*, 8 December 1985, 8.

46. Smith, "In Praise of Waitresses," 8; Elder and Rolens, *Waitress*, 7–8, 17–18, 33, 59, 64, 82.

47. Smith, "In Praise of Waitresses," 8; Elder and Rolens, *Waitress*, 7–8, 17–18, 33, 59, 64, 82; Creighton, "Tied by Double Apron Strings," 59–64; MacDougall, *The Secret of Successful Restaurants*, 193, 216–18; O. Henry, "The Brief Debut of Tildy," in *The Complete Works of O. Henry* (New York, 1937), 101–2; Stanley Hollander, "A Historical Perspective on the Service Encounter," in *The Service Encounter: Managing Employee-Customer Interaction in Service Businesses*, ed. John Czepiel, Michael Solomon, and Carol Surprenant (Lexington, Mass., 1985), 50–53, 59.

48. Whyte, *Human Relations in the Restaurant Industry*, 171–88; MacDougall, *The Secret to Successful Restaurants*, 66–68; Elder and Rolens, *Waitress*, 9–10; Hughes, "Girl with a Tray," 8; Langdon, *Orange Roofs, Golden Arches*, 30–31; Lucius Boomer, *Hotel Management: Principles and Practice* (New York, 1931), 330; Butler and Skipper, "Working the Circuit," 23; Elaine J. Hall, "Serving Side by Side? The Organi-

zational Stratification of Waiters and Waitresses Between and Within Restaurants," unpublished working paper, Sociology Department, University of Connecticut, 1989; interview with Florence Farr.

49. HM, April 1918, 61; Lilian Gunn, *Table Service and Decoration* (Philadelphia, 1928), 16–20; Eleanor Marchant, *Serving and Waiting: Modern Methods of Table Preparation* (New York, 1905), 10, 21, 42; George Chappell, *The Restaurants of New York* (New York, 1925), 131; Mars and Nicod, *The World of the Waiter*, 104; interview with Clela Sullivan.

50. Erving Goffman, "The Nature of Deference and Demeanor," *American Anthropologist* 58 (1956): 473–502; Maud Younger, "The Diary of an Amateur Waitress," pt. 1 *McClure's Magazine* (March 1907): 543–52, pt. 2 (April 1907): 665–77; NYT, 20 December 1987; Whyte, *Human Relations in the Restaurant Industry*, 92–97, 282; Douglas Bauer, "The Prime of Miss Jean Brody," *Esquire*, June 1985, 118; Elder and Rolens, *Waitress*, 69; interview with Clela Sullivan.

51. Elder and Rolens, *Waitress*, 69, 72; NYT, 20 May 1928; HM, June 1930, 83; Strakosch, *Job Study of Waitresses*, 7; MacDougall, *The Secret of Successful Restaurants*, 80; Smith, "In Praise of Waitresses," 8; Hughes, "Girl with a Tray," 8; Helmi Koivisto, "Subprofessional Jobs for Women with Limited Home Economic Training," *Journal of Home Economics* 37 (October 1945): 496; Dahl, *Dining Room Management for Head Waitresses and Hostesses*, 3, 34; William F. Whyte, "When Workers and Customers Meet," in *Industry and Society*, ed. Whyte (New York, 1946), 142–43; *Today's Waitress*, prepared by Bolt, Beranek and Newman Inc. (New York, 1971); MHBRR, December 1950, 3; "No Hashers: Waitresses Now Must Have Tact and Charm," *Literary Digest*, 1 May 1937, 26–27.

52. Carol Zisowitz Stearns and Peter Stearns, *Anger: The Struggle for Emotional Control in America's History* (Chicago, 1986), 110–56; Benson also discusses this new service ideal in *Counter Cultures*, 12–30, 134.

53. J. O. Dahl, *The Efficient Waitress Manual* (New York, 1935), 52–55; Arlie Hochschild, *The Managed Heart: The Commercialization of Human Feeling* (Berkeley, 1983), 7; interview with Clela Sullivan; Elder and Rolens, *Waitress*, 32–33; Rose Kennedy, "Dreamscape," *Tables*, April 1986, 29–35; C. Wright Mills, *White Collar* (New York, 1951), 187–88; Greta Foff Paules, "Behind the Lines: Strategies of Self-Perception and Protection Among Waitresses in New Jersey," Ph.D. diss., Princeton University, 1990, 199.

54. Hochschild found that male flight attendants received less abuse from customers because men were perceived as having higher status and more authority, *The Managed Heart*, 174–81. For examples of the same phenomenon operating in the food service industry, see LaPointe, "Waitressing," 5; Elder, *Waitress*, 12; and Howe, *Pink-collar Workers*, 116.

55. "Waitress Work in Summer Hotels By One Who Has Tried It," 62; Gunn, *Table Service and Decoration*, 17; Marchant, *Serving and Waiting*, 13, 21; Dahl, *The Efficient Waitress Manual*, 5; NYT, 20 May 1928; Louis Garfunkel, *Sandwich Shops, Drive-ins and Diners: How to Operate* (New York, 1955), 233; interviews with Helene Powell, Florence Douglas, and Jackie Walsh; Langdon, *Orange Roofs, Golden Arches*, 64–65; Woods, "Waitressing," 88; MHBRR, September 1939, 10; *Hotels and Restaurants International*, February 1984, 58–61; (Detroit, Michigan) *The Wage-Earner*, December 1951, 4–5; "Houston's Drive-in Trade Gets Girl Show with Its

Hamburgers," *Life*, 26 February 1940, 84–87; Sara Rapport, " 'I'm Cheryl—Fly Me to Court': Flight Attendants vs. the Airlines, 1960–1976," unpublished seminar paper, Rutgers University History Department, September 1986. The phrase "personality and pulchritude" is from *MHBRR*, September 1939, 10.

56. Tanner, "Glimpses at the Mind of a Waitress," 49–52.

57. Consumers' League of New York City, *Behind the Scenes in a Restaurant*, 7.

58. Bemelmans, *Hotel Bemelmans*, 115–16; "Being a Waitress in a Broadway Hotel," 322–25; Wolfe, *The Lodging House Problem in Boston*, 9; Donovan, *The Woman Who Waits*, 124; Gordon, "The Forgotten Industry," 516; Hamilton, *Employer-Employee Relations in Hotels*, 115–19; U.S. National Youth Administration, Illinois, *Restaurant Occupations*, 18; Mary Lee Spence, "They Also Serve Who Wait," *Western Historical Quarterly* 17 (January 1983): 4–28; *Hotel Monthly*, September 1927, 70; T. S. Chivers, "The Proletarianization of the Service Worker," *Sociological Review* 21 (November 1973): 647; interview with Blanche Copenhaver; Elder and Rolen, *Waitress*, 61; Strakosch, *Job Study of Waitresses*, 12; Lorine Pruette, "The Casual Woman Laborer," *Survey*, 15 September 1924, 624.

59. Butler and Skipper, "Working the Circuit," 30; Orwell, *Down and Out in Paris and London*, 25; *NYT*, 8 July 1923; R. N. Elliot, *Tea Room and Cafeteria Management* (Boston, 1935); Mary Dutton, "Restaurant Management," in *An Outline of Careers for Women*, ed. Doris E. Fleischman (Garden City, 1929); Catherine Filene, ed. *Careers for Women* (Boston, 1920, rept., New York, 1974), 209–13; Donald Lundberg, *The Restaurant: From Concept to Operation* (New York, 1985), 286; Strakosch, *Job Study of Waitresses*, 10–13; Whyte, *Human Relations in the Restaurant Industry*, 15, 153, 273–76; *NYT*, 20 May 1928; Erma Hubbell, *The Hostess and Social Executive* (Los Angeles, 1930), 63; San Francisco Board of Education, Attendance and Guidance Bureau, *The Restaurant Industry in San Francisco* (San Francisco, 1932), 45–48; Ann Seidman, ed. *Working Woman* (Boulder, 1978), 95.

60. U.S. Department of Labor, Women's Bureau, *Women's Occupations Through Seven Decades*, Bulletin no. 218, by Janet M. Hooks (Washington, D.C., 1947), 182–83; U.S. National Youth Administration, Illinois, *Restaurant Occupations*, 2, 16; Frances Willard, *Occupations for Women* (New York, 1897), 120; Donovan, *The Woman Who Waits*, 96; Consumers' League of New York City, *Behind the Scenes in a Restaurant*, 26; Charles Brecher, *Upgrading Blue-collar and Service Workers* (Baltimore, 1972), 36; interview with Idoniea Duntley.

61. Edna Ferber, "Our Very Best People," in *Mother Knows Best* (New York, 1927), 171–201.

62. My notion of culture has been shaped by the work of Herbert Gutman, *Work, Culture, and Society in Industrializing America* (New York, 1974); E. P. Thompson, *The Making of the English Working Class* (New York, 1966); Clifford Geertz *The Interpretation of Cultures* (New York, 1973); and Michael Merrill's two interviews with Thompson and Gutman in *Visions of History* (New York, 1976), 3–26, 185–216.

63. Although sociologists were studying group practices on the shopfloor as early as the 1920s, labor historians did not focus on informal organization and worker culture(s) until the 1970s. For an early article on occupational cultures, see Everett C. Hughes, "Personality Types and the Division of Labor," in *Personality and the Social Group*, ed. Ernest W. Burgess (Chicago, 1929, rept., Freeport, 1969), 78–94. Studies of work cultures in occupations other than waitressing include Cynthia Costello,

" 'WEA're Worth It': Work Culture and Conflict at the Wisconsin Education Association Insurance Trust," *Feminist Studies* 11 (Fall 1985): 497–518; Benson, *Counter Cultures*, 227–83; Patricia A. Cooper, *Once a Cigar Maker: Men, Women, and Work Culture in American Cigar Factories, 1900–1919* (Urbana, 1987); and Seymour Martin Lipset, Martin Trow, and James Coleman, *Union Democracy: The Internal Politics of the Typographical Union* (Glencoe, 1956). A summary of work pertaining to women's work culture is found in Micaela di Leonardo, "Women's Work, Work Culture, and Consciousness," *Feminist Studies* 11 (Fall 1985): 491–95.

64. Di Leonardo, "Women's Work, Work Culture, and Consciousness," 492–95; Benson, *Counter Cultures*, 227–83; George Kirstein, *Stores and Unions: A Study of the Growth of Unionism in Dry Goods and Department Stores* (New York, 1950). Waitresses did divide along racial lines but theirs was not a class-stratified occupational culture such as that of nurses. See Susan Reverby, *Ordered to Care: The Dilemma of American Nursing, 1850–1945* (New York, 1987).

65. For the quotes, see Della Yoe and Jennette Edwards, "Snappy Feeding," in Works Progress Administration, *These Are Our Lives: As Told by the People and Written by the Members of the Federal Writers Project of the WPA in North Carolina, Tennessee, and Georgia* (Chapel Hill, 1939), 347; and Studs Terkel *Working: People Talk About What They Do All Day and How They Feel About What They Do* (New York, 1972), 390. For other examples, see Chumley, "Hotel, Restaurant and Domestic Workers," n.p.; Bernard Rosenberg and Saul Weinman, "Young Women Who Work: An Interview with Myra Wolfgang," *Dissent* 86 (Winter 1972): 29; Robert Itzin, "Starting Over," *Tables*, July 1986, 33; Angela M. Bowery, *The Sociology of Organizations* (London, 1976), 137; Whyte, *Human Relations in the Restaurant Industry*, 10–16, 369; Elder and Rolens, *Waitress*, 11, 42, 46, 78–81, 84; Patricia Stoll, "Occupational Alienation: The Case of the Cocktail Waitress," master's thesis in sociology, University of Missouri-Kansas City, 1973, 17–20; Amy Short, "Waitressing," *Glamour*, August 1979, 154–57; Sondra Dahmer and Kurt Kahl, *The Waiter and Waitress Training Manual* (Boston, 1974), 1–2; Barbour, "Wages, Hours, and Unionization," 100; LaPointe, "Waitressing," 15; Trueblood, "Household versus Shop and Factories," 2692; and Becky Sukovsky, "Waiting: The Other Side of the Counter," *Northwest Passage*, August 19–September 9, 1980, 11–12.

66. Joseph O. Dahl, *Soda Fountain and Luncheonette Management* (New York, 1930), 7; Scott, *The Itching Palm*, 97.

67. Terkel, *Working*, introduction and 393; Yoe and Edwards, *These Are Our Lives*, 343; Elder and Rolens, *Waitresses*, 84; Hansen, "Don't Kid the Waitress," 67.

68. Chapters 3 and 4 of this volume discuss employers' attitudes toward unionization. Donald Lundberg, *The Hotel and Restaurant Business* (Boston, 1979), 40; HM, January 1930, 56–57; NYT, 20 May 1928; interview with Clela Sullivan; Susan Dietz, *The Correct Waitress* (New York, 1952), 9, 11.

69. NYT, 12 May 1929; MHBRR, March 1945; Henry, "The Brief Debut of Tildy," 102; Bauer, "The Prime of Miss Jean Brody," LaPointe, "Waitressing," 12; Benson, *Counter Cultures*, 268.

70. Researchers have found that while "friendly rapport" and other strategies failed to augment tips, "the promoting waitress" increased her tips to a statistically significant degree. Suellen Butler and William Snizek, "The Waitress-Diner Relationship," *Sociology of Work and Occupations* 3 (May 1976): 209–22.

71. Sociologists disagree over the degree of autonomy waitresses exercise at the workplace. Some emphasize the lack of formal authority held by waitresses and the increasing rationization of food service; others stress waitresses' control over tipping and the "shared arsenal of tactics" by which they have resisted management intrusion. See Stoll, "Occupational Alienation," 27–30, 50–61; Woods, "Waitressing," 84–88; Butler and Skipper, "Working the Circuit," 25–26, and Butler and Snizek, "The Waitress-Diner Relationship," 212–15, 222; Paules, "Behind the Lines," iv, 24–25, chs. 3, 5.

72. George Ritzer, *Working: Conflict and Change* (Englewood Cliffs, 1977), 288–97; Women's Legal Defense Fund, *The Waitress Handbook: A Guide to the Legal Rights of Waitresses and Other Restaurant Workers* (Washington, D.C., 1986), 7. On food service worker individualism, see Donovan, *The Woman Who Waits*, 128; Mars and Nicod, *The World of Waiters*, 9, 124–40; Butler and Skipper, "Working the Circuit," 24; Paules, "Behind the Lines," 181–88.

73. See the discussion in Theodore Caplow, *The Sociology of Work* (Minneapolis, 1954), 46–52 in which he examines the evaluation of particular occupations by the Census Bureau and various social scientists. The Census classification used by A. M. Edwards in *Comparative Occupational Statistics for the U.S. 1870–1940* places all servants at the very bottom of the occupational heap, below farm laborers and unskilled industrial workers. The Minnesota Occupational Scale is somewhat kinder, putting most servants among the "slightly" skilled and waiters and waitresses among the semiskilled.

74. Matthews, *Women in Trade Unions in San Francisco*, 33; Donovan, *The Woman Who Waits*, 211.

75. Whyte, *Human Relations in the Restaurant Industry*, 65–81, 92–128, 282–87; William F. Whyte, "The Social Structure of the Restaurant," *American Journal of Sociology* 54 (January 1949): 305–11; William F. Whyte, *Men at Work* (Homewood, 1961), 125–35; and Whyte, "When Workers and Customers Meet."

76. H. L. Hearn and Patricia Stoll, "Continuance Commitment in Low-Status Occupations: The Cocktail Waitress," *Sociological Quarterly* 16 (Winter 1975): 112.

77. Donovan, *The Woman Who Waits*, 94; Hansen, "Don't Kid the Waitress," 14; Hughes, "Personality Types and the Division of Labor," 78–94; "Being a Waitress in a Broadway Hotel," 317; Mars and Nicod, *The World of the Waiter*, 126; Whyte, Hamilton, and Wiley, *Action Research for Management*, 44; Whyte, *Human Relations in the Restaurant Industry*, 153–56; interview with Valentine Webster; Stoll, "Occupational Alienation," 71–73; interview with Kathryn Dewing; Maryellen Kennedy, "The Kitchen Man," *Tables*, August 1986, 7; Hope Dlugozima, "Waitressing: The Thrills and Spoils," *Seventeen* 45 (June 1986): 146–47; Elder and Rolens, *Waitress*, 82.

78. Whyte, *Human Relations in the Restaurant Industry*, 65–81; James Spradley and Brenda Mann, *The Cocktail Waitress: Women's Work in a Man's World* (New York, 1975); LaPointe, "Waitressing," 23–24.

79. Younger, "The Diary of An Amateur Waitress," pt. 1, 543; Donovan, *The Woman Who Waits*, 21; Dwight Macdonald, "Your Waiter Looks at You," *Harper's Magazine*, April 1941, 517; Dahl, *Dining Room Management for Head Waitresses and Hostesses*, 8; Hughes, "Girl with a Tray," 8; interview with Clela Sullivan; Hughes, "Personality Types and the Division of Labor," 78–94; Kennedy, "The Kitchen Man," 8; "No Hashers: Waitresses Now Must Have Tact and Charm," 26–27; *MHBRR*, May 1946; John Riordan, "Soda Fountain Lingo," *California Folklore Quarterly* 4 (January

1945): 50–57; Lewis Mennerick, "Client Typologies: A Method of Coping with Conflict in the Service Worker-Client Relationship," *Sociology of Work and Occupations* 1 (November 1974): 396–418; Runcie, "Occupational Communication as Boundary Mechanism," 423. For other examples of culinary language, see *NYT* 3 May 1981 and *Newsweek*, 31 July 1989.

80. Orwell, *Down and Out in Paris and London*, 75; Mars and Nicod, *The World of the Waiter*, 105–8, 111–23; interview with Idoniea Duntley; Migler, "The Philadelphia Waitress," 108; Creighton, "Tied by Double Apron Strings," 59–64; "Being a Waitress in a Broadway Hotel," 317; *NYT*, 20 May 1928.

81. Whyte, "The Social Structure of the Restaurant," 305–11; LaPointe, "Waitressing," 17–18; Paules, "Behind the Lines," 188; interview with Valentine Webster; Ritzer, *Working*, 351–53.

82. *NYT*, 5 May 1928, 10 August 1932; Mars and Nicod, *The World of the Waiter*, 59, 79, 83–98; Migler, "The Philadelphia Waitress," 108; MacDonald, "Your Waiter Looks at You," 519; Hughes, "Girl with a Tray," 8; Younger, "The Diary of an Amateur Waitress," pt. 2, 670; *MHBRR*, February 1951, 2, November 1944, 5. See also Hansen, "Don't Kid the Waitress," and Maud Younger, "Taking Orders: A Day as a Waitress in a San Francisco Restaurant," *Sunset*, October 1908, 518–22 for further examples of group strategies for handling customers.

83. Donovan, *The Woman Who Waits*, 16, 20, 26–28, 80–81.

84. See, for example, Tentler, *Wage-earning Women.*

85. The sexually experienced, cynical waitress is a stock character in fiction and in the media; for example, Flo on the television series "Alice" or the waitress in Arthur Penn's movie *Five Easy Pieces.* Tentler, *Wage-earning Women*, 71–80; *Time*, 3 June 1985, 13; Donovan, *The Woman Who Waits*, 136–37, 219–20.

86. Ritzer, *Working*, 352–53; O. Henry, "Cupid à la Carte," in *The Complete Works of O. Henry* (New York, 1937), 186, 188.

87. Although the remainder of this book focuses primarily on formal or union approaches to workplace governance, waitresses continued to exert their collective power informally as well. In many workplaces, the two approaches (formal and informal) were not mutually exclusive. They existed side by side, with the particular problem determining the most appropriate tactic.

Part II. Waitresses Turn to Political and Economic Organization

1. Leo Wolman, *Growth of American Trade Unions, 1880–1923* (New York, 1924), 85, 137–45; Marten Estey, *The Unions: Structure, Development, and Management* (New York, 1981), 2–4.

2. For the statistics, see Ruth Milkman, "Organizing the Sexual Division of Labor: Historical Perspectives on 'Women's Work' and the American Labor Movement," *Socialist Review* 49 (January–February 1980): 96, 120–21: for the obstacles women faced in organizing, see Alice Kessler-Harris, "Where Are the Organized Women Workers?" *Feminist Studies* 3 (1975): 92–110, and *Out to Work: A History of Wage-Earning Women in the United States* (New York, 1980), 152–71. See Philip S. Foner, *Women and the American Labor Movement: From Colonial Times to the Eve of World War I* (New York, 1979), 277–89 passim, and Foner, *Women and the American Labor Movement: From World War I to the Present* (New York, 1980), 59–79 passim for an overview of women's labor struggles.

3. Stephen Norwood, *Labor's Flaming Youth: Telephone Operators and Worker Militancy, 1878–1923* (Urbana, 1990); Sharon Strom, " 'We're no Kitty Foyles': Organizing Office Workers for the Congress of Industrial Organizations, 1937–50," in *Women, Work, and Protest: A Century of U.S. Women's Labor History*, ed. Ruth Milkman (Boston, 1985), 226; George Kirstein, *Stores and Unions: A Study of the Growth of Unionism in Dry Goods and Department Stores* (New York, 1954).

4. See Tables 5B, 5C, 6, and 8.

Chapter 3. The Emergence and Survival of Waitress Unionism, 1900–1930

1. "Story of a Waitress," *Independent*, 18 June 1908, 1381.

2. See, for example, Ruth Milkman, "Organizing the Sexual Division of Labor," *Socialist Review* 49 (January–February 1980): 95–150, Alice Kessler-Harris, "Where Are the Organized Women Workers?" *Feminist Studies* 3 (Fall 1975): 92–110; and Nancy Schrom Dye, *As Equals and as Sisters: Feminism, the Labor Movement and the Women's Trade Union League of New York* (Columbia, 1980).

3. See, for example, Dana Frank, "Housewives, Socialists and the Politics of Food: The New York City Cost of Living Protests," *Feminist Studies* 11 (Summer 1985): 255–85; and Patricia Cooper, *Once a Cigar Maker: Men, Women and Work Culture in American Cigar Factories, 1900–1919* (Urbana, 1987).

4. Ira B. Cross, *A History of the Labor Movement in California* (Berkeley, 1935), 177 and 33n.; Grace Heilman Stimson, *Rise of the Labor Movement in Los Angeles* (Berkeley, 1955), 66; Matthew Josephson, *Union House, Union Bar: A History of the Hotel and Restaurant Employees and Bartenders International Union, AFL-CIO* (New York, 1956), 7–12; Robert Hesketh, "Hotel and Restaurant Employees," *American Federationist* 38 (October 1931): 1269–71; "Brief History of Our Organization," *The Federation News*, 25 January 1930; Henry C. Barbour, "Wages, Hours, and Unionization in Year-Round Hotels," unpublished study, School of Hotel Administration, Cornell University, 1948, 115–16; Paul Frisch, "Gibralter of Unionism: The Development of Butte's Labor Movement, 1878–1900," *The Speculator* (Summer 1985): 12–20. For a discussion of the relation between the Knights of Labor and culinary workers, see MS, April 1904, 5–7.

5. Since 1981 the official name of the union has been the Hotel Employees and Restaurant Employees. For official HERE membership figures see the HERE Officers' Report, 1947, 17–18, Table 5A, and Figure 1 in the Appendix. The major published accounts of the history of the International include Josephson, *Union House, Union Bar*; Jay Rubin and M. J. Obermeier, *Growth of a Union: The Life and Times of Edward Flore* (New York, 1943); Morris A. Horowitz, *The New York Hotel Industry* (Cambridge, 1960), 21–65 passim; and John P. Henderson, *Labor Market Institutions and Wages in the Lodging Industry* (East Lansing, 1965), 129–59.

6. An examination of the IWW Collection, WRL-WSU and various IWW newspapers such as *Industrial Worker* and *Solidarity* revealed only scattered organizing efforts among culinary workers. For references to IWW culinary organizing outside New York before World War I, see "To the Workers Who Feed the World," Box 174; 10 October 1906–15 September 1911, General Executive Board Minutes, Box 7, file 1; "Address to the Hotel and Restaurant Workers," *Industrial Union Bulletin*, 4 January 1908, Box 156; Foodstuff Workers Industrial Union, Local 460, Box 69—all in IWW Collection, WRL-WSU. Also see *Industrial Worker*, 21 May 1910, 13 August 1910, 24 Septem-

ber 1910, 11 June 1910, 18 June 1910; *Solidarity*, 28 June 1913; 16 August 1913; and Guy Louis Rocha, "Radical Labor Struggles in the Tonopah-Goldfield Mining District, 1901–22," *Nevada Historical Society Quarterly* 20 (Spring 1977): 10–11. For IWW organizing in New York, see note 27.

7. Mabel Abbott, "The Waitresses of Seattle," *Life and Labor* 4 (February 1914): 48–49. After 1920, the majority of newly organized waitresses entered mixed-gender hotel service locals, miscellaneous culinary unions (composed of cooks, waiters, waitresses, and bartenders), or mixed-craft locals of waiters and waitresses. Waitress organizing before the New Deal, however, is essentially the story of separate waitress locals—their activities, leadership, strategies, and tactics.

8. Early discussions of gender separatism include Belva Mary Herron, "The Progress of Labor Organizations Among Women, Together with Some Considerations Concerning Their Place in Industry," *University Studies* 1 (May 1905): 443–511; Alice Henry, *The Trade Union Woman* (New York, 1915); Alice Henry, *Women and the Labor Movement* (New York, 1923); and Teresa Wolfson, *The Woman Worker and the Trade Unions* (New York, 1926). For more recent analyses see Roger Waldinger, "Another Look at the ILGWU: Women, Industry Structure and Collective Action," and Alice Kessler-Harris, "Problems of Coalition-building: Women and Trade Unions in the 1920s," both in *Women, Work, and Protest: A Century of Women's Labor History*, ed. Ruth Milkman (Boston, 1985), 86–138; and Susan Glenn, *Daughters of the Shtetl: Life and Labor in the Immigrant Generation* (Ithaca, 1990).

9. In *Daughters of the Shtetl*, ch. 6, Glenn notes that her work draws on Mary Jo Buhle's distinction between native-born varieties of feminism and urban-immigrant varieties. See Buhle, *Women and American Socialism 1870–1920* (Urbana, 1981), chs. 2, 3, passim.

10. In "The Progress of Labor Organizations Among Women," 66, Herron suggests that men prefer mixed locals in trades in which direct competition exists; separatism is advocated where competition is minimal. In the culinary industry sex segregation lessened direct competition but did not eliminate it. Hence, it is not surprising that men were divided in their attitudes toward separatism.

11. MS, May 1902, 5; June 1905, 84.

12. Ibid., June 1900, 7; November 1902, 20–21; December 1902, 38; *240 News*, February 1954, 3 on Reel 342, LUR, HERE Files; Abbott, "The Waitresses of Seattle," 48–49; Esther Taber, "Women in Unions: Through Trade Union Organization Waitresses Have Secured Marked Improvements in Conditions," *American Federationist* 12 (December 1905): 928. For biographical nuggets on the early Seattle leaders see MS, June 1903, 19; November 1904, 30; CIE, May 1931; December 1938; December 1939, 25; June 1942, 30; November 1940, 26; and Erika Gottfried, "Thank Lord for the 8-hour Day," *Seattle Post-Intelligencer*, 18 July 1976. For discussions of the "equal rights" tradition and female unionists, see, for example, Thomas Dublin, *Women at Work: The Transformation of Work and Community in Lowell, Massachusetts, 1826–1860* (New York, 1979), ch. 6, and Mary Blewett, "Work, Gender, and the Artisan Tradition in New England Shoemaking, 1780–1860," *Journal of Social History* 17 (Winter 1983): 221–48.

13. Lillian Ruth Matthews, *Women in Trade Unions in San Francisco* (Berkeley, 1913), 76; MS, April 1901, 6; April 1906, 28; SFLC, 23 January 1906; *San Francisco Examiner*, 3 April 1901.

14. *CIE*, June 1900, 7; April 1940, 35; August 1946, 37; April 1947, 40; October 1948, 37; *SFLC*, 9 January 1903; 4 December 1904; 7 July 1905; 23 January 1906; 1 May 1908; 10 July 1908; 1 January 1909; 24 February 1911; 25 June 1915; 24 August 1928; 22 February 1946; 5 December 1947; *San Francisco Call*, 5 July 1909. For additional details on LaRue and Younger, see Susan Englander, "The San Francisco Wage-earners' Suffrage League: Class Conflict and Class Coalition in the California Women's Suffrage Movement, 1907–1912," master's thesis, San Francisco State University, 1989, ch. 3.

15. Interview with Gertrude Sweet; Marion Dickerman and Ruth Taylor, ed., *Who's Who in Labor* (New York, 1946), 346; *Fifty Years of Progress: A Brief History of Our Union, 1891–1914*, foreword by Hugo Ernst and Harry Fox (Cincinnati, 1941), 13–14.

16. Bob Hesketh to JL Sullivan, 29 September 1921 and Harley Johnson to JL Sullivan, 1 October 1921, Reel 415, LUR, HERE Files; MS March 1919, 45.

17. *CIE*, December 1938, 55; interview with Gertrude Sweet; Dickerman and Taylor, ed. *Who's Who in Labor*; see *MS*, February 1927, 59–60; January 1929, 37.

18. For background on the Butte labor movement, see Frisch, "Gilbralter of Unionism" and Margaret Olsen, "How the Unions Went Underground in Early-Day Butte," *Montana Magazine*, November–December 1981. Information on the early Women's Protective Union can be found in Mary Murphy, untitled guide, WPU, BSBA; *MS*, October 1907, 35; *CIE*, April 1954, 19; and Laura Weatherby and Margaret Harrington, "Bucket Girl, Yard Girl: The Women Who Worked in Butte," *CIE*, October 1975, 22–23. Information on the early affiliations and jurisdiction of the WPU is in WPU Minutebook, 1 January 1903—31 December 1905, Box 13, file 13, WPUC-174, MHS. The description of Bridget Shea is from Marilyn Maney, BSBA staffperson.

19. Local 457 Minutebook, 24 June 1921, 2 September 1921, 16 September 1921, Local 457 Files; Local 457 Minutebook, 1 September 1922, 31 August 1922, 6 July 1923, 25 April 1924, 1 May 1925, 17 September 1926, 1 October 1926, 19 August 1927, Box 14-1, WPUC-174, MHS.

20. *MS*, January 1908, 43–44.

21. Reel 526, LUR, HERE Files; S. M. Franklin, "Elizabeth Maloney and the High Calling of the Waitress," *Life and Labor* 3 (February 1913): 36–40; John Andrews and W. D. P. Bliss, *A History of Women in Trade Unions*, vol. 10 of the *Report on the Condition of Women and Child Wage-Earners in the United States*, Senate Document 645, 61st Cong., 2d sess. (Washington, 1911, rept. New York, 1974), 186–87; *MS*, February 1903, 40; October 1905, 28, 32; December 1905, 28; Taber, "Women in Unions," 927–28; Emily Barrows, "Trade Union Organization Among Women in Chicago," master's thesis, University of Chicago, 1920, 55–57, 148–52; Luke Grant, "Women in Trade Unions," *American Federationist*, August 1903, 655–56. For background on women's unionism in Chicago, see Meredith Tax, *The Rising of the Women: Feminist Solidarity and Class Conflict, 1880–1917* (New York, 1980), 38–89.

22. U.S. Commission on Industrial Relations (1912), "Industrial Conditions and Relations in Chicago," *Final Report and Testimony* 4 (Washington, 1916), 3244–59, 3389–91; (Chicago) *City Club Bulletin* 8 no. 14, 13 June 1914, 189–204 in Office Files of Chicago HERE Local 1; Barrows, "Trade Union Organization Among Women in Chicago," 153–56; *MS*, December 1911, 53; November 1914, 73; December 1914, 65–69; January 1915, 3–9; June 1915, 51–56; August 1914, 35–36; Mary Anderson as told to Mary Winslow, *Women at Work: The Autobiography of Mary Anderson* (Minneapo-

lis, 1951), 54–55; Agnes Nestor, *Woman's Labor Leader: Autobiography of Agnes Nestor* (Rockford, 1954), 157–58.

23. *San Francisco Examiner*, 4 May 1901, 6 May 1901; MS, November 1902, 35; *San Francisco Chronicle*, 12 August 1917; SFLC, 18 December 1903; Robert E. L. Knight, *Industrial Relations in the San Francisco Bay Area 1900–1918* (Berkeley, 1960), 67–72, 136; Matthews, *Women in Trade Unions in San Francisco*, 78; Ed Rosenberg, "The San Francisco Strikes of 1901," *American Federationist* (1902): 15–18.

24. SFLC, 18 August 1905, 27 October 1905, 19 June 1906, 10 August 1906, 6 September 1907, 26 March 1909, 13 August 1909, 27 August 1915; Knight, *Industrial Relations in the San Francisco Bay Area*, 164–65; Louise Margaret Ploeger, "Trade Unionism Among the Women of San Francisco," master's thesis, University of California, 1920, 107–8.

25. SFLC, 19 May 1916, 21 July 1916, 11 August 1916, 25 August 1916; Ploeger, "Trade Unionism Among the Women of San Francisco," 108–11.

26. See Table 6 for examples of other locals that disappeared. See Andrews and Bliss, *A History of Women in Trade Unions*, 147, for New York City female culinary membership from 1902–9. See Gary M. Fink, ed., *Biographical Dictionary of American Labor* (Westport, 1984), 56–57, 599–600 for a description of Maud Younger's activities. Dye, *As Equals and as Sisters*, 61–65, 76–80; "Story of a Waitress."

27. Offshoots of the New York movement also appeared in Buffalo, Boston, Philadelphia, and elsewhere. For IWW organizing in New York City, see Frank Bohn, "The Strike of the New York Hotel and Restaurant Workers," *International Socialist Review* 13 (February 1913): 620–21; "Workers of the World Now Run Affairs for New York Waiters," *Square Deal* 12 (February 1913): 29–32, 87; *Solidarity* 14 and 21 February 1914; 15 June 1912, 2; 15 February 1913, 4; Hugo Ernst, "The Hotel and Restaurant Workers," *American Federationist* 53 (June 1946), 20–21, 29; New York Hotel and Motel Trades Council, *The Story of the First Contract* (New York, 1974), 19–25; NYT, 8, 10, 14, 20, 31 May 1912; 2, 4, 22 June 1912; 4 July 1912; 13–14, 25 January 1913; 1–2 February 1913; 14–15 May 1914; 9, 21, 28 December 1915; 29 October 1918; 7 and 27 December 1918.

28. Organizing can be traced in SFLC, 16 November 1917, 21 June 1918, 7 March 1919, 4 August 1919; NYT, 7 and 27 December 1918; "Department Store Waitresses Win Increase," *Life and Labor Bulletin*, July 1918, 141.

29. For HERE female membership figures, see Table 7. For IWW organizing attempts during World War I and the 1920s, see "Wake Up! Hotel, Restaurant, and Cafeteria Workers," n.d. [ca. 1920s], Box 177, IWW, WRL-WSU; Charles Devlin, "Help Organize Hotel, Restaurant, and Domestic Workers," *One Big Union Monthly* 2 (February 1920): 49; Devlin, "Who Does Not Work Neither Shall He Eat," *One Big Union Monthly* 2 (August 1920): 56–57; "Who Will Feed Us When Capitalism Breaks Down?" *One Big Union Monthly* 2 (November 1920): 40–42; "The Servant Girl Rediscovered," *One Big Union Monthly* 2 (January 1920): 53–54; L. S. Chumley, "Hotel, Restaurant, and Domestic Workers," 1918, Box 163, IWW, WRL-WSU.

30. Ernst categorizes Denver in this fashion, see MS, July 1923, 38. The term also is used by Max Kniesche in "Schroeder's Cafe and the German Restaurant Tradition in San Francisco, 1907–1976," an interview by Ruth Teiser conducted in 1976 for the Regional Oral History Office, Bancroft Library, UCB.

31. Interview with Charles Paulsen; Rubin and Obermeier, *The Growth of a Union*, 164–80.

32. Following World War I, employers linked the open-shop concept with Americanism by dubbing it the "American Plan." The "yellow-dog contract" was a pledge by the employee that he or she would not join or support a union. Some employers required these contracts from all newly hired workers. For a general account that includes particulars on HERE, see Irving Bernstein, *The Lean Years* (Boston, 1960), 85, 117, 336. See also Lawrence Nelson to Lena Mattausch, 28 January 1922, letter stuck in Local 457 Minutebook, 1916–22, Local 457 Files.

33. Barrows, "Trade Union Organization Among Women in Chicago," 148, 155; MS, June 1920, 24; July 1920, 25–26; July 1923, 32–37; December 1929, 14; (Chicago) *WTUL Bulletin*, June 1920, in Reel 9, C-9, WTUL Papers. See Rubin and Obermeier, *The Life and Times of Edward Flore*, 168–69, for an account of the 1920–21 lockout in St. Louis hotels and restaurants affecting Waitresses' Local 249.

34. MS, April 1923, 52; March 1925, 51. For the growth of California's locals, see California (State) Industrial Welfare Commission, *Fourth Biennial Report for 1919–1920* (Sacramento, 1924); *Fifth Biennial Report for 1922–24* (Sacramento, 1927); *Sixth Biennial Report for 1926–1928* (Sacramento, 1929); and Reel 628, LUR, HERE Files.

35. Local 457 Minutebook, 26 March 1920, 2 April 1920, 14 May 1920, 24 September 1920, 2 September 1921, Local 457 Files. Local 457 Minutebook, 30 April 1926, 28 May 1926, Box 14-1, WPUC-174, MHS.

36. *Proceedings*, 1921 Convention, HERE, 177; *Proceedings*, 1923 Convention, HERE, 178–80, 185; Local 457 Minutebook, 20 January 1922, Local 457 Files.

37. MS, May 1917, 29; April 1918, 28; May 1918, 62; December 1918, 18; January 1921, 17; October 1928, 14; March 1932, 10.

38. Ibid., January 1906, 15; March 1906, 16.

39. Ibid., April 1906, 15; October 1908, 42; January 1909, 59–60.

40. *Proceedings*, 1915 Convention, HERE, 110; *Proceedings*, 1909 Convention, HERE, 111; MS, April 1911, 17; May 1912, 23; February 1913, 59.

41. Favorable editorials by Sullivan and Ernst on this topic can be found in ibid., May 1918, 48; August 1918, 26; and January 1919, 54. Examples of male ambivalence toward organizing females are in ibid., April 1911, 17; May 1912, 23; and February 1913, 59.

42. The editorial ends ruefully: "the organizing of waitresses has not been general enough to warrant pointing with pride to results, but where we have succeeded in enlisting their [male] support, men have been benefited and the women have obtained conditions and wage scales which were regarded as unobtainable a few years ago." Ibid., June 1913, 40; March 1918, 49–50.

43. Ibid., January 1915, 69; March 1918, 23–24; April 1918, 64.

44. Ibid., November 1919, 19–20; December 1919, 23. Brooklyn also established a waitress branch in the same year, ibid., December 1919, 23.

45. SFLC, 12 October 1923; MS, July 1923, 35–39; February 1924, 2–3; January 1925, 4, 69; March 1925, 3–4; December 1925, 46.

46. *Proceedings*, 1925 Convention, HERE, 40, 181.

47. CIE, May 1930, 11; July 1923, 30; St. Louis Waiters Local 20 to Hugo Ernst, 27 July 1923, MJM, HERE Files.

48. *CIE*, June 1930, 36.

49. Ibid., September 1932, 8; Gertrude Sweet interview, 41; typed notes by Marian Fitch based on an interview with Ida Peterson on 9 April 1954, MJM, HERE Files.

50. MS, July 1923, 32–35; October 1915, 26; April 1917, 30; June 1919, 22; *NYT*, 24 January 1921; MHBRR, April 1946, 4; typed reports, file—"Waitresses Local 48," Carton 40, SFLCR-UCB.

51. For the history of the WTUL, see Gladys Boone, *The Women's Trade Union Leagues in Great Britain and the United States of America* (New York, 1942); also see Dye, *As Equals and as Sisters*, 5–6, passim; MS, November 1909, 8.

52. Ibid., December 1921, 6–7; October 1908, 25; June 1929, 27; "Official Minutes of the St. Louis WTUL," November 1911 Meeting, Reel 9, C-9, WTUL Papers. On this same reel the (Chicago) *WTUL Bulletin* documents the fluctuating nature of WTUL support for waitresses. For remembrances of Maloney, see Mary Anderson as told to Winslow, *Women at Work*, 54–55; Nestor, *Woman's Labor Leader*, 157–58, 222–24, 233–35; and Mary Drier, *Margaret Dreier Robins: Her Life, Letters and Work* (New York, 1950), 172–73. For biographical backgrounds on Addams and Breckinidge, see *Notable American Women: A Biographical Dictionary*, ed. Edward T. James (Cambridge, 1971), vol. 11, 16–22, 233–36; on Starr, ibid., vol. 3, 351–53; on Henry, ibid., vol. 12, 183–84.

53. MS, July 1908, 22.

54. Ibid., January 1915, 61; May 1912, 61–62.

55. Reformers favoring welfare work essentially believed that workplace problems could be alleviated by enhancing the workers general well-being through recreational activities, improved workplace conditions, and other health and welfare benefits. Fundamental authority at the workplace, however, would be retained by the employer.

56. MS, February 1920, 30.

57. Ibid., May 1917, 35; October 1921, 18–19; June 1929, 40; *CIE*, June 1930, 37; Ploeger, "Trade Unionism Among the Women of San Francisco," 122.

58. 1905 Constitution, HERE, in MS, June 1905, 89; Josephson, *Union House, Union Bar*, 226–27; Sterling Spero and Abram Harris, *The Black Worker* (New York, 1931, rept., New York, 1968), 73–74; Ira De A. Reid, *The Negro Population of Denver, Colorado* (New York, 1929), 18.

59. MS, November 1918, 19–20; July 1919, 79. HERE also chartered black "domestic worker" unions in this period. See Elizabeth Haynes, "Negroes in Domestic Service in the U.S.," *Journal of Negro History* 8 (October 1923): 435.

60. MS, October 1907, 35; Barrows, "Trade Union Organization Among Women in Chicago," 156; Taber, "Women in Unions," 927; Waitresses' Local 48 Constitution and By-Laws, n.d., Bancroft Library, UCB.

61. *CIE*, April 1935, 6. The International did allow local unions to admit Asian workers (although their right to transfer from one local to another was denied); front cover, MS, April 1905; *CIE*, July 1925, 31; February 1937, 54.

62. Ibid., September 1932, 121–23; April 1935, 6. Some distinctions among Asian workers were made. The strictest exclusionary policies applied to the Chinese and Japanese; Filipino workers, probably because they were few in number, were admitted to more local unions. Ibid., July 1937, 54; *Proceedings*, HERE Convention, 1938.

63. MS, November 1905, 30; May 1917, 41; *Proceedings*, 1923 Convention, HERE,

131. Ernst also favored organizing Japanese culinary workers. See *SFLC*, 18 August 1916. The Butte response is illuminated in the following: Frisch, "Gilbralter of Unionism," 14–15; Rose Hum Lee, *The Growth and Decline of Chinese Communities in the Rocky Mountain Region* (Ph.D. diss., Department of Sociology, University of Chicago, 1947, rept., New York, 1978), 104–16, 187; Local 457 Minutebook, 21 June 1918, Local 457 Files; Local 457 Minutebook, 8 January 1926 and 5 March 1926, Box 14-1, WPUC-174, MHS.

64. See *MS*, November 1929, 39 for one example of the difficulty of organizing among New York City cafeteria workers and the employer's use of cultural and social divisions to keep unions out of the industry.

65. Ibid., May 1917, 23; July 1919, 79; four-page typed manuscript by Ethel M. Smith, "The Union Waitress Interprets," n.d., 2, Reel 2, C-2, WTUL Papers; William Whyte, *Human Relations in the Restaurant Industry* (New York, 1948), 192.

66. See Table 4 in the Appendix.

67. Frances Donovan, *The Woman Who Waits* (Boston, 1920), 134; Chumley, "Hotel, Restaurant, and Domestic Workers."

68. Although the labor movement had taken the lead in the nineteenth-century drive for shorter hours, by the early twentieth century their response was more ambivalent. The AFL's voluntaristic viewpoint discouraged state interference and touted free collective bargaining as the better method for improving working conditions, especially for adult men. They objected less to maximum hour legislation than minimum wage legislation, however, because wage rates fluctuated much more rapidly than did standards for hours, and the minimum wage might more easily become the maximum. The historic struggle for hours legislation in the nineteenth century also ameliorated the AFL voluntaristic sentiment in regard to hours; no such legacy existed in relation to wage legislation. For a discussion of the relation between the labor movement and protective legislation see Susan Lehrer, *Origins of Protective Labor Legislation for Women, 1905–1925* (Albany, 1987), 144–83.

69. For an overview of the campaigns to secure protective legislation, see Elizabeth Brandeis, "Organized Labor and Protective Labor Legislation," in *Labor and the New Deal,* ed. Milton Derber and Edwin Young (Madison, 1961); Barbara A. Babcock, et al., *Sex Discrimination and the Law: Causes and Remedies* (Boston, 1975); and Judith Baer, *The Chains of Protection: The Judicial Response to Women's Labor Legislation* (Westport, 1978). For the seminal role of middle-class organizations, especially on the East Coast, see U.S. Department of Labor, Women's Bureau, *History of Labor Legislation for Women in Three States,* Bulletin no. 66, by Clara Beyer (Washington, D.C., 1929) and Consumers' League of New York City, *Behind the Scenes in a Restaurant: A Study of 1017 Women Restaurant Employees* (New York, 1916).

70. Lord did, however, thank the women's clubs and societies, "all of whom gave their support," as well as organized labor throughout the state. Joseph Frederick Tripp argues that momentum for the law grew after women's suffrage passed in 1909. Tripp, "Progressive Labor Laws in Washington State, 1900–1925," Ph.D. diss., University of Washington, 1973, 81–90; *MS*, February 1907, 39; April 1911, 40; April 1909, 55; November 1910, 52; typed notes by Marian Fitch based on an interview with Ida Peterson, MJM, HERE Files; *Local 240 News,* February 1954, 3, Reel 342, LUR, HERE Files; Abbott, "The Waitresses of Seattle," 48–49; Gottfried, "Thank Lord for the 8-hour Work Day."

71. Franklin, "Elizabeth Maloney and the High Calling of the Waitress," 36–40; Andrews and Bliss, *A History of Women in Trade Unions*, 216; pamphlet entitled *The Eight Hour Fight in Illinois by the Girls Who Did the Work* (Chicago, 1909), 4; *WTUL Annual Report*, 1913, 19 and (Chicago) *WTUL Bulletin*, June 1916, in C-9, Reel 9, WTUL Papers; U.S. Commission on Industrial Relations, "Industrial Conditions and Relations in Chicago," 3252, 3256; Anderson, *Women at Work*, 76; Nestor, *Woman's Labor Leader*, 90–93; Drier, *Margaret Dreir Robins*, 61.

72. For the California struggle for hours legislation, see Dorothy Sue Cobble, "Sisters in the Craft: Waitresses and Their Unions in the Twentieth Century," Ph.D. diss., Stanford University, 1986, 167–68; Lucile Eaves, *A History of California Labor Legislation* (Berkeley, 1910), 316; Earl Clarkson Crockett, "The History of California Labor Legislation, 1910–1930," Ph.D. diss., University of California, 1932; Matthews, *Women in Trade Unions*, 90–91; SFLC, 20 August 1909, 3 February 1911. Ronnie Steinberg Ratner notes that the California State Federation was unusual in its support of maximum hour legislation. See Ratner, "The Paradox of Protection: Maximum Hours Legislation in the U.S.," *International Labour Review* 119 (March–April 1980): 185–98.

73. MS, September 1916, 63–64; February 1917, 39; April 1915, 69. The International union endorsed the legislative activities of their women members in promoting maximum hour statutes covering female workers; *Proceedings*, 1907 Convention, HERE, 145; *Proceedings*, 1909 Convention, HERE, 99, 163.

74. Consumers' League of New York, *Behind the Scenes in a Restaurant*, 7, 36; SFLC, 24 February 1911.

75. Consumers' League of New York, *Behind the Scenes in a Restaurant*, 36; MS, April 1909, 55; July 1911, 34; U.S. Department of Labor, Women's Bureau, *History of Labor Legislation for Women in Three States*, 123; SFLC, 3 February 1911, 3; Crockett, "The History of California Labor Legislation," 12–14.

76. Nancy Dye discusses similar divisions among working-class women in the WTUL in Dye, *As Equals and as Sisters*, 146–52. She notes that sex-specific minimum wage laws were harder to justify than similar hours legislation because "there was no physiological reason for women to earn a specified wage." By the 1920s, however, the working-class women within the league united in favor of protective legislation, emphasizing the social and economic conditions that necessitated protection.

77. Tripp, "Progressive Labor Laws in Washington State, 1900–1925," 88; MS, November 1912, 51; *Proceedings*, 1923 Convention, HERE, 196–97. The notably poor enforcement sections of most minimum wage laws confirm Lord's assessment. Minimum rates for women in Massachusetts, for example, were advisory only; enforcement relied not on legal penalties but on the publication of the names of offending employers. See Robert Ingalls, "New York and the Minimum Wage Movement, 1933–37," *Labor History* 15 (Spring 1974): 181.

78. *Coast Seamen's Journal*, 22 January 1913, 6; SFLC, December 20, 27, 1912, 2; U.S. Department of Labor, Women's Bureau, *History of Labor Legislation for Women in Three States*, 130–31n; Crockett, "The History of California Labor Legislation," 12–14.

79. California (State) Industrial Welfare Commission, *Fifth Biennial Report for 1922–24*, 12; California (State) Industrial Welfare Commission, *What California Has Done to Protect the Women Workers* (Sacramento, 1929); Ploeger, "Trade Unionism

Among the Women of San Francisco," 115–19; California (State) Industrial Welfare Commission, *Fourth Biennial Report for 1919–20* (1924), 130.

80. MS, August 1924, 18–19.

81. California (State) Industrial Welfare Commission, *Fifth Biennial Report for 1922–24*, 18; handwritten notes, Box 4, File, "Calif. DIW Misc.," SFLCR-UCB; Crockett, "The History of California Labor Legislation," 72–73, 90–94.

Chapter 4. The Flush of Victory, 1930–1955

1. Gertrude Sweet to Robert Hesketh, 13 April 1937, Reel 416, LUR, HERE Files.

2. Quote from Henry Pelling, *American Labor* (Chicago, 1960), 178. For labor union membership growth during the 1930s and World War II, see Marten Estey, *The Unions: Structure, Development, and Management* (New York, 1981), 11–12.

3. See Tables 5A–5C and Figure 1 for statistics on union membership among food service workers.

4. The Hotel Employees and Restaurant Employees did not record the membership totals for individual crafts; thus, the exact number of organized waitresses can only be estimated. Nonetheless, the membership figures for waitress locals provide some guidance (Tables 7 and 8).

5. Philip Taft, "Brief Review of Other Industries," in *How Collective Bargaining Works*, ed. Harry A. Millis (New York, 1942), 924; CIE, August 1933, 28.

6. Ibid., January 1935, 25; Matthew Josephson, *Union House, Union Bar: History of the Hotel and Restaurant Employees* (New York, 1956): 193–98. The participation of the left-wing unions, AFW and FWIU, is mentioned in Grace Hutchins, *Women Who Work* (New York, 1934). For an account of the involvement of the Women's Bureau, see the correspondence between Edward Flore and Mary Anderson, File "HERE," Box 865, RG-86, NA.

7. See the Restaurant Industry Basic Code, submitted by the National Restaurant Association, approved 10 August 1933; Hugo Ernst to John O'Connell, 20 December 1933, F-"Culinary Misc.," Box 8, SFLCR-UCB; Lafayette G. Harter, Jr., "Master Contracts and Group Bargaining in the San Francisco Restaurant Industry," master's thesis, Stanford University, 1948, 42.

8. A sizable group within the International resisted these sentiments and clung to a more exclusive craft unionism, but they were outvoted and outmaneuvered. *Proceedings*, HERE Convention, 1941, 206; *Proceedings*, HERE Convention, 1932, 130–31; *Proceedings*, HERE Convention, 1938, 10. The description of Flore is from Irving Bernstein, *Turbulent Years: A History of the American Worker 1933–41* (Boston, 1970), 116.

9. CIE, February 1936, 4.

10. CIE, December 1932, 19; July 1935, 30. Mary Anderson to John Fitzpatrick, 26 April 1934, File-HERE, Box 865, RG-86, NA; CIE, May 1932, 31.

11. Ibid., December 1933, 31; January 1932, 32.

12. Ibid., January 1932, 18; December 1933, 23.

13. For an overview of San Francisco's union traditions, see Michael Kazin, *Barons of Labor: The San Francisco Building Trades and Union Power in the Progressive Era* (Urbana, 1987), ch. 1.

14. CIE, September 1933, frontispiece; October 1933, 28; February 1934, 21; LJEB Minutes, 20 December 1933, Local 2 Files.

15. LJEB Minutes, 20 December 1933, Local 2 Files; typed ms., "Findings of Fact and Conclusions of Law," B. J. Della Valle v. Cooks, Waitresses and Miscellaneous Employees, 4, File "Cooks vs. Valle," Box 7, SFLC R, BL-UCB.

16. LJEB Minutes, 15 May 1934, Local 2 Files; File 170-9742, RG-280, NA.

17. LJEB Minutes, January 1933–December 1934, in particular, 13 July 1934, Local 2 Files; interview with William G. Storie, 24 January, 31 March, 7 April, 1959, 53; *SFLC*, 3 August 1934. For accounts of the General Strike, see Bernstein, *Turbulent Years*, 252–98 and Bruce Nelson, *Workers on the Waterfront: Seamen, Longshoremen, and Unionism in the 1930s* (Urbana, 1990), ch. 5.

18. David Selvin, *Sky Full of Storm* (San Francisco, 1975), 50; interview with Lou Goldblatt; *CIE*, October 1934, 33; September 1935, 15; Membership Records, HERE Files.

19. Only one hotel in San Francisco was unionized at this point, the Whitcomb Hotel. Ernst to James Vahey, 5 March 1935, File "HERE," Box 8, SFLC R, BL-UCB; *CIE*, October 1934, 33; March 1936, 33; *SFLC*, 8 January 1937; LJEB Minutes, 3 October 1933, 21 January 1936, 15 January 1937, 6 April 1937, 15 April 1937, 1 May 1937, Local 2 Files; Van Dusen Kennedy, *Arbitration in the San Francisco Hotel and Restaurant Industries* (Philadelphia, 1952), 13; telegram, Matthewson to Hugh Kerwin, 19 April 1937 and 28 May 1937, Case file 182-2408, RG-280, NA. Local 283, chartered in March of 1937, demanded recognition and working conditions comparable to the other organized crafts. George O. Bahrs, *The San Francisco Employers' Council* (Philadelphia, 1948); *CIE*, June 1937.

20. Josephson, *Union House, Union Bar*, 264–69; "Summary Report," Matthewson to Kerwin, 28 July 1937; "Final Report," 28 July 1937, by Matthewson; telegram, Matthewson to Kerwin, 17 July 1937. All in Case file 182-2408, RG-280, NA. LJEB Minutes, 15 April 1937, Local 2 Files; transcript, "Award of Fred Athearn, Arbitrator, to the San Francisco LJEB and San Francisco Hotel Operators," San Francisco, 1937, Local 2 Files; Harter, "Master Contracts and Group Bargaining in the San Francisco Restaurant Industry," 52–64; Kennedy, *Arbitration in the San Francisco Hotel and Restaurant Industry*, 13–14, 29–32, passim.; press release, 22 December 1937, and Ernst to Clarence Johnson, 4 January 1938, LJEB Correspondence Folder, Local 2 Files.

21. LJEB Minutes, 27 August 1937; *SFLC*, 10 December 1937. Arbitration Proceedings between the San Francisco LJEB and Owl Drug Co. before George Cheney, Union Opening Brief, 16 December 1943, SFLCR, BL-UCB, 2–3; S.F. clubs to LJEB, October 1937 and Ernst to Hesketh, 9 December 1937, LJEB Correspondence Folder, Local 2 Files.

22. Warren G. Desepte to C. C. Coulter, 10 February 1935, 26 February 1935, 30 August 1936, 11 September 1936, Reel 1, RCIA Records; Ernst to O'Connell, 13 October 1934, File "HERE," Box 8, SFLC R, BL-UCB.

23. In part because of the actions of local AFL unionists like Ernst, San Francisco department stores remained within the AFL, unlike those in New York and other major cities.

24. Strike Board Minutes, 9 November 1940, Local 2 Files. For further details see Dorothy Sue Cobble, "Sisters in the Craft: Waitresses and Their Unions in the Twentieth Century," Ph.D. diss., Stanford University, 1986, 199–201.

25. Local 48 EB Minutes, 19 July 1938, and Local 48 MM Minutes, 20 April 1938, Local 2 Files; *CIE*, February 1940, 26–27.

26. *B/G Organizer Bulletin*, 11 October 1941; Union Brief and Exhibits, Arbitration Proceedings between the San Francisco LJEB and the Hotel Employers' Association before Edgar Rowe, 18 August 1942, 2, Local 2 Files.

27. LJEB Minutes, 15 October 1936 and 17 June 1941, Local 2 Files.

28. Petition, 13 September 1937, San Francisco Employers to Ernst; Ernst to O'Connell, 21 July 1939, LJEB Correspondence Folder and LJEB Minutes, 16 October 1934 and 6 November 1934, Local 2 Files.

29. Ernst to SFLC Delegates, 15 March 1933 and 25 July 1933, and T. K. Bronson to O'Connell, 9 October 1939, File-"HERE," Box 8, SFLCR, BL-UCB; Duchess Sandwich Co. President to C. T. McDonough, 14 December 1940, LJEB Correspondence Folder, Local 2 Files.

30. LJEB Minutes, 4 June 1940 and 16 July 1940, Local 2 Files.

31. *Department Store Strike Bulletin*, 3 October 1941, and "Score Card," San Francisco Strikes and Lockouts Collection, Box 1, BL-UCB.

32. *Department Store Strike Bulletin*, 3 November 1941; 18 November 1941; interview with Carmen Lucia.

33. Stafford to SFLC, 16 December 1938, File "Local 1100," Box 15, SFLCR, BL-UCB; *CIE*, January 1939, 43; interview with Helen Jaye.

34. In imitation of union practices, employer members who refused to abide by group decisions were fined, harassed, and shunned. See Josephson, *Union House, Union Bar*, 295–96.

35. Interview with William G. Storie, 154; Kennedy, *Arbitration in the San Francisco Hotel and Restaurant Industry*, 11; Bahrs, *The San Francisco Employers' Council*, iii; binder entitled "House Card Agreements 1938–1946," Local 2 Files; interview with Paul St. Sure, 487–89.

36. Rubenstein to Ernst, 18 November 1937, 20 November 1937, and leaflet signed by David Rubenstein, n.d. [ca. November 1937], LJEB Correspondence Folder, Local 2 Files.

37. LJEB Minutes, 2 August 1938, 6 June 1939, 5 March 1941, and Rubenstein to LJEB, 26 February 1938, LJEB Correspondence Folder, Local 2 Files.

38. Bahrs, *The San Francisco Employers' Council*, 10; LJEB Minutes, 6 May 1941, 20 May 1941, 10 June 1941, Local 2 Files. Interview with William G. Storie, 154–56.

39. Ibid.; Andrew Gallagher to John Steelman, 3 July 1941 and n.d. [ca. July 1941], Case File 196-6257A, RG-280, NA; Harter, "Master Contracts and Group Bargaining in the San Francisco Restaurant Industry," 67, and Edward Eaves, "A History of the Cooks and Waiters' Unions of San Francisco," Ph.D. diss., University of California, Berkeley, 1930, 98.

40. Interview with William G. Storie; LJEB Minutes, 25 August 1941. This first master restaurant contract subsequently became the universally accepted scale for organized restaurants whether or not they belonged to the association. Copies of both the old and new house card agreements can be found in the binder entitled "House Card Agreements 1938–1946," Local 2 Files.

41. For a detailed account of the 1941 San Francisco hotel strike consult Josephson, *Union House, Union Bar*, 293–96, and Harter, "Master Contracts and Group Bargain-

ing in the San Francisco Restaurant Industry," 73–101. See also Case File F-196-2066, RG-280, NA. In other cities, hotel employers also turned to association bargaining. Gertrude Sweet wrote the International of this new employer technique much feared by the unions. Sweet to Hesketh, Reel 416, LUR, HERE Files.

42. For further comments on the remarkable stability of San Francisco culinary labor relations and the unprecedented use of arbitration machinery, see Kennedy, *Arbitration in the San Francisco Hotel and Restaurant Industry*, 1–19, 100–109; and Harter, "Master Contracts and Group Bargaining in the San Francisco Restaurant Industry," 128–33.

43. Only four large unions for waitresses were chartered after 1930, even though the female membership of the International increased dramatically (Tables 6 and 7).

44. For information on Detroit's culinary unions before the 1930s consult *Detroit Labor News*, 8 August 1957; *Detroit Times*, 27 July 1927; MHBRR, February 1937, 1, and January 1941, 6; campaign broadside for Louis Koenig and unidentified newspaper clipping, scrapbooks, Local 705 Files.

45. The Koenig quote is from *Detroit Free Press*, 22 January 1956. See also interview with Charles Paulsen; MHBRR, February 1937, 6; Jay Rubin and M. J. Obermeier, *Growth of a Union: The Life and Times of Edward Flore* (New York, 1943), 259–61; Josephson, *Union House, Union Bar*, 144, 169–70.

46. Jean Pitrone, *Myra: The Life and Times of Myra Wolfgang, Trade Union Leader* (Wyandotte, 1980), 7, 23, 53; Myra Wolfgang Collection, WRL-WSU; interview with Charles Paulsen; Josephson, *Union House, Union Bar*, 271. In 1941 Mira changed the spelling of her first name to Myra and later took her husband's last name, Wolfgang. MHBRR, January 1936, 1.

47. MHBRR, March 1937, 1, 8; Steve Babson and Dave Elsila, *Union Town: A Labor History Guide to Detroit* (Detroit, 1980), 8, 10, 15, and Steve Babson, *Working Detroit: The Making of a Union Town* (New York, 1984), 77–79; Carlos A. Schwantes, "'We've Got 'em on the Run, Brothers': The 1937 Non-Automotive Sit Down Strikes in Detroit" *Michigan History* 55 (Fall 1972): 179–99; interview with Charles Paulsen; Pitrone, *Myra*, 23–35. The *Detroit Free Press*, 24 July 1966, credits Wolfgang with blowing the Woolworth strike whistle.

48. Wolfgang to Josephson as quoted in Josephson, *Union House, Union Bar*, 271.

49. Scrapbooks and clipping files, Local 705 Files; "Fiftieth Anniversary Ball Program, Local 705, Hotel and Restaurant Employees, AFL-CIO," 22 February 1965, Local 705 Files.

50. MHBRR, June 1943; Pitrone, *Myra*, 51–52; Schwantes, "'We've Got 'em on the Run, Brothers'," 189; interview with Charles Paulsen; Babson and Elsila, *Union Town*, 15; *Detroit Times*, 28 February 1937; *Detroit Free Press*, 28 and 29, February 1937.

51. MHBRR, July 1937, 7, and August 1937, 8; Pitrone, *Myra*, 40; Rubin and Obermeier, *Growth of a Union*, 263; interview with Charles Paulsen. See MHBRR, 1941–42 for examples of Teamster cooperation. The 1946–47 restaurant strike was more problematic. See *Detroit Times*, 22, 26, 27 January 1947. See Myra Wolfgang Collection, WRL, WSU for later IBT-HERE relations and the friendship between Hoffa and Wolfgang.

52. MHBRR, July 1937, 7, and August 1937, 8; Pitrone, *Myra*, 40; Rubin and Obermeier, *Growth of a Union*, 263; interview with Charles Paulsen.

53. *CIE*, July 1938, 27; Rubin and Obermeier, *Growth of a Union*, 251–53.

54. The history of the two left unions can best be traced through their newspapers: *Free Voice*, published by the Amalgamated Food Workers from 1921–35 and the *Food Worker*, the official organ of the Food and Packing House Workers Industrial League, affiliated with the Trade Union Unity League. The slight stirrings of the IWW among New York City food service workers in the 1920s and early 1930s can be glimpsed in Foodstuff Workers Industrial Union Daybook, Box 69, IWW Collection, WRL-WSU. The *NYT*, 14 December 1988, published a short article on the Greenwich Village radical L. S. Chumley and his IWW-oriented bar.

55. Hutchins, *Women Who Work*, 94; *Food Worker*, December 1931, 6.

56. *CIE*, September 1935, 40.

57. See Rubin and Obermeier, *Growth of a Union*, 225–42 passim; Josephson, *Union House, Union Bar*, 216–33; and Harold Seidman, *Labor Czars* (New York, 1935), 199–213 for fuller details on the rise and fall of gangsterism in New York and Chicago and in the International union.

58. New York WTUL Organization Committee Minutes, 9 November 1933, 27 January 1935; New York WTUL Organization Report, October 1933, by Beatrice Bilyieri; New York WTUL Organization Report, April 1934, by Eleanor Mishnun; New York WTUL Executive Board Minutes, 14 June 1934. All on Reel 3, C-4, WTUL Papers.

59. New York WTUL, *Annual Report, 1933–4* (New York, 1934), 9; "Convention Report, 1935–36," 23, Reel 8, C-9, WTUL Papers.

60. New York WTUL, "Organizing Report, May 1934" and Testimony of Eleanor Mishnun before the Minimum Wage Board, 5 August 1935, Reel 3, C-4, WTUL Papers; New York WTUL Executive Board Minutes, April 1937, Reel 4, WTUL Papers.

61. See Leo Wolman, *Ebb and Flow in Trade Unionism* (New York, 1936), 144–45 for membership figures. David J. Saposs, *Communism and American Unions* (New York, 1959), 59; *Free Voice*, June 1934, July 1934; *Food Worker*, April 1933, May 1935, January 1936.

62. See the Subject/Correspondence Files and the Report of the Investigation Committee at a Special Business Meeting of Local 16, 6 April 1937, Local 16 Minutes, Local 6 Files.

63. Seidman, *Labor Czars*, 205.

64. New York WTUL Organization Committee Minutes, 17 July 1937, and New York WTUL Executive Board Minutes, 27 September 1937, Reel 4, C-4, WTUL Papers; Garriga to Flore, 3 July 1937 and Garriga to Flore, 9 July 1937, Subject/Correspondence Files, Local 6 Files; New York WTUL *Monthly Bulletin*, October 1937, Reel 8, C-9, WTUL Papers; *CIE*, November 1937.

65. Ironically, union leaders as well as some hotel executives, advocated a separate industrial union, but many hotel service workers opposed the idea. Garriga to Flore, 4 January 1938, 21 June 1937, and n.d. [ca. December 1937], Subject/Correspondence Files, Local 6 Files; Flore to William Albertson, 13 October 1937, in Local 16's Minute Book, Local 6 Files.

66. *CIE*, June 1938, 46; December 1937, 51; Garriga to Flore, 1 September 1937, Subject/Correspondence Files, Local 6 Files.

67. For biographical information on Lane, see *CIE*, May 1945, 20; October 1951, 25; December 1953, 16–17; *The Office Worker* (New York City), February 1935, in "Strikes and Department Store Organizing," Collection 2, Box 1, RWA-NYU; *NYT*, 23 November 1953; interview with Charlotte Stern; Josephson, *Union House, Union Bar*, 280–83.

68. The sessions included: "special problems of the service industries and comparison with those of factory industries; organizational methods and suggestions for service workers; labor legislation for women; minimum wage legislation and its impact; presenting cases before government boards; the organizing campaign and the law; and the WTUL-its purposes." Mimeo sheet, "Program for Apprentice Organizers on Special Problems of Women in Industry," n.d. [ca. 1938], Reel 3, WTUL Papers; New York WTUL "Annual Election Report," 27 April 1942, Reel 4, WTUL Papers. See also *Life and Labor Bulletin*, March 1940, 3 for an explanation of the league's officer training.

69. Whether for ideological or financial reasons, Local 6 lapsed into nonpayment of Blanchard's salary. See letters exchanged between the league and Local 6, 3 April 1939 and 12 August 1939 on Reel 13, C-4, WTUL Papers. By 1942, Helen Blanchard was vice-president of the league and two of the eight Executive Board members of the New York chapter were from culinary locals.

70. Typed transcript entitled "Summary of Discussion at Women's Bureau Conference, October 30–31, 1946," 180-1, File "Conf. 10/46," Box 207, RG-86, NA.

71. *HCV*, 9 October 1943, 1; New York Hotel and Motel Trades Council, *The Story of the First Contract* (New York, 1974), 31–33. For a complete account, see Josephson, *Union House, Union Bar*, 276–83, and Morris Horowitz, *The New York Hotel Industry* (Cambridge, 1960), 21–65.

72. Newspaper clipping, no identification, n.d., Case File 199-334, RG-280, NA.

73. New York WTUL Organization Committee Minutes, August 1937, Reel 4, C-4, WTUL Papers; interview with Loretta Szeliga; Robert Bruere to Steelman, 17 January 1938, Case File 199-334, RG-280, NA; Garriga to Flore, 11 August 1937, Subject/ Correspondence Files, Local 6 Files; *Cafeteria Call*, July 1939, 5; July 1940, 7; October–November 1943, 1; *CIE*, May 1942, 5; leaflet, To Horn and Hardart Employees, n.d. [ca. 1950], Reel 409, LUR, HERE Files. Horn and Hardart finally signed an agreement in 1966. See "Footnote to Labor History: After 30 Years the Automats Are Organized," *Industrial Bulletin* (New York State) 45 (May 1966): 10–11.

74. Attempts to organize Schrafft's proved fruitless until the early 1950s, when a change in management and rumors of lay-offs opened the shop to the union message. The local consciously slanted its campaign to predominantly conservative older Irish Catholic waitresses: union radio shows opened and closed with Gaelic poetry and Irish melodies, union spokesmen assured the waitresses that the Association of Catholic Trade Unionists supported the campaign, and that "the elected officers . . . are pledged . . . to keep our union free of any Communist influence." Officials also promised job protection for older waitresses. See Grace Hutchins, *Women Who Work* (New York, 1934), 94; and, for the early drives, minutes of Schrafft's Organizing Committee, 25 March 1946 and 30 June 1947, Local 6 Files; typed reports, Schrafft's Folder, Local 6 Files; handwritten sheet, "Schrafft's Group Meeting," 3 February 1945, Local 6 Files; *HCV*, 10 August 1940; 1 November 1947, 1; and 14 February 1948, 8, Local 6 Files. For the later campaigns, see Newsletter, "Schrafft's Organizer," December 1952,

vol. 1, no. 9; transcript, WABC Radio Show no. 3, 22 February 1953, 5; and transcript, WABC Radio Show no. 4, 8 March 1953, 4, all in Schrafft's Folder, Local 6 Files; *CIE,* April 1951; Louise Howe, *Pink Collar Workers* (New York, 1977), 118–21.

75. Local 42 to New York LJEB, 24 April 1940, Subject/Correspondence Files, Local 6 Files; *HCV,* 23 March 1941, 8; *New York Post,* 10 April 1941; typed report by Helen Blanchard, 7 April 1941, "Organizing" Folder, Local 6 Files.

76. New York City's pattern of greater union penetration in the male-dominated sector of the culinary industry, for example, large downtown hotels and first-class restaurants, was typical. Agreements providing for closed-shop, wage increases, vacations with pay, and other advances were secured with Hotel Employer Associations representing a sizable proportion of the downtown hotels in Chicago, St. Louis, Pittsburg, Kansas City, Milwaukee, and Washington, D.C., for example; yet in none of these cities was there comparable union strength in lower-priced hotels and restaurants. *CIE,* June 1941, 23; August 1949, 13–16; Taft, "Brief Review of Other Industries," 924–95; Josephson, *Union House, Union Bar,* 262–63, 272–76.

77. Francois Somlyo, "A Short History of the Hotel and Restaurant Workers of Washington, D.C.," Washington, 1984, 1, unpublished typewritten paper in possession of the author; correspondence between Local 781 and Robert Hesketh, Reel 690, LUR, HERE Files; *CIE,* September 1936, 35; January 1937, 53; April 1937, 44; *Washington Evening Star,* 9 March 1937.

78. (Washington) *WTUL News,* March 1937 and May 1937, Reel 9, C-9, WTUL Papers.

79. Federal Mediator Report by Edmund McGrady, Case File 182-2257, RG-280, NA; *CIE,* February 1938, 18.

80. According to James McNamara, the hotel local's financial secretary, many of Washington's culinary locals withheld financial aid and organizing assistance from the hotel drives because a large proportion of the hotel workers were black and female. McNamara to Hesketh, 12 September 1937, Reel 229, LUR, HERE Files; *CIE,* September 1938, 53.

81. See Case File 199-3221, RG-280, NA, for a detailed account of the strike.

82. *CIE,* May 1939, 43; (Washington) *WTUL Banner,* July 1939, Reel 9, Collection C-9, WTUL Papers; *Washington Post,* 19 March 1939. The Federal mediator reported that "wages weren't even an issue in the strike." Howard T. Calvin's Final Report, 23 March 1939, Case File 199-3221, RG-280, NA.

83. Federal Mediator Report by Edmund McGrady, Case File 182-2257, RG-280, NA; *CIE,* February 1938, 18.

84. Carter to Flore, 1 April 1939, Reel 229, LUR, HERE Files.

85. Membership Records, HERE Files; *CIE,* December 1941, 16; June 1943, 27; August 1949, 19; Transcript, *Arbitration Proceedings Between San Francisco LJEB and the Hotel Employers Association of San Francisco,* July 1953, 732, San Francisco LJEB Minutes, 16 December 1947, and Board of Business Agent Minutes, 17 November 1947, all in Local 2 Files. California (State) Department of Industrial Relations, Division of Statistics and Research, *Union Labor in California* (1941–59) details the statewide figures for female HERE membership.

86. Membership Records, HERE Files; *Proceedings,* HERE Convention, 1941, 131; *HCV,* 15 January 1949, 2–3; Wolfgang Report to Labor Advisory Committee Meeting,

May 1950, 4, File-"Econ Resp." Box 1695, RG-86, NA; Local 705, Hotel and Restaurant Employees, "Fiftieth Anniversary Ball Program," 22 February 1965, Local 705 Files; Pitrone, *Myra*, 52–56; *Detroit Times*, 26 and 27 January 1947; 3 August 1951, 12 and 13 November 1952.

87. *CIE*, January 1945, 33, 40; March 1946, 14; interview with Blanche Copenhaver; interview with Valentine Webster.

88. *CIE*, January 1939, 42; October 1938.

89. Membership Records, HERE File; *CIE*, June 1937, 48; February 1932, 19; April 1941, 27; Stoneman to Flore, 1 September 1944, *Southland Waitress*, November 1944, and newspaper clipping on Stoneman, n.d., Reel 628, LUR, HERE Files; reports by Ethel Erickson, 1950, Box 698, RG-86; *NYT*, 9 December 1942, 35.

90. *CIE*, November 1944, 27; February 1945, 34; February 1940, 39; October 1944, 17; March 1940, 46. See January 1943, 34 for description of walkout of Chattanooga waitresses.

91. *MHBRR*, November 1936, 1; December 1936, 1; March 1937, 1; April 1937, 1; September 1937, 1; October 1937, 8; April 1940, 7; August 1941, 1; March 1948, 7; April 1950, 4; Local 705, Hotel and Restaurant Employees, "Fiftieth Anniversary Ball Program," 22 February 1965, Local 705 Files; *Wage Earner* (Detroit), December 1951, 4–5.

92. Hugo Ernst to George Holbert, 19 January 1946 and Correspondence between Ernst and Walter White, R-10, DUR, HERE Files. For the Southern campaigns, see *CIE*, 1945–60.

93. In contrast to the progress among Chinese and other minority groups, cooperation between Japanese and white culinary workers halted abruptly during World War II, as the union closed its doors to Japanese. When approached in 1943 by a government representative from the War Relocation Authority who requested HERE assistance in placing interned Japanese Americans in hotel and restaurant jobs, Flore refused, stating that he would not willingly agree to the "invasion of our industry by evacuating Japanese and would protest their placement in any hotel or restaurant under contractual relations with our International union." Flore's policy engendered the feeblest of protests from local unions. *CIE*, June 1943, 2–3; Edward Flore to Joseph Fox, 20 August 1943, Reel 302, DUR, HERE Files.

94. For more details, see Josephson, *Union House, Union Bar*, 227; Herbert R. Northrup, *Organized Labor and the Negro* (New York, 1944), 98; *CIE*, November 1939, 38; September 1938, 47; October 1938, 11; Gertrude Sweet to Edward Flore, 25 March 1939, Reel 416, LUR, HERE Files; interview with Beulah Compton.

95. *CIE*, November 1946, 33.

96. 23 August 1940, 30 August 1940, 4 December 1942, 8 January 1943, WPU Minutebook, 1940–43, Box 14-2, WPUC-174, MHS; 7 January 1944, 11 February 1944, WPU Minutebook, 1943–46, Local 457 Files.

97. John P. Henderson, *Labor Market Institutions and Wages in the Lodging Industry* (East Lansing, 1965), 129–59.

98. The almost unrelenting hostility of working-class men was emphasized in the early influential work of Heidi Hartman, see "Capitalism, Patriarchy, and Job Segregation by Sex," in *Women and the Workplace: The Implications of Occupational Segregation*, ed. Martha Blaxall and Barbara Reagan (Chicago, 1976), 137–69. The "immutable"

character of that opposition was first questioned by Ruth Milkman in "Organizing the Sexual Division of Labor," 105–7.

99. The reluctance of skilled workers to support the organizing of unskilled workers within their own trade while simultaneously offering aid to those outside their trade has been documented in other situations as well, even in those where gender was not an issue. See Kim Voss, "Labor Organization and Class Alliance: Industries, Communities, and the Knights of Labor," *Theory and Society* 17 (1988): 329–64.

Chapter 5. Uplifting the Sisters in the Craft

1. *CIE*, June 1900, 7.

2. Jane Morgan, "Love Letter from One Waitress to Local 705," *MHBRR*, no date, in clipping file, Local 705 Files.

3. For discussions of the practices and philosophy of male craft unionists, see, Nick Salvatore, *Eugene V. Debs: Citizen and Socialist* (Urbana, 1982), 27–30; David Bensman, *The Practice of Solidarity: American Hat Finishers in the Nineteenth Century* (Urbana, 1985), ch. 4; Seymour Martin Lipset et al., *Union Democracy: The Internal Politics of the Typographical Union* (Glencoe, 1956), 25–32, passim; David Montgomery, *The Fall of the House of Labor* (New York, 1987), 191–99; Michael Kazin, *Barons of Labor: The San Francisco Building Trades and Union Power in the Progressive Era* (Urbana, 1987), chs. 4 and 6; and Selig Perlman, *A Theory of the Labor Movement* (New York, 1928, repr. Philadelphia, 1979), 254–79.

4. Bylaws, Waitresses' Local 249, 1961, Reel 350, DUR, HERE Files.

5. Preamble to Bylaws, Waitresses' Local 112, 1915–44, Reel 20, DUR, HERE Files; Bylaws, Waitresses' Local 347, 1960, Reel 441, LUR, HERE Files. For Butte bylaws see Bylaws, Waitresses' Local 457, 1946 and 1964, Reel 970, LUR, HERE Files and Bylaws, Local 457, 1954, Box 13-8, WPUC-174, MHS. Reels 342–43, 415, 525, 970–71, LUR, HERE Files contain the most complete run of waitress bylaws and union agreements and provide further examples of many of the achievements and practices detailed in chs. 5 and 6.

6. For the reliance on "motherhood" by middle-class black and white women activists, see Eileen Boris, "The Power of Motherhood: Black and White Activist Women Redefine the 'Political,'" *Yale Journal of Law and Feminism* 2 (Fall 1989): 25–49.

7. It should be kept in mind that the achievements of waitress locals in collective bargaining and in the legislative arena upgraded the working conditions of unorganized workers as well as organized. For a discussion of this "spillover" phenomenon, see *MS*, June 1920, 48; February 1922, 55; Louise Ploeger, "Trade Unionism Among the Women in San Francisco, 1920," master's thesis, University of California, Berkeley, 1920, 44–48; Lillian Matthews, *Women in Trade Unions in San Francisco*, Publications in Economics, vol. 3, no. 1 (Berkeley, 1913), 89; Frances Donovan, *The Woman Who Waits* (Boston, 1920), 192.

8. *MS*, August 1902, 14; John Andrews and W. D. P. Bliss, *A History of Women in Trade Unions*, vol. 10 of *Report on the Condition of Woman and Child Wage-Earners in the US*, Senate Document 645, 61st Cong., 2d sess. (Washington, D.C., 1911), 228–29; Esther Taber, "Women in Unions: Through Trade Union Organization Waitresses Have Secured Marked Improvements in Conditions," *AF* 12 (December 1905): 927–28; Robert Hesketh, "Hotel and Restaurant Employees," *AF* 38 (October 1931):

1271; "Story of a Waitress," *SFLC*, 6 September 1907, 12–13. For Butte conditions, see Minutebooks, Local 457, 10 June 1903, 28 June 1903, 10 July 1903, WPUC-174, MHS.

9. The statistics on union contract coverage were culled from HERE convention proceedings from 1905 to 1929. At every convention, reports were tabulated from each local indicating average weekly hours and wages. See also *MS*, January 1915, 69; March 1903, 16. Butte women generally enjoyed the best conditions nationwide; see Scale of Wages and Working Rules, Local 457, Box 70 (Loose Contracts), RG-257, NA and Minutebook, 4 September 1924, WPUC-174, MHS; 10 November 1916 and 2 November 1917, Local 457 Minutebook, Local 457 Files. For an overview of legislative coverage, see Ronnie Steinberg, *Wages and Hours: Labor and Reform in Twentieth Century America* (New Brunswick, 1982), 94, 220.

10. The fourteen states were Arkansas, California, Colorado, Kentucky, Minnesota, Nevada, New York, North and South Dakota, Ohio, Oklahoma, Oregon, Washington, and Wisconsin. The District of Columbia, Puerto Rico, and Alaska also had legislation covering hotel and restaurant workers by 1942. Women's Bureau, Department of Labor, *State Minimum Wage Laws and Orders, 1 July 1942–1 March 1953*, Bulletin no. 249 (Washington, D.C., 1953), 6–7; Pennsylvania (State) Bureau of Hours and Minimum Wages, Department of Labor and Industry, *Report to the Wage Board for Restaurants on Employment of Women and Minors in Restaurants and Other Eating Places* (Philadelphia, 1938), 102–3; Labor Research Association, *Labor Fact Book No. 5* (New York, 1941), 66; *Woman Worker*, January 1940, 7; Mabel Smythe, "Tipping Occupations as a Problem in the Administration of Protective Labor Legislation," Ph.D. diss., University of Wisconsin, 1942, 60–65; Women's Bureau Release, 11 January 1950, Survey Material for Bulletin 227, Box 991, RG-86, NA.

11. Typed note by Matthew Josephson on Tampa, Florida, Local 104, in unmarked folders at HERE headquarters, MJM, HERE Files; *CIE*, June 1956, 16; Philip Taft, "Brief Review of Other Industries," in *How Collective Bargaining Works*, ed. Harry Millis (New York, 1942), 925. For the superior conditions achieved by the stronger locals, see Dorothy Sue Cobble, "Sisters in the Craft: Waitresses and Their Unions in the Twentieth Century," Ph.D. diss., Stanford University, 1986, 270–72.

12. HERE Officers' Report, 1947, 15; *CIE*, September 1953, 8.

13. *MS*, March 1903, 16 and January 1915, 69; Wage Scale and Work Rules, 1931, Local 249, Box 70, RG-270, NA; Minutebook, Local 457, 29 October 1943, Local 457 Files; Transcript of the Arbitration Proceedings between San Francisco LJEB and the San Francisco Hotel Employers Association, July 1953, 538, Local 2 Files; HCV, 22 June 1946, 31; Wage Scale and Working Agreement, San Francisco LJEB, September 1951, Local 2 Files.

14. For early examples, see CC, May 1938, 1 and San Francisco LJEB Minutes, 1945, Local 2 Files. For the analysis of recent contracts, see California (State) Department of Industrial Relations, *Union Contract Provisions: Eating and Drinking Places* (San Francisco, January 1961), 1–6.

15. For example, see Scale of Wages and Working Rules, 1922, Local 457, Box 70, RG-257, NA.

16. *DRE*, February 1955, 5. For Wolfgang's activities and philosophy in regard to protective legislation, see MW, WRL-WSU, in particular "Statement of Policy Regarding Hours Legislation for Women Workers," and "Statement Re States Protective

Legislation for Women," Box 1, File 8 and letter, Wolfgang to Representative James Del Rio, 31 May 1968, Box 1, File 3.

17. Andrews and Bliss, *A History of Women in Trade Unions*, 228–29; Taber, "Women in Unions," 927; U.S. Commission on Industrial Relations, "Industrial Conditions and Relations in Chicago," *Final Report and Testimony* 4 (Washington, 1916), 3254–55; Minutebook, Local 457, 26 March 1920, 2 April 1920, 14 May 1920, Local 457 Files; MS, June 1921, 58–59; June 1920, 48; Contract and Agreement between Helena Hotel and Restaurant Keepers Association and Hotel and Restaurant Employees, Local 612, 1 October 1920, Box 29, File "Hotel-C-M," RG-257, NA; "Wages and Hours of Labor," *MLR* 9 (September 1919): 196; Connecticut (State), *Report of the Bureau of Labor on the Conditions of Wage-Earning Women and Girls* (Hartford, 1916), 99–100.

18. LJEB Minutes, 1955, Local 2 Files; Reel 342, LUR, HERE Files. A 1961 survey of food service wage rates revealed the greater the degree of unionization, the higher the wage rate. See U.S. Department of Labor, Bureau of Labor Statistics, *Industry Wage Survey: Eating and Drinking Places, June 1961,* Bulleton no. 1329 (Washington, D.C., June 1962), 2–25; U.S. Department of Labor, Bureau of Labor Statistics, "Summary Release: Earnings of Hotel Employees, Summer 1955" (Washington, D.C., 1955).

19. *CIE*, January 1950, 18.

20. New York State minimums in 1953 were still only 52 cents an hour for service employees and 75 cents for nonservice. *HCV*, 24 August 1939; New York (State) Department of Labor, Division of Industrial Relations, *Wages and Hours in the Restaurant Industry, 1938–1946* (Albany, October 1946); New York State Department of Labor, Division of Research and Statistics, *Wages and Hours in the Restaurant Industry*, Bulletin 30 (Albany, May 1950), 5; *HCV*, 15 June 1940, 8.

21. Agreement between San Francisco Hotel Owners Association and Locals 283 and 14, 4 January 1947–1 January 1949, Local 2 Files; see also Reels 342–43, 415, 441, 525, 970–71, LUR, HERE Files.

22. See, for example, California (State) Industrial Welfare Commission, *Fourth Biennial Report for 1919–1920 and 1921–1922* (Sacramento, 1924), 131; MS, June 1920, 37; U.S. Department of Labor, Wage and Hour and Public Contracts Division, *Hotels and Motels: Data Pertinent to an Evaluation of the Need for and Feasibility of Applying Statutory Minimum Wage and Maximum Hours Standards* (Washington, D.C., February 1962), 23–30.

23. Andrews and Bliss, *A History of Women in Trade Unions*, 228–29; MS, December 1924, 54–55; CC, June 1938, 5; Working Rules and Regulations, Local 30 and Local 48, 1 January 1940, Local 2 Files; Wage Scales and Working Conditions, San Francisco LJEB and Golden Gate Restaurant Association, 1 September 1950–1 September 1955, Local 2 Files; San Francisco LJEB Minutes, 1945, Local 2 Files; Union Brief and Exhibits in the Arbitration Proceedings between San Francisco LJEB and the San Francisco Hotel Employers Association, 18 August 1942, 78–79, Local 2 Files; *HCV*, 19 September 1944, 2. See also Wage Scale and Work Rules, Local 249, St. Louis, Box 70, RG-257, National Archives.

24. MS, December 1929, 40. For other early examples of regulation see Taber, "Women in Unions," 928; Minutebooks, Local 457, 2 May 1919, 25 April 1919, Local 457 Files; Wage Scale and Work Rules, Local 249, St. Louis, Box 70, loose contracts, RG-257, NA.

25. California Industrial Welfare Commission, *Fourth Biennial Report for 1919–20 and 1921–22*, 13; transcript of IWC Hearing 6 July 1929, 13, in File "Calif. IWC Misc.," Box 4, SFLCR, BL-UCB; California State Federation of Labor, *Report on Labor Legislation* (San Francisco, 1931), 2–8. See typed transcript of the 1946 Conference of Women Trade Unionists, 206, Box 8897, RG-86, NA, for the New York situation.

26. Local 48 MM, 2 April 1941, Local 2 Files; U.S. Department of Labor, Bureau of Labor Statistics, *Industry Wage Survey: Eating and Drinking Places, June 1961*, Bulletin no. 1329, 5–6.

27. Wage Scale and Working Rules, Sacramento LJEB, 16 February 1942, Wage Scales and Working Conditions, San Francisco LJEB and San Francisco Golden Gate Restaurant Association, 1 September 1950–1 September 1955, transcript of the arbitration proceedings between the San Francisco LJEB and the San Francisco Hotel Operators before Fred Athearn, 1937, 37, San Francisco LJEB Correspondence, 21 December 1939, San Francisco LJEB Minutes, 15 August 1939, all Local 2 Files; *HCV*, 15 September 1945, 3.

28. Taber, "Women in Unions," 928; *MS*, August 1902, 14; September 1902, 26–27; Andrews and Bliss, *A History of Women in Trade Unions*, 228–29.

29. For examples, see earlier discussion in ch. 2, 42.

30. Clipping stuck in minutebook and 19 August 1927 Minutes, Minutebook, 1922–30, Box 14-1, WPUC-174, MHS; unidentified clipping concerning tipping, Local 705 Newsclipping file; *NYT*, 28 December 1915; *CIE*, January 1945, 27.

31. Unlike HERE, the IWW consistently made the abolition of tipping central to their organizing. See *NYT*, 14 January 1913; *Solidarity*, 25 January 1913; L. S. Chumley, "Hotel, Restaurant, and Domestic Workers," Box 163 and "Wake Up! Hotel, Restaurant and Cafeteria Workers," Box 177, IWW Collection, WRL-WSU. The only example of implementation I found, however, was in San Francisco. There, IWW Local 460 printed up "tip chips" in 1924; these were to be left with the customer's bill to discourage tipping. See Foodstuff Workers Industrial Union, Local 460, Box 69, 1924–25, WRL-WSU.

32. Carroll Morris Powers, "Methods of Labor Adjustment in the San Francisco Bay Region," master's thesis in economics, University of California at Berkeley, 1921, 720–23; Sidney Cohn et al., "Memo to establish that tips of New York hotel employees are part of wages for Social Security purposes," n.d. [ca. 1964], Reel 37, GOR, HERE Files; *CIE*, January 1939, 24; Union Brief for the Arbitration Proceedings between San Francisco LJEB and the San Francisco Hotel Employers Association, 18 August 1942, 47, Local 2 Files; *Detroit News*, 25 February 1943. See *CIE*, February 1946, 23 for an interesting article suggesting an alternative commission system to the existing "beggar system" of tipping.

33. *Voice of Local 1*, January 1950, 1.

34. In addition to New York, early regulatory laws in Wisconsin, Oregon, and Washington stated that tips could not be deducted from the minimum. S. M. Franklin, "Elizabeth Maloney and the High Calling of the Waitress," *Life and Labor* 3 (February 1913): 36–40; *MS*, March 1921, 52; Smythe, "Tipping Occupations as a Problem in the Administration of Protective Labor Legislation," 24–33, passim; *CIE*, June 1951, 12–13.

35. *MS*, April 1920, 55–6; transcript of Ninth Minimum Wage Conference, No-

vember 1939, 1–5, Box 904, RG-86, NA; *Woman Worker*, November 1939, 8; *CIE*, July 1943, 28.

36. See Bylaws, Waitresses' Local 227, 1952 and 1962, Reel 39, DUR, HERE Files. See also Bylaws, Waitresses' Local 112, 1915–44, Reel 20, DUR, HERE Files.

37. The regulation of training and job performance will be discussed in chapter 6.

38. For example, Waitresses' Local 803 in Dallas succeeded in having the week of August 10, 1941 set aside to honor the work of waitresses in the community, but the proclamation signed by the mayor asked the community to "unite in being considerate to the little ladies who serve the citizenry its bacon, eggs, and steaks." *CIE*, September 1941, 44.

39. They note: "Far from being an objective economic fact, skill is often an ideological category imposed on certain types of work by virtue of the sex and the power of the workers who perform it." Anne Phillips and Barbara Taylor, "Sex and Skill: Notes Towards a Feminist Economics," *Feminist Review* 6 (1980): 79.

40. Franklin, "Elizabeth Maloney and the High Calling of the Waitress," 36–40; also see the account of the evolution of the craft idea among food service workers in MS, April 1904, 5–7 and the division of mixed locals along craft lines decreed by the Fourth Annual HERE Convention in "Brief History of Our Organization," *The Federation News*, 25 January 1930.

41. MS, December 1924, 54–55; January 1929, 10; April 1927, 16; Local 48 Wage Rates and Work Rules, n.d. [pre-1935], Local 2 Files. See also Local 457 Minutebook, Box 14-2, 19 June 1942, WPUC-174, MHS, and Local 457 Minutebook, 29 October 1943, Local 457 Files; and *MHBRR*, December 1938, 1.

42. The best record of this incorporation can be found in the Women's Protective Union records. See Local 457 Minutebook, 1943–46, 13 September 1944, letter from Lena Mattausch to George Martin, Local 457 Files and 1943, 1946, and 1950 Contract, Box 13-8, WPUC-174, MHS in particular.

43. See, for example, Wage Scale and Working Conditions, San Francisco LJEB, 7 July 1942, 1 October 1945, 1 September 1946, 1 September 1950, 1 September 1951, 1 September 1956, Local 2 Files.

44. Bylaws of Cooks, Waiters, Waitresses and Miscellaneous Help, Local 180, San Jose, California, 1 October 1937, Wage Rates and Working Conditions, Local 347 and 549, 15 April 1942, both Local 2 Files; Local 1 Work Rules, n.d., Reel 134, LUR, HERE Files; *Voice of Local 1*, December 1948, 3.

45. Interview with Valentine Webster; interview with Clela Sullivan.

46. Employer Brief and Exhibits, Arbitration between San Francisco LJEB and San Francisco Hotel Operators before Fred Ahearn, 1937, 250–56, and Wage Scale and Work Rules, Local 30 and Local 48, 1941, Local 2 Files; undated agreement, Local 1, Box 70, loose contracts, RG 257, NA; Waiters and Waitresses' Local 1 Agreement, New York City, 1934–35, Box 29, File-"Hotels, N-P," RG 257, NA.

47. See Hannah Creighton, "Tied by Double Apron Strings: Female Work Culture and Organization in a Restaurant," *The Insurgent Sociologist* 11 (Fall 1982): 59–64; interviews with Valentine Webster and Clela Sullivan.

48. For evidence of the persistence of racial and ethnic segregation within the industry, see Thomas Bailey, "A Case Study of Immigrants in the Restaurant Industry," *Industrial Relations* 24 (Spring 1985): 205–21.

49. Salvatore characterizes the craft brotherhoods on the railroads in this fashion. Salvatore, *Eugene Debs*, 30.

50. Bylaws, Local 639, 1941, Reel 627, LUR, HERE Files. For other examples, see Bylaws, San Francisco Waitresses' Local 48, n.d. [pre-1938], File, "Local 48-Misc," Box 22, SFLCR, BL-UCB; Bylaws, Rochester Waitresses' Local 227, 1952, Reel 39, DUR, HERE Files; Bylaws, Local 457, n.d., Reel 441, LUR, HERE Files; Bylaws, Local 249, 1961, Reel 350, DUR, HERE Files; Bylaws, Local 112, n.d., Reel 20, DUR, HERE Files.

51. Waitress locals also took responsibility for upgrading the skills of waitresses. Apprentice and training programs will be discussed in chapter 6.

52. Maud Younger, "The Diary of an Amateur Waitress," *McClure's Magazine*, March 1907 and April 1907, 543–52 and 665–77; typed reports, File-"Local 48, 1943," Box 46, SFLCR, BL-UCB; John Murphy, *An Appraisal and Abstract of Available Literature on Waiters and Waitresses* (New York City, 1937), 4; Local 48 EBM, 7 January 1941 and Local 48 MM, 27 October 1948, 1 November 1938, 24 June 1952, both in Local 2 Files.

53. San Francisco's local, for example, under pressure from the International and the LJEB organizer for San Francisco, C. T. McDonough, voted in 1938 to "rescind our former action relative to [not] accepting colored girls," to "organize the colored girls," and to delete the word *white* from the bylaws. See Local 48 MM, 3 March 1937, 25 November 1936, 14 July 1937, 8 December 1937, 27 April 1938; LJEB Minutes, 2 March 1937; Local 48 EBM, 10 May 1938, 21 June 1938, all in Local 2 Files.

54. Local 48 MM, 27 April 1938; Local 48 EBM, 10 May 1938, 21 June 1938, Local 2 Files.

55. Local 48 EBM, 9 January 1945, 11 August 1943, 17 August 1943; LJEB Minutes, 17 August 1943; Business Agent Board Minutes, 24 August 1942, Local 2 Files.

56. Ibid.; Arthur M. Kezer, "The Problem of Upgrading in a Multi-Racial Service Industry," master's thesis, University of California, Berkeley, 1956, 39.

57. Kezer, "The Problem of Upgrading," 38.

58. Edward Flore to Frances Metz, Secretary Local 347, 21 November 1949, Reel 441, LUR, HERE Files; Field Reports, n.d. [1950], Box 698, RG-86, NA; interview with Beulah Compton; *Local 240 News*, September 1953, R-342, HERE Files; oral history interview with Nellie Stone Johnson, 7–8; Telegram, 23 June 1952, Reel 36, HERE Files; Edward C. Koziara and Karen S. Koziara, *The Negro in the Hotel Industry* (Philadelphia, 1968). For other examples, letter, Local 507 to International, 23 August 1955, R-543, DUL, HERE.

59. Kazin, *Barons of Labor*, ch. 6; Alexander Saxton, *Indispensable Enemy: Labor and the Anti-Chinese Movement in California* (Berkeley, 1971).

60. See HCV, 1936–55 for the racial policies of New York's Local 6; "Fiftieth Anniversary Ball Program, 22 February 1965," Local 705 Files; Francis Kornegay to Robert Alpert, 7 May 1976, MW Collection, Box 1, file 5, WRL-WSU; and *MHBRR*, 1936–55 for the Detroit local.

61. Quote is from Buffalo waitresses' Local 347, 1960, Reel 441; LUR, HERE Files; the "respectable/rough" dichotomy is from Ellen Ross, "'Not the Sort that Would Sit on the Doorstep': Respectability in Pre-World War I London Neighborhoods," *International Labor and Working Class History* 27 (Spring 1985): 39–59.

62. The desire for conformity to middle-class definitions of respectability may have been more characteristic of union activists and waitress labor officials than rank-and-file waitresses. For a similar analysis positing a more assimilated male leadership in the early nineteenth century, see Paul Faler, "Cultural Aspects of the Industrial Revolution: Lynn, Massachusetts Shoemakers and Industrial Morality, 1826–1860," *Labor History* 15 (1974): 367–94.

63. Quote is from Ross, " 'Not the Sort that Would Sit on the Doorstep,' " 45. For other treatments that posit a distinct working-class definition of respectability see, for example, Kathy Peiss, *Cheap Amusements: Working Women and Leisure in Turn-of-the-Century New York* (Philadelphia, 1986); Jacquelyn Dowd Hall, " 'Disorderly Women': Gender and Labor Militancy in the Appalachian South," *Journal of American History* 73 (September 1986): 354–82; and Joanne Meyerowitz, *Women Adrift: Independent Wage-Earners in Chicago, 1880–1930* (Chicago, 1988).

64. Franklin, "Elizabeth Maloney and the High Calling of the Waitress," 36–40. In San Francisco, the Executive Board rebuked waitresses for using language in the headquarters before new members that was "unbecoming a member of Local 48." One sister apologized and said she "felt rather badly that she had spoken the way she did." Local 48 EB Minutes, 24 January 1948, Local 2 Files.

65. MS, 15 March 1927, 64; Franklin, "Elizabeth Maloney and the High Calling of the Waitress," 36–40.

66. Interview with Kathryn Wetzel Newton Dewing; Hall, " 'Disorderly Women,' " 354–82; see also interviews with Lucy Kendall and Loretta Szeliga.

67. Local 48 MM, 24 February 1937; 3 March 1937; 5 January 1938; Local 48 EBM, 17 May 1938; 18 May 1938; 8 October 1940; Local 48 MM, 24 May 1944, Local 2 Files.

68. Edward Eaves, "A History of the Cooks and Waiters Unions of San Francisco," master's thesis, University of California, Berkeley, 1930, 313; Matthews, *Women in Trade Unions in San Francisco,* 81.

69. The question of when and where waitresses could serve and mix liquor was a complicated one. Many locals did not admit cocktail waitresses, or women who served only liquor, until the 1940s. Female bartenders, or women who *mixed* drinks, were forbidden until the 1970s (ch. 7).

70. CIE, April 1937, 36.

71. Interview with Florence Farr.

72. Lois Banner, *American Beauty* (New York, 1983), 3, 13, 15–16.

73. See MHBRR, December 1939, 6–7 for the first beauty contest in Detroit. Subsequent contests and photographs of the winners appear in the clipping and photograph files of Local 705. For Los Angeles and New York, see *Southland Waitress,* October 1959 and October 1950, Reel 628, LUR, HERE Files; and CC, July 1940, 5; September 1940, 5.

74. The quote is from MS, December 1921, 7. For an overview of enforcement of Title VII of the Civil Rights Act, see Karen Maschke, *Litigation, Courts, and Women Workers* (New York, 1989), ch. 3.

75. MS, April 1927, 2–4.

76. HCV, 6 July 1940, 2; 15 June 1940, 2; 29 June 1940, 2.

77. LAT, 13 October 1967. In a similar case in San Francisco, an arbitrator sustained the discharge of a long-service waitress, despite the "quite vague" employer

rationale because "management was attempting to dispose of a delicate personnel problem"—the issue of an aging waitress. Decision 102, 6 February 1941, quoted in Van Dusen Kennedy, *Arbitration in the San Francisco Hotel and Restaurant Industries* (Philadelphia, 1952), 79. For examples of other unresolved complaints over age discrimination see letter, 14 February 1934, Berns to Hesketh, R-39, and letter, 5 May 1960, R-535, HERE Files.

78. Unidentified newspaper clipping, Box 1, Folder 1, MW, WRL-WSU; *DRE*, February 1964, 5, March 1964, 1, 8; Bernard Rosenberg and Saul Weinman, "Young Women Who Work: An Interview with Myra Wolfgang," *Dissent* 86 (Winter 1972): 34–36; Jean Pitrone, *Myra: The Life and Times of Myra Wolfgang, Trade Union Leader* (Wyandotte, 1980), 122–28.

79. See the citations in note 78, as well as San Francisco Playboy Club Agreement, 19 January 1966, Appendix A, Local 283 Materials, Box 12, Local 2 Files; In the Matter of the Arbitration between Playboy Club International, Inc. Detroit Division and Local 705, Federal Mediation and Conciliation Service File no. 72A/9255, October 1972, Local 705 Files.

80. *NYT*, 16 February 1966; 20 August 1970, 41; 13 February 1971; 15 November 1973; 17 November 1974, 45. *DRE*, September 1970, 1; October 1970, 1; March 1971, 1; December 1973, 8.

81. "Bunny Jo Wins Back Tail—It's Solid Gold," Local 705 news release, 20 October 1972, Local 705 Files.

82. See Susan Porter Benson, *Counter Cultures: Saleswomen, Managers, and Customers in American Department Stores, 1890–1940* (Urbana, 1986), 235–38, for a discussion of the attitudes of retail women.

83. Interview with Clela Sullivan.

84. Andrews and Bliss, *A History of Women in Trade Unions*, 228–29; MS, December 1924, 54–55; Local 457 Minutebook, 20 August 1926, Box 14-1, WPUC-174, MHS; Article 9, Rochester Waitresses' Bylaws, 1952, Reel 39, DUR, HERE Files.

85. For example, see *Voice of Local 1*, December 1948, 3.

86. Local 48 MM, 7 February 1939 and 8 March 1939, Local 2 Files.

87. *HCV*, 4 December 1948, 2; see also *Southland Waitress*, October 1959, LUR, HERE Files and *HCV*, 12 October 1946, 1. The Buffalo waitresses forbade the wearing of "large earrings, fancy pins, and large rings while on duty" until 1964, but the intent appears to have been reducing safety hazards rather than diminishing waitresses' decorative flourishes. Bylaws, Buffalo Local 347, 1958 and 1964, Reel 441, LUR, HERE Files.

88. *HCV*, 2 November 1946, 2; Jack Parmley, business agent, Houston Local 808, *CIE*, June 1939, 32.

89. *HCV*, 5 April 1947, 5.

90. Sara Rapport, " 'I'm Cheryl—Fly Me to Court': Flight Attendants v. the Airlines, 1960–1976," unpublished paper, Graduate Women's History Seminar, Rutgers University, September 1986, 12; David Montgomery in *Workers' Control in America* notes that male craft workers resisted policies interfering with their male identities (13–14); what would be an affront to female dignity and identity has been less explored.

91. Franklin, "Elizabeth Maloney and the High Calling of the Waitress," 37; interview with Valentine Webster; Mary Murphy, "Woman's Work in a Man's World," *The*

Speculator: A Journal of Butte and Southwest Montana History 1 (Winter 1984): 23;
Local 48 EB Minutes, 1 March 1938, and Board of Business Agent Minutes, 4 November 1940, Local 2 Files; *HCV*, 25 November 1944, 3; 9 December 1944, 3. See also
LJEB Correspondence File, September 11, 1940, Local 2 Files and letter dated June 10,
1948, Reel 690, DUR, HERE Files.

92. MS, March 1924, 24.

93. A majority of the cocktail waitresses interviewed by Patricia Stoll in 1973, for
example, said they preferred their own clothes to cocktail waitress uniforms because
they "felt more like an individual" and because there were "fewer advances toward
them." Stoll, "Occupational Alienation: The Case of the Cocktail Waitress," master's
thesis, Sociology Department, University of Missouri, Kansas City, 1973, 34.

94. Interview with Clela Sullivan.

95. For the Detroit case see Steve Babson, *Working Detroit: The Making of a Union
Town* (New York, 1984), 205; Local 705 Grievance Files, 1978–79; notes taken by
Bob Dixon on April 11 and April 30, 1979 hearing asking for injunctive relief, Local
705 Files.

96. For a discussion of management rights, see Edna Elkouri and Frank Elkouri,
How Arbitration Works, 4th ed. (Washington, 1985), 457–62, 553–57, passim. For
the current legal situation regarding Title VII and sexually provocative uniforms, see
Anthony Marshall, "It's Risky to Require Risque Outfits on Your Waitresses," *Hotel
and Motel Management*, June 30, 1986, 12; G. Withiam, "Too Hot to Handle," *Cornell
Hotel Restaurant Administration Quarterly* (May 1986): 6; Eric Matusewitch, "Tailor
Your Dress Codes," *Personnel Journal*, February 1989, 86–91; for the Sizzleboard example, see statement of Patricia Welch, 10 February 1972 in Liza Bingham, Meredith
Golden, and Holly Newman, "Harvard Square Waitresses Strike," *Second Wave* 1
(1972): 4.

97. Susan Englander, "The San Francisco Wage Earners' Suffrage League: Class
Conflict and Class Coalition in the California Woman Suffrage Movement, 1907–
1912," master's thesis, History Department, San Francisco State University, 1989,
94–99.

98. Benefit unionism is often associated with such craft unionists as Samuel
Gompers, who saw it as a way of binding members to the organization. But a recent
study makes it clear that "radical" industrial unionists also practiced benefit unionism. See Alan Derickson, *Workers' Health, Workers' Democracy: The Western Miners'
Struggle, 1891–1925* (Ithaca, 1989).

99. MS, June 1905, 49, for excerpts from the 1905 Constitution, HERE; *SFLC*,
1 November 1906, 4; 24 January 1908, 4; Andrews and Bliss, *A History of Women
in Trade Unions*, 203; Franklin, "Elizabeth Maloney and the High Calling of the
Waitress," 38; Esther Taber, "Women in Unions," 928; Abbott, "The Waitresses of
Seattle," 48.

100. Bylaws, Waitresses' Local 249, n.d., 8–9, Reel 350, DUR, HERE Files and
discussion of Local 457's fund, Reel 970, LUR, HERE Files.

101. *Proceedings*, HERE convention, 1953, 52–58; Matthews, *Women in Trade
Unions in San Francisco*, 79, 91; Local 48 MM, 8 July 1936 and 25 February 1948, Local
2 Files; Teresa Staggenburg to Ed Horne, 22 May 1939, Reel 39, DUR, HERE Files;
Taber, "Women in Unions," 928.

102. Interview with Beulah Compton; see also the thoroughly documented activities of Local 457's sick committee in the Minutebooks of the local located at the MHS, BSBA, and the offices of Local 457.

103. Waitresses' Local 305, for example, did not set up death benefits for its members until 1947. Waitresses' Local 48, unlike their brother union, Local 30, never had a pension fund for older members, although many waitresses worked long years in the trade, stopping work in their sixties or even later.

104. Male-dominated trade union organizations from the Cigar Makers to the Piano and Organ Workers also denied sick benefits to pregnant women. Teresa Wolfson, *The Woman Worker and the Trade Unions* (New York, 1926), 215–19.

105. Bylaws, Waitresses' Local 48, 1938; Bylaws, Waitresses' Local 48, January 1943; Revised Wage Scales and Working Conditions, San Francisco LJEB, 1 September 1946; Wage Scale and Working Conditions, San Francisco LJEB, 1 September 1951—all in Local 2 Files; Bylaws Local 457, 1954, Box 13-8, WPUC-174, MHS; Bylaws, Waitresses' Local 112, 1944, Reel 20, DUR, HERE Files; Bylaws, Waitresses' Local 781, Reel 690, LUR, HERE Files; Bylaws, Waitresses' Local 507, 1955 and 1962, Reel 543, LUR, HERE; Bylaws, Waitresses' Local 347, 1958, and 1964, Reel 441, LUR, HERE. See also Bylaws, Waitresses' Local 48, 1943, File "Local 48, 1943," Box 46, SFLCR, BL-UCB.

106. Jeri Powell, "Goals and Achievements of San Francisco Waitresses' Local 48," talk presented to the Twelfth Annual Southwest Labor Studies Conference, 14 March 1986, San Francisco State University, San Francisco, tape recording in possession of the author; Flo Douglas, "The Impact of Merger on San Francisco Waitresses' Local 48," presented to the Twelfth Annual Southwest Labor Studies Conference; LJEB Minutes, 5 September 1950 and 15 July 1952, and Elizabeth Kelley Correspondence Folder, Local 2 Files. For the activities of New York waitresses, see CC, February 1952, 6. The California law was changed before the 1978 amendments to Title VII mandated that pregnancy be treated no worse than other disabilities. Thus, the shift in California cannot be credited simply to a changing legal climate.

107. CIE, December 1951, 14; HCV, 24 March 1945, 5. For further details on the development of employer-paid benefits in the culinary industry, see Cobble, "Sisters in the Craft," 313–14.

108. File-"Committee on the Care of Children of Working Mothers, 1942," File-"Local 110, 1943," File-"Committee on the Care of Children of Working Mothers, 1943," File-"LJEB, 1951," all in Box 65; File-"LJEB, 1953," Box 74, File-"Waitresses, 1953–4," Box 75, all in SFLCR, BL-UCB; Local 48 MM, 10 August 1949, 26 July 1950, 9 July 1952, 12 May 1954, and LJEB Minutes, 5 September 1950, 16 January 1951, all in Local 2 Files; CIE, July 1953, 30. For New York's involvement, see HCV, 14 February 1948, 8 and 25 June 1949, 4.

109. Local 48 MM, 9 February 1949, 22 March 1936, Local 2 Files; Local 240 Records, 1951–543 and 240 News, February 1954, Reel 342, LUR, HERE Files; interview with Beulah Compton; HCV, 7 September 1940, 8 and 23 March 1946, 2.

110. Andrews and Bliss, *A History of Women in Trade Unions*, 187; Younger, "The Diary of an Amateur Waitress," 671.

111. MS, January 1912, 18; Local 48 MM and EBM, 1936–58, Local 2 Files; Local

457 Minutebooks, 29 September 1904, WPUC-174, MHS for an early dance in Butte. See also MS, March 1904, 64, 69 and MS, January 1916, 71 for other examples.

112. Local 48 EBM, 19 August 1941; Local 48 MM, 1 August 1940.

113. MS, October 1905, 32; Women's Trade Union League, *Tri-annual Report*, 1926–1929 (Chicago, 1929), 5–6, Collection 9, Reel 9, WTUL Papers; MS, May 1912, 23. For San Francisco waitresses see *SFLC*, 13 August 1909.

114. MS, September 1913, 33–34; July 1911, 37. Seattle waitresses had a second home bequeathed to them in the 1920s which they planned to use as a retirement center; see MS, January 1929, 20. For an example of an East Coast local influenced by Seattle's work, see MS, October 1918, 61.

Chapter 6. Waitress Unionism

1. Interview with Valentine Webster.

2. A. J. Muste, "Factional Fights in Trade Unions," in *American Labor Dynamics*, ed. J. B. S. Hardman (New York, 1928), 332, as quoted in James Wallihan, *Union Government and Organization in the United States* (Washington, 1985), 212.

3. Other mobile and dispersed occupations have relied on these mechanisms with varying degrees of success. For example, for domestic workers and the use of union-run employment offices, see letter Jane Street to Fellow Worker, 1917 reproduced in " 'We Have Got Results': A Document on the Organization of Domestics in the Progressive Era," ed. Daniel T. Hobby, *Labor History* 17 (Winter 1976): 103–8, and Amy Dudley, "Domestic Workers' Organizations in California," *Life and Labor*, September 1919, 217–18; for carpenters, see Morris Horowitz, *The Structure and Government of the Carpenters' Union* (New York, 1962), 1–9, and Michael Kazin, *Barons of Labor: The San Francisco Building Trades and Union Power in the Progressive Era* (Urbana, 1987), 82–99. More stable groups such as railroad workers also used a modified hiring hall in which the union "plug board" or dispatch system acted as a work-sharing device and as a way of giving workers more control over when and how much they worked. Interview with W. E. Cobble, Business and Legislative Representative, Brotherhood of Locomotive Engineers, 7 August 1990, Atlanta.

4. Minutebook, 1903–5, 28 January 1904, 18 February 1904, 14 April 1904, and clipping stuck in book, Box 13-13, MHS. See also "Address to Hotel and Restaurant Workers," in *Industrial Union Bulletin*, Box 156, IWW, WRL-WSU.

5. *LAT*, 13 October 1967.

6. Closed-shop provisions were more typical of the restaurant than the hotel industry. Hotel locals often accepted preferential hiring and union shop provisions in lieu of closed shop because the employers had more bargaining leverage and a closed shop was not deemed as critical for the successful operation of unionism among a work force concentrated in large establishments with longer-term, more permanent hiring practices.

7. MS, February 1902, 21; September 1916, 7; May 1917, 29; October 1928, 14; March 1932, 10; survey forms in Box 3, folder 25, JR, WRL-WSU.

8. For examples, see contracts in Box 29 and Box 70, RG-257, NA and the agreements governing union halls maintained by the California State Department of Employment in Box 3, folders 25 and 27, JR, WRL-WSU.

9. Quote from L. S. Chumley, "Hotel, Restaurant, and Domestic Workers," Box 163, IWW, WRL-WSU; other examples in Minutebook, 1903–5, Box 13, folder 13, WPUC-174, MHS.

10. For examples, see Box 3, folder 27, and Box 4, folders 3, 4, 5, JR, WRL-WSU. For the evolution of one local's hiring hall, see *MHBRR*, September 1936, 1, March 1940, 1, October 1940, 1, May 1949, 3.

11. I first encountered this distinction in Ronald Schatz, *The Electrical Workers: A History of Labor at General Electric and Westinghouse, 1920–1960* (Urbana, 1983).

12. Quote is from the U.S. Commission on Industrial Relations, "Industrial Conditions and Relations in Chicago," 4 *Final Report and Testimony* (Washington, 1916), 3254. For other examples of work-sharing, see Agreement, adopted June 1921, Local 48; Bylaws, Buffalo, Local 347, 1958, Reel 441, LUR, HERE Files. Also see the excellent discussion of this phenomenon in Schatz, *Electrical Workers*, 108, 158–60.

13. Agreement, June 1921, Waitresses' Local 48; Local 48 EBM, 15 February 1937; 4 May 1938; San Francisco LJEB Minutes, 13 November 1944; Joint Wage Scale, Local 30 and Local 48, n.d. [ca. 1938], all in Local 2 Files. See also Minutebook, 1 June 1917, Local 457 Files; Scale of Wages and Working Rules, 1922, Local 457, Box 70, RG-257, NA; Minutebook, Local 457, 10 July 1903, WPUC-174, MHS; Minutebook, 9 August 1946, 11 April 1947, and Minutebook, 23 November 1973, Local 457 Files.

14. Wage Scale and Working Rules, Local 305, 1932, Box 29, and Scale of Wages and Working Rules, Local 457, 1922, Box 70, RG-257, NA. See also Contract, Local 457 and Silver Bow Employers Association, 1943, 1946, and 1950, Box 13, folder 8, WPUC-174, MHS.

15. Lillian Matthews, *Women in Trade Unions in San Francisco*, Publications in Economics (Berkeley, 1913), 79–80; Agreement, Local 48, June 1921, HERE Files; Local 48 EBM, 11 August 1943, 23 May 1944, Local 2 Files. See also Local 550 Agreement, Bakersfield, California, Box 122, RG-257, NA.

16. The benefit funds discussed in chapter 5 are another example of how the rights and protections of culinary workers transcended any one job-site. Like employment security, welfare funds were portable protections as long as waitresses maintained their membership in good standing. The funds bound members emotionally as well as financially to the union; the tie with the employer was deemphasized.

17. The criteria used for membership selection is discussed more fully in chapter 5. The quote is from typed mss., Reel 30, Section on Apprenticeship, GOR, HERE Files.

18. MS, November 1925, 49; *Serving America*, January 1951, 3; May–June 1951, 5; January 1954, 1; May–June 1966, 8; *CIE*, February 1947, 19, March 1941, 48; interview with Beulah Compton. For other examples: letter, Secretary Local 427 to Secretary Local 457, 9 November 1959, Minutebook, Local 457, Box 17, folder 2, WPUC-174, MHS; Contract, Local 457 and Silver Bow Employers Association, 1975–78, WPU Collection, BSBA; "Fiftieth Anniversary Ball Program," 22 February 1965, Local 705 Archives.

19. Culinary Alliance, Local 258, Marion, Illinois, July 1925, Box 29, File-"Hotel: C-M," RG-257, NA; Agreement, Local 529, Bellingham Washington, 1938, Box 122, RG-257, NA.

20. Contract, Local 457 and Silver Bow Employers Association, 1943 and 1946,

Box 13, folder 8, WPUC-174, MHS; Wage Scale, 1929, Local 659, Box 70, loose contracts, RG-257, NA.

21. Maud Younger, "Taking Orders: A Day as a Waitress in a San Francisco Restaurant," *Sunset Magazine*, October 1908, 521. See, for example, "Rules and Regulations," St. Louis Waitresses' Local 249, Reel 350, LUR, HERE Files; San Francisco LJEB to San Francisco Restaurant Association, 25 October 1933, LJEB Correspondence Folder, Local 2 Files; Wage Scale and Working Rules between Portland LJEB and Portland Restaurant Association, 1 October 1950, 21–22, MJM, HERE Files.

22. Typed reports, File-"Local 48, 1943," Box 46, SFLCR, BL-UCB; Local 48 EBM, 7 January 1941; Local 48 MM, 27 October 1948, 1 November 1938, 24 June 1952, Local 2 Files.

23. "Sample Agreement, Local 484," n.d. [ca. 1909] reproduced in John P. Andrews and W. D. P. Bliss, *A History of Women in Trade Unions*, vol. 10 of *Report on Conditions of Woman and Child Wage-Earners in the United States* (Washington, 1911), 228–29; Bylaws and Union Agreements, Chicago Waitresses' Local 484, 1909–1962, Reel 525, LUR, HERE Files; Local 48 Wage Scale, 1907, in *San Francisco Call*, 8 September 1907, 27; Local 48 Wage Scale, 1913, Local 48, Local 2 Files; *Proceedings*, 1921, HERE, 179; Hotel, Motel, Restaurant Employees, and Bartenders' Local 20, August 1977, Tacoma, Washington, Box 3, Folder 22, IWW, WRL-WSU.

24. "Sample Agreement, Local 484," n.d. [ca. 1909] reproduced in Andrews and Bliss, *A History of Women in Trade Unions*, 228–29. Bylaws and Union Agreements, Chicago Waitresses' Local 484, 1909–1962, Reel 525, LUR, HERE Files; Bylaws, Rochester Waitresses' Local 227, 1952, Reel 39, Working Rules, Portland Waitresses' Local 305, n.d., Reel 415, Bylaws, Waitresses' Local 507, 1955, and 1962, Reel 543, all in DUR, HERE Files. See also Wage Scale, 1928, Hotel and Restaurant Employees Alliance, Local 781, Box 30, RG-257, NA.

25. Agreement, Local 670, 1925–6, Box 29, File: "Hotel, C-M," RG-257, "Sample Agreement, Local 484," n.d. [ca. 1909] reproduced in Andrews and Bliss, *A History of Women in Trade Unions*, 228–29; Local 48 EBM, 13 February 1951, Local 2 Files.

26. HCV, 23 December 1944, 3.

27. Local 48 EBM, 9 March 1944, 25 June 1945, 27 February 1945, 7 March 1944, 13 July 1943, Local 2 Files; Minutebook, 9 May 1919, Local 457 Files. See also Minutebook, 19 October 1928, Box 14, folder 1, WPUC-174, MHS.

28. Local 457 Minutebook, 12 March 1943 and 2 October 1942, 14-2, WPUC-174, MHS.

29. Local 48 EBM, 9 March 1944, 25 June 1945, 27 February 1945, 7 March 1944, 13 July 1943, Local 2 Files; see 18 August 1942 and 7 March 1944 for additional examples of disputes between waitresses and members of other culinary locals.

30. HCV, 23 December 1944, 3; MS, December 1924, 54–55, January 1923, 50; Andrews and Bliss, *A History of Women in Trade Unions*, 228–29.

31. Minutebook, Report of the Executive Board, 10 February 1950, Box 15-2, WPUC-174, MHS. Local 48 EBM, 7 March 1944, 25 May 1942, 29 May 1947, 13 February 1951, Local 2 Files. For a case involving the distribution of tips, see Local 48 BM, 9 November 1943, Local 2 Files.

32. Local 107, Cleveland, Reel 19, DUR, HERE Files; HCV, 29 April 1950, 4;

MS, December 1924, 54–55; Local 16 Minutes, 14 September 1937, 4 November 1937, Local 6 Files. See also the Washington LJEB Agreement, 1939 requiring all employers to rotate stations, Case File 199-3221, RG-280, NA.

33. Local 48 EBM, 12 May 1942, Local 2 Files. See R-30, GOR, HERE Files for a description of rules pertaining to passive membership.

34. "Rules and Regulations," n.d. Waitresses' Local 249, Reel 350, LUR, HERE Files. See also San Francisco LJEB to San Francisco Restaurant Association, 25 October 1933, LJEB Correspondence Folder, Local 2 Files; Wage Scale and Working Rules between Portland LJEB and Portland Restaurant Association, 1 October 1950, 21–22, MJM, HERE Files; Local 457 Minutebook, 6 July 1905, WPUC-174, MHS.

35. Minutebook, Local 457, 24 October 1941, Box 14, File 2, WPUC-174, MHS, NA; Local 48 EBM, 19 April 1938, 7 June 1938, 22 March 1938; Local 48 MM, 3 February 1937, 25 February 1948; Bylaws, Waitresses' Local 48, 1953, Local 2 Files. See also Bylaws, St. Louis Waitresses' Local 249, n.d., Reel 350, LUR, HERE Files.

36. Employer Brief and Exhibits, 30 September 1937, prepared for the arbitration proceedings between the San Francisco LJEB and the San Francisco Hotel Operators before Fred Athearn, 25–26, Local 2 Files; Bylaws, Waitresses' Local 507, 1955 and 1962, Reel 543, LUR, HERE Files. See Local 48 EBM, 11 October 1938, Local 2 Files for an example of the removal of an entire crew; see also Local 457 Minutebook, 7 February 1946, WPUC-174, MHS.

37. Interview with Beulah Compton, 19; see, for example, Local 48 MM, 2 February 1937, Local 2 Files; "Rules and Regulations," Waitresses' Local 249, Reel 350, LUR, HERE Files; Bylaws, Waitresses' Local 484, 1951, Reel 525, HERE Files; Wage Scale and Working Conditions, San Francisco LJEB, 7 July 1942; Dairy Lunch and Cafeteria Wage Scale and Working Conditions, San Francisco LJEB, 1 October 1942; Wage Scale and Working Conditions, San Francisco LJEB, 1 October 1945; Revised Wage Scale and Working Conditions, San Francisco LJEB, 1 September 1946, all in Local 2 Files.

38. Local 48 MM, 19 April 1939, Local 2 Files; "Trial Committee, Local 240" to Edward Flore, 14 March 1949, Reel 342, LUR, HERE Files. For the expulsion of the member who crossed the picket lines, see Local 48 MM, 11 February 1942, Local 2 Files. For other discussions of picket duties of Local 48 members see Local 48 EBM, 22 July 1941 and Local 48 MM, 3 April 1938. For regulations concerning meeting attendance, see Bylaws, Section 25, St. Louis Waitresses' Local 249, n.d., Reel 350, LUR, HERE Files.

39. Bylaws, Waitresses' Local 457, 1946 and 1952, Reel 970, LUR, HERE Files.

40. Minutebook, 10 November 1916, 27 July 1917, Local 457 Files; Bylaws, Waitresses' Local 457, 1964, Reel 970-971, LUR, HERE Files; Bylaws, Waitresses' Local 347, 1958, Reel 441, LUR, HERE Files; Local 48 MM, 25 February 1948, Local 2 Files; Local 48 Bylaws, 5 January 1943, Box 46, File-"#48-1943," SFLCR, BL-UCB; Local 48 EBM, 7 November 1938, 11 September 1945, 7 March 1944, Local 2 Files; Gertrude Sweet to Edward Flore, 25 December 1938, Reel 416, LUR, HERE Files.

41. MS, March 1901, 7. See LJEB Minutes, 7 June 1949, 21 June 1949, 3 September 1949 for cases waitresses appealed to the LJEB.

42. Local 48 EBM, 14 November 1938; see also Local 48 Minutes of February an

March 1936 for examples of other members reprimanded before the entire body for working six days a week and for accepting wages below scale.

43. U.S. Commission on Industrial Relations, "Industrial Conditions and Relations in Chicago," *Final Report and Testimony* 4 (Washington, 1916), 3257.

44. Seattle LJEB and Washington State Restaurant Association, 4 June 1937, CIE, June 1937, 35; Agreement, Local 670, 1925–26, Box 29, File-"Hotel: C-M," RG-257, NA; Bylaws, Waitresses' Local 639, 1962, Reel 627, LUR, HERE Files; interview with Charles Paulsen; Local 48 bylaws, 1921–48, Local 2 Files.

45. Younger, "Taking Orders," 521; Local 457 Bylaws, 1964, BSBA; Agreement, Local 670, 1925–26, Box 29, File-"Hotel: C-M," RG-257, NA; Bylaws, Local 126, Box 87, SFLCR, BL-UCB; Bylaws Local 347, 1960, Reel 441, LUR, HERE Files; Bylaws, Local 227, 1952, Reel 39, DUR, HERE Files; Bylaws, Local 507, 1954, Reel 543, LUR, HERE Files.

46. The openness of hotel locals to mass-production unionism derived in part from the historical period in which they were organized—few existed until the 1930s—and in part from the more factorylike nature of the hotel sector compared to the restaurant.

47. Agreement, Waiter and Waitresses' Local 1, 1 June 1930, Box 70, RG-257, NA. See Morris Horowitz, *The New York Hotel Industry* (Cambridge, 1960) and the HCV, 1936–50, for the emphasis on seniority and discharge protection by Hotel Workers' Local 6 in New York; HCV, 23 December 1944, 3 for quote.

48. See, for example, San Francisco LJEB Minutes, 20 June 1939 and Agreement between the San Francisco LJEB and the Golden Gate Restaurant Association, 1 December 1959, Local 2 Files.

49. CIE, December 1951, 14; HCV, 24 March 1945, 5; for further details, see Dorothy Sue Cobble, "Sisters in the Craft: Waitresses and Their Unions in the Twentieth Century," Ph.D. diss., Stanford University, 1986, 313–14.

50. Bylaws, Waitresses' Local 347, 1958, Reel 441, LUR, HERE Files and Bylaws Local 457, 1954, WPUC-174, Box 13, folder 8, MHS. The following contracts illustrate the longevity and pervasiveness of clauses giving unions the right to determine the work week: Wage Scale and Working Conditions, San Francisco LJEB, 7 July 1942, 1 September 1946, 1 September 1950, 1 September 1954, and 1 September 1956; Minimum Wage Scale and Working Conditions, Local 41, 1 October 1945; Wage Scale and Working Conditions, Las Vegas LJEB and Employers' Association of Southern Nevada; all in Local 2 Files.

51. For example, see Local 457 Minutebook, 23 November 1973, Local 457 Files; see also the contracts between Local 457 and the Silver Bow Employers Association, 1943, 1946, 1950, 1959, and 1961 in WPUC-174, Box 13, folders 8 and 9, MHS and in particular, the single-sheet supplementary agreement, "Notice—Hiring Procedure," 20 March 1959 in Box 13, folder 9. A clause on "seniority and discharge" was not added to the Butte contract until 1961.

Chapter 7. "Women's Place" in the Industry

1. CIE, June 1935, 48.

2. "Some of the Problems of Eve," talk given to the AFL-CIO Conference on Women and Work, 13 March 1971, Box 1, File 6, MW Collection, WRL, WSU.

3. Mae Stoneman to Ed Miller, 30 September 1959; Grievance Committee Report, 31 August 1959 and 10 October 1957; John L. Cooper, President, Los Angeles LJEB to Miller, 13 October 1959; Ed Miller to Mae Stoneman, 10 November 1959, all on Reel 628, LUR, HERE Files.

4. The phenomenon of men advocating equal pay to maintain their own working standards and jobs is not unique to the culinary industry. For example, see Ruth Milkman, *Gender at Work: The Dynamics of Job Segregation by Sex During World War II* (Urbana, 1987), 42–48, 74–77, and Nancy Gabin, "Women Workers and the UAW in the Post-World War II Period: 1945–54," *Labor History* 21 (Winter 1979–80): 9.

5. MS, January 1918, 53; *Proceedings*, HERE Convention, 1919, 245.

6. For an overview of pay practices in the culinary industry which reveals the frequencies of pay inequities before the 1930s, see "Wages and Hours of Union Hotel and Restaurant Employees," *Monthly Labor Review* 37 (August 1933): 350–54. For examples of individual contracts with considerable wage inequities, see "Contract and Agreement between Helena Hotel/Restaurant Keepers Association and HERE Local 612," 1 October 1920, Box 29, File-"Hotel-C-M" and Agreement, Waiters and Waitresses, Local 1, 1 June 1930, Box 70, loose contracts, both RG-257, NA. For early attempts to close the wage gap, see MS, July 1903, 50; January 1920, 23; April 1922, 57, and *Industrial Unionist*, 23 May 1925.

7. "GEB Report 1923–25," *Proceedings*, HERE convention, 1925, 98, 185; 1927, 168; and 1929, 146–47.

8. The transcript of the convention proceedings belies Matthew Josephson's contention that during the conventions of the 1920s "a goodly number of women members spoke in behalf of equal rights and equal pay for women." Matthew Josephson, *Union House, Union Bar: The History of the Hotel and Restaurant Employees and Bartenders International Union* (New York, 1956), 159–60.

9. *Proceedings*, HERE Convention, 1927, 168–71. For continuing problems once equal pay was enacted, see Kitty Amsler to Hugo Ernst, 25 March 1946, Ernst to Amsler, 11 July 1946, Ernst to Keller, 28 March 1946, all Reel 229, LUR, HERE Files.

10. *Proceedings*, HERE Convention, 1925, 185; 1927, 168–71; 1929, 146–47; Josephson, *Union House, Union Bar*, 159–60. Butte waitresses judged equal pay "injurious" to women workers in the 1920s. See Minutebook, 1922–30, 29 May 1925, 11 September 1927, 7 June 1929, 14-1, WPUC-174, MHS.

11. *CIE*, September 1936, 88, 146–47. Waitresses' Local 48 sponsored the resolution and spoke fervently in its behalf; they had opposed equal pay before 1936. See the debates in LJEB Minutes, 1929–36, LJEB Correspondence Folder, and Joint Wage Scale for Locals 30 and 48, n.d. [ca. 1936–38], all Local 2 Files.

12. *CIE*, December 1942, 33.

13. Waitresses were not the only female activists who shifted their policy in the 1930s. Alice Kessler-Harris argues that for social feminists especially, the depression proved to be a "watershed in which opinions began to change." The Fair Labor Standards Act challenged the need for basing legislation on arguments of difference and the economic impact of the depression undercut the idea of economic security deriving from one male breadwinner. Alice Kessler-Harris, "The Debate over Equality for Women in the Workplace," in *Women and Work* 1, ed. Laurie Larwood et al. (Beverly Hills, 1985), 148–49.

14. LJEB Minutes, 4 October 1937; "Closing Brief for the Union in the Arbitration between the San Francisco LJEB and the San Francisco Hotel Operators before Fred Athearn in 1937," "Brief in Behalf of the Hotel Employers Association of San Francisco before the 1938 Wage Board, Robert Littler, Chair," 157, "Employer Brief and Exhibits in the Arbitration between the San Francisco LJEB and the San Francisco Hotel Operators before Fred Athearn, 1937," "Athearn Award in the Arbitration between the San Francisco LJEB and the San Francisco Hotel Operators, 1937," all Local 2 Files.

15. For a fuller discussion of negotiating equal pay during the wartime period, see Dorothy Sue Cobble, "Sisters in the Craft: Waitresses and Their Unions in the Twentieth Century," Ph.D. diss., Stanford University, 1986, 404–8.

16. Working-class women historically have divided in their support of the family wage concept. Although no systematic study has been done, my research and that of Mary Blewett suggest that the positions taken by working-class women correlate closely with their family status, with single, divorced women and others outside the patriarchial family economy least inclined to support the "family wage" idea. See Mary H. Blewett, *Men, Women and Work: Class, Gender, and Protest in the New England Shoe Industry, 1780–1910* (Urbana, 1988), 121–41. For other discussions of the family wage, see Jane Humphries, "The Working-Class Family, Women's Liberation and Class Struggle: The Case of Nineteenth Century British History," *Review of Radical Political Economics* 9 (Fall 1977): 25–41, and Martha May, "Bread Before Roses: American Workingmen, Labor Unions and the Family Wage," in *Women, Work and Protest: A Century of Women's Labor History*, ed. Ruth Milkman (Boston, 1985), 1–21.

17. Interview with Gertrude Sweet, 22–41.

18. Stapled pamphlet, "Contract Wage Rates for Selected Job Classifications as of April, 1948," prepared by the Department of Research and Education, HERE, Cincinnati, July 1948, 2, HERE Files; California (State) Department of Industrial Relations, Division of Labor Statistics and Research, *Union Contract Provisions: Eating and Drinking Places* (San Francisco, 1961), 1–6. Although this survey was conducted in 1961, the clauses governing wage scales had been in place for a number of years.

19. *CIE*, August 1941, 46; July 1942, 22; *Woman Worker*, September 1941, 12.

20. For details on waitress activities, see Cobble, "Sisters in the Craft," 408–16; the participation of other groups is reconstructed in Cynthia Harrison, *On Account of Sex: The Politics of Women's Issues, 1945–1968* (Berkeley, 1988), 39–51, 89–105. See also Doris Cochrane to Rose Schneiderman, 6 February 1945, and Anne Larrabee to Blanch Freedman, 14 January 1946, Reel 13, C-4, WTUL Papers.

21. *CIE*, June 1949, 17; April 1949, 15; Dorothy S. Brady, "Equal Pay for Women Workers," *Annals of the American Academy of Political and Social Sciences* 251 (May 1947): 54; Alice K. Leopold, "Federal Equal Pay Legislation," *Labor Law Journal* 6 (January 1955), 21–22; Ronnie Steinberg, *Wages and Hours: Labor and Reform in Twentieth Century America* (New Brunswick, 1982), 94, 220.

22. Transcript, "Women's Bureau Conference for Women Trade Union Leaders, 1946," Box 897, Memo from Alice Angus to Frieda Miller, 21 August 1944, Box 901, Mary Anderson to Blanch Freedman, Executive-Secretary, New York WTUL, 7 June 1944, File "WTUL," Box 852, all in RG-86, NA. Leopold's article "Federal Equal Pay Legislation" is an excellent example of the comparable worth concerns of the early

equal pay advocates. See also Elaine Johansen, *Comparable Worth: The Myth and the Movement* (Boulder, 1984), 30–34, and Frances C. Hutner, *Equal Pay for Comparable Worth: The Working Women's Issue of the 1980s* (New York, 1986).

23. New York (State) Department of Labor, Division of Research and Statistics, *Some Aspects of the Nightwork Problem with Special Reference to the Restaurant Industry*, Publication B-23, by Vera Freeman and Harry Newman (Albany, 1949), 56–58, passim. Ironically, the New York statute language closely conformed to Women's Bureau recommendations. The law provided that "no employee shall, because of sex, be subjected to any discrimination in the rate of her or his pay." See *HCV*, 29 April 1944.

24. Because most houses hired either men or women, equal pay legislation had little effect on the waiting work force. As the New York state case illustrates, in the small number of houses with mixed crews, reasons for inequitable wages often were found.

25. The gap between male and female tip income in 1970 was much greater than that between their wage income. At full-course restaurants waitresses made only 68 percent of the tips made by waiters; in contrast, waitresses made nearly 90 percent of the hourly wages paid waiters. Computed from charts published in U.S. Department of Labor, Bureau of Labor Statistics, *Wages and Tips in Restaurants and Hotels, March 1970*, Bulletin no. 1712 (Washington, D.C., 1971), 26.

26. Milkman, *Gender at Work*, 47.

27. The argument that men became less interested in equal pay after the war and more focused on the reestablishment of occupational segregation is ably presented in Milkman, *Gender at Work*, ch. 7. Hartmann makes suggestions along the same lines in her discussion of the declining AFL support for equal pay legislation by 1948. Susan Hartmann, *The Home Front and Beyond: American Women in the 1940s* (Boston, 1982), 134.

28. *MS*, February 1903, 37; Butte Montana Ordinance no. 499, 1898, Record Books, BSBA; *Industrial Worker*, 18 June 1910. For further examples of such laws, see Mary Lee Spence, "Waitresses in the Trans-Mississippi West: 'Pretty Waiter Girls,' Harvey Girls and Union Maids," in *The Women's West*, ed. Susan Armitage and Elizabeth Jameson (Norman, 1987), 224–25, and Sophonisba Breckinridge, "Legislative Control of Women's Work," *Journal of Political Economy* 14 (January 1906): 110–11.

29. For a discussion of the controversy over the California statute, see Ira Cross, *A History of the Labor Movement in California* (Berkeley, 1935), 313n; Lucile Eaves, *A History of California Labor Legislation* (Berkeley, 1910), 312–13; and Elizabeth Baker, *Protective Labor Legislation with Special Reference to Women in the State of New York* (New York, 1925), 58. For the response of waitresses, see *MS*, April 1911, 11, May 1913, 49, and Susan Englander, "The San Francisco Wage Earners' Suffrage League: Class Conflict and Class Coalition in the California Woman Suffrage Movement, 1907–1912," master's thesis, San Francisco State University, 1989, 61.

30. Not all waiters supported these policies. For example, Brother Sesma, an International organizer, considered a petition prohibiting the employment of women where liquor was served "a dastardly and nefarious proposition, which, if adopted, would have thrown out of employment many of our members." He started a campaign against its enactment. *MS*, April 1915, 28.

31. *CIE*, March 1934, 37; August 1935, 17.

32. A biographical portrait of Kitty Donnelly can be found in *MS*, September 1921,

150, and *CIE*, January 1930. Donnelly's quote is from *CIE*, May 1933, 27. The other quotes are in ibid., June 1935, 27, 48, and August 1935, 17. See also ibid., May 1933, 17, 27; April 1935, 30; and May 1935, 32.

33. *CIE*, April 1935, 30; *Proceedings*, HERE, 1941, Resolution 38 introduced by San Francisco Local 48.

34. *CIE*, May 1933, 17, 27.

35. EB Minutes, Local 48, 27 October 1942, and LJEB Minutes, 17 March 1942, Local 2 Files; *CIE*, March 1936, 25. Butte waitresses also stated that "any place where food is not served, we don't allow girls to fill in as barmaids," Minutebook, 5 December 1941, Box 14, File 2, WPUC-174, MHS.

36. Chartered in 1926, Local 444 had allowed dues payments to lapse. General Secretary-Treasurer to McNeal, President 444, 2 August 1944 and General Secretary-Treasurer to Virginia Blanton, Secretary 444, 7 May 1934, Reel 10, DUL, HERE Files.

37. The details of the dispute are chronicled in *Chicago Defender*, 31 March 1934, 4; 7 April 1934, 4; 14 April 1934, 1, as well as in the archival material cited in subsequent notes.

38. *Chicago Defender*, 31 March 1934, 4; 7 April 1934, 4; 14 April 1934, 1; Ethel Erickson to Elizabeth Christman, 6 August 1934, and Ethel Erickson to John Fitzpatrick, 6 August 1934, R-2, C-2, WTUL Papers.

39. George McLane, president of the Chicago Bartenders Local, has been described by Matthew Josephson and others as part of the "Al Capone syndicate" which moved from illicit rum-running to pushing various racketeer-owned liquor at bars where they controlled the teamster and culinary locals. Most likely, St. Louis Kelly was tied in with McLane and thus desired to have "his men" working there instead of women because of the greater ease in conducting his illegal scams. He needed "experienced" union waiters in the taverns, for instance, to push certain brands of beer. For a fuller discussion of the racketeering elements in Chicago, see Jay Rubin and M. J. Obermeier, *The Growth of a Union: The Life and Times of Edward Flore* (New York, 1943), 48–73, passim, and Josephson, *Union House, Union Bar*, 211–15, 234–61.

40. Ethel Erickson to John Fitzpatrick, 6 August 1934; Oscar De Priest to Mary Anderson, 26 April 1934; Mary Anderson to John Fitzpatrick, 26 April 1934, all in File "HERE," Box 865, RG-86, NA.

41. Memo from Ethel Erickson to Mary Anderson, 6 August 1934 and Ethel Erickson to John Fitzpatrick, 6 August 1934, File "HERE," Box 865, RG-86, NA.

42. *Chicago Defender*, 21 April 1934; Edward Flore to Mary Anderson, 20 August 1934; Fitzpatrick to Erickson, 25 August 1934, both in HERE File, Box 865, RG-86, NA.

43. *CIE*, June 1935, 30.

44. Standard Agreement Local 302, 1934, Reel 62, DUR, HERE Files. The 1938 and 1941 contracts reiterated the union's control over the sex of employees, limiting the ratio of female to male employees. CC, June 1938, 5–6, July 1941, 7; see also Agreement between the Delicatessen and Restaurant Countermen, Local 60, New York City, 1937–38, Box 122, RG-257, NA.

45. Agreements, Waiters and Waitresses' Local 1, 1930 and 1936, Box 70, loose contracts, RG-257, NA; Agreement, Waiters and Waitresses' Local 1, n.d. [1942], Reel 134, DUR, HERE Files; *Voice of Local 1*, June 1950, 3.

46. For example, at the end of the war when it seemed they would be replaced, women in Local 1 urged each other to file grievances based on the infamous Clause 12 of their contract; *Voice of Local 1*, 1944–47.

47. For example, the LJEB rejected requests from ball-park concessioners to employ women because the jobs had "been equally divided between waiters, waitresses, and bartenders in the past years," but they allowed food purveyors at the downtown War Memorial Building to change to waitresses because purveyors "originally had girls there." In another case, the LJEB permitted the displacement of waiters in San Francisco night clubs because they agreed with the employers that the change might help business and prevent the closing of union night clubs. The waiters objected, but their motion was defeated "after quite a lengthy debate." LJEB Minutes, 19 September 1940, 8 June 1938, 13 November 1944, 4 April 1939, 18 April 1939, 6 May 1941, Local 2 Files. For further examples, see LJEB Minutes, 1 May 1934, 19 June 1934, 3 July 1934, 27 January 1938, 28 December 1937, and Local 48 Minutes, 18 October 1939, 25 October 1939, all Local 2 Files.

48. For decisions against the waitresses, see LJEB Minutes, 5 December 1944, 18 September 1945, 2 October 1945, 15 January 1946, 16 July 1946, 5 May 1947, 19 May 1947, 19 August 1947, 20 January 1948, 2 March 1948, all Local 2 Files.

49. For waitresses' opinions of wartime LJEB policies, see Local 48 Minutes for June and July 1942 and 3 November 1944, all Local 2 Files. See LJEB Minutes, 5 December 1944 and 15 January 1946, Local 2 Files for instances of waitress protests.

50. Walsh to Ernst, 22 June 1949, Reel 10, DUR, HERE Files.

51. For information on the occupations of the women in the Butte local, see Laura Weatherly and Margaret Harrington, "Bucket Girl, Yard Girl: The Women Who Worked in Butte," *CIE*, October 1975, 22–23; Mary Murphy, untitled introduction to the WPU Collection, BSBA.

52. Minutebook, 16 September 1921, Local 457 Files; Minutebook, 31 August 1922, 25 April 1924, 1 May 1925, 4 March 1927, 19 November 1926, 16 November 1928, Box 14, File 1, WPUC-174, MHS.

53. By 1920, six states outlawed night work for all working women, while an additional twelve states prohibited night work in some occupations. These legislative drives relied primarily on the energies of the National Consumers' League and other middle-class female reform groups. For an overview of the night work issue, see Sheila Rothman, *Women's Proper Place: A History of Changing Ideals and Practices* (New York, 1978), 156–65; Baker, *Protective Labor Legislation with Special Reference to Women in the State of New York*, 233–51; Judith Baer, *The Chains of Protection: The Judicial Response to Women's Labor Legislation* (Westport, 1978), 86–88; U.S. Department of Labor, Women's Bureau, "Night Work Laws in the U.S.," Bulletin no. 7 (Washington, D.C., 1920); U.S. Department of Labor, Women's Bureau, "Labor Laws for Women in the States and Territories," Bulletin no. 98, by Florence P. Smith (Washington, D.C., 1932); U.S. Department of Labor, Women's Bureau, "History of Labor Legislation for Women in Three States," Bulletin no. 66, by Clara M. Beyer (Washington, D.C., 1929); and Steinberg, *Wages and Hours.*

54. Since 1917, the New York night work statute had applied to all female restaurant workers over the age of sixteen in first- and second-class restaurants in cities with more than fifty thousand. Singers and performers, attendants in ladies' cloak rooms

and parlors, as well as women employed in hotel dining rooms were exempt, however. See Baker, *Protective Labor Legislation with Special Reference to Women in the State of New York*, 71–72, 138, 189–91; New York (State) Department of Labor, Division of Research and Statistics, *Some Aspects of the Nightwork Problem*, 13–14; MS, February 1929, 35; *Monthly Bulletin*, New York WTUL, March 1932, Reel 22, C-4 and New York WTUL, 1926–29 *Convention Report*, 14, Reel 8, C-9, WTUL Papers; Consumers' League of New York, *The Forty-Eight Hour Law: Do Working Women Want It?* (New York, 1927); Mary Murray, "The Hearing on the Kirkland-Jenks Bill," *Equal Rights*, 15 March 1930, 43–45.

55. MS, March 1929, 43; CIE, June 1930, 36–37, March 1930, 19; Murray, "The Hearing on the Kirkland-Jenks Bill," 43–45; Vee Terry Perlman, "The Minimum Wage Muddle" (pamphlet, 1934), File "Min wage/1934," Box 906, RG-86, NA.

56. CIE, October 1930, 36–37; MS, June 1929, 43; May 1928, 69.

57. NYT, 27 February 1930; the director of inspection for the New York State Department of Labor confessed to Elizabeth Baker in the 1920s that enforcement of night work prohibitions was difficult because the "women themselves are not in sympathy with being deprived of work at night when tips are higher." Baker, *Protective Labor Legislation with Special Reference to Women in the State of New York*, 336.

58. CIE, May 1935, 32; June 1935, 48. For other cases of waitress opposition to night work restrictions see MS, June 1929, 43; May 1928, 69; Minutebook, 23 September 1929, Box 14, folder 1, WPUC-174, MHS.

59. During World War II, protective legislation, including night work laws, was perceived as hampering the war effort; as a result, all but five states exempted women from the laws. See Philip S. Foner, *Women and the American Labor Movement: From World War I to the Present* (New York, 1980), 353–54.

60. In the postwar era, male culinary unionists replaced the NCL and other middle-class women's groups as the principal proponents of the legislation. Working-class women appeared as a major element in the coalition favoring repeal. See Cobble, "Sisters in the Craft," 427–45.

61. MS, May 1928, 69; CIE, May 1945, 29; New York (State) Department of Labor, Division of Research and Statistics, *Some Aspects of the Nightwork Problem*, 33.

62. HCV, 16 August 1941, 2; CIE, May 1945, 29; Miguel Garriga to Ed Miller, 13 May 1948, File "HERE," Box 865, RG-86, NA; typed mss, "Women and Night Work in Restaurants," n.d. [ca. 1948], no author, "Night Work" folder, Local 6 Files.

63. Brief submitted by New York State Culinary Alliance, 7 December 1950, 6–7, 11–12, 14–17, "Night Work" folder, Local 6 Files. See *Muller v. Oregon*, 208 U.S. 412 (1908) for the text of the Brandeis brief. Other reasons cited included "the correlation between juvenile delinquency and broken homes—where the mother is out of the home because of nightwork"—and "the opportunities and inclination for crime, including sexual crimes, [being] greater after midnight than in broad daylight."

64. Freeman and Newman found that of 139 restaurant workers interviewed, only 16 favored restrictions for women. New York (State) Department of Labor, Division of Research and Statistics, *Some Aspects of the Nightwork Problem*, 13–14, 32–33; transcript, "Women's Bureau Conference for Women Trade Union Leaders, 1946," 252–56, Box 897 and transcript, "Women's Bureau Conference for Trade Union Women, 1945," 252–58, Box 898, RG-86, NA; Minutes of Women Bureau's Labor Advisory

Committee Meeting, 4 June 1946, 2, Box 1529, RG-86, NA; Memo, Constance Williams to Frieda Miller, 29 April 1947, File "Bulletin no. 233," Box 991, RG-86, NA; Gertrude Lane to Hugo Ernst, 12 November 1946, Reel 145, LUR, HERE Files; _HCV_, 26 March 1949, 1; _Voice of Local 1_, August 1949, 7; July 1950, 1; "Night Work" folder, Local 6 Files.

65. In Connecticut, according to Darling, the women members urged the union to support the relaxation of night work restrictions because they "don't make anything" on day shifts. "At night they . . . make more money because they get more in tips at dinner, banquets or from persons drinking, and consequently they 'don't mind' night work." Interview with Charles Darling, Hartford, Connecticut, 25 June 1947 by Women's Bureau Agent Martha Ziegler, Box 676, RG-86, NA.

66. New York (State) Department of Labor, Division of Research and Statistics, _Some Aspects of the Nightwork Problem_, 2, 33–34, 100.

67. Wage-earning women on both sides of the night work debate claimed their position was consistent with fulfilling women's responsibilities at home. See synopsis of night work studies in transcript, "Women's Bureau Conference for Women Trade Union Leaders, 1946," 237, Box 897, RG-86, NA; mimeo, "Summary of Material on Effect of Night Work," file "Trade Union Women's Conference, October 1946," Box 1696, RG-86, NA; _Voice of Local 1_, October 1948, 2; interview with Kathryn Dewing.

68. In the long run, however, male workers misperceived their own economic interest because they were undermining their own working standards and trade union organizations by competing with their female co-workers. By reinforcing an artificial division of labor among food servers, night work legislation crowded women workers into lower-paying, daytime jobs in which women worked for less, undermined conditions within the industry, and encouraged the displacement of men.

69. _CIE_, June 1949, 32; interview with Charles Darling; U.S. Department of Labor, Women's Bureau, "Night Work for Women in Hotels and Restaurants," Bulletin no. 233, 12; New York (State) Department of Labor, Division of Research and Statistics, _Some Aspects of the Nightwork Problem_, 2; Baer, _The Chains of Protection_, 86–87.

70. Cobble, "Sisters in the Craft," 427–45 traces the controversy over night work in the WTUL and the Women's Bureau.

71. New York (State) Department of Labor, Division of Research and Statistics, _Some Aspects of the Nightwork Problem_, 19–20, 26; Steinberg, _Wages and Hours_, 220.

72. Before World War I, the U.S. Census reported a mere handful of female bartenders, and with the passage of the 18th Amendment neither men nor women pursued the craft. As late as 1940, women were less than 3 percent of all bartenders. U.S. Department of Commerce, Bureau of the Census, _Sixteenth Census of the U.S., 1940: Comparative Occupational Statistics_ by A. M. Edwards (Washington, D.C., 1943), 56, Table 14, 165 and Table 15, 172. State statutes were passed as early as the 1890s banning women from bartending. See U.S. Department of Labor, Women's Bureau, "History of Labor Legislation for Women in Three States," 109; Joint Committee on the Employment of Barmaids, "Women as Barmaids," London, 1905, 44–45.

73. Boycott card, n.d. [ca. 1937–38], File "Local 41 Bartenders," Box 2, SFLCR, BL-UCB. See also Business Agent Board Minutes, 26 August 1940, Local 2 Files for examples of picketing directed against employers who hired women bartenders. Other

prewar legislative activity by bartender locals can be found in *CIE*, July 1936, 37; October 1936, 35; December 1936, 42; February 1937, 51; October 1940, 33; November 1940, 43; *HCV*, 16 August 1941, 2; *MHBRR*, October 1936, 4; May 1940, 1; September 1941, 1.

74. At times, the term *barmaid* was used to describe women who served liquor; here it refers solely to women who mixed liquor.

75. Some bartender locals closed down rather than dispatch women even on a temporary basis, but a few opened their ranks to women and encouraged the training of women in the craft. *CIE*, January 1943, 29; April 1943, 30; May 1943, 4, 8; *HCV*, 11 December 1943; *NYT*, 11 December 1942, 25; *HCV*, 14 August 1943; 30 October 1943; 11 December 1943; Edith Carroll, "Barmaids Come Back," *NYT Magazine*, 18 March 1945, 27.

76. Officers' Report, HERE, 1947, 41; *CIE*, September 1942, 37; March 1946, 31, 39; for an example of a postwar strike against women bartenders see July 1949, 26.

77. See U.S. Supreme Court decision dated December 20, 1948, *Goesaert v. Cleary*, no. 49, October Term, 1948 and the discussion of this case in Hartmann, *The Home Front and Beyond*, 131; *NYT*, 21 December 1948, 27; Baer, *The Chains of Protection*, 111–21.

78. "Anti-Barmaid Laws," December 1948, by Hotel and Restaurant Employees International Union, 3, Reel 30, GOR, HERE Files; *Proceedings*, HERE Convention, 1953. See Barbara Babcock et al., *Sex Discrimination and the Law: Causes and Remedies* (Boston, 1975), 261.

79. The gallantry behind these laws is suspect, of course. As the historian Susan Hartmann has argued, female bartenders may actually be subject to fewer moral and physical dangers than cocktail waitresses who lack the protection of a bar between them and the patrons. Hartmann, *The Home Front and Beyond*, 132. In addition, the higher status of female bartenders helps insulate them from customer abuse.

80. *CIE*, December 1936, 42; February 1937, 51; March 1937, 38; April 1939, 45; October 1942, 18; January 1943, 29; February 1943, 31; April 1943, 30; *HCV*, 15 January 1947, 4; *Voice of Local 1*, October 1950, 3; Officers' Reports, 1949, 26; Carroll, "Barmaids Come Back," 27; *MHBRR*, June 1936, 1; May 1940, 1–7.

81. *MHBRR*, July 1942, 1–2; *CIE*, February 1935, 21, 36; *Proceedings*, HERE Convention, 1938.

82. The quotes are from Jon M. Kingsdale, "The 'Poor Man's Club': Social Functions of the Urban Working-class Saloon," *American Quarterly* 25 (October 1973): 472–89; Carroll, "Barmaids Come Back," 27; and Robert Popham, "The Social History of the Tavern," *Research Advances in Alcohol and Drug Problems* 4, ed. Yedy Israel et al. (New York, 1978), 282. James Spradley and Brenda Mann, *The Cocktail Waitress: Women's Work in a Man's World* (New York, 1975), contains an extended anthropological analysis of male and female tensions in bars and the American male bartender's tenacious protection of his "sacred male space" behind the bar; see esp. 1–14, 144–48. For an excellent historical discussion of the centrality of taverns to American working-class male culture, see Roy Rosenzweig, *Eight Hours for What We Will: Workers and Leisure in An Industrial City, 1870–1920* (Cambridge, 1983), 35–65, 93–126.

83. *CIE*, December 1934, 25. The strong taboos in relation to women "behind the bar" seem to be derived from the American experience, as barmaids are common

in Europe. See Ernest M. Porter, *Hotel and Restaurant Careers for Women* (London, 1931), 60–64, and Joint Committee on the Employment of Barmaids, "Women as Barmaids," London, 1905 for a discussion of the prevalence of barmaids in other cultures, particularly in England and Australia.

84. See *CIE* 1940–53 and Correspondence Files, HERE Files.

85. *CIE*, June 1941, 3; February 1941, 32; Mae Stoneman to Bob Wasson, 25 April 1944; contract between the Restaurant Hotel Employers Council of Southern California and Los Angeles LJEB HERE, 1962–67, all Reel 628, LUR, HERE Files.

86. *CIE*, June 1949, 15; "Brief in Support of Legislation to Prohibit Employment of Women Bartenders in Ohio," 3, n.d. [ca. 1949], Reel 30, GOR, HERE Files.

87. Amsler to Ernst, 5 January 1949; Ernst to Amsler, 7 January 1949; Reel 229, LUR, HERE Files; Hotel and Restaurant International League of America, *Fifty Years of Progress: A Brief History of Our Union, 1891–1941* (Cincinnati, 1941), 68.

88. Sociological studies of social relations among food service employees in the workplace as well as my own research suggest that another factor relevant to the hesitancy of waitresses may have been the real power exercised by the bartender. A waitress literally cannot perform her work if the bartender does not cooperate. Waitresses, it appears, perceived waiters more as equals; bartenders were seen as having greater authority and status. See "Sisters in the Craft," 98–108, 509–13 and earlier accounts of food service workers such as William Whyte's classic *Human Relations in the Restaurant Industry* (New York, 1948).

89. Interview with Gertrude Sweet, 21; interview with Florence Farr.

90. Interview with Jackie Walsh.

91. "1955 Report," typed sheet attached to letter, Local 356 to General President (GP), 14 October 1958; Local 444 to GP, 13 May 1952; Murray Washington to GP, 3 July 1954; Willis Thomas, "On the Job: Bartenders Training Program," (Manual published by Local 356, n.d. [ca. 1958]), 1; all in Reel 10, DUR, HERE Files. At this point, another union, Local 356 had absorbed the nine-hundred-member Local 444.

92. For the long tradition of black protest based on "motherhood" see Eileen Boris, "The Power of Motherhood: Black and White Activist Women Redefine the 'Political,' " *Yale Journal of Law and Feminism* 2 (Fall 1989): 25–49.

93. (Chicago) *New Crusader*, 11 February 1961, 18 February 1961.

94. Mrs. Leila Adkins, et al. to Ed Miller, 23 February 1961, and Miller to Leila Adkins, 2 March 1961, Reel 30, GOR, HERE Files.

95. U.S. Department of Commerce, Bureau of the Census, *Sixteenth Census of the U.S.*, 1940, 56, Table 14, 165, and Table 15, 172; U.S. Department of Commerce, Bureau of the Census, *Seventeenth Census of Population: 1950*, vol. 4, *Special Reports*, pt. 1 (Washington, 1953), 1B-21; U.S. Department of Commerce, Bureau of the Census, *Eighteenth Census of Population: 1960*, *Subject Reports, Occupational Characteristics* (Washington, D.C., 1963), 8, 13.

96. For the statistics on the changing ambiance of bars and the decline of unionization, see Linda Detman, "Women Behind Bars: The Feminization of Bartending," in Barbara Reskin and Patricia Roos, *Job Queues, Gender Queues: Explaining Women's Inroads into Male Occupations* (Philadelphia, 1990), 241–56.

97. Baer, *The Chains of Protection*, 111–21; Hartmann, *The Home Front and Beyond*, 131–33; Babcock, et al., *Sex Discrimination and the Law*, 269–71 for accounts

of litigation related to women mixing liquor. *San Francisco Chronicle*, 28 May 1971, 5 June 1971.

98. Reskin and Roos, *Job Queues, Gender Queues*, Table 1.6, 17.

99. The concept of emotional labor is from Arlie Hochschild, *The Managed Heart: The Commercialization of Human Feeling* (Berkeley, 1983), 3–12, passim.

100. The concern evidenced by waitresses over protecting the jobs of their union brothers can be seen as deriving in part from this working-class tradition. The concept of "moral economy" was first developed by E. P. Thompson in "The Moral Economy of the English Crowd in the Eighteenth Century," *Past and Present* 50 (February 1971): 79. Maurine Greenwald argues that Seattle working-class women subscribed to this concept in determining who had a legitimate claim to wage work in "Working-class Feminism and the Family Wage Ideal: The Seattle Debate on Married Women's Right to Work in the Era of the First World War," *Journal of American History* 76 (June 1989): 118–49.

101. James Henretta's insights in "The Study of Social Mobility: Ideological Assumptions and Conceptual Bias," *Labor History* 18 (1977): 165–78 are also helpful in thinking about the decisions of waitresses. Historians, Henretta points out, have ignored the possibility that many in the working-class may have not desired upward mobility with the same intensity as the middle class. Waitresses, it appears, defined their highest priorities not as upward mobility and job opportunity but as meeting their obligations as breadwinners, parents, spouses, and union sisters and as creating jobs that granted them economic security and a measure of respect.

Chapter 8. *"Women's Place" in the Union*

1. Reprinted in *CIE*, March 1936, 7.

2. For an analysis of the position of women in trade unions in the early twentieth century, see Alice Henry, *The Trade Union Woman* (New York, 1915), and her later work, *Women and the Labor Movement* (New York, 1923). See also B. M. Herron, "The Progress of Labor Organizations Among Women, Together with Some Considerations Concerning Their Place in Industry," *University Studies* 1 (May 1905): 443–511; and Teresa Wolfson, *The Woman Worker and the Trade Unions* (New York, 1926).

3. Eli Ginzberg concluded in 1948, for example, that "the role of women in many respects parallels that of the Negroes . . . their voice in union affairs generally has been less than their numerical strength would have warranted." See Eli Ginzberg, *The Labor Leader: An Exploratory Study* (New York, 1948), 49.

4. Naomi Baden, "Developing an Agenda: Expanding the Role of Women in Unions," *Labor Studies Journal* 10 (Winter 1986): 229–30, 236–37. For related articles on the contemporary status of women within the labor movement, see Ruth Milkman, "Women Workers, Feminism and the Labor Movement," in *Women, Work, and Protest: A Century of U.S. Women's Labor History*, ed. Ruth Milkman (Boston 1985), 305–7, 319n; and Ruth Needleman, "Women Workers: A Force for Rebuilding Unionism," *Labor Research Review* 11 (Spring 1988): 1–13.

5. For comparison with other unions see the works cited in note 2 as well as Roger Waldinger, "Another Look at the ILGWU: Women, Industry Structure and Collective Action," and Alice Kessler-Harris, "Problems of Coalition-building: Women and Trade Unions in the 1920s," both in *Women, Work, and Protest*, ed. Milkman, 86–

138; Susan A. Glenn, *Daughters of the Shtetl: Life and Labor in the Immigrant Generation* (Ithaca, 1990); ch. 6; Michael Harrington, *The Retail Clerks* (New York, 1962); Marten Estey, "The Retail Clerks," in *White-Collar Workers*, ed. Albert A. Blum (New York, 1971); Barbara Wertheimer and Anne H. Nelson, *Trade Union Women: A Study of Their Participation in New York City* (New York, 1975); and Mary Margaret Fonow, "Women in Steel: A Case Study of the Participation of Women in a Trade Union," Ph.D. diss., Ohio State University, 1977.

6. See, for example, Nancy MacLean, *The Culture of Resistance: Female Institution Building in the ILGWU 1905–1925*, Michigan Occasional Paper 21 (Winter 1982), and Nancy Gabin, *Feminism in the Labor Movement: Women and the United Auto Workers, 1935–1975* (Ithaca, 1990).

7. Virginia Bergquist, "Women's Participation in Labor Organizations," U.S. Department of Labor, Bureau of Labor Statistics Reprint 2997 (Washington, D.C., 1974), 5–6. Charts used in her article excluded HERE because the "figure was not reported to the Bureau or not available." Bergquist noted that statistical data below the national level is usually not included in surveys because of the difficulty in surveying thousands of locals.

8. For an analysis emphasizing the role of separate female locals, see MacLean, *The Culture of Resistance*. For discussions of the variety of attitudes toward separate locals held by working-class women activists, see Sherna Gluck, "The Changing Nature of Women's Participation in the American Labor Movement, 1900–1940: Case Studies from Oral History," paper presented at the Southwest Labor History Conference, Arizona State University, Tempe, March 5, 1977, and Glenn, *Daughters of the Shtetl*, ch. 6. The controversy over the impact of separate female institutions is by no means limited to the trade-union activities of women. One of the more illuminating essays is by Estelle B. Freedman, "Separatism as Strategy: Female Institution Building and American Feminism, 1870–1930," *Feminist Studies* 5 (Fall 1979): 512–29.

9. For instance, see Meredith Tax, *The Rising of the Women: Feminist Solidarity and Class Conflict, 1880–1917* (New York, 1980).

10. For a discussion of these, see Wolfson, *The Woman Worker and the Trade Unions*; Ruth Milkman, "Gender and Trade Unionism in Historical Perspective," in *Women, Politics and Change*, ed. Louise A. Tilly and Patricia Gurin (New York, 1990), 87–107; Waldinger, "Another Look at the International Ladies Garment Workers' Union"; Kessler-Harris, "Problems of Coalition-building"; and Glenn, *Daughters of the Shtetl*, ch. 6.

11. The women's locals in the garment industry, for example, cut across occupational and ethnic lines, taking in all women within a given geographical location. Glenn, *Daughters of the Shtetl*, ch. 6, and Waldinger, "Another Look at the ILGWU," 99. The term *occupational homogeneity* is from Wolfson, *The Woman Worker and the Trade Unions*, 164. Wolfson notes that when women's locals "not only represent a separation of sex but a separation of crafts," they are more successful than when "the locals are made up of women of different crafts of one industry." Herron makes a similar point in "The Progress of Labor Organizations Among Women," 445–46.

12. For analyses that link household arrangements and collective action, see Louise Tilly, "Paths of Proletarianization: Organization of Production, Sexual Division of Labor, and Women's Collective Action," *Signs* 7 (Winter 1981): 400–417; Carole

Turbin, "Beyond Conventional Wisdom: Women's Wage Work, Household Economic Contribution, and Labor Activism in a Mid-Nineteenth-Century Working-Class Community," in *"To Toil the Livelong Day": America's Women at Work, 1780–1980*, ed. Carol Groneman and Mary Beth Norton (Ithaca, 1987), 47–67; Ronald Schatz, "Union Pioneers: The Founders of Local Unions at GE and Westinghouse, 1933–37," *Journal of American History* 66 (1979): 586–602; and Alice Kessler-Harris, "Organizing the Unorganizable: Three Jewish Women and Their Union," *Labor History* 17 (Winter 1976): 5–23.

13. Although the numbers are not available for every convention year, in many cases separate locals sent a higher proportion of the female delgates than their numbers warranted. This line of argument concerning the importance of separate locals is at odds with those made by Matthew Josephson in *Union House, Union Bar: The History of the Hotel and Restaurant Employees and Bartenders International Union* (New York, 1956). Josephson states that during the 1930s the character of the unions transformed, with many female officers coming to the fore for the first time. The women he names (225), Gertrude Sweet, Pauline Newman, Bee Tumber, Mae Stoneman, and others, however, were all from separate locals that had existed before the 1930s.

14. For comparison with other unions, see works cited in notes 2, 5 and 6.

15. In 1915, for example, at the Eighteenth HERE Convention in San Francisco, women comprised 13 percent of committee members and 7.5 percent of the delegates. Again, in 1919 and in 1932, their committee influence out-distanced their actual numbers at the conventions. HERE Convention Records, 1915, 1919, 1932.

16. From 1909 to 1938 women held one seat on a board numbering between ten and twelve; in 1938, women captured three seats on an eighteen-member board. During the 1940s and 1950s women continued to hold two and sometimes three seats. The composition of the GEB is listed year by year in the HERE national journals, MS and CIE.

17. CIE, April 1940, 35. When the Women's Bureau selected female culinary workers for their 1950 Women's Bureau Labor Advisory Committee, three of the four selected were from separate locals.

18. CIE, October 1938, 31; January 1938, 34; May 1938, 36; see July 1947, 22 for other examples.

19. Wolfson, *The Woman Worker and the Trade Unions*, 178; CIE, March 1944, 18.

20. Interview with Gertrude Sweet. In general, the record of East Coast waitresses fell behind that of the Midwest and West—in part because of the larger proportion of male workers in the industry and the smaller number of separate-sex locals.

21. Marion Dickerman and Ruth Taylor, *Who's Who in Labor* (New York, 1946), 187; CIE, June 1942, 30 and May 1948, 29; San Francisco LJEB Minutes, 17 January and 7 March 1950; CIE, December 1956, 22 and April 1940, 35.

22. More than 50 percent of the delegates to the 1940 Oregon Hotel, Restaurant, and Beverage Employees Alliance meeting were women. Some 33 percent of the Washington State Culinary Alliance in the 1940s was female, while Wyoming culinary locals sent an equal number of male and female delegates to the Wyoming Labor Convention in August of 1940. Many of the top-level executive positions were held by women as well. See "Proceedings of the Sixth Annual Convention of the California State Council of Culinary Workers, Bartenders, and Hotel Service Employees," held

at Mayfair Hotel, Los Angeles, California, 27–28 August 1949, Box 3, file 23, BMC-CHS; *CIE*, January 1933, 44; August 1940, 46; August 1940, 41; Gertrude Sweet to G. S. T., 25 March 1939, Reel 416, LUR, HERE Files.

23. *MS*, January 1906, 8.

24. Alexander's own local had "chosen two of the best women talkers" as their first delegates to the International Convention of 1905 and subsequently had sent delegations to as many conventions as they could. See *MS*, 15 May 1904, 64; *Proceedings*, HERE Convention, 1927, 172. For the Butte vote, see, Minutebook, 1922–30, 1 October 1926, B14-F1, WPUC-174, MHS.

25. *SFLC*, 7 December 1906, 4.

26. *Chicago Tribune*, 23 March 1962; letter from Executive Board members, Local 484 to Ed Miller, 14 February 1963; Anne Steward to Miller, 6 September 1963; Miller to Anne Steward, 11 September 1963, all Reel 525, LUR, HERE Files.

27. Alice Lord to the Editor, *MS*, April 1906, 15. Tellingly, Lord apologized for her audaciousness the first time she wrote a letter to the national journal, but she hinted that she would not be intimidated. "Now, this is my first letter and I trust that you will not deem it too long. If you knew me . . . well, I imagine I could hear you say: 'Deliver me from hearing that woman talk.' You may hear from me again." Her closing line proved prophetic. *MS*, August 1903, 69.

28. Ibid., July 1901, 12; *CIE*, March 1940, 27; back cover, Local 639 Bylaws, 1954–59, Reel 627, DUR, HERE Files.

29. *CC*, January 1939, 4, mentions that three thousand of the membership of Local 302 was female. *CC*, May 1938, 2, lists nine thousand paid-up members in the entire local; thus, women were a third of the membership. Gertrude Lane, general organizer for Local 6, estimated that 40 percent of her local's membership was female. See *Proceedings*, HERE Convention, 1941, 131.

30. For example, see the listing of the 1942 officers and staff of Local 6 in *CIE*, February 1942, 25, or see *HCV*, 7 February 1942, 1.

31. *CC*, January 1939, February–March 1944, March–April 1947, February 1949. For data on Local 1, see *Voice of Local 1*, December 1947, 2; June 1948, 1; November 1949, 6.

32. In 1939, the New York LJEB appeared to have one female member on a council of roughly fifty members. See New York LJEB Minutes, 6 November 1939, Local 6 Files. In 1943, two of its thirty members were female. *CIE*, February 1943, 37.

33. Besides women's own "stage fright" and the discouragement they faced from men, Brown argued that the low level of female participation stemmed from the many new women members in the local and their lack of familiarity with trade-union procedures and practices. *Voice of Local 1*, January 1950, 2; *CC*, November 1940, 7.

34. New York WTUL Minutes, 9 November 1942, 31 January 1943, 28 April 1943, 29 March 1944, C-4, Reel 4, WTUL Papers; *CIE*, June 1938, 31, January 1939, 49, December 1942; *CC*, June 1938, 9, March 1939, 4, January 1940, 5, January 1942, 7; *HCV*, 26 April 1941, 6–7, 1 January 1944, 8.

35. *HCV*, 15 February 1941, 7; *Voice of Local 1*, November 1948, 5; *CC*, 1938–45.

36. *CC*, June 1943, 2; *Voice of Local 1*, August 1954, 7. See the *Dining Room Employee*, 1954–55, the successor to the *Voice of Local 1*.

37. Women were continually being called upon to "do their share" and "to shoul-

der the load"; see *HCV*, 24 August 1940, 1–8; "Listen Sister" columns written by Charlotte Ferris throughout 1940 and 1941; *Voice of Local 1*, November 1948, 5.

38. Bylaws, Local 6, 1947 and 1951, 4–5, Tamiment Vertical Files, RWA-NYU; *Voice of Local 1*, April 1950, 8.

39. CC, November 1940, 7.

40. New York LJEB Minutes, 6 and 20 November 1939, Local 6 Files.

41. CC, January 1940, 5; February 1940, 7; April 1941, 5; June 1938, 8–9; see also May 1938, 7, and June 1938, 8.

42. Ibid., March 1942, 5.

43. CC, 1938–44.

44. See *HCV*, 24 August 1940, 1–8; ibid., 28 May 1949, 8; 4 June 1949 for a brief revival of the committee.

45. See *Voice of Local 1*, March 1948, 2, and 1949–51.

46. Ibid., June 1949, 3; July 1949, 3; March 1951, 1 for a discussion of problems soliciting women contributors.

47. *Proceedings*, HERE Convention, 1909, 145, and 1921, 116, 171.

48. Women may have felt less singled out and demeaned by these policies of special board seats because quotas were now being applied to women, and to dining-car workers, and hotel service workers. *Proceedings*, HERE Convention, 1938, 144–48; CIE, September 1938, 13.

49. Bee Tumber of Waitresses' Local 639 in Los Angeles and Olivia Moore from Local 567 in Olympia, Washington, filled the vice-presidential positions reserved for women. Gertrude Sweet became the first woman to win a board seat in open competition with men; she secured a regular vice-presidential slot as the representative of the Pacific Northwest District. CIE, October 1938, 33; Hotel and Restaurant Employees International Alliance and the Bartenders International League of America, *Fifty Years of Progress: A Brief History of Our Union, 1891–1941* (Cincinnati, 1941), 14.

50. *Proceedings*, HERE Convention, 1941, 130–33.

51. Myra Wolfgang and Gertrude Sweet represented their districts throughout this period; see the GEB minutes as reprinted in CIE, March 1953, 26; and CC, June 1941, 5.

52. In contrast, female telephone workers resided in a separate division within the IBEW during the Progressive Era. More recently, flight attendants and clerical workers also have experimented with separate national unions or divisions. See Stephen Norwood, *Labor's Flaming Youth: Telephone Operators and Worker Militancy, 1878–1923* (Urbana, 1990); Georgia Painter Nielsen, *From Sky Girl to Flight Attendant: Women and the Making of a Union* (Ithaca, 1982); and Anne Hill, "District 925: A New Union for Office Workers," *Socialist Review* 11 (September–October 1981): 142–46.

53. See William Whyte, *Human Relations in the Restaurant Industry* (New York, 1948), 65–81, 92–128, 282–87; Whyte, "The Social Structure of the Restaurant," *American Journal of Sociology* 54 (January 1949): 305–11; and the earlier discussion of waitress work culture in chapter 2.

54. The structure of the clerical workplace seems to reinforce such qualities as acquiescence to authority and passivity. See Margery Davies, *Woman's Place Is at the Typewriter* (Philadelphia, 1982); and Roberta Lynch, "Organizing Clericals: Problems and Prospects," *Labor Research Review* 8 (Spring 1986): 91–101.

55. Tilly, "Paths of Proletarianization"; Turbin, "Beyond Conventional Wisdom"; Schatz, "Union Pioneers," 586–602, and Ronald W. Schatz, *The Electrical Workers: A History of Labor at General Electric and Westinghouse, 1923–60* (Urbana, 1983), 80–101.

56. Schatz, "Union Pioneers," and Schatz, *The Electrical Workers*, 80–101.

57. Tilly, "Paths of Proletarianization," 411–17. Turbin, in "Beyond Conventional Wisdom," 59–63 includes an excellent summary of literature that supports these suppositions.

58. For information on Donnelly, see MS, September 1921, 150; CIE, March 1936, 7; *Proceedings*, HERE Convention, 1947, 198; The data on Florence Farr were gathered in an interview by the author on June 28, 1989 in Detroit.

59. Data were gathered on approximately forty waitress officials whose careers spanned the twentieth century. Roughly half of the women were born between 1880 and 1901 and began their careers in the Progressive Era and the 1920s; the other half, born between 1902 and 1920, led the union in the 1930s and after. The primary sources used in compiling the detailed biographical material on waitress leaders were Dickerman and Taylor, *Who's Who in Labor*; Gary Fink, ed., *Biographical Dictionary of American Labor* (Westport, 1984); and CIE, plus interviews conducted by the author, the California Historical Society, Tamiment Library, and the Institute of Industrial Relations, University of Michigan (see Tables 10A–10D).

60. Lillian Sandberg to Jack Weinberger, 20 April 1948, Reel 342, LUR, HERE Files.

61. Interview with Charles Paulsen. As Paulsen's remarks indicate, and as numerous photographs underscore, waitress leaders were often heavy-set and matronly. See CIE, March 1935, 32; June 1941, 44; March 1952, 21, for photographs of waitress officials.

62. Kessler-Harris, "Organizing the Unorganizable"; Fink, ed., *Biographical Dictionary of American Labor*; Schatz, "Union Pioneers"; and Schatz, *The Electrical Workers*, 80–101.

63. In general, historical studies of labor activists have focused on agitational leaders, middle-class reformers, and Jewish immigrant women—all of whom tended to enter labor organizing at an early age when they were single, but later found they had to choose between their work and their family life. Thus, their careers were either brief and superseded by marriage, or they chose to remain single. Several studies of contemporary women union leaders, however, note a disproportionate number of older, divorced activists. See Wertheimer and Nelson, *Trade Union Women*, and Patricia Cayo Sexton, *The New Nightingales: Hospital Workers, Unions, New Women's Issues* (New York, 1982), 84–85.

64. Gary Fink finds fewer women labor leaders who married and fewer women with children because the biographical data in his study are skewed toward middle-class women reformers and immigrant women leaders from the garment trades. In the 1925 sample, no women from the service sector were included. Twenty-six percent of the women were from the needle trades, 17.9 percent from professional unions, and 19.6 percent from the Women's Trade Union League. The 1946 and 1976 samples were better, but still not balanced. Fink, ed., *Biographical Dictionary of American Labor*, xiii–xviii; Table 7, 29; Table 10, 32; 3–79.

65. Kessler-Harris, "Organizing the Unorganizable." The literature on middle-class career women who chose to remain single is enormous. For an analysis of the tension between marriage and careers for women in the twentieth century, see Nancy Cott, *The Grounding of Modern Feminism* (New Haven, 1987), 180–211.

66. One waitress press secretary reported in 1903 that one of the officers of her local had married, but that "we have no objections as she is still as active member of Local 249." *MS*, September 1903, 47. Gertrude Sweet, a full-time labor officials from 1925 until her retirement in the late 1970s, raised four children with the help of her mother and a housekeeper. Sweet felt, however, that she "wouldn't have succeeded had it not been for my deep belief in God and knowing that I had guidance when I needed it." Interview with Gertrude Sweet, 31, 47.

67. *CIE*, November 1955, 23; Rothring to Ernst, 16 September 1953, Reel 33, GOR, HERE Files.

68. Fink, ed., *Biographical Dictionary of American Labor*, xiii–xviii; Table 7, 29; Table 10, 32; 3–79. For concurring portraits of male labor leaders see Lois MacDonald, *Leadership Dynamics and the Trade Union Leader* (New York, 1959), 108, and Fink, ed., *Biographical Dictionary of American Labor*, 7–10.

69. In a striking illustration of the bias in compiling information on women labor leaders, Maud Younger, a San Francisco upper-class feminist, suffragist, and labor activist in the Progressive Era, is featured as a San Francisco waitress leader in the *Biographical Dictionary of American Labor*. She is erroneously identified as the "organizer of the waitresses' union in San Francisco" and its president for three terms. Working-class leaders like Louise LaRue and others are not included. Fink, ed., *Biographical Dictionary of American Labor*, 56–57, 599–600. For biographical details on Younger and LaRue, see Susan Englander, "The San Francisco Wage-Earners' Suffrage League: Class Conflict and Class Coalition in the California Women Suffrage Movement, 1907–1912," master's thesis, San Francisco State University, 1989.

Epilogue

1. Interview with Kathryn Dewing, 55–58.

2. As quoted in Leon Elder and Lin Rolens, *Waitress: America's Unsung Heroine* (Santa Barbara, 1985), 43.

3. Ann Japenga, "Granny Waitresses' Picket Restaurant to Reclaim Jobs," *LAT*, 23 February 1984, pt. 5, 1, 7; Table 5C and 8 herein; *LAT*, 13 October 1967; telephone interview conducted by the author with Maria Durazo, executive officer, HERE Local 11, Los Angeles, 2 May 1990.

4. Table 8 herein; interview with Beulah Compton, 29–30.

5. See *CIE* 1970–80 for the changing sexual composition of the GEB. See Tables 7 and 9 for the feminization of union membership and the proportionate decline of female representation at conventions. The lack of data on female leadership at the local level prohibits a definitive assessment.

6. As in many unions, the McCarthy period took its toll on left-leaning culinary officials: some lost their posts as a result of the ouster of Communist party members and sympathizers; others survived the purges but reined in their rhetoric and circumscribed their activities to fit the new temper of the fifties. Noncommunist leftists also lost their titles and found themselves red-baited out of the union.

7. Maurice B. Better, "Recent Unionism Among the Unskilled in the South: The Retail and Wholesale Trades and Service and Public Service Workers," in *Southern Workers and Their Unions, 1880–1975*, ed. Merl E. Reed et al. (Westport, 1981); John P. Henderson, *Labor Market Institutions and Wages in the Lodging Industry* (East Lansing, 1965), 181–99; CIE, 1940–59, in particular June 1940, 25; September 1946, 20; May 1949, 32; and John P. Henderson, "Collective Bargaining Elections and the Hotel Industry," *Labor Law Journal* 13 (August 1962): 658–75. For a broader perspective on the problems of organizing in the South, see Barbara S. Griffith, *The Crisis of American Labor: Operation Dixie and the Defeat of the CIO* (Philadelphia, 1988).

8. For the expansion and structural transformation of the industry, see Stan Luxenberg, *Roadside Empires: How the Chains Franchised America* (New York, 1985), 13–50, passim; Philip Langdon, *Orange Roofs, Golden Arches: The Architecture of American Chain Restaurants* (New York, 1986), 188–89; and Kurt Andersen, "Good Bad Taste and Bad Good Taste," *San Francisco Examiner*, 31 May 1986.

9. The unionization of chains is not impossible. HERE organized the Playboy Clubs nationally and secured national agreements with such airport-based food chains as Sky-Chef, *Dining Room Employee*, February 1986, 1. The United Food and Commercial Workers also succeeded in organizing grocery store chains. See David Brody, *The Butcher Workmen: A Study of Unionization* (Cambridge, 1964). Nevertheless, the fast-food empires seem virtually untouchable. See Luxenberg, *Roadside Empires*, 162–63, and Food and Allied Service Trades Department, AFL-CIO, *A Profile of the Fast Food Industry* (Washington, D.C., October 1985), 31–33.

10. For the declining use of the union hiring hall by employers and their preference for nonunion employees, see, for example, Jeri Powell, "Goals and Achievements of San Francisco Waitresses," and Flo Douglas, "The Impact of Merger on San Francisco Waitresses' Local 48," remarks presented to the Twelfth Annual Southwest Labor Studies Conference, San Francisco State University, 14 March 1986, tape recording in possession of author.

11. The hotel and restaurant industry did not fall under Taft-Hartley initially because of the low volume of interstate commerce. A 1955 Supreme Court action "brought a segment of the industry's labor relations under federal supervision"; a National Labor Relations Board ruling extended the coverage. See Henderson, *Labor Market Institutions and Wages in the Lodging Industry*, 44; *Dining Room Employee*, November 1959, 3; *Proceedings*, HERE Convention, 1957; Floridan Hotel of Tampa, Inc., 124 NLRB 261, 44 LRRM 1345 (1959).

12. Disciplinary actions by unions against their own members became difficult to enforce once unions could remove workers from a job only for nonpayment of dues. Local 6 in New York, for example, had to give up its contract provision requiring employers to discharge any employee who was suspended or expelled from the union. Morris Horowitz, *The New York Hotel Industry* (Cambridge, 1960), xviii–xix. See also Ed Miller to Blanche Copenhaver, 10 August 1961; Union Minutes, 24 August 1961, 4 October 1961, WPU Minutebook, 15-4, WPUC-174, MHS; Local 457 and Silver Bow Employers Association Contract, 1972–75, BSBA.

13. Interview with Clela Sullivan; also, for example, see John Krosky to Arthur Morgan, 25 February 1967, Box 3, File 26, JRC, WRL-WSU; Contracts, 1943–61,

Local 457, and Silver Bow Employers Association, WPUC-174, Box 13, Folders 8 and 9, MHS.

14. As discussed in chapter 5, the transition for some locals began in the late 1940s. Jointly run benefit plans were mandated for all locals once the industry came under Taft-Hartley.

15. The forces prompting this shift to part-time workers in the hotel and restaurant industry have not been analyzed systematically. Both supply and demand factors were involved: employers sought a more flexible, lower-paid work force and the number of part-time job seekers also expanded.

16. Barbara C. Job, "Employment and Pay Trends in the Retail Trade Industry," *Monthly Labor Review* 103 (March 1980): 40–43; Richard Carnes and Horst Brandt, "Productivity and New Technology in Eating and Drinking Places," *Monthly Labor Review* 100 (September 1977): 9–15; Donald E. Lundberg, *The Hotel and Restaurant Business* (Boston, 1979), 203; Luxenberg, *Roadside Empires*, 168–69.

17. Carnes and Brandt, "Productivity and New Technology in Eating and Drinking Places," 11; Raymond Pedderson, et al., *Increasing Productivity in Food Service* (Chicago, 1973); Leon Ullensvang, "Food Consumption Patterns in the 1970s," *Vital Speeches of the Day* 36 (February 1, 1970): 240–46; Wickham Skinner and Kishore Chakraborty, *The Impact of New Technology: People and Organizations in Service Industries* (New York, 1982).

18. U.S. Bureau of the Census, 1967, Table 2 and 1977, Table 4 as quoted in Thomas Bailey, "A Case Study of Immigrants in the Restaurant Industry," *Industrial Relations* 24 (Spring 1985): 205–21.

19. For analyses of the fast-food sector, see sources cited in notes 8 and 9, as well as Bureau of National Affairs, "Special Supplement: Employee Relations in the Fast Food Industry," *Retail Services Labor Report*, pt. 2, June 10 1985 (Rockville, 1985); Jeffrey Man, "Toward Service Without a Snarl," *Fortune*, March 3, 1981, 58–66; Job, "Employment and Pay Trends in the Retail Trade Industry," 40–43; Daryl Wyckoff and W. Earl Sasser, *The Chain Restaurant Industry* (Lexington, Mass., 1978); George Ritzer, "The 'McDonaldization' of Society," *Journal of American Culture* 6 (Spring 1983): 101–8.

20. *Boston Magazine*, September 1984, 28; interview with Ira Wood by Maryellen Kennedy, *Tables Magazine*, August 1986, 7; Amy Short, "Waitressing," *Glamour*, August 1979, 154–57.

21. The degree to which food service has rationalized overall is debated, but I find Thomas Bailey's schema convincing. He categorizes eating establishments as either (1) fast-food (routinized work, part-time, teenage work force); (2) intermediate (table and counter service, mix of part-time and full-time, older and younger work force, heavily female); or (3) full service (more formal service, male, long-term work force). Intermediate and full service combined comprise a majority of the industry according to his calculations. Bailey, "A Case Study of Immigrants in the Restaurant Industry," 206–13. For further indications of the resistance of certain sectors of food service to rationalization, see Thomas F. Powers, "Industry Dynamics: An Institutional View" in *The Future of Food Service: A Basis for Planning*, ed. Thomas F. Powers (University Park, 1974); Donald Lundberg, *The Restaurant: From Concept to Operation* (New

York, 1985), 119; Greta Foff Paules, "Behind the Lines: Strategies of Self-Perception and Protection Among Waitresses in New Jersey," Ph.D. diss., Princeton University, 1990, 105–33.

22. *Nation's Restaurant News* 21, 30 March 1987, 3, 11; *Today's Waitress*, prepared by Bolt Beranek and Newman Inc. (New York, 1971); Sondra Dahmer and Kurt Kahl, *The Waiter and Waitress Training Manual*, 2d ed. (Boston, 1982); Donald Lundberg, *The Restaurant: From Concept to Operation* (New York, 1985), 281.

23. Hope Dlugozima, "Waitressing: The Thrills and Spoils," *Seventeen* 45 (June 1986), 146–47; Becky Sukovsky, "Waiting: The Other Side of the Counter," *Northwest Passage*, August 19–September 9, 1980, 12.

24. Business Agent Reports, WPU Minutebooks, 1950–75, Local 457 Files; quote is from 22 January 1971.

25. See, for example, the files of Waitresses' Local 507 and Local 227 from the late 1940s to the early 1960s, Reel 39, DUR, HERE Files; Local 484 Correspondence 1949–1952, Reel 525, LUR, HERE Files; and Local 48 Correspondence File, Local 2 Files.

26. By the 1950s, waitress unions also were subject to problems associated with the maturing of any organization: a decline in overall membership participation, a gulf between the founders and the newcomers, and an increased bureaucratic rigidity. For a discussion of these phenomenon, see Richard Lester, *As Unions Mature: An Analysis of the Evolution of American Unionism* (Princeton, 1958); and Leonard Sayles and George Strauss, *The Local Union* (New York, 1953).

27. The trusteeship of the three waitress locals can be followed in the HERE Files; see Reel 19, DUR for the history of Cleveland's Local 107; Reels 970–71, LUR, for the situation of Butte's Local 457; and Reel 350, DUR, for the charges against Local 249 of St. Louis. See also interviews with Clela Sullivan, Valentine Webster, and Blanche Copenhaver.

28. Interview with Helen Jaye, 1–3, 5.

29. Local 48 Minutes, 10 March 1948; "Election leaflet," n.d. [ca. 1950], Box 1, File 1, BMC, CHS; Newsletter, "Lets Face It," n.d. [ca. 1950]; Pamphlets and Election Cards [1948–52], issued by Local 48's "Green Slate Candidates," in possession of Lillian Caldwell, Local 48 reform candidate for office.

30. Ibid.; interview with Helen Jaye, 1–3, 5; interview with Lucy Kendall.

31. Waitress leaders demanded extreme personal loyalty from their members and personalized criticism. Their behavior contrasts in interesting ways with that of male officials under challenge. The gender differences in conflict resolution within unions is an important, understudied area.

32. Local 629 Correspondence, 1949–59, Reel 628, LUR; Local 249 Correspondence, 1956, Reel 350, DUR; and Local 457 Correspondence, 1951–61, Reel 970, LUR, all HERE Files. Moreover, some officers used their powers to punish rivals. Those responsible for job dispatching could withhold employment—especially extra work and banquet work. Incumbent-dominated executive boards could heap punishment and fines on uncooperative reformers. Business agents, responsible for ensuring employer and employee compliance with the labor agreement, might ignore establishments where dissenters were employed, allowing conditions to lapse below union standards.

33. Initially, the EEOC had allowed employers wide discretion in behavior. See Ann Corinne Hill, "Protection of Women Workers and the Courts: A Legal Case History," *Feminist Studies* 5 (Summer 1979): 261–63; Karen Maschke, *Litigation, Courts, and Women Workers* (New York, 1989), ch. 3.

34. *NYT*, 11 November 1976, 45; 20 December 1977, 32; 11 June 1977, 7; Louise Howe, *Pink-Collar Workers: Inside the World of Women's Work* (New York, 1977), 125–27. Indeed, some locals had proposed clauses that forbade race discrimination but not sex. For an early example, see San Francisco LJEB Minutes, 19 March 1946, Local 2 Files.

35. Interview with Florence Farr; University Parking, Inc. d.b.a. Seattle Hilton Downtown and Seattle Local Joint Executive Board, HERE, *Labor Arbitration Reports* 57 (November 18, 1971): 876–83; San Mateo County Restaurant-Hotel Owners Association and Bartenders and Culinary Workers Union, Local 340, *Labor Arbitration Reports* 59 (November 10, 1972): 997–1003; Al Richmond, "The San Francisco Hotel Strike," *Socialist Review* 57 (May–June 1981): 98–99.

36. For an incisive overview of feminist activism in these years, see Cynthia Harrison, *On Account of Sex: The Politics of Women's Issues, 1945–1968* (Berkeley, 1988). For an example of waitresses arguing with middle-class women's groups over protective legislation, see newspaper clipping, n.d. [ca. 1957], BMC, Box 23, File 24, CHS.

37. For the divisions within the labor movement over protective legislation, see Alice Cook, "Women and American Trade Unions," *Annals of the American Academy of Political and Social Science* 375 (January 1968): 127. For the growth of "equal rights" feminism among UAW women and others, see Nancy Gabin, "Trade Union Feminism: Advocating Women's Rights and Gender Equity in the UAW, 1935–1975," paper presented at the 81st Annual OAH Convention, Reno, March 1988; Harrison, *On Account of Sex*, 169–211; Carol Kates, "Working-class Feminism and Feminist Unions: Title VII, the UAW, and NOW," *Labor Studies Journal* 14 (Summer 1989): 28–45.

38. Myra Wolfgang, "Some of the Problems of Eve," talk to the AFL-CIO Conference, "Women at Work," 13 March 1971, MWC, Box 1, File 6, WRL-WSU; *MHBRR*, October 1969; press release, "Wolfgang Routs Friedan," 22 October 1970, Local 705 Files; see also MWC, Box 1, files 3 and 8, WRL-WSU.

39. *Evans v. Sheraton Park Hotel*, 5 FEP Cases 393, 396 (D.D.C. 1972).

40. Minutebook 1972–73, letters, 29 April 1973, 14 May 1973, 1 August 1973, 27 September 1973, Memo, 21 August 1973, Minutes of Special Meeting 21 August 1973, and 24 August 1973, all in Local 457 Files; interviews with Valentine Webster, Blanche Copenhaver, and Clela Sullivan.

41. *San Francisco Chronicle*, 6 July 1973. See for example, the mergers in Detroit, *Detroit News*, 18 January 1974, Vertical Files, Labor Unions, A–Z, WRL-WSU.

42. A number of participant observation studies of waitresses posit a solidaristic work culture among waitresses but see waitresses as indifferent and sometimes actively opposed to the culinary unions that currently exist. See Hannah Creighton, "Tied by Double Apron Strings: Female Work Culture and Organization in a Restaurant," *Insurgent Sociologist* 11 (Fall 1982): 59–64; Paules, "Behind the Lines," and Eleanor La Pointe, "Still Waiting: Gender and Job Power Among Waitresses," Ph.D. diss., Rutgers University, 1991.

43. Sarah Little, "One Waitress's Story," *Rank and Filer* (San Francisco), 1 July

1974. On Harvard Square organizing, see Liza Bingham, Meredith Golden and Holly Newman, "Harvard Square Waitresses Strike," *Second Wave* 1 (Winter 1972): 3–5; June Gross and Judith Hoffman, "Turning the Tables and Serving the People," *Second Wave* 3 (Spring 1974): 5–6; E. Frye, "Waitresses Win Strike," *Off Our Backs* 8 (June 1978): 4, and Wendy Stevens, "A Pinch too Much," *Off Our Backs* 8 (May 1978): 10.

44. See previously cited material and pamphlets in IWW Collection, Box 3, File 21 and 27 February 1973 letter in Box 5, File 28 WRL-WSU; (New Jersey) *Communications Workers of America*, August/September 1986, 15; Paules, "Behind the Lines," 105–33, 177–99.

45. Creighton, "Tied by Double Apron Strings," 59–64; Bernard Rosenberg and Saul Weinman, "Young Women Who Work: An Interview with Myra Wolfgang," *Dissent* 86 (Winter 1972): 31.

46. Leaflets issued by HERE Local 2, October–December 1984, Local 2 Files; Cindy Mahan Young, "The Current Concerns of Waitresses," comments delivered at the Twelfth Annual Southwest Labor Studies Conference, San Francisco State University, 14 March 1986, tape recording in possession of the author; "San Francisco Operators Battle Strike," *Nation's Restaurant News*, 24 September 1984, 1; see also Imbert Matthee, "Is City Losing Taste for Unions?" *Seattle Times*, 15 August 1985, 1.

47. See *In These Times*, 13 August 1980, 4; Karen Guma, "6,000 Strike City Hotels," *Union Wage* 61 (September–October 1980): 1; Diane Sandrowski, "Hotel Stonewalls," *Union Wage* 58 (March–April 1980): 16, for Local 2's affirmative action emphasis. For sexual harassment cases picked up by the media, see, for example, Carol Conitas, "We Fought Back and Won," *Good Housekeeping* (February 1986): 83–86; *LAT*, 28 May 1986, sect. 2, 1, 6. For employer attitudes and actions, see *Restaurant Hospitality* 69 (May 1985): 38; *50 Plus*, February 1986, 11 and November 1987, 16; Thomas Bailey, "A Case Study of Immigrants in the Restaurant Industry," 205–21. The Oakland, California, case is discussed in the *San Francisco Chronicle*, 5–8 February 1980, 11 March 1980, 5 April 1980.

48. For descriptions of Chiesa's leadership style and the activities of Local 2, see *San Francisco Chronicle*, 7 and 20 January 1988, 15 May 1988, and Young, "The Current Concerns of Waitresses"; for Durazo, see *CIE*, June 1990, 9.

Index

Addams, Jane, 75

Affirmative action, 12

AFL: attitudes toward maximum hour and minimum wage legislation, 83, 255n; consensus among historians on political nature of, 226n; criticisms of sit-in tactic by, 99; and department store unionization, 258n; and early food service workers unions, 61; and HERE, 71; and labor's resurgence in 1930s, 7; new revisionist scholarship on, 7; organizing successes with women workers in 1930s and 1940s, 59

Age: at first marriage of waitress leaders and all women labor leaders, 216, 217; of waitresses compared with other women workers, 30–31; of women workers, 189

Alexander, Carrie, 179

Allies of waitresses unions, 73–77; Jewish kosher restaurant customers, 74; in large heterogenous urban areas, 74; male unionists, 74; middle-class customers, 74; middle-class reformers, 75–76; tactics used in unionized communities, 73–74; Young Men's Christian Association, 76. See also Middle-class women's groups; Waiters' unions; Women's Trade Union League

Amalgamated Food Workers (AFW), New York City, 87, 99; absorption into HERE, 101–2

American Beauty (Banner), 127

American plan, 18; impact on culinary unions, 69

Amsler, Kitty, 88–89, 153, 157, 168, 177

Anderson, Mary, 155, 159

Andrews, Minnie, 64

Apprenticeship, 141

Arbitration, minimized by occupational unionism, 147

Arbitration boards, 89

Arden, Eve, 34

Argo, Madge, 73, 74

Asian culinary workers, 124; exclusion by HERE, 77–78; exclusion by waitresses unions, 12; during World War II, 109–10, 264n. See also Chinese culinary workers; Japanese culinary workers; Filipina waitresses; Filipino workers

Atlantic City waitresses, 77

Atlantic Monthly, 42

Attendance and punctuality, self-regulation by union, 142

Automat. See Horn and Hardart chain

Autonomy of waitresses, 8, 247n; tipping and, 43; and work culture, 51–52

Bakersfield, California, Cooks and Waiters' Local 550, 177

Bakery workers, 83; and Horn and Hardart organizing campaign, 104

Banner, Lois, 127

Banquet work, 165; and night work restrictions for waitresses, 162; and sex discrimination suit, 198, 200

Barmaids: bar owner's wives and daughters as, 168; number of, 170; and Title VII sex discrimination lawsuits, 170; use of term, 223n, 287n; waitress unions' attitudes toward, 126, 158, 168. See also Bartenders, female; Bartenders' unions; Black cocktail waitresses; Black women bartenders; Cocktail waitresses; Night work

Chicago Labor Temple, 66, 135
Chicago Restaurant Keepers Association,
    66–67
Chicago Tribune, 179
Chicago Urban League, 159
Chicago Waitress Club, 88
Chicago Waitress League, 88
Chiesa, Sherri, 202
Childbearing and childrearing: choice of
    waitressing occupation and, 33, 52; and
    equal pay issue, 153; and protective
    legislation, 82, 83; and union goals, 116;
    and women union leaders, 190–91,
    216, 217
Child care: sponsored by waitresses'
    unions, 132, 134; and waitresses' support
    for night work restrictions, 162
Childs Dairy Lunch chain, New York City,
    21, 101; "charm course" for employees,
    47; unionization drives, 102; and
    waitresses assisting with organizing other
    chains, 105
Chinese culinary workers, 109–10, 124.
    See also Asian culinary workers
Chinese Restaurant Association of
    Alameda County, 110
Chinese restaurants, unionization of, 110
Christman, Elizabeth, 81
CIO: and Detroit culinary workers union,
    99; impact on AFL of organizing drives
    in late 1930s, 103; new revisionist
    scholarship on, 7; organizing successes in
    1930s and 1940s, 59; organizing tactics,
    98; and upsurge in waitress unions in
    1930s, 86. *See also* Industrial unionism;
    Worksite unionism
Civil Rights Act of 1964, Title VII: and
    merger of waiters' and waitresses' locals,
    200; and new younger waitresses, 198–
    99; and pregnancy, 274n; and sexual
    discrimination, 128
Class backgrounds: and definitions of
    feminism, 228n; and sex separatism in
    leisure pursuits, 228n; of waitress union
    leaders, 191, 217. *See also* Working class;
    Working women
Class loyalties, 11
Cleaning, forbidden by union rules, 121
Clerical work, clerical workers: culture and
    management control, 51–52;
    demographic data compared with

waitressing, 30; feminization of, 28;
    structure of workplace, activism and,
    293n; waitressing preferred over, 52;
    unions, 59–60, 86
Cleveland Federation of Labor, 174
Cleveland Plain Dealer, 174
Cleveland Waitresses' Local 107, 63, 88;
    157, 174, 189; and union rules, 119, 121;
    and work hour reductions, 116
Clinton's Cafeteria chain, San
    Francisco, 91
Closed-shop agreements: and control over
    labor supply, 138–39; and hotel industry,
    275n
Cocktail waitresses, union ban on, 158,
    271n. *See also* Barmaids; Bartenders,
    female; Black cocktail waitresses; Liquor
    service
Coffee shops, defined, 232n
Collective bargaining: in culinary locals
    compared with auto and steel, 225n; and
    effort to slow feminization of food
    catering industry, 160–61; and
    waitresses' unions in San Francisco,
    94–96
Collectivity, vs. individual upward
    mobility, waitresses and, 10–11
College students, as part-time waitresses,
    50, 195, 196. *See also* Part-time waiters
    and waitresses; Student workers in food
    industry
Collier's Magazine, 55
Colonial America, public food service
    in, 18
Colorado waitresses, and protective
    legislation, 81
Committee for Enforcement of the
    Minimum Wage, San Francisco, 83–84
Communist party, and Food Workers
    Industrial Union, 99
Compagnon, Ruth, 128
Comparable worth movement, 12; and
    equal pay for equal work slogan, 154
Competency: and union membership, 120;
    and wages related to skills, 141
Compton, Beulah, 134, 193
Consumer groups, opposition to
    unionization drives, 108
Consumers' League, 49, 82; on waitresses
    living apart from families, 31
Cooks' helpers, 100

134–35; and union recreation and rest
homes, 135
Swearing, 125
Sweeney, Margaret, 105
Sweet, Gertrude, 64, 65, 86, 88, 141,
145–46, 168, 177, 293n
Szeliga, Loretta, 44

Tacoma Waitresses' Local 61, and equal
pay issue, 155
Taft-Hartley Act: extension to hotel and
restaurants industry in 1955, 194–95,
296n
Taylor, Barbara, 121
Tea Room Guild, San Francisco, 92
Tea rooms, unionization in San Francisco,
92, 232n
Technological innovations, and
feminization of work force, 28
Telephone operators, female, unionization,
59, 293n
Ten-hour day, winning of, 116
Thompson's cafeteria chain, New York
City, replacement of male day crews
with women, 100
Tilly, Louise, 188
Tipping, Tips: amount of, 40–41;
attractiveness and, 127; autonomy and,
43, 247n; customer abuse and, 44–45;
dependence on, and public attitude
toward waitressing, 24; HERE and IWW
on, 268n; impact on wages, 43; and
income stratification, 43; laws against,
42; methods of augmenting, 246n; and
minimum wage standards, 42, 268n; and
night work, 164; and Playboy Club
management, 129; and preference for
waitressing, 52; and public perception of
waitressing, 25–26; recommended rates,
42–43; reform movement opposed to,
41–42; and sexually explicit uniforms,
130; in union contracts, 119–20
Toledo waitresses, struggle for maximum
hour legislation, 81–82
Tomlins, Christopher, 7
Trade Union Unity League, New York
City, 103
Training programs, union-sponsored, 53,
120, 270n; apprenticeship model, 141; of
bartenders, in Chicago, women and,

169; decline of, 195; and employers'
attitudes toward union, 146; and
increased demand for waitresses in
1930s, 26; introduction of, 25, 26; and
new service ideal, 47–48; and older
waitresses, 56–57; and "restaurant
vernacular," 55–56
Travelers, and development of inns and
hotels, 18
Tremont House, Boston, 18
Tumber, Bee, 73, 84, 109, 121, 151, 157,
177, 293n
Turbin, Carole, 188
Turnover rates, occupational tenure and,
32–33
Two-income families, growth of, and
growth of food service industry, 27

Unemployment: and employment security
vs. job security, 139–40; and exclusion
of women from bartending, 166; and
night work restrictions for
waitresses, 164
Uniforms: costs of, 38; elimination of
deductions for, 118; explicitly sexual,
130, 131; and male opposition to night
work for waitresses, 163; and new service
ideal, 48; and sexuality, 129–30, 131; in
union agreements, 92; union rules
on, 119
Union buttons, 74; and educational
campaigns, 94; and group loyalty, 145;
prohibition against Asians wearing, 78
Union consciousness: demographic
characteristics of waitresses and, 33; loss
of, and decline of waitresses' unions,
194. *See also* Group loyalty to union
Union contracts, craft rules in, 121–22
Union headquarters, social role of, 135
Union house cards, 74; reduced power to
attract customers, 194
Unionization of food service
establishments: extent of, 212; regional
variations in, 1961, 213
Unionization of waitresses: and affiliation
with HERE, 3–4; in chain restaurants,
296n; compared with other occupational
groups, 59–60; compared with
unionization of waiters, 5–6; cross-class
alliances with other women, 6; and

Index

323

establishments, 234n; as "feminists," 10–13, 228n; and gender expectations, 2; goals of, and male-dominated labor movement, 5; and informal collective power, 248n; job sites for, compared with waiters, 20–24; lack of social life, 49; legislative activism, 6; living apart from families, 31–32; marital status, 30–31; marital status compared with all working women, 1910–60, 211; and middle-class morality, 10; in mixed culinary locals, 3–4; occupational tenure of, 32–33; opportunities for advancement, 50–51; opposition to bans on women bartending, 167–68; percentage full- and part-time, 1940–70, 211; as primary earners, 31–33; as "professional nurturers," 2; and promotion of better tips, 246n; race and nativity, 1900–1970, 208; relationships with bartenders, 288n; relationships with customers, 1–2, 6, 53–54, 187–88, 195–96; as semi-prostitutes, 24–26; and sex-based protective legislation, 11; sexual division of labor in food service industry, 27–28; status of, sexuality and, 6; stock character in fiction and the media, 248n; and success of restaurant, 53–54; support for bans on women tending bar, 167–69; and traditional male bastions during World War II, 27; use of term, 223n

Waitresses, participation in HERE activities and leadership, 174–91; class background and, 191; compared with other unions, 174–75; and craft unionism, 176; and decline of waitress unionism, 193; extent of, 176–78; family characteristics of waitress leaders, 216; family characteristics of all women labor leaders, 217; and family life, 188; and female representatives on General Executive Board, 291n; historical data on waitress officials, 294n; and household responsibilities, 182; and leadership in mixed gender locals, 177–78; life histories of waitress officials, 188–91; and Local Joint Executive Boards, 178; and merger of segregated locals, 200–201; and middle-class women's movement, 175; nativity of

waitress leaders, 217; occupation of fathers of waitress leaders, 217; participation at selected HERE conventions, 1901–76, 216; and preference for separate locals, 178–80; and quota system for woman's seats on General Executive Board, 184–86, 293n; and separate waitress locals, 175–76, 291; and separate waitress locals vs. women's committees, 184; and state culinary alliances, 178; and strategic dilemmas on national level, 184–86; and women's committees of mixed-gender locals, 180–84; and work culture of waitresses, 186–88
Waitressing crews, 50
Waitressing work: bias against Jews and Italians in, 30; and blacks, 23–24; demographic data compared with teaching and waitressing, 30; employers' attitude toward, 52–53; enhancing status of, 269n; feminization and segregation of, 26–29; introduction of training courses in, 25, 26; prejudices against, 17; reasons for choice of, 24; and shortage of male labor during World War I, 19; as sixth largest occupation for women, 27; skills involved in, 52–53; unionism and elevation of moral and social status of, 120–21; and women's history research, 9–13. See also Waiting work; Waitresses; Waitressing work, rise of; Waitressing work culture; Waitressing work conditions
Waitressing work, rise of, 17–24; and change in public attitude toward occupation, 24–26; and changes in restaurant decor, 22; and commercialization of food service, 17–24; and labor shortages, 24; and Prohibition, 22–23
Waitressing work conditions, 34–57; arbitrary management and demanding public, 44–46; and boarding, 39; changes in 1940s, 36–37; comparisons with domestic labor, 36; and costs of uniforms, 38; customer abuse of waitresses, 44–46; and downward mobility, 51; dress codes and daily inspections, 38; and employer fines, 37–38; and employer service ideals, 46–48;

Books in the Series
The Working Class in American History

Worker City, Company Town:
Iron and Cotton-Worker Protest in Troy
and Cohoes, New York, 1855–84
Daniel J. Walkowitz

Life, Work, and Rebellion in the Coal Fields:
The Southern West Virginia Miners, 1880–1922
David Alan Corbin

Women and American Socialism, 1870–1920
Mari Jo Buhle

Lives of Their Own:
Blacks, Italians, and Poles in Pittsburgh, 1900–1960
John Bodnar, Roger Simon, and Michael P. Weber

Working-Class America:
Essays on Labor, Community, and American Society
Edited by Michael H. Frisch and Daniel J. Walkowitz

Eugene V. Debs: Citizen and Socialist
Nick Salvatore

American Labor and Immigration History, 1877–1920s:
Recent European Research
Edited by Dirk Hoerder

Workingmen's Democracy:
The Knights of Labor and American Politics
Leon Fink

The Electrical Workers:
A History of Labor at General Electric
and Westinghouse, 1923–60
Ronald W. Schatz

The Mechanics of Baltimore:
Workers and Politics in the Age of Revolution, 1763–1812
Charles G. Steffen

The Practice of Solidarity:
American Hat Finishers in the Nineteenth Century
David Bensman

The Labor History Reader
Edited by Daniel J. Leab

On the Line:
Essays in the History of Auto Work
Edited by Nelson Lichtenstein and Stephen Meyer III

Upheaval in the Quiet Zone:
A History of Hospital Workers' Union, Local 1199
Leon Fink and Brian Greenberg

Labor's Flaming Youth:
Telephone Operators and Worker Militancy, 1878–1923
Stephen H. Norwood

Another Civil War:
Labor, Capital, and the State in the
Anthracite Regions of Pennsylvania, 1840–68
Grace Palladino

Coal, Class, and Color:
Blacks in Southern West Virginia, 1915–32
Joe William Trotter, Jr.

For Democracy, Workers, and God:
Labor Song-Poems and Labor Protest, 1865–95
Clark D. Halker

Dishing It Out: Waitresses and Their
Unions in the Twentieth Century
Dorothy Sue Cobble

Books in the Series
Women in American History

Women Doctors in Gilded-Age Washington:
Race, Gender, and Professionalization
Gloria Moldow

Friends and Sisters: Letters between Lucy Stone
and Antoinette Brown Blackwell, 1846–93
Edited by Carol Lasser and Marlene Deahl Merrill

Reform, Labor, and Feminism: Margaret Dreier Robins
and the Women's Trade Union League
Elizabeth Anne Payne

Private Matters: American Attitudes toward Childbearing
and Infant Nurture in the Urban North, 1800–1860
Sylvia D. Hoffert

Civil Wars: Women and
the Crisis of Southern Nationalism
George C. Rable

I Came a Stranger: The Story of a Hull-House Girl
Hilda Satt Polacheck
Edited by Dena J. Polacheck Epstein

Labor's Flaming Youth: Telephone Operators and
Worker Militancy, 1878–1923
Stephen H. Norwood

Winter Friends: Women Growing Old
in the New Republic, 1785–1835
Terri L. Premo

Better Than Second Best:
Love and Work in the Life of Helen Magill
Glenn C. Altschuler

Dishing It Out: Waitresses and Their Unions
in the Twentieth Century
Dorothy Sue Cobble

A Note on the Author

DOROTHY SUE COBBLE received her Ph.D. in American history from Stanford University in 1986. She is an assistant professor at the Institute of Management and Labor Relations at Rutgers University, where she teaches courses in history, women's studies, and labor studies.

Winner of the 1992 Herbert G. Gutman Award

Dishing It Out
Waitresses and Their Unions in the Twentieth Century

Dorothy Sue Cobble

"In this imaginative study of waitresses, work, and unionism, Cobble challenges us all to rethink the conventional wisdom about the relationship between craft unionism and the possibilities for women workers' collective action. Women's labor history will never be the same." — Ruth Milkman, author of *Gender at Work: The Dynamics of Job Segregation by Sex during World War II*

"Remarkable on several grounds—first, of course, for rescuing from history's indifference a very special battalion of working women and, second, for probing deeply and imaginatively into some of the big questions in American labor and women's history. In unexpected ways, we are henceforth going to see both craft unionism and working-class feminism differently because of Sue Cobble's fine book." — David Brody, author of *Workers in Industrial America: Essays on the 20th Century Struggle*

"Rich in detail, studded with telling anecdotes, *Dishing It Out* is just as vivid and evocative as its title suggests. . . . This book speaks with clarity and good sense to the major debates in the history of work and gender and will become a landmark in our growing understanding of the relationships between the two." — Susan Porter Benson, author of *Counter Cultures*

DOROTHY SUE COBBLE is an associate professor in the Rutgers University Labor Education Center.

AN ILLINI BOOK FROM THE UNIVERSITY OF ILLINOIS PRESS

9 780252 061868